PRESIDENTS OF THE CHURCH

"They That Move the Cause of Zion"

Student Manual (Rel. 345)

Prepared by the Institutes of Religion of the
Church Educational System

Published by
The Church of Jesus Christ of Latter-day Saints
Salt Lake City, Utah

TABLE OF CONTENTS

INTRODUCTION

Philosophical Basis of the Approach

The course shall be based on a definition of the word *prophet,* and shall include the following elements: A prophet is a person who knows by personal revelation from the Holy Ghost that Jesus Christ is the Son of God, "for the testimony of Jesus is the spirit of prophecy." (Revelation 19:10.) While all who have testimony of Jesus are prophets, this course shall be concerned only with that succession of presiding prophets who have been divinely appointed to stand at the head and preside among the Lord's people in this final dispensation. On the foundation of that testimony which the presiding prophet has received by the manifestations of the Holy Ghost, he may press forward to receive other revelations by the Holy Ghost, which may qualify him to speak on any and all subjects that may come under his consideration; and "whatsoever they shall speak when moved upon by the Holy Ghost shall be scripture, shall be the will of the Lord, shall be the mind of the Lord, shall be the word of the Lord, shall be the voice of the Lord, and the power of God unto salvation." (D&C 68:4.)

The president of the Church is not sent to foretell as much as he is sent to tell forth. He is to announce boldly and without equivocation the will and designs and desires of the Lord. He is a seer to whom the veil becomes merely a curtain. Seership is intrinsic to the prophetic call, "and a gift which is greater can no man have." (Mosiah 8:16.) He may be permitted to see things which are past, and also things which are to come. It may be his privilege, as the Lord permits, to see truth in all of its dimensions, for "truth is knowledge of things as they are, and as they were, and as

they are to come" (D&C 93:24), but he may not be permitted to declare all that he knows. His knowledge, understanding, and perspective of eternal things, gained through revelation, are the foundation of his position as the Lord's mouthpiece, but prophets are "laid under a strict command that they shall not impart only according to the portion of his word which he doth grant unto the children of men, according to the heed and diligence which they give unto him." (Alma 12:9.) They are generally permitted to reveal only piecemeal, "line upon line, precept upon precept, here a little and there a little" (2 Nephi 28:30), all according to the direction of Him whose Church it is.

"The duty of the President of the office of the High Priesthood is to preside over the whole church, and to be like unto Moses—

"Behold, here is wisdom; yea, to be a seer, a revelator, a translator, and a prophet, having all the gifts of God which he bestows upon the head of the church." (D&C 107:91, 92.) As President Joseph F. Smith has said, "The house of God is a house of order, and not a house of confusion. In this house, God himself is the supreme head, and He must be obeyed. Christ is in the image and likeness of His being, His begotten Son, and He stands as our Savior. . . . We must walk in His paths, and observe His precepts to do them, or we will be cut off. Next unto God and Christ, in the earth is placed one unto whom the keys of power and the authority of the Holy Priesthood are conferred, and unto whom the right of presidency is given. He is God's mouthpiece to His people, in all things. . . . " (*CR,* Apr. 1898, p. 68.)

Presidents of the Church are prophets, seers, and revelators,

who by their divine appointment hold keys and powers and prerogatives which make them the Lord's mouthpiece in the earth, such that the Lord may say to them, "Whatsoever you seal on earth shall be sealed in heaven; and whatsoever you bind on earth, in my name and by my word, saith the Lord, it shall be eternally bound in the heavens." (D&C 132:46.) Thus, "his word ye shall receive, as if from mine own mouth" (D&C 21:5), and whether it be "by mine own voice or by the voice of my servants, it is the same" (D&C 1:38). Jacob, who was accountable as a prophet, declared, "We did magnify our office unto the Lord, taking upon us the responsibility, answering the sins of the people upon our own heads if we did not teach them the word of God with all diligence; wherefore, by laboring with our might their blood might not come upon our garments." (Jacob 1:19.)

Prophets are watchmen, of whose position between God and man the word of the Lord to Ezekiel is instructive, "So thou, O son of man, I have set thee a watchman unto the house of Israel; therefore thou shalt hear the word at my mouth, and warn them from me.

"When I say unto the wicked, O wicked man, thou shalt surely die; if thou dost not speak to warn the wicked from his way, that wicked man shall die in his iniquity; but his blood will I require at thine hand." (Ezekiel 33:7, 8.) Latter-day prophets build upon the foundations and prophetic ministries that have preceded theirs, but their responsibilities are intrinsic to all the stewardships associated with this great and last dispensation. The Lord said that they hold their powers and keys and are therefore accountable "in connection with all those who have

received a dispensation at any time from the beginning of the creation;

"For verily I say unto you, the keys of the dispensation, which ye have received, have come down from the fathers, and last of all, being sent down from heaven unto you.

"Verily I say unto you, behold how great is your calling. Cleanse your hearts and your garments, lest the blood of this generation be required at your hands." (D&C 112:31-33.) Thus, while they are men, their appointment is a divine one, for which they must answer to God, and "that person is not truly converted until he sees the power of God resting upon the leaders of this church, and until it goes down into his heart like fire." (Cited in Harold B. Lee, "The Strength of the Priesthood," *Ensign,* July 1972, p. 103.)

The course shall not presume to present an exhaustive biography of the presidents of the Church. Selected incidents from their lives shall be included to show evidence of the divine hand in preserving them and preparing them to assume the high position they would occupy. Representative statements expressing their testimony of the divine life and mission of Jesus Christ shall be presented so that students may understand that the presidents of the Church stand first and foremost as witnesses of the Master. Examples of their loyalty, obedience, humanity, courage, faith, steadiness in trial, and purity of life shall be noted so that the students will be brought to acknowledge that although they are mortal men, the calling they have received is a divine one, and places them in a position where mankind generally, and the Church specifically, must receive them and honor them or be "cut off from among the people." (D&C 1:14.)

In the course the prophets will not be compared to each other. Some of the peculiar gifts, talents, and inspiration of each will be noted, and the host of spiritual and worldly conditions against which their ministries were arrayed will be briefly chronicled, so that the students will perceive the Church as a dynamic kingdom—building temples, resisting wickedness, warning the world, providing for its own, worshiping the Lord and extending to man the only plan under heaven whereby man can be saved. But all this will be done on the foundation of eternal principles which the prophets announce and which remain everlastingly the same.

The course will not be a history of the Church per se, but a view and an explanation of that history through the administrations of those who have been called forth and appointed to lead. Some of the specific decisions and actions of the prophets will be noted as evidence of how the Lord works through them to carry out his purposes in the earth. Of course, the limits of time and space preclude consideration of all the decisions or even more than a mere sampling of their actions.

By considering only representative acts and teachings from the ministries of the prophets, the day-to-day progress of the kingdom will be overshadowed by the larger perspective of a heaven-inspired Church overcoming obstacles, spreading throughout the earth, and responding to the will of heaven. Thus, the students may learn to consider carefully and thoroughly the words and actions of the living prophets and recognize that safety and happiness and glory and exaltation can be had only by obedience to all that the Lord may require through the living prophet.

The orderly plan of apostolic succession shall be noted near the commencement of the course so that an understanding of the principles which govern the succession and selection of the prophets may underlie and circumscribe the whole of any student's participation in the course.

The course will not be a doctrinal course in the sense of presenting an exhaustive treatment of the doctrines of the kingdom; but it will highlight particular doctrines or policies, the establishment of which seem to be inherently tied to the ministry of a particular president. Thus, the concept of the nature of God—that he was once a man, that he became what he is now by obedience and faithfulness, and that man may obey the gospel and become like God—may be presented as one of the major themes of President Lorenzo Snow. Brigham Young's loyalty to the Prophet Joseph Smith, and thereby his example and teaching to the Saints of the respect and esteem and obedience that are appropriate with regard to how the Saints look upon the presidents, may be considered in one of the chapters on Brigham Young. The development of concepts relating to the Church correlation program would be highlighted in the chapters that emphasize the administrations of President David O. McKay and President Harold B. Lee. Thus, the presidents will be viewed as men whom God has called and prepared and brought forth to accomplish specific missions.

The Purpose of the Student Manual

Personal study is a source of progress and spiritual growth. Prayerful study is necessary for any appreciable understanding of

spiritual laws and principles. Prayerful study, under the direction of an inspired teacher, enhances and accelerates such growth. This manual is used in class by the instructor as an aid to the teaching process. However, in the event you have no teacher, you will find that your student manual is written in such a way that it will be your teacher. Use it as an aid to your effort, letting it become a springboard to take you to complete sources and texts that can enlighten you with a fulness and coverage not possible here. Determine to peruse these pages in the spirit of the exciting adventure it can be, whether that adventure be on your own or with a teacher.

How This Manual Was Organized

There are twenty-eight chapters in the manual, grouped into fourteen units. The first unit deals with the concept of Zion and how it has inspired the prophets of all dispensations, including our own. The last unit examines Zion as it pertains to modern Israel. Each of the other units treats one of the twelve presidents of the Church.

There are two chapters dealing with each president. One is a study of the man, his background, and the preparation by which the Lord brought him to the leadership of the Church. The other deals with his ministry as president and prophet. It is intended that you study the chapter on the life of a president before proceeding with a study of his ministry; hence, the order is deliberate.

Each unit is introduced with a short overview. To maintain a rapid and

easy flow for the reader, there has been a deliberate effort to avoid the use of references in the overview. However, each quote has a footnote number, and the sources are listed in the back of the manual.

A concerned effort has been made to illustrate the manual with sufficient pictures of the early life of each president so that the student will gain an appreciation for the times in which each prophet lived, the people with whom he associated, the accomplishments he made, and the historical events in which he had an instrumental part.

Criteria Used in Material Selection for This Manual

Substantial research has been expended for the writing of these chapters. It has sounded the depths of some sources and has sampled broadly from others, for example, personal diaries, the Historical Department of the Church, books that are now out of print, and interviews with some of the living relatives of the presidents.

It has been the rule that primary sources have been used or quoted in preference to secondary ones, and to quote rather than to paraphrase when referring to a statement by one of the presidents in order to better maintain the flavor of his character and life.

What to Expect in Your Study

In the process of your study, and especially as you complete this course, you will be keenly aware that the presidents of The Church of Jesus Christ of Latter-day Saints were real men and that they too

were human. You will thrill at the realization that you have actually gained a personal relationship with them.

Be careful not to rush your study, but savor each new understanding and vicarious experience you may have with these servants of the living God. Many of the things you will learn will never be forgotten; but, more importantly, you will never be the same if your study is genuine and prayerful.

Note: With the addition of new scriptures to the Pearl of Great Price on April 3, 1976, a change in the method of citation was also instituted. The books of Moses and Abraham were not affected, but the writings of Joseph Smith and the new additions are now cited as follows:

Joseph Smith 1 is now Joseph Smith—Matthew (abbreviated JS-M).

Joseph Smith 2 is now Joseph Smith—History (abbreviated JS-H).

The new addition entitled "Joseph Smith—Vision of the Celestial Kingdom" will be cited as Joseph Smith—Vision (abbreviated JS-V).

The new addition entitled "Joseph F. Smith—Vision of the Redemption of the Dead" will be cited as Joseph F. Smith—Vision (abbreviated JFS-V).

Articles of Faith will be A of F.

Most of these changes have been implemented in this manual; however, the complete titles of the two new additions to the Pearl of Great Price have been cited.

UNIT ONE
THE LAST DISPENSATION

OVERVIEW

Except for times of extreme wickedness, the Lord has provided prophets throughout the history of the world to gather the righteous and lead them as near to the ideal society called Zion as they are and were willing to be led. Generally these prophets have not been recognized as prophets by the world and have been rejected even by the house of Israel.[1] And the establishment of a Zion society rarely has been realized. However, the Lord has always held the ideal of Zion before his prophets and has promised them, in every age, that Zion would be established in the last days to flourish a thousand years.[2]

In the authority and power of the priesthood and under the direction of the Holy Ghost, Adam was told to teach all of his posterity that they must repent or they could never expect to merit an inheritance in the kingdom of God, for no unclean thing could return and dwell in the presence of God.[3]

Adam taught earnestly the truths of salvation to his family through almost the entire millennium of his life. Many believed and became the sons of God. And many did not believe, and they perished in their sins.

Centuries after his own ministry had commenced, Adam, who held the presidency of all dispensations, commissioned his grandson Enos to lead the righteous away from the land of Shulon and into a land of promise. Enos named that new promised land Cainan, after his own son, and established righteousness and peace there so successfully that 350 years later, Enoch, the seventh from Adam, was born there and commenced his ministry from there, and it was still a land of righteousness.[4]

Enoch went forth and stood upon the hills and high places, and called upon all people to repent. He led the people of God and they "were blessed upon the mountains, and upon the high places, and did flourish."[5] Enoch established Zion as a defense and a refuge from the evil of his day. After many years Adam called Enoch and the presiding prophets and all of his righteous posterity into a conference and bestowed upon them his last blessing. "And the Lord appeared unto them, and they rose up and blessed Adam. . . ."[6] Adam died three years later; but his blessing and desire did not die, for 122 years later Enoch and his city were translated and taken into heaven, and "from thence went forth the saying, ZION IS FLED."[7]

After the righteous had been caught up by the powers of heaven unto Zion and the wicked had been destroyed in the Flood, Noah labored, and so did Melchizedek after him, to bring the people into the presence of God.

Abraham walked throughout the length and breadth of the land that the Lord had promised to give him for an everlasting possession, a land that was filled with other peoples. Abraham contemplated the latter day when a new and glorious Zion would arise within the borders of his everlasting inheritance. For his faithfulness and holiness, Abraham received this plaudit from God: "For I know him, that he will command his children and his household after him, and they shall keep the way of the Lord. . . ."[8]

Moses, Elijah, Nathan, John—all the prophets—sought to gather the righteous out from the fetters and chains of a corrupt world and establish them in lands of promise. They sought to purify them so that God could dwell with them. They sought to raise cities "which hath foundations, whose builder and maker is God."[9] But although they struggled mightily and valiantly, with few exceptions they failed to bring their people into the presence of God. And they themselves endured their allotment of years as outcasts, despised and forsaken, and as strangers in the world. "These all died in faith, not having received the promises, but having seen them afar off, and were persuaded of them, and embraced them, and confessed that they were strangers and pilgrims on the earth."[10]

But they were comforted by visions and strengthened by revelations that in a latter day, the Zion they sought would come. After their death, and as immortal beings, they would return and empower a prophet and people with keys and priesthoods, with glories and honors, and Zion would be. Zion would be!

Reformation's dawn would begin to dispel the night of blackness, and scores of valiant, noble souls would seek to kindle the light but would die before the morning came. Slowly, quietly, the first rays of sunlight would peek over the mountains and filter into the world. Almost imperceptibly, the light would increase. Men who loved the darkness would rage and resist, but the light would not be denied. The morning would break. The shadows would flee. The sun would mount up, dazzling, brilliant, and march resolutely to the meridian. That day of glory so long sought would come! Zion would be established and light and truth would cover the earth. "And they shall not teach every man his neighbour, and every man his brother, saying, Know the Lord: for all shall know me, from the least to the greatest."[11] That day the prophets looked for shall come, for "no unhallowed hand can stop the work from progressing; persecutions may rage, mobs may combine, armies may assemble, calumny may defame, but the truth of God will go forth boldly, nobly, and independent, till it has penetrated every continent, visited every clime, swept every country, and sounded in every ear, till the purposes of God shall be accomplished. . . ."[12] "For the earth shall be filled with the knowledge of the glory of the Lord, as the waters cover the sea."[13] And all men and creation shall know thy God reigneth!

CHAPTER 1

THEY LOOKED FOR A CITY WHOSE BUILDER AND MAKER IS GOD

INTRODUCTION

"What was the highest point of spiritual perfection ever attained among mortal men? When did hosts of living saints ascend those heights of spiritual knowledge and personal righteousness which made them as near one with Deity as men can be and yet remain in mortality?

"True, Our Lord was perfect and some prophets have walked with God in perfect faith, but they are isolated examples of men standing virtually alone in a godless world; and true, a whole nation of Nephite Saints so lived that not one soul was lost, all were saved in the kingdom of God. (3 Ne. 27:30-31.) But only in Enoch's day and among the inhabitants of his city was that perfection found which caused the Lord himself to come down, dwell 'with his people,' and then take them from this mortal sphere into his heavenly realms. (Moses 7:16-21.) Surely life in the City of Zion reached the highest spiritual pinnacle of the ages.

"Is it any wonder, then, that righteous people of succeeding generations looked back with longing for like blessings, and for that matter that God commanded them so to do? To Abraham the Lord said: 'Remember the covenant which I make with thee; for it shall be an everlasting covenant; and thou shalt remember the days of Enoch thy father.' (*Inspired Version*, Gen. 13:13.) And remember them he did, as he and his children after him sought an habitation in that greatest of all cities—the City of Zion." (Bruce R. McConkie,

Doctrinal New Testament Commentary, 3:201-2.)

"The building up of Zion is a cause that has interested the people of God in every age; it is a theme upon which prophets, priests and kings have dwelt with peculiar delight; they have looked forward with joyful anticipation to the day in which we live; and fired with heavenly and joyful anticipations they have sung and written and prophesied of this our day; but they died without the sight. . . . " (Joseph Smith, *Teachings of the Prophet Joseph Smith*, p. 231.)

Why should you begin a course of study on the presidents of the Church by talking about those who through the ages have sought for Zion?

Speaking of Joseph Smith, the Lord said, "Him have I inspired to move the cause of Zion in mighty power for good. . . . " (D&C 21:7.) Such a description is appropriate for all the presidents of the Church; they were and are movers of the cause of Zion. So it is that you begin your study by examining the concept that has

motivated the servants of God since the beginning of time, a concept that has been a primary concern of each president of the Church that you will study in this course. (See also the article in Appendix A by Bruce R. McConkie, "Come: Let Israel Build Zion.")

ALL HOLY MEN BEFORE THE FLOOD SOUGHT FOR A DAY OF RIGHTEOUSNESS

(1-1) This Is Why Adam Called His Righteous Posterity into a Conference

"I saw Adam in the valley of Adam-ondi-Ahman. He called together his children and blessed them with a patriarchal blessing. The Lord appeared in their midst, and he (Adam) blessed them all, and foretold what should befall them to the latest generation.

"This is why Adam blessed his posterity; he wanted to bring them into the presence of God. They looked for a city, etc., 'whose builder and maker is God.' (Hebrews 11:10.)" (Smith, *Teachings*, pp. 158-59.)

And although Adam died three years after that conference, his last great wish and blessing did not die, for approximately 125 years later Enoch and his city were taken to heaven. (For an explanation of what *translation* means, see Smith, *Teachings*, pp. 170-71, and Joseph Fielding Smith, *Doctrines of Salvation*, 1:107-11.)

Adam was the father of the human race. We have learned that in the premortal spirit world he was called Michael, the archangel, and that he led the hosts of the Lord when Lucifer and his followers were cast out.

Valley of Adam-ondi-Ahman

(See Revelation 12:7; D&C 107:54.) Adam's great concern was the preservation of his posterity; therefore, he sought their conversion through the gospel and held out hope for a Zion in this life, if they were sufficiently righteous, and an eternal inheritance with their Heavenly Father.

If you will now read Moses 6 and D&C 107:49-56, you will add to your insight regarding Adam's greatness and his concern for his posterity. As you read, consider the following questions:

1. What does the phrase "residue of his posterity who were righteous" mean?

2. How many of the righteous in the earth at the time were not present at the conference?

3. Why do you suppose that the assembled hosts learned of Adam's premortal identity?

4. What was the purpose of the conference?

5. What did Adam desire to do?

(1-2) Enos, the Son of Seth, Sought to Establish the Righteous of His Day in a Land of Promise

Approximately 325 years after the Fall, Adam, who held the keys of the First Presidency, commissioned his grandson Enos to lead the righteous people into a land of promise. Enos named that new land of promise Cainan, after his son. There Enos succeeded in establishing righteousness and peace of such quality that Cainan was still a land of righteousness 350 years later. (See Moses 6:17, 41.)

If you would now read Moses 6:1-41, it would help you to catch some of the perspective of this chapter and of the whole course for the presidents of the Church. As you read, note how quickly the effects of the Fall were felt. In spite of the presence of Adam and Eve, with their great knowledge, men and women fell away in large numbers into all manner of iniquity. This helps show why President

David O. McKay so often quoted Emerson's statement about character being greater than intellect. (For example, see *Church News*, 24 Aug. 1963, p. 13.) You probably have noticed that most of the time when you break the commandments, you know better.

As you read, also note that the Lord sent prophets from the very beginning. These prophets preached repentance and held out hope for an immediate Zion. But, in large measure, Zion failed to materialize because the people rejected the prophets, just as most people do today. However, there was some success. The land of Cainan is one example; it continued to be righteous. (See Moses 6:41.) There will be other examples noted in the pages which follow. Also, the Lord periodically showed the prophets—for example, Adam, Enoch, Noah, and Abraham—visions of a Zion in the last days that would flourish for a thousand years. (See Moses 7:64.) Thus you can begin to see that much of the great hope of antiquity comes to focus and fruition in the lives and ministries of the prophets of the last dispensation.

(1-3) Enoch Was Commissioned to Gather the Righteous

When Enoch was sixty-five years old, he journeyed from the land of Cainan and along the borders of the "sea east," where he saw a glorious vision of the Lord. For the next 365 years, Enoch "walked with God" and taught the righteous of his day to do likewise. Approximately 1,050 years after the Fall, Enoch and his people were translated and taken into heaven. (See Moses 7:68, 69.)

(1-4) Enoch Gathered the Righteous to Adam-ondi-Ahman

Enoch gathered the righteous to the land of Adam-ondi-Ahman, the land where Adam dwelt, and there he commenced to build the "City of Holiness." Of this, Elder Bruce R. McConkie has written:

"In our popular Latter-day Saint hymn which begins, 'Glorious things are sung of Zion, Enoch's city seen of old,' we find William W. Phelps preserving the doctrine that '*In Adam-ondi-Ahman, Zion rose where Eden was.*' And in another hymn, written by the same author in the days of the Prophet Joseph Smith, we find these expressions: . . .

"We read that Enoch walk'd with God,
Above the power of mammon,
While Zion spread herself abroad,
And Saints and angels sang aloud,
In Adam-ondi-Ahman."
(*Mormon Doctrine*, p. 20.)

The scriptures give considerable information about the ministry of Enoch. The following passages and questions will help you see why Enoch and the Zion

he established have been important in the minds of the prophets ever since his day.

D&C 107:48, 49. How many years did the Zion of Enoch's day continue in the earth? (Compare Moses 7:68.) What happened to Enoch when he was twenty-six years of age? What three great events occurred in Enoch's life when he was sixty-five years old? How many years, therefore, did Enoch "walk with God"?

Moses 6:31, 32, 40. What significant burden did Enoch have, in addition to others? What did Mahijah have reference to when he taunted Enoch, "Tell us plainly who thou art"?

Moses 7:2-4. What great privilege and qualification did Enoch, who was pure in heart, receive? (Compare D&C 107:49.)

Moses 7:12-21. What do these passages reveal about the ministry of Enoch? What happened to his city?

(*Note:* Have you ever noticed the information that has been restored by revelation to the story of Enoch as given in the book of Moses? It amounts to approximately 111 consecutive verses [Moses 6:26-27:68], which fall between Genesis 5:21 and Genesis 5:22.)

(1-5) Enoch and His People Achieved a Holiness in the Flesh That Was Seldom Equalled

"Away back before the flood Enoch, to a generation vexed with wars and bloodshed, taught the gospel of Jesus Christ in mighty power, including the procedure required by the celestial law in loving one's neighbor as one's self. Those who believed it, lived it, with the result that 'the Lord came and dwelt with [them] and they dwelt in righteousness. . . . And the Lord called his people ZION, because they were of one heart and one mind, and dwelt in righteousness; and there was no poor among them' (Moses 7:16-18).

"Now, my brethren and sisters, they did not remove the poor from among them by turning them over to be cared for through some dole system sponsored by the warring nations. They provided for their own in the prescribed manner. By full observance of the law of Enoch, they became equal in all things, temporal and spiritual, thereby obtaining that 'union required by the law of the celestial kingdom.'" (Marion G. Romney, *Look to God and Live,* pp. 179-80.)

(1-6) Zion Is the Pure in Heart

According to the design of God and through the exercise of his own free agency, Adam opened the way for the hosts of premortal spirits to leave their heavenly home and receive a body and a probation in a finite, fallen world. In the plan of

Prophets warn the wicked

life it was necessary that the mortal probation be lived by faith and not by sight. Adam and Eve were shut out from the presence of God; but they were given commandments and ordinances and power by which they, and those of their children who would, might go back again into the presence of God. It was not necessary, and they understood it was not necessary, for a person to die before he could return to the presence of God. They were taught that if they would strive mightily to live as God directed, he would come down and dwell with them. They would have to do more than believe or know; they would also have to do. Their living of the law would have to be an accomplished fact before they could hope to be restored to the presence of God. They would have to be obedient to the servants

appointed to preside. They could not please God if they did not labor, sacrifice, serve, or gather with other saints, as God may command their leaders to direct them to do. Obedience would be the first condition of their becoming pure; and they would have to be pure, for no unclean thing could go into the presence of God. (See Moses 6:57.) But always they could respond to the ageless promise, "Blessed are the pure in heart: for they shall see God." (Matthew 5:8.) And in that way this mortal world could become more like conditions that may be found in heaven. Therefore, the Lord said, "Let Zion rejoice, for this is Zion—THE PURE IN HEART." (D&C 97:21.) (See also the article in Appendix B by Spencer W. Kimball, "Becoming the Pure in Heart.")

MELCHIZEDEK ESTABLISHED RIGHTEOUSNESS IN SALEM AND WAS CALLED THE KING OF PEACE

(1-7) Melchizedek Preached to His People in the Power and Majesty of the Holy Priesthood

Melchizedek was a man who lived sometime between the time of Noah and the time of Abraham. He was a king with legitimate authority and power in the patriarchal system, "and he did reign under his father." (Alma 13:18.) When he was still a child, long before his actual ministry commenced, "he feared God, and stopped the mouths of lions, and quenched the violence of fire." (Genesis 14:26, JST.) For his righteousness he was approved by God, and he received ordination to the holy priesthood "after the

God spoke to Abraham

order of the covenant which God made with Enoch, it being after the order of the Son of God." (Genesis 14:27, 28, JST.) That is, he received the Holy Priesthood after the Order of the Son of God. He attained the order and calling "by faith, to break mountains, to divide the seas, to dry up waters, to turn them out of their course; To put at defiance the armies of nations, to divide the earth, to break every band, to stand in the presence of God; to do all things according to his will, according to his command, subdue principalities and powers; and this by the will of the Son of God." (Genesis 14:3, 31, JST. Compare Hebrews 11:32-34.) When Melchizedek assumed the throne, the kingdom was in disarray, for "his people had waxed strong in iniquity and abomination; yea, they had all gone astray; they were full of all manner of wickedness." (Alma 13:17.) Melchizedek preached repentance to his people in the power and dignity of the holy priesthood, and they did repent insomuch that the kingdom of Salem was established and peace was settled throughout all the land administered by Melchizedek.

(1-8) Under Melchizedek, the People of Salem Wrought Righteousness and Obtained Heaven

Melchizedek lived at a time when an awareness of the development and destiny of Enoch's Zion had not been completely lost and when "men having this faith, coming up unto this order of God, were translated and taken up into heaven. And now, Melchizedek was a priest of this order; therefore he obtained peace in Salem, and was called the Prince of peace." (Genesis 14:32, 33, JST.) It appears that Melchizedek was not his given name, but was, rather, a name title that his people conferred upon him after he had succeeded in helping

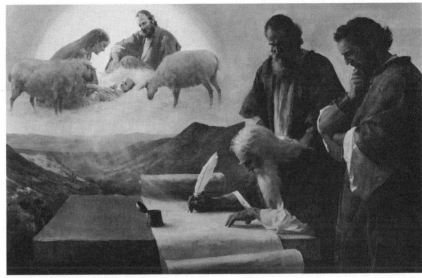

Isaiah foretold Christ's mission

them achieve such marvelous heights. The passages that speak of him say he was called the "prince of peace" or "king of peace" or the "king of Salem" *because* of what he had done. "And this Melchizedek, having thus established righteousness, was called the king of heaven by his people, or, in other words, the King of peace." (Genesis 14:36, JST.) And all those titles, by interpretation, mean "Melchizedek." (See Hebrews 7:1, 2.)

PROPHETS AND HOLY MEN HAVE LOOKED FORWARD TO THIS LAST DISPENSATION OF TIME

(1-9) Although They Were Rejected in Their Day, the Ancient Prophets Prophesied of a Day When Men Would Gather and Zion Would Arise

"Moses sought to bring the children of Israel into the presence of God, through the power of the Priesthood, but he could not. In the first ages of the world they tried to establish the same thing; and there were Eliases raised up who tried to restore these very glories, but did not obtain them; but they prophesied of a day when this

glory would be revealed. Paul spoke of the dispensation of the fullness of times, when God would gather together all things in one, etc.; and those men to whom these keys have been given, will have to be there; and they without us cannot be made perfect." (Smith, *Teachings,* p. 159.)

(1-10) All the Prophets Were Inspired by Their Assurance That Zion Would Come

[Read Hebrews 11 and D&C 45:11-14.]

Yes, it is a cause that has interested the people of God in every age. They wandered about in sheepskins. They were murdered, tortured, afflicted, mocked, scourged, and stoned. They died without seeing the rise of Zion. But in all of their difficulty, in all of their loneliness, they looked forward with an eye of faith to that day when Zion would arise and shine forth and be a standard for the nations to follow. These saints all died in faith, not having received the promised Zion but having seen it afar off, and were persuaded of it; and because of their knowledge,

they determined that they would forsake the worldliness of men and await the day when, in their flesh, they would be privileged to enter that far better land of promise.

(1-11) Each of the Modern Prophets Was Inspired by the Concept of Zion and Sought to Further Its Reality for the Saints

Our modern prophets have differed in many ways. Some were reared in financial hardship; others, in more comfortable circumstances. Some came into rural settings and knew plowing, planting, milking, and harvesting; others were born in the city and learned the meaning of work by clerking in the stores or by assisting in the business world. They varied in size, appearance, and boyhood interests. Each brought unique gifts to the office of President of The Church of Jesus Christ of Latter-day Saints.

But though they were different in many ways, in every prophet of this dispensation we find two common qualities: first, each one demonstrated a lifelong commitment to Christ, seeking diligently to be more like him on a daily basis; and, secondly, each has been driven by a vision and desire to build the kingdom of God. Like the prophets of old, they have willingly endured deprivation, hardships, persecutions, and imprisonment; they have even accepted the possibility of martyrdom rather than let the vision of a better world lie dormant or die. Like Adam, Enoch, and so many others, these are the men who have been inspired to move the cause of Zion in mighty power. One of the great blessings of this last dispensation is that once again we have those called by the Lord to do that very thing. (See articles in Appendixes A and B.)

The following talk by President Spencer W. Kimball is an appeal to all Latter-day Saints to ever keep the perspective of Zion uppermost in their minds, as the prophets of old have done.

"Now, brothers and sisters, would you put aside for a moment the pressing demands of this day and this week, and permit me to establish some very important perspectives. . . . For many years we have been taught that one important end result of our labors, hopes, and aspirations in this work is the building of a Latter-day Zion, a Zion characterized by love, harmony, and peace—a Zion in which the Lord's children are as one.

"The vision of what we are about and what should come of our labors must be kept uppermost in our minds as we learn and do our duty in the present implementation of welfare service. This applies equally to all Church activities. . . .

"This day will come; it is our destiny to help bring it about! Doesn't it motivate you to lengthen your stride and quicken your pace as you do your part in the great sanctifying work of the kingdom? It does me. It causes me to rejoice over the many opportunities for service and sacrifice afforded me and my family as we seek to do our part in establishing Zion. . . .

Prophets guide God's children

". . . Zion can be built up only among those who are the pure in heart, not a people torn by covetousness or greed, but a pure and selfless people. Not a people who are pure in appearance, rather a people who are pure in heart. Zion is to be in the world and not of the world, not dulled by a sense of carnal security, nor paralyzed by materialism. No, Zion is not things of the lower, but of the higher order, things that exalt the mind and sanctify the heart. . . .

". . . May I suggest three fundamental things we must do if we are to 'bring again Zion,' three things for which we who labor for Zion must commit ourselves.

"First, we must eliminate the individual tendency to selfishness that snares the soul, shrinks the heart, and darkens the mind. . . .

"Second, we must cooperate completely and work in harmony one with the other. There must be unanimity in our decisions and unity in our actions. . . .

"Third, we must lay on the altar and sacrifice whatever is required by the Lord. We begin by offering a 'broken heart and a contrite spirit.' We follow this by giving our best effort in our assigned fields of labor and callings. We learn our duty and execute it fully. Finally we consecrate our time, talents, and means as called upon by our file leaders and as prompted by the whisperings of the Spirit. In the Church, as in the welfare system also, we can give expression to every ability, every righteous desire, every thoughtful impulse. Whether a volunteer, father, home teacher, bishop, or neighbor, whether a visiting teacher, mother, homemaker, or friend—there is ample

opportunity to give our all. And as we give, we find that 'sacrifice brings forth the blessings of heaven!' (*Hymns*, no. 147.) And in the end, we learn it was no sacrifice at all.

"My brothers and sisters, if we can do this, then we will find ourselves clothed in the mantle of charity 'which is the greatest of all, for all things must fail—

" 'But charity is the pure love of Christ, and it endureth forever; and whoso is found possessed of it at the last day, it shall be well with him.' (Moro. 7:46-47.)

"Let us unite and pray with all the energy of heart, that we may be sealed by this bond of charity; that we may build up this latter-day Zion, that the kingdom of God may go forth, so that the kingdom of heaven may come. This is my prayer and testimony in the name of Jesus Christ. Amen." ("Becoming the Pure in Heart," *Ensign*, May 1978, pp. 80-81.)

CHAPTER 2

THEY THAT MOVE THE CAUSE OF ZION

INTRODUCTION

Fallen men in a fallen world quite often look upon this world as their home and all that there is. But those who have become informed about the joy of the Saints and the hope of eternal life "[look] for a city which hath foundations, whose builder and maker is God." (Hebrews 11:10.) They hope to return to realms of glory and escape the sin and sorrow of this world.

Babylon is the name the scriptures give the city that men build on a sandy foundation. Its brick and mortar are the political, social, and economic systems men create to seek security in their sins and in their rebellion against the King who reigns in all eternity. Zion is the name of the "city which hath foundations." It is the home of the pure in heart who seek security in obedience to the King and in his laws and in the society he creates for the believers.

In chapter one you reviewed some of the history of the hope of Zion that motivated the Saints in antiquity. You read about some who founded a Zion that was caught up to a heavenly home, and of others who were comforted by the promise that a latter-day Zion would be built and that the old Zion would come down and dwell together with the new Zion.

Did you notice that the hope of Zion was promulgated and the building of Zion was accomplished through prophets? You read about such prophets as Adam, Enos, Enoch, Noah, Melchizedek, Abraham, and Moses. What was their relationship to the Lord

and to his saints? Were they not the voice of the Lord to the saints? And did not the saints have to come unto the Lord and his city by obeying the voice of the prophet? There was no other way. And there is no other way.

In the first dispensation it was Adam. In our dispensation it is Joseph Smith. Then it was Enoch or Noah or Melchizedek. Now it is Brigham Young or Heber J. Grant or Spencer W. Kimball—whoever the Lord has placed at the head to move the cause of Zion.

PROPHETS ARE MEN WHOM GOD HAS LIFTED OUT OF THE WORLD AND HAS PREPARED AND PURIFIED

(2-1) The Prophets, Apostles, and Saints of All Ages Have Been Motivated by the Concept of Zion

The saints of God were men and women. They were mortal. They had to eat and sleep and wash their clothes. They were subject to sickness, heartache, and death. And they were subject to the joys and satisfactions of life in the world. They had no easier access to spiritual blessings than their fellowmen. The records noting their great spiritual accomplishments are simple witnesses to the fact that they paid the price demanded in obedience,

sacrifice, and service. They, with all the hosts in any age, would have to learn and obey the law that was decreed in the heavens before and upon which all blessings are predicated. Prayer, obedience, holiness—these would be required of them then just as they are required of us now. Revelation was sought for and revelation was obtained, but not without price; not without obedience, restraint, and repentance; and not without service. They loved their children and their families. They loved God. And that was their hope, their quest, and their burning desire—not to master the world but to master the heavens, not to live with men or things but to live with God! (See D&C 45:11-14 and Hebrews 11.)

(2-2) The Divine Messengers of the Lord Are Rejected with Various Excuses Because They Too Are Mortals

"Various excuses have been used over the centuries to dismiss these divine messengers. There has been denial because the prophet came from an obscure place. 'Can there any good thing come out of Nazareth?' (John 1:46.) Jesus was also met with the question, 'Is not this the carpenter's son?' (Matt. 13:55.) By one means or another, the swiftest method of rejection of the holy prophets has been to find a pretext, however false or absurd, to dismiss the man so that his message could also be dismissed. Prophets who were not glib, but slow of speech, were esteemed as naught. Instead of responding to Paul's message, some saw his bodily presence as weak and regarded his speech as contemptible. Perhaps they judged Paul by the timbre of his voice or by

his style of speech, not the truths uttered by him. . . .

"These excuses for rejection of the prophets are poor excuses. The trouble with using obscurity as a test of validity is that God has so often chosen to bring forth his work out of obscurity. He has even said it would be so. (See D&C 1:30.) Christianity did not go from Rome to Galilee; it was the other way around. In our day the routing is from Palmyra to Paris, not the reverse. Just because something is in our midst does not mean that we have been in the midst of it. We can daily drive by a museum or an art gallery but know nothing of what is inside.

"The trouble with rejection because of personal familiarity with the prophets is that the prophets are always somebody's son or somebody's neighbor. They are chosen from among the people, not transported from another planet, dramatic as that would be!" (Spencer W. Kimball, "Listen to the Prophets," *Ensign*, May 1978, pp. 76-77.)

THE LORD SPEAKS HIS WILL AND INITIATES HIS WORK THROUGH HIS PROPHETS

(2-3) In Some Matters of Communication, the Prophet Shall Be to Us "Instead of God"

"As we read the story of how Aaron was called, we find this classic statement regarding authority: 'And no man taketh this honour unto himself, but he that is called by God, as was Aaron.' (Hebrews 5:4.) God said, defining the relationship that Moses would have to God and that Aaron would have to Moses:

" 'And thou shalt speak unto him, and put words in his [Aaron's] mouth: and I will be with thy mouth, . . . and will teach you what ye shall do. And . . . he shall be to thee instead of a mouth, and

Ezekiel foretold the Book of Mormon

thou shalt be to him instead of God.' (Exodus 4:15-16.)

"Now that is as clear a relationship as I think we can find anywhere—the relationship of the prophet of the Lord and the president of the Church, the prophet, seer, and revelator, to others of us to whom he may delegate authority." (Harold B. Lee, *Stand Ye in Holy Places*, pp. 155-56.)

(2-4) Only the Living Prophet Has the Right to Revelation for the Church

"I bear witness to you, my brothers and sisters, that God sustains him, and no one else in the world today but him, because he has the holy calling of prophet, seer, and revelator, representing the Lord upon the earth in our time. *He only has the right to revelation for the people of the Church,* and if all people would understand that, they would not be tossed about by those who would seek to divert their

minds from the Church and its glorious principles. . . .

" . . . they will be fortified against false teachers and anti-Christs, and we do have them among us." (Delbert L. Stapley in *CR*, Oct. 1953, p. 70. Italics added.)

(2-5) No One Has the Right to Take His Place

"Sometimes we have brethren who become a little irritated because they are not consulted and are not asked their opinions on certain high-level matters. I have said to them, rather gently—having had a few years more experience and perhaps lessons that they may have if they live as long as I have—'I choose not to be excited over things that are none of my business.' Usually they say, 'Well, it is our business.' And I have said, 'You just think it is your business. It becomes our business when the president of the Church delegates to us some of the keys which he

holds in fulness. Until he gives us the authority, it is not our business and we do not have the right to take his place.' " (Lee, *Stand Ye in Holy Places*, p. 156.)

(2-6) God Will Never Allow His Mouthpiece to Lead the Saints Astray

"Yes, we believe in a living prophet, seer, and revelator, and I bear you my solemn witness that we have a living prophet, seer, and revelator. We are not dependent only upon the revelations given in the past as contained in our standard works—as wonderful as they are—but here in 1964 we have a mouthpiece to whom God is revealing his mind and will. *God will never permit him to lead us astray.* As has been said, God would remove us out of our place if we should attempt to do it. You have no concern. Let the management and government of God, then, be with the Lord. Do not try to find fault with the management and affairs that pertain to him alone and by revelation through his prophet—his living prophet, his seer, and his revelator, I pray humbly, in the name of Jesus Christ. Amen." (Harold B. Lee, "The Place of the Living Prophet, Seer, and Revelator," Address to Seminary and Institute of Religion Personnel, Brigham Young University, 8 July 1964, p. 13. Italics added.)

THE KEY TO PEACE AND SAFETY IN THE LAST DAYS LIES IN FOLLOWING THE MEN WHOM GOD HAS CALLED AS HIS LIVING PROPHETS

(2-7) The Prophet Is the One Who Will Guide Us Through the Frightening Events to Come

" . . . the Lord has clearly placed the responsibility for directing the work of gathering in the hands of the leaders of the Church, to whom He will reveal His will where and when such gatherings would take place in the future. It would be well, before the frightening events concerning the fulfillment of all God's promises and predictions are upon us, that the Saints in every land prepare themselves and look forward to the instruction that shall come to them from the First Presidency of this church as to where they shall be gathered. They should not be disturbed in their feelings until such instruction is given to them as it is revealed by the Lord to the proper authority." (Harold B. Lee, *Ye Are the Light of the World*, p. 167.)

(2-8) What Following a Living Prophet Means

"It is an easy thing to believe in the dead prophets, but it is a greater thing to believe in the living prophets. I will give you an illustration.

"One day when President Grant was living, I sat in my office across the street following a general conference. A man came over to see me, an elderly man. He was very upset about what had been said in this conference by some of the Brethren, including myself. I could tell from his speech that he came from a foreign land. After I had quieted him enough so he would listen, I said, 'Why did you come to America?'

" 'I came here because a prophet of God told me to come.'

" 'Who was the prophet?' I continued.

" 'Wilford Woodruff.'

" 'Do you believe Wilford Woodruff was a prophet of God?'

" 'Yes,' said he.

" 'Do you believe that his successor, President Lorenzo Snow was a prophet of God?'

" 'Yes, I do.'

" 'Do you believe that President Joseph F. Smith was a prophet of God?'

" 'Yes, sir.'

"Then came the 'sixty-four dollar question.' 'Do you believe that Heber J. Grant is a prophet of God?'

"His answer, 'I think he ought to keep his mouth shut about old age assistance.'

Noah forewarned destruction

"Now I tell you that a man in his position is on the way to apostasy. *He is forfeiting his chances for eternal life. So is everyone who cannot follow the living prophet of God.*" (Marion G. Romney in *CR*, Apr. 1953, p. 125. Italics added.)

(2-9) Safety Lies in Following the Word of the Living Prophet "As If from Mine Own Mouth"

"Now the only safety we have as members of this church is to do exactly what the Lord said to the Church in that day when the Church was organized. We must learn to give heed to the words and commandments that the Lord shall give through his prophet, 'as he receiveth them, walking in all holiness before me; . . . as if from mine own mouth, in all patience and faith.' (D&C 21:4-5.) There will be some things that take patience and faith. You may not like what comes from the authority of the Church. It may contradict your political views. It may contradict your social views. It may interfere with some of your social life. . . .

" . . . Your safety and ours depends upon whether or not we follow the ones whom the Lord has placed to preside over his church. He knows whom he wants to preside over this church, and he will make no mistake. The Lord doesn't do things by accident. . . .

"Let's keep our eye on the President of the Church. . . . " (Harold B. Lee in *CR*, Oct. 1970, pp. 152-53.)

(2-10) The Gates of Hell Will Not Prevail Against Church Members Who Follow the Word of the Living Prophet

"So on the day the Church was organized, the Lord said this: 'Wherefore, meaning the church'—and that was addressed not just to the few on that day, but to all who have been or who will be members of this church—'thou shalt give heed unto all his words and commandments which he shall give unto you as he receiveth them, walking in all holiness before me;

" 'For his word [meaning the president of the Church] ye shall receive, as if from mine own mouth, in all patience and faith.'

"Now note the promise if we will be thus obedient to seek counsel and to accept counsel from the proper channels: 'For by doing these things the gates of hell shall not prevail against you; yea, and the Lord God will disperse the powers of darkness from before you, and cause the heavens to shake for your good, and in his name's glory.' (D&C 21:4-6.)

The First Vision opened a new dispensation

18

"To you Latter-day Saints everywhere, that promise will be yours if you will follow the leadership the Lord has placed within the Church, giving heed to their counsel in patience and faith; this promise to you and yours is that the gates of hell will not prevail against you, that the Lord will disperse the powers of darkness from before you and will cause the heavens to shake for your good and his name's glory." (Harold B. Lee, "The Way to Eternal Life," *Ensign,* Nov. 1971, pp. 11-12.)

A great lesson about prophets is found in the story of how the Israelites began to be ruled by kings rather than by the prophet-judge, Samuel. Samuel told the Lord that the people had rejected him and wanted a king. The Lord answered, "They have not rejected thee, but they have rejected me, that I should not reign over them." (1 Samuel 8:7.) There are two ideas here. One is that we reject the Lord when we reject the prophets, and the other is that we end up with less than we had before.

THROUGH THE PROPHETS OF THIS LAST DISPENSATION, THE LORD WILL RESTORE EVERYTHING GIVEN FROM ADAM DOWN TO THE LATEST DAY

(2-11) A Dispensation Is a Period of Time When Gospel Knowledge and Priesthood Power Are Made Available to Men

The word *dispensation* is taken from the word *dispense,* which means to give out, to distribute, to deal out in an orderly manner, or to make available. A dispensation of the gospel is a giving out of the gospel, or a distribution of the gospel. It is to make the gospel available. Since God's kingdom is a kingdom of order, and since nothing can be

done in his kingdom unless it is done by someone authorized to do it, then a dispensation of the gospel necessarily involves someone with God's authority to dispense the gospel during a specified time through God's people. (See Moses 7:12, 68, 69.) We therefore speak of Adam, Enoch, Noah, Abraham, and others as being heads of dispensations.

(2-12) The Last Dispensation Involves Privileges, Authorities, and Powers Unknown to Other Dispensations

"The principles of the gospel were taught from the beginning among the children of Adam. Some believed and accepted them; many others rejected them, bringing down upon their heads the wrath of God, for his anger was kindled against them because of their rebellion. In course of time, when the inhabitants of the earth were sufficiently corrupt, he caused the floods to come upon them, sweeping them off the earth. Noah, who was a preacher of righteousness, continued to preach these saving principles. The gospel was also taught to Abraham, and has always been among men when they were prepared to receive it. . . .

"While the saints in former dispensations were granted every privilege and power by which they, through their faithfulness, could obtain exaltation even to the fulness, the fact remains that the Lord has reserved many privileges, authorities, powers, and much knowledge for the dispensation of the fulness of times, into which all things are to be eventually gathered and made perfect in the consummation of the purposes of the Lord towards the earth and its inhabitants." (Joseph Fielding Smith, *Doctrines of Salvation,* 1:160.)

(2-13) The Last Dispensation Shall Embrace the Sanctification of the

Human Family and the Renovation of the Earth

"This is the Kingdom of God on the earth. The people that sit before me, in connection with the many thousands that are upon the earth, are the people of God. If we have become so taught that the Lord sees that we shall be capable of managing, governing, and controlling the Kingdom of God upon the earth in a more perfect manner than it has been heretofore, you may rest assured that this people are bound to victory. Just as fast as we are capable of rightly dispensing the principles of power, of light, of knowledge, of intelligence, of wealth, of heaven, and of earth, just so fast will they be bestowed upon this people.

"If this Gospel goes to the uttermost parts of the earth and fulfils its destiny as predicted by the Prophets, by Jesus and by the Apostles, it will eventually swallow up all the good there is on the earth; it will take every honest, truthful and virtuous man and woman and every good person and gather them into the fold of this Kingdom. . . .

"What will be the final result of the restoration of the Gospel, and the destiny of the Latter-day Saints? If they are faithful to the Priesthood which God has bestowed upon us, the Gospel will revolutionize the whole world of mankind; the earth will be sanctified, and God will glorify it, and the Saints will dwell upon it in the presence of the Father and the Son." (Brigham Young, *Discourses of Brigham Young,* p. 438.)

(2-14) "The Kingdom Shall Not Be Left to Other People . . . and It Shall Stand Forever" (Daniel 2:44.)

"He has given to us the kingdom. *He has made us the promise that the*

enemy of the kingdom shall not overcome. We may have trouble. We have had trouble. We may meet with opposition, but that *opposition shall fail in its endeavor to destroy the work of God.* . . .

"The gospel has been restored, and the kingdom given to his saints according to the prophecy of Daniel. *It is not again to be removed, destroyed, or given to other people, and in his own way and time he is going to break down all other systems, that his kingdom may prevail* and that he may come and reign as Lord of lords and King of kings upon the face of the whole earth. . . .

"The Lord has called attention to the fact that *he is going to destroy systems and organizations and combinations that are false. And how is he going to do it? By giving their members the truth, if they will receive it;* by giving them the privilege of coming out of those organizations to receive the truth and have every opportunity to come into his kingdom, for his hand is outstretched ready to greet them. *If they will not come; if they will not receive his message; then, of course, they must fall with their systems. Truth will prevail; truth will stand when all else is removed, and it is destined to cover the face of the earth.*" (Smith, *Doctrines of Salvation,* 1:241.)

Section 128 of the Doctrine and Covenants catches much of the spirit and breadth of the last dispensation. Study the following verses and consider what significance they have for the fact that you now live in the age that all the prophets longed to see.

D&C 128:18 What was beginning to usher in? What does the word *complete* mean? What is the inspiration of the Lord making clear by the phrase "whole and complete and perfect union, and welding together"? Could any dispensation be omitted? Would any key be forgotten? What does the verse say must be done with the "powers and glories" that have been on the earth from the days of Adam down to 1842? What would occur from 1842 to the winding up scene?

D&C 128:21 What does the word *all* mean? Do the words *whole* and *complete* and *perfect* that appeared in the previous verse contribute to our understanding of this verse? What did "all" the angels who came do? Would there be any right, key, assignment, labor, gift, calling, power, or anything else pertaining to the work of God in the earth throughout its long history that would not be established again in the earth in the last dispensation? Would it all be restored at once? Why, or why not? What does this suggest about your privilege to be on the earth in these favored years? What does it suggest about the greatness of the prophets of this dispensation?

ALL OF THE LORD'S PLANS AND PROMISES FOR THIS WORLD ARE COMING TO FRUITION IN THE MINISTRIES OF THE LATTER-DAY PROPHETS

(2-15) It Was Decreed Before in the Heavenly Councils That Joseph Smith Would Be the Prophet of the Restoration

" . . . Joseph Smith, jr., was ordained to this great calling before the worlds were. . . . It was decreed in the counsels of eternity, long before the foundations of the earth were laid, that he should be the man, in the last dispensation of this world, to bring forth the word of God to the people and receive the fullness of the keys and power of the Priesthood of the Son of God. The Lord had his eye upon him, and upon his father, and upon his father's father, and upon their progenitors clear back to Abraham, and from Abraham to the flood, from the flood to Enoch and from Enoch to Adam. He has watched that family and that blood as it has circulated from its fountain to the birth of that man. He was foreordained in eternity to preside over this last dispensation. . . . " (Brigham Young, cited in *Deseret News* [Weekly], 26 Oct. 1859, p. 266.)

(2-16) Joseph Stands at the Head and Will Throughout All Eternity

" . . . Joseph, the head of this dispensation, Prophet, Seer and Revelator, whom God raised up, received from all these different sources, according to the mind and will of God, and according to the design of God concerning him; he received from all these different sources all the power and all the authority and all keys that were necessary for the building up of the work of God in the last days, and for the accomplishment of His purposes connected with this dispensation. He stands at the head. He is a unique character, differing from every other man in this respect, and excelling every other man. Because he was the head God chose him, and while he was faithful no man could take his place and position. He was faithful, and died faithful. He stands therefore at the head of this dispensation, and will throughout all eternity, and no man can take that power away from him. If any man holds these keys, he holds them subordinate to him." (George

Joseph Smith established the foundation of Zion

Q. Cannon, cited in *Deseret News* [Weekly], 21 Feb. 1883, p. 66.)

(2-17) All the Modern Prophets Were Ordained in the Premortal World

Speaking of the premortal appointment of all the prophets in general, and of President Spencer W. Kimball in particular, Elder Bruce R. McConkie said:

"May I say that there is no chance in the call of these brethren to direct the Lord's work on earth. His hand is in it. He knows the end from the beginning. He ordained and established the plan of salvation and decreed that his everlasting gospel should be revealed to man in a series of dispensations commencing with Adam and continuing to Joseph Smith. And he—the Almighty—chooses the

prophets and apostles who minister in his name and present his message to the world in every age and dispensation. He selects and foreordains his ministers; he sends them to earth at the times before appointed; he guides and directs their continuing mortal preparations; and he then calls them to those positions they were foreordained to receive from before the foundations of the earth.

"May I take President Spencer W. Kimball as an illustration and pattern of one who was prepared, foreordained, and called to leadership among the Lord's people. He was, it is true, born in the household of faith. Like Jacob, who inherited spiritual talents from Isaac and Abraham, so is he endowed by natural inheritance with those talents and abilities that

prepare him for his present position of apostolic presidency.

"But more than mortal birth, more than mortal preparation are involved. He was born in the household of faith for a reason, and it was not this life alone that prepared him to stand as a minister of light and truth and salvation to his fellow mortals. The fact is, he is a spirit son of God who was called and chosen and foreordained before the foundations of the earth were laid, and he is now fulfilling the destiny designed for him from the preexistence, and promised him, in our presence, as we sat with him in the grand council when God himself was there. . . .

" . . . President Kimball now wears the mantle of Joseph Smith and was a participant in the operation of the same law of foreordination." (*CR*, Apr. 1974, p. 101.)

(2-18) Each of the Presidents of the Church Had Special Gifts and Talents That Qualified Him to Act as the Lord's Mouthpiece

"On the sacred occasion three months ago when I began to sense the magnitude of the overwhelming responsibility which I must now assume, I went to the holy temple. There, in prayerful meditation, I looked upon the paintings of those men of God—true, pure men, God's noblemen—who had preceded me in a similar calling.

"A few days ago in the early morning hours, in my private study at home and all alone with my thoughts, I read the tributes paid to each of the Presidents by those who had been most closely associated with each of them.

"Joseph Smith was the one whom the Lord raised up from boyhood and endowed with divine authority and taught the things

necessary for him to know and to obtain the priesthood and to lay the foundation for God's kingdom in these latter days.

"There was President Brigham Young, who was foreordained before this world was, for his divine calling to lead the persecuted Saints in fleeing from the wrath that threatened the Saints in those early gathering places in Missouri and Illinois and to pioneer the building of an inland commonwealth in the tops of these majestic mountains, to fulfill God's purposes.

"To look upon the features of President John Taylor was to gain a realization that here was one, as President Joseph F. Smith spoke of him, 'One of the purest men I ever knew. . . .'

"As I saw the sainted face of President Wilford Woodruff, I was aware that here was a man like Nathanael of old, in whom there was no guile, and susceptible to the impressions of the Spirit of the Lord, by whose light he seemed to almost always walk 'not knowing beforehand the thing he was to do.'

"While President Lorenzo Snow had but a brief administration, he had a special mission to establish his people on a more solid temporal foundation by the determined application of the law of sacrifice, to relieve the great burdens placed upon the Church because of mistakes and errors which had unwittingly crept in.

"When I want to seek for a more clear definition of doctrinal subjects, I have usually turned to

the writings and sermons of President Joseph F. Smith. As I looked upon his noble stature, I thought of the nine-year-old boy helping his widowed mother across the plains and the 15-year-old missionary on the slopes of Haleakala on the isle of Maui being strengthened by a heavenly vision with his uncle, Joseph Smith. It was he who presided during the stormy days when an antagonistic press maligned the Church, but his was the steady arm by the Lord's appointment to carry off the Church triumphantly.

"I suppose I never drew closer to the meaning of a divine calling than when President Heber J. Grant placed his hands upon my shoulders and, with a deep feeling akin to mine, announced my calling to be an apostle of the Lord Jesus Christ. As his picture looked down upon me, there came again to my mind the prophetic words of his inspired blessing when I was ordained in the holy temple under his hands.

"President George Albert Smith was a disciple of friendship and love. He was indeed a friend to everyone. My gaze at his likeness seemed to give me a warmth of that radiance which made every man his friend.

"Tall and impressive was President David O. McKay, as he now looked at me with those piercing eyes, which always seemed to search my very soul. Never was I privileged to be in his presence but that I felt for a brief moment, as I had done on so many occasions, that I was a better man for having been in his company.

"To him who sought no earthly honors, but whose whole soul delighted in the things of the spirit, President Joseph Fielding Smith was there with his smiling face, my

The Melchizedek Priesthood was restored

beloved prophet-leader who made no compromise with truth. As 'the finger of God touched him and he slept,' he seemed in that brief moment to be passing to me, as it were, a sceptre of righteousness as though to say to me, 'Go thou and do likewise.' " (Harold B. Lee in *CR*, Oct. 1972, pp. 18-19.)

You are about to embark on a study of the lives of those men whom God has called to preside over the Saints of this dispensation, the men whom God has inspired to move his cause forth with great power, the men who provide the key to our own spiritual and temporal safety. As you study each life, ponder this question: What is it that brought them to such a high and holy calling? In the answer to that question you will find a great model for you to follow. We live in the last days. We live in the dispensation that will finally see Zion triumphant. Elder Wilford Woodruff commented thus:

"There never was a generation of the inhabitants of the earth in any age of the world who had greater events awaiting them than the present. . . . And an age fraught with greater interest to the children of men than the one in which we live never dawned since the creation of the world." (*JD*, 18:110-11.)

In a similar mood, the Prophet Joseph said this:

"The blessings of the Most High will rest upon our tabernacles, and our name will be handed down to future ages; our children will rise up and call us blessed; and generations yet unborn will dwell with peculiar delight upon the scenes that we have passed through, the privations that we have endured; the untiring zeal that we have manifested; the all but insurmountable difficulties that we have overcome in laying the foundation of a work that brought about the glory and blessing which they will realize; a work that God and angels have contemplated with delight for generations past; that fired the souls of the ancient patriarchs and prophets; a work that is destined to bring about the destruction of the powers of darkness, the renovation of the earth, the glory of God, and the salvation of the human family." (Joseph Smith, *Teachings of the Prophet Joseph Smith*, p. 232.)

Now study carefully the lives of those who were called by God as his leaders in this last tremendous age. And ask yourself, What can I learn from the presidents of the Church?

JOSEPH SMITH
And the Restoration

OVERVIEW

Mighty, foreordained, he was a noble spirit. He was tutored in the mansions of eternity, chosen before he was born and numbered with the elect. Obedience and holiness before his mortal birth in rural New England in 1805 prepared him for his earthly mission. He was raised a farm boy. His parents moved often and they were poor. Joseph worked with his family, sought religion, loved his parents and suffered their hardships. They were disadvantaged by crop failure, made victims of land fraud, and betrayed in investment. Adversity would become his common lot. Stricken by disease at age seven, he was left lame and limping for years, years filled with farm work and family moves. At eleven he was forced to walk much of the way as the family moved from Vermont to Palmyra, New York. At fourteen, he was fired upon by an intended assassin.

In the spring of 1820 he was visited by the Father and the Son and persecuted thenceforward for his witness that God had spoken to him. The heavens opened again in 1823; Moroni came, followed by a host of other heavenly messengers, "all declaring their dispensation, their rights, their keys. . . . "[1] Instructed by the resurrected Christ, tutored by angels, custodian of great truths (some of which he was forbidden to teach), and empowered through the return of ancients who had held the keys themselves, he was a man whose mind swelled broad as eternity.

In the face of relentless opposition, he had custody of the sacred plates for about eighteen months. During this hectic time, he married Emma Hale in 1827, buried his firstborn son in 1828, translated the plates in the first months of 1829, and published the Book of Mormon to a hostile world in 1830. In

that same year the tiny seed was planted. With a great vision of what would eventually be, and by divine appointment, Joseph Smith planted the seed and then set about to make it grow. Revelation followed revelation; a Book of Commandments was issued in Missouri in 1833, newspapers were established, property purchased, crops planted, businesses chartered, industry commenced, temples planned and cornerstones set. But Zion was not to be—yet. The revelations were issued in the Doctrine and Covenants at Kirtland in 1835, a temple was raised, quorums ordained, dozens sent to lift the warning voice, and thousands heard—in Britain, Scandinavia, the United States—thousands gathered to Illinois, cities were laid out, and a university planned.

Mobbed, beaten—Joseph would bear scars of abuse to his grave. Over forty-six lawsuits were brought against him. He spent months in jail on trumped up charges. Five of his and Emma's nine children died in infancy. Persecution raged. Members of the Church were driven from New York, Ohio, Missouri, and after his death, from Illinois.

There were prophets before, but here was the Prophet of the Restoration. Joseph had the spirit and power of all the prophets. He taught of the Creation, the Fall, the Atonement, of the history of God's dealings from Adam to John the Baptist, and of the life and ministry of Christ and the apostles—in Asia and America. He seemed to be as familiar with the ancients as though he had spent his life among them. He taught about the apostasy, and of the restoration through him of every key and power by which God designed to perfect the Saints and bear off the kingdom triumphant. He became God's instrument. Of Joseph the Lord said,

"Him have I inspired to move the cause of Zion in mighty power for good, and his diligence I know, and his prayers I have heard. Yea, his weeping for Zion I have seen, and I will cause that he shall mourn for her no longer. . . . "[2]

Selfless in his associations, zealous in his call, and loyal to his brethren, valiant against evil, fearless in his march to destiny ("I shall not live [to be] forty," he often said),[3] this forged instrument of heaven could not rest. Converts were welcomed, plans for the prophesied trek west were discussed. He was president, prophet, priest, mayor, soldier, friend, brother, husband, and father—father to his own children and father to his people. There were many places: Palmyra, Colesville, Thompson, Hiram, Kirtland, Far West, Jackson, Caldwell, and Commerce, renamed Nauvoo. To Nauvoo—the City of Joseph—he gathered the Saints, dispensed holy ordinances, instructed, preached, buried his father, prophesied, rolled off the burden of the kingdom onto the shoulders of the Twelve and sent them away to avoid the imminent storm. And then he went like a lamb to the slaughter, and died innocent at Carthage. Yes, finally there was Carthage, with mobbers, assassins, and traitors. On a summer afternoon they rushed the jail, armed and resolute. His years had not been numbered less. His last words were, "Oh Lord, my God!"[4]

"I obtained power," he said, "on the principles of truth and virtue, which would last when I was dead and gone."[5] "For how knoweth a man the master," the Book of Mormon said, "whom he has not served, and who is a stranger unto him, and is far from the thoughts and intents of his heart?"[6] Certain it is that Joseph knew his Master, that Redeemer who had said to him before, "You shall dwell with me in glory."[7]

CHAPTER 3
THE YOUTH AND EDUCATION OF THE PROPHET

INTRODUCTION

The year was 1812. Napoleon was desperate for a victory in Russia, and all of Europe waited in a hush for news from the wars. In America, Plattsburg and Fort Detroit were familiar names—the United States was deadlocked in war with Great Britain.

But the fate of nations seemed remote to the obscure village of Lebanon in central New Hampshire. There a seven-year-old boy named Joseph Smith struggled to endure an unusually severe infection that appeared to center in his left leg. During the weeks that dragged along before the infection cleared, twelve-year-old Hyrum kept a faithful and comforting vigil near the bed of his younger brother. As they passed those long hours together, Joseph suffering and Hyrum attending, foreordinations began to focus and bonds of love and trust and mutual help were forged. Three decades hence, Joseph Smith would be Prophet and President of The Church of Jesus Christ of Latter-day Saints, Mayor of Nauvoo (the fastest growing and one of the largest cities in Illinois at that time), Lieutenant General of the Nauvoo Legion, and candidate for the presidency of the United States. Hyrum Smith would be Associate President of the Church, Vice-Mayor of the city of Nauvoo, and Major-General of the Nauvoo Legion. "In life they were not divided. . . . " (D&C 135:3.) But as they were in 1812, farm boys of rural New England, who on the earth would have guessed the high destiny that beckoned them?

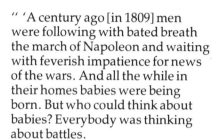

Lebanon would not hold Joseph Smith. Family moves would take him to Palmyra, New York, where divine appointments would be kept. Translation of the Book of Mormon and the organization of the restored church would carry the name Joseph Smith throughout New England. His people would build temples and cities that would attract the attention of the nation. He would announce his candidacy in the presidential election of 1844. America would know of Joseph Smith, but the Lord had said, "The ends of the earth shall inquire after thy name." (D&C 122:1.) The tide of restored truth would burst from the Americas. For that same Jesus, whose servant he was, had commanded holy men in an earlier age, "Go ye therefore, and teach all nations, baptizing them in the name of the Father, and of the Son, and of the Holy Ghost." (Matthew 28:19.) Joseph Smith, whose ministry would lay the foundation for that mighty effort in the last days, was born in New England, on a winter day in 1805.

JOSEPH SMITH WAS A PURE YOUNG MAN

(3-1) God Sends Babies to Fulfill His Purposes

"About sixty years ago, F. M. Bareham wrote the following:

" 'A century ago [in 1809] men were following with bated breath the march of Napoleon and waiting with feverish impatience for news of the wars. And all the while in their homes babies were being born. But who could think about babies? Everybody was thinking about battles.

" 'In one year between Trafalgar and Waterloo there stole into the world a host of heroes: Gladstone was born in Liverpool; Tennyson at the Somersby Rectory; and Oliver Wendell Holmes in Massachusetts. Abraham Lincoln was born in Kentucky, and music was enriched by the advent of Felix Mendelssohn in Hamburg.'

"Quoting Bareham further:

" 'But nobody thought of babies, everybody was thinking of battles. Yet which of the battles of 1809 mattered more than the babies of 1809? We fancy God can manage His world only with great battalions, when all the time he is doing it with beautiful babies.

" 'When a wrong wants righting, or a truth wants preaching, or a continent wants discovering, God sends a baby into the world to do it.'

"While most of the thousands of precious infants born every hour will never be known outside their own neighborhoods, there are great souls being born who will rise above their surroundings. . . .

" . . . One mother gives us a Shakespeare, another a Michelangelo, and another an Abraham Lincoln, and still another a Joseph Smith.

"When theologians are reeling and stumbling, when lips are pretending and hearts are wandering, and people are

'running to and fro, seeking the word of the Lord and cannot find it'—when clouds of error need dissipating and spiritual darkness needs penetrating and heavens need opening, a little infant is born. Just a few scattered neighbors in a hilly region in the backwoods even know that Lucy is expecting. There is no prenatal care or nurses; no hospital, no ambulance, no delivery room. Babies live and die in this rough environment and few know about it.

"Another child for Lucy! No trumpets are sounded; no hourly bulletins posted; no pictures taken; no notice is given; just a few friendly community folk pass a word along. It's a boy! Little do the brothers and sisters dream that a prophet is born to their family; even his proud parents can little suspect his spectacular destiny. No countryside farmers or loungers at the country store, no village gossips even surmise how much they could discuss, did they but have the power of prophetic vision." (Spencer W. Kimball, *Faith Precedes the Miracle,* pp. 323-25.)

Lucy Mack Smith

(3-2) Joseph Smith Was a Boy of Courage and Resolve

In describing the time when his leg was seriously infected, Joseph's mother said:

"[Joseph's] leg soon began to swell and he continued to suffer the greatest agony for the space of two weeks longer. . . .

" . . . we laid Joseph upon a low bed and Hyrum sat beside him, almost day and night for some considerable length of time, holding the affected part of his leg in his hands and pressing it between them, so that his afflicted brother might be enabled to endure the pain which was so excruciating that he was scarcely able to bear it. . . .

" . . . we deemed it wisdom to call a council of surgeons. . . .

"The principal surgeon, after a moment's conversation, ordered cords to be brought to bind Joseph fast to a bedstead; but to this Joseph objected. The doctor, however, insisted that he must be confined, upon which Joseph said very decidedly, 'No, doctor, I will not be bound, for I can bear the operation much better if I have my liberty.' 'Then,' said Dr. Stone, 'will you drink some brandy?'

" 'No,' said Joseph, 'not one drop.'

" 'Will you take some wine?' rejoined the doctor. 'You must take something, or you can never endure the severe operation to which you must be subjected.'

" 'No,' exclaimed Joseph, 'I will not touch one particle of liquor, neither will I be tied down; but I will tell you what I will do—I will have my father sit on the bed and hold me in his arms, and then I will do whatever is necessary in order to have the bone taken out.'

Looking at me, he said, 'Mother, I want you to leave the room, for I know you cannot bear to see me suffer so; father can stand it, but you have carried me so much, and watched over me so long, you are almost worn out.' Then looking up into my face, his eyes swimming in tears, he continued. 'Now, mother, promise me that you will not stay, will you? The Lord will help me, and I shall get through with it.' . . .

"The surgeons commenced operating by boring into the bone of his leg, first on one side of the bone where it was affected, then on the other side, after which they broke it off with a pair of forceps or pincers. They thus took away large pieces of the bone. When they broke off the first piece, Joseph screamed. . . .

"Joseph immediately commenced getting better, and from this onward, continued to mend until he became strong and healthy." (Lucy Mack Smith, *History of Joseph Smith*, pp. 55-58.)

(3-3) Even at an Early Age the Adversary Seemed Bent on Destroying Joseph

"I shall say nothing respecting him until he arrived at the age of fourteen. . . . I suppose, from questions which are frequently asked me, that it is thought by some that I shall be likely to tell many very remarkable incidents which attended his childhood; but, as nothing occurred during his early life except those trivial circumstances which are common to that state of human existence, I pass them in silence.

"At the age of fourteen an incident occurred which alarmed us much, as we knew not the cause of it. Joseph being a remarkably quiet, well-disposed child, we did not suspect that any one had aught against him. He was out one evening on an errand, and, on returning home, as he was passing through the dooryard, a gun was fired across his pathway with the evident intention of shooting him. He sprang to the door much frightened. We immediately went in search of the assassin, but could find no trace of him that evening. . . . We have not as yet discovered the man who made this attempt at murder, neither can we discover the cause thereof." (Smith, *History of Joseph Smith*, pp. 67-68.)

JOSEPH SMITH SAW THE FATHER AND THE SON

(3-4) Joseph Was Acutely Sensitive to the Unusual Excitement About Religion That Prevailed in His Area

There were so many churches, and the pageantry of the opposing sects was paraded before this young boy. Each of the many contended against all the rest. Who was right? Who could be trusted? Who could be believed? Did God have a true religion? How could anyone know—for sure?

Joseph Smith, Sr.

Please stop now and carefully read Joseph Smith—History 5-20, wherein he records his story of the First Vision. You may be tempted to think you have read it many times before, but read it again now as you study the life of Joseph Smith, for it is one of the most significant events in the history of mankind.

(3-5) In Another Account of the First Vision, Joseph Indicated in More Detail the Events Which Led Him to the Grove

During his ministry, Joseph Smith had occasion to prepare accounts of the First Vision other than the one recorded in the Pearl of Great Price. In one such account, he explained his concern about which church was right and about the troubling questions that eventually led him to ask God.

"At about the age of twelve years my mind became seriously impressed with regard to the all-important concerns for the welfare of my immortal soul, which led me to searching the scriptures, believing as I was taught, that they contained the word of God. Thus, applying myself to them and my intimate acquaintance with those of different denominations led me to marvel exceedingly, for I discovered that they did not adorn their profession by a holy walk and godly conversation agreeable to what I found contained in that sacred depository. This was a grief to my soul. Thus from the age of twelve years to fifteen I pondered many things in my heart concerning the situation of the world of mankind, the contentions and divisions, the wickedness and abominations and the darkness which pervaded the minds of mankind. My mind became exceedingly distressed, for I became convinced of my sins, and by searching the scriptures I found that mankind did not come unto the Lord but that they had apostatized from the true and living faith. And there was no society or denomination that built upon the gospel of Jesus Christ as recorded in the New Testament. And I felt to mourn for my own sins and for the sins of the world, for I learned in the scriptures that God was the same yesterday, today, and forever, that he was no respecter of persons, for he was God. For I looked upon the sun—the glorious luminary of the earth—and also the moon, rolling in their majesty through the heavens, and also the stars shining in their courses, and the earth also upon which I stood, and the beasts of the field and the fowls of heaven and the fish of the waters, and also man walking forth upon the face of the earth in majesty and in the strength of beauty. . . . And when I considered upon these things, my heart exclaimed, 'Well hath the wise man said, "It is a fool that saith in his heart there is no God." 'My heart exclaimed, 'All these bear testimony and bespeak an omnipotent and omnipresent power, a being who maketh laws and decreeth and bindeth all things in their bounds, who filleth eternity, who was and is and will be from all eternity to eternity.' And when I considered all these things, and that that being seeketh such to worship him as worship him in spirit and in truth, therefore I cried unto the Lord for mercy, for there was none else to whom I could go and obtain mercy. And the Lord heard my cry in the wilderness and while in the attitude of calling upon the Lord, in the 15th year of my age, a pillar of light above the brightness of the sun at noon day came down from above and rested upon me and I was filled with the spirit of God.

Four churches in Palmyra

And the Lord opened the heavens upon me and I saw the Lord and he spake unto me saying, 'Joseph, my son, thy sins are forgiven thee. Go thy way, walk in my statutes and keep my commandments. Behold, I am the Lord of glory. I was crucified for the world that all those who believe on my name may have eternal life. Behold, the world lieth in sin at this time, and none doeth good, no not one. They have turned aside from the gospel and keep not my commandments. They draw near to me with their lips while their hearts are far from me. And mine anger is kindling against the inhabitants of the earth to visit them according to this ungodliness and to bring to pass that which hath been spoken by the mouth of the prophets and apostles. Behold and lo, I come quickly, as is written of me, in the cloud, clothed in the glory of my Father.' And my soul was filled with love and for many days I could rejoice with great joy and the Lord was with me but could find none that would believe the heavenly vision." (Joseph Smith, "Kirtland Letter Book" [MS, LDS Historian's Library], 1829-1835, pp. 1-6, as cited in Dean C. Jessee, "The Early Accounts of Joseph Smith's First Vision," *BYU Studies*, vol. 9, no. 3, Spring 1969, pp. 279-80. The original spelling, punctuation, and grammar have been altered to conform to contemporary usage.)

The Sacred Grove

(3-6) The Father and Son Came Personally to the Boy Prophet

There were parliaments and congresses, but God would not speak through them. Kings reigned and prime ministers sat. There were presidents, professors, priests—but this was not to be the work of man. There were temples, universities, cathedrals—but this was to be no slight altering of the human system. This was to be a

restoration, direct from heaven. This was a work of God. And the foundations for this mighty work were laid by God himself. He came, the morning broke, and the shadows fled.

When President Harold B. Lee visited the Sacred Grove July 28, 1973, he said: "I know this is the place where *the Father and the Son came.*" (*Church News*, 4 Aug. 1973, p. 3. Italics added.)

(3-7) After the Visit of the Father and the Son, Joseph Smith Was Persecuted and Ridiculed for His Witness That God Had Spoken to Him

Joseph's mother wrote, "From this time until the twenty-first of September, 1823, Joseph continued, as usual, to labor with his father, and nothing during this interval occurred of very great importance—though he suffered

every kind of opposition and persecution from the different orders of religionists.'' (Smith, *History of Joseph Smith*, p. 74.) Now here is a marvelous thing. A world against which the heavens had remained closed for almost two millennia had been revisited. Revelation, so long absent, had returned. The masses of men were groping, their leaders pretending to search. Why, then, would the sincere claim of new revelation incur such immediate and universal wrath? Joseph Smith himself recorded:

[**Read Joseph Smith—History 21-26.**]

(3-8) Joseph Smith Never Pretended to Be Anything More Than a Man Who Had Been Called by God

Here was new revelation. The heavens had opened again, and Joseph Smith had seen the Father and the Son. Here was opportunity aplenty to claim superior holiness. Here was the first real justification in centuries to vaunt oneself and encourage the adulation of the masses. But Joseph Smith said instead:

[**Read Joseph Smith—History 27, 28.**]

Some enemies of the Prophet and the Church have tried to infer from Joseph's honest evaluation of himself that he was not worthy of his calling by his own declaration. On another occasion, Joseph answered those critics by saying this:

''During this time, as is common to most, or all youths, I fell into many vices and follies; but as my accusers are, and have been forward to accuse me of being guilty of gross and outrageous violations of the peace and good order of the community, I take the occasion to remark that, though as I have said above, 'as is common to most, or all

youths, I fell into many vices and follies.' I have not, neither can it be sustained, in truth, been guilty of wronging or injuring any man or society of men; and those imperfections to which I allude, and for which I have often had occasion to lament, were a light, and too often, vain mind, exhibiting a foolish and trifling conversation.

''This being all, and the worst, that my accusers can substantiate against my moral character, I wish to add that it is not without a deep feeling of regret that I am thus called upon in answer to my own conscience, to fulfil a duty I owe to myself, as well as to the cause of truth, in making this public confession of my former uncircumspect walk, and trifling conversation and more particularly, as I often acted in violation of those holy precepts which I knew came from God. . . . I do not, nor never have, pretended to be any other than a man 'subject to passion,' and liable, without the assisting grace of the Savior, to deviate from that perfect path in which all men are commanded to walk.'' (*HC*, 1:10.)

JOSEPH SMITH WAS VISITED FREQUENTLY BY ANGELS

When Joseph Smith first prepared a record of those years that had preceded the organization of the restored church, he related a sequence of four events that had occurred, events by which the foundation of the great latter-day work had been laid. These included (1) the testimony from on high, or the First Vision; (2) the ministering of angels in bringing forth the Book of Mormon; (3) the restoration of the Aaronic Priesthood; and (4) the restoration of the Melchizedek

Priesthood. (See ''Kirtland Letter Book'' [MS, LDS Historian's Library], 1829-1836, p. 1.) In September 1823, the ministry of angels commenced. Again we ask you to read the story of the angel Moroni's visits, though you may be familiar with it. It should still have great power for you, for it too records one of history's most important events. Please read Joseph Smith—History 29-50.

(3-9) Joseph's Mother Records What Happened the Morning Following Moroni's Visit

''The next day, my husband, Alvin, and Joseph, were reaping together in the field, and as they were reaping, Joseph stopped quite suddenly, and seemed to be in a very deep study. Alvin, observing it, hurried him, saying, 'We must not slacken our hands or we will not be able to complete our task.' Upon this Joseph went to work again, and after laboring a short time, he stopped just as he had done before. This being quite unusual and strange, it attracted the attention of his father, upon which he discovered that Joseph was very pale. My husband, supposing that he was sick, told him to go to the house, and have his mother doctor him. He accordingly ceased his work, and started, but on coming to a beautiful green, . . . he was so weak he could proceed no further. He was here but a short time, when the messenger whom he saw the previous night, visited him again, and . . . he said . . . 'Why did you not tell your father that which I commanded you to tell him?' Joseph replied, 'I was afraid my father would not believe me.' The angel rejoined, 'He will believe every word you say to him.'

''Joseph then promised the angel that he would do as he had been

Moroni's visit

that was to be performed in the latter days.'' (Orson Pratt, *Deseret News* [Weekly], 2 Oct. 1872. Italics added.)

''The principles which he had placed him in communication with the Lord, and not only with the Lord, but with the ancient apostles and prophets; such men, for instance, as Abraham, Isaac, Jacob, Noah, Adam, Seth, Enoch, and Jesus, and the Father, and the apostles that lived on this continent, as well as those who lived on the Asiatic continent. He seemed to be as familiar with these people as we are with one another.'' (John Taylor, *The Gospel Kingdom*, p. 353.)

''Joseph Smith has often been termed an illiterate, unlearned man. He was a farmer's son, and had very small chance of education. What primer had he to reveal the fullness of the Gospel to the world? None at all, only as he was taught by the administration of angels from heaven, by the voice of God and by the inspiration and power of the Holy Ghost.'' (Wilford Woodruff in *JD*, 16:34-35.)

Consider the special circumstances of Joseph Smith's youthful preparation. Educated by heavenly tutors, untainted by the biases and prejudices so skillfully engendured by mortal educators, the boy Joseph was wiser in spiritual matters than his adult contemporaries. Is it any wonder that his father and his brothers saw in this unusual boy the qualities of greatness? Joseph Smith, Sr., ever believed, encouraged, and blessed his son. Alvin charged Joseph to be true to the trust God had placed in him and to bring forth the record of Moroni. Hyrum stood firmly by his side even unto death. Are there many mortals in whom you

commanded. Upon this, the messenger departed, and Joseph returned to the field. . . . '' (Smith, *History of Joseph Smith*, p. 79.)

(3-10) Moroni Became Young Joseph's Teacher, and During the Four Years from 1823 to 1827, While Awaiting the Time for Possessing the Plates, Many Other Angels Came to Teach Him

''Joseph Smith was an unlearned youth, so far as the learning of the world is concerned. *He was taught by the angel Moroni.* He received his education from above, from God Almighty, and not from man-made institutions; but to charge him with

being ignorant would be both unjust and false; no man or combination of men possessed greater intelligence than he, nor could the combined wisdom and cunning of the age produce an equivalent for what he did. He was not ignorant, for he was taught by him from whom all intelligence flows. He possessed a knowledge of God and of his law, and of eternity. . . . '' (Joseph F. Smith, *Gospel Doctrine*, p. 484. Italics added.)

'' . . . during these four years he was *often* ministered to by the angels of God, and received instruction concerning the work

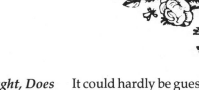

could put such trust? Who was this Joseph Smith to have commanded such loyalty from those who knew him best? Why had God chosen him? What was his great mission? Meditate upon these things as you proceed.

THROUGH HEAVENLY PREPARATION JOSEPH SMITH ESTABLISHED THE KINGDOM OF GOD

(3-11) Joseph Smith Was Encouraged to Be Strictly Obedient in Order to Retain the Favor of Heaven

From the time Joseph first told his father about his visions and assignments from heavenly messengers, Joseph Smith, Sr., gave his son unqualified support. Some of his support came in the form of fatherly warnings that he must be very careful not to fail in his important mission. But as the years rolled along and the restoration of the truth began to be firmly established, the Prophet's father learned by revelation that Joseph would continue faithful and live to fulfill his mission completely. In his dying blessing to Joseph he said:

" 'Joseph, my son, you are called to a high and holy calling. You are even called to do the work of the Lord. Hold out faithful and you shall be blest and your children after you. You shall even live to finish your work.' At this Joseph cried out, weeping, 'Oh! my father, shall I?' 'Yes,' said his father, 'you shall live to lay out the plan of all the work which God has given you to do. This is my dying blessing upon your head in the name of Jesus. I also confirm your former blessing upon your head; for it shall be fulfilled. Even so. Amen.' " (Cited in Smith, *History of Joseph Smith*, pp. 309-10.)

(3-12) The World Has Sought, Does and Will Seek the Name Joseph Smith Because of the Saving Truths of the Gospel He Restored

The heavens were opened, and earth was never to be the same. Old ideas began to crumble as new revelations of eternal principles brought truths that would begin to change the world. The world could not help but note him; indeed, it has been impelled to reckon with the Prophet.

"Joseph Smith was a prophet, called in these last days to receive by revelation the saving truths of the gospel and to stand as a legal administrator, having power from on high, to administer the ordinances of the gospel.

"Since these truths revealed through him are the ones which shall go forth to every nation before the Second Coming, it is little wonder that we find Moroni saying to Joseph Smith that his 'name should be had for good and evil among all nations, kindreds, and tongues, or that it should be both good and evil spoken of among all people.' (Joseph Smith 2:33.)

"Nor is it any wonder when we later find the Lord saying to the Prophet: 'The ends of the earth shall inquire after thy name, and fools shall have thee in derision, and hell shall rage against thee;

" 'While the pure in heart, and the wise, and the noble, and the virtuous, shall seek counsel, and authority, and blessings constantly from under thy hand.' (D&C 122:1-2.)

"The ends of the earth are now beginning to inquire after the name of Joseph Smith, and many people in many nations are rejoicing in the gospel restored through his instrumentality." (Joseph Fielding Smith in *CR*, Oct. 1970, p. 6.)

It could hardly be guessed that the model organization formed in a farmhouse in Fayette, New York, by six members on April 6, 1830, would grow to become a powerful worldwide organization. Elder LeGrand Richards reminded a body of priesthood, however, that such a fact was common knowledge to him who laid the foundation of the kingdom of God on earth.

"I would like to give you an illustration of prophecy in our day. In the general conference of the Church in 1898, President Wilford Woodruff told about when he first met the Prophet Joseph Smith. He said he met the Prophet for the first time when he attended a meeting where many of the brethren bore testimony of the Restoration. When they got through, the Prophet said, 'Brethren, I have been very much edified and instructed in your testimonies here tonight, but I want to say to you before the Lord that you know no more concerning the destiny of this church and kingdom than a babe upon his mother's lap.' It is only a little handful of priesthood you see here, and yet our last priesthood meeting during April conference was broadcast in 1,050 different buildings all over the land. Is there anything else like it in this world? Has there ever been anything like it in the world, as far as the priesthood of God is concerned? The Prophet Joseph understood all of this, and he said, 'It is only a little handful of priesthood you see here tonight, but this Church will fill North and South America. It will fill the world. It will fill the Rocky Mountains.' (This was fourteen years before our people came to the Rocky Mountains.)" (LeGrand Richards, "The Prophets and the Scriptures," *Speeches of the Year*, 28 Sept. 1976, pp. 159-60.)

Three Witnesses of the Book of Mormon

Yet in the brief space of twenty years preceding his death he accomplished what none other has accomplished in an entire lifetime. He translated and published the Book of Mormon, a volume of 522 pages which has since been retranslated into more than a score of languages and which is accepted by millions across the earth as the word of God. The revelations he received and other writings he produced are likewise scripture to these millions. The total in book pages constitutes the equivalent of almost the entire Old Testament of the Bible, and it all came through one man in the space of a few years." (Gordon B. Hinckley in *CR*, Apr. 1977, pp. 95-96.)

(3-14) The Kingdom of God Restored Through Joseph Smith Testifies of His Great Vision

"In this same period he established an organization which for almost a century and a half has withstood every adversity and challenge, and is as effective today in governing a worldwide membership of more than three and a half million as it was 145 years ago in governing a membership of three thousand. There are those doubters who have strained to explain this remarkable organization as the product of the times in which he lived. That organization, I submit, was as peculiar, as unique, and as remarkable then as it is today. It was not a product of the times. It came as a revelation from God." (Gordon B. Hinckley in *CR*, Apr. 1977, p. 96.)

(3-15) The Extent of Joseph Smith's Vision of the Gospel Plan and Its Application Testify to His Greatness

"Joseph Smith's vision of man's immortal nature reached from an existence before birth to the eternities beyond the grave. He

In summary, President Harold B. Lee has succinctly said that "Joseph Smith was the one whom the Lord raised up from boyhood and endowed with divine authority and taught the things necessary for him to know and to obtain the priesthood and to lay the foundation for God's kingdom in these latter days." (*CR*, Oct. 1972, p. 18.)

(3-13) The Accomplishments of Joseph Smith Testify to His Greatness

"The story of Joseph's life is the story of a miracle. He was born in poverty. He was reared in adversity. He was driven from place to place, falsely accused, and illegally imprisoned. He was murdered at the age of thirty-eight.

taught that salvation is universal in that all men will become the beneficiaries of the resurrection through the atonement wrought by the Savior. But beyond this gift is the requirement of obedience to the principles of the gospel and the promise of consequent happiness in this life and exaltation in the life to come.

"Nor was the gospel he taught limited in application to those of his own and future generations. The mind of Joseph Smith, tutored by the God of heaven, encompassed all mankind of all generations. Both the living and the dead must have the opportunity to partake of gospel ordinances.

"Peter of old declared: 'For this cause was the gospel preached also to them that are dead, that they might be judged according to men in the flesh, but live according to God in the spirit.' (1 Pet. 4:6.) In the case of the dead there must be vicarious work if they are to be judged according to men in the flesh, and in order to accomplish this they must be identified; hence the great genealogical program of The Church of Jesus Christ of Latter-day Saints. It was not established to satisfy the interests of a hobby, but to accomplish the eternal purposes of God.

"Within the space of that twenty years preceding his death, Joseph Smith set in motion a program for carrying the gospel to the nations of the earth. I marvel at the boldness with which he moved. Even in the infant days of the Church, in times of dark adversity, men were called to leave homes and families, to cross the sea, to proclaim the restoration of the gospel of Jesus Christ. His mind, his vision encompassed the entire earth.

"Seated in this hall today are those from North, Central, and South America; from the British Isles and Africa; from the nations of Europe; from the islands and continents of the Pacific; and from the ancient lands of Asia. You who have come from far and near, you are the flowering of the vision of Joseph Smith, the prophet of God. He was indeed a mighty seer, who saw this day and greater days yet to come as the work of the Lord moves over the earth." (Gordon B. Hinckley in *CR*, Apr. 1977, p. 96.)

The organization of the Church at Fayette

(3-16) The Keys of Presidency of the Kingdom of God on Earth Were Received by and Passed Down Through Joseph Smith

"May I now say—very plainly and very emphatically—that we have the holy priesthood and that the keys of the kingdom of God are here. They are found only in The Church of Jesus Christ of Latter-day Saints.

"By revelation to Joseph Smith, the Lord said that these keys 'belong always unto the Presidency of the High Priesthood' (D&C 81:2), and also, 'Whosoever receiveth my word receiveth me, and whosoever receiveth me, receiveth those, the First Presidency, whom I have sent' (D&C 112:20).

"In this same connection the Prophet Joseph Smith said: 'You must make yourselves acquainted with those men who like Daniel pray three times a day toward the House of the Lord. Look to the Presidency and receive instruction.' " (Joseph Fielding Smith in *CR*, Apr. 1972, p. 99.)

(3-17) We Do Not Worship the Prophet but Owe Him a Great Debt of Gratitude

"We do not worship the Prophet. We worship God our Eternal Father, and the risen Lord Jesus Christ. But we acknowledge him, we proclaim him, we respect him, we reverence him as an instrument in the hands of the Almighty in restoring to the earth the ancient truths of the divine gospel, together with the priesthood through which the authority of God is exercised in the affairs of his church and for the blessing of his people." (Gordon B. Hinckley in *CR*, Apr. 1977, p. 95.)

Who is Joseph Smith? What kind of man has the power to shape the destiny of nations yet unborn? What can be said of a prophet who has been responsible for more written scripture than any other? What kind of being was the prophet who laid the foundation—for the establishment of Zion, even for the second coming of the Lord Jesus Christ? Singular, indeed, is the Prophet Joseph Smith.

Could you but take his hand, look into his eye, and feel of his spirit, your soul would be filled to the very depths with this truth declared by President John Taylor: "Joseph Smith, the Prophet and Seer of the Lord, has done more, save Jesus only, for the salvation of men in this world, than any other man that ever lived in it." (D&C 135:3.) Make no mistake, we all stand in this last dispensation indebted to a prophet whom God prepared, even in his youth, to do for us what we could not do for ourselves. "The ends of the earth shall inquire after thy name" (D&C 122:1), the Lord has said. And all who inquire earnestly and honestly will find not a mere farm boy or a pretender, but will discover the mighty prophet of the last dispensation, even Joseph Smith, the Prophet of the living God.

CHAPTER 4
RESTORER WITNESS MARTYR

INTRODUCTION

Joseph got the plates in 1827. He would have them for about eighteen months, but he would be allowed peace to translate them during only three of those months.

Fourteen hundred years before, a holy prophet named Moroni had made a shallow excavation near the top of a long sloping hill in what is now western New York, and lined it with stone slabs joined with a type of cement so as to fashion a stone box. Into that box Moroni had laid the sacred records of his nation, an abridgment written on plates of gold and bound together by three rings, and had sealed the box over with a stone lid, rounded on the top.

There had been no question in Moroni's heart about the destiny of those sacred plates or the audience to whom they would someday be published. Writing to people who would live centuries later, Moroni said:

[**Read Ether 12:38, 39, 41.**]

War and desolation had swept the continent, as a mighty civilization with vast numbers of people had crumbled to ruin. But the plates were hidden. War and strife wracked the continent for centuries afterward, until only a shadow of their former mighty civilization remained. But the sacred plates remained secure, through long seasons of rain and snow and sun, hidden, unnoticed by any who happened on the hill in which they lay, under the apparent care of Moroni, empowered from his vantage point outside of mortality to watch and guard.

In time, Moroni was raised from the dead by the power of the resurrection. Still bearing the divine stewardship for the care of the plates, he was instructed and empowered in the presence of God, and was sent from that glorious heaven to answer the prayer of a humble boy in a wilderness cabin in September, 1823. Under the direction of the Father, Moroni taught and prepared that boy through four years. Always during those years, as in the preceding fourteen hundred, the plates were secure under the protection of divine power and immortal guardians. But now they would be placed in the care of a mortal man, and one not yet twenty-three years of age.

IN THE COMING FORTH OF THE BOOK OF MORMON JOSEPH CAME TO UNDERSTAND SOMEWHAT THE PRINCIPLE OF SUFFERING AND TRUE PENITENCE

(4-1) Joseph Finally Allowed Martin Harris to Take the 116 Manuscript Pages That Had Been Translated from the Plates

"Some time after Mr. Harris had begun to write for me, he began to importune me to give him liberty to carry the writings home and show them; and desired of me that I would inquire of the Lord, through the Urim and Thummim, if he might not do so. I did inquire, and the answer was that he must not. However, he was not satisfied with this answer, and desired that I should inquire again. I did so, and the answer was as before. Still he could not be contented, but insisted that I should inquire once more. After much solicitation I again inquired of the Lord, and permission was granted him to have the writings on certain conditions; which were, that he show them only to his brother, Preserved Harris, his own wife, his father and his mother, and a Mrs. Cobb, a sister to his wife. In accordance with this last answer, I required of him that he should bind himself in a covenant to me in a most solemn manner that he would not do otherwise than had been directed. He did so. He bound himself as I required of him, took the writings, and went his way." (Joseph Smith, *HC*, 1:21.)

(4-2) A Few Days After Martin Had Left with the Manuscript, a Son Was Born to Joseph and Emma, but He Died the Same Day

"Joseph did not suspect but that his friend would keep his faith, consequently, he gave himself no uneasiness with regard to the matter.

"Shortly after Mr. Harris left, Joseph's wife became the mother of a son, which, however, remained with her but a short time before it was snatched from her arms by the hand of death. And the mother seemed, for some time, more like sinking with her infant into the mansion of the dead, than remaining with her husband

Martin Harris lost 116 pages of the manuscript

(4-3) Martin Had Lost the Manuscript

"Notwithstanding, however, the great restrictions which he had been laid under, and the solemnity of the covenant which he [Martin Harris] had made with me, he did show them to others, and by stratagem they got them away from him, and they never have been recovered unto this day." (Smith, *HC*, 1:21.)

(4-4) The Lord Withdrew His Spirit from Both Joseph and Martin

"When Joseph had taken a little nourishment, . . . he requested us to send immediately for Mr. Harris. This we did without delay. And when we had given the stranger his breakfast, we commenced preparing breakfast for the family; and we supposed that Mr. Harris would be there, as soon as it was ready, to eat with us, for he generally came in such haste when he was sent for. At eight o'clock we set the victuals on the table, as we were expecting him every moment. We waited till nine, and he came not—till ten, and he was not there—till eleven, still he did not make his appearance. But at half past twelve we saw him walking with a slow and measured tread towards the house, his eyes fixed thoughtfully upon the ground. On coming to the gate, he stopped, instead of passing through, and got upon the fence, and sat there some time with his hat drawn over his eyes. At length he entered the house. Soon after which we sat down to the table, Mr. Harris with the rest. He took up his knife and fork as if he were going to use them, but immediately dropped them. Hyrum, observing this, said, 'Martin, why do you not eat; are you sick?' Upon which Mr. Harris pressed his hands upon his temples, and cried out in a tone of deep anguish, 'Oh, I have lost my soul! I have lost my soul!'

among the living. Her situation was such for two weeks, that Joseph slept not an hour in undisturbed quiet. At the expiration of this time she began to recover, but as Joseph's anxiety about her began to subside, another cause of trouble forced itself upon his mind. Mr. Harris had been absent nearly three weeks, and Joseph had received no intelligence whatever from him, which was altogether aside of the arrangement when they separated. But Joseph kept his feelings from his wife, fearing that if she became

acquainted with them it might agitate her too much.

"In a few days, however, she mentioned the subject herself, and desired her husband to go and get her mother to stay with her, while he should repair to Palmyra, for the purpose of learning the cause of Mr. Harris' absence as well as silence. At first Joseph objected, but seeing her so cheerful, and so willing to have him leave home, he finally consented." (Lucy Mack Smith, *History of Joseph Smith*, p. 125.)

"Joseph who had not expressed his fears till now, sprang from the table, exclaiming, 'Martin, have you lost that manuscript? Have you broken your oath, and brought down condemnation upon my head as well as your own?'

" 'Yes; it is gone,' replied Martin, 'and I know not where.'

" 'Oh, my God!' said Joseph, clinching his hands. 'All is lost! all is lost! What shall I do? I have sinned—it is I who tempted the wrath of God. I should have been satisfied with the first answer which I received from the Lord; for he told me that it was not safe to let the writing go out of my possession.' He wept and groaned, and walked the floor continually.

"At length he told Martin to go back and search again.

" 'No'; said Martin, 'it is all in vain; for I have ripped open beds and pillows; and I know it is not there.'

" 'Then must I,' said Joseph, 'return with such a tale as this? I dare not do it. And how shall I appear before the Lord? Of what rebuke am I not worthy from the angel of the Most High?' . . .

"The next morning, he set out for home. We parted with heavy hearts, for it now appeared that all which we had so fondly anticipated, and which had been the source of so much secret gratification, had in a moment fled, and fled forever." (Smith, *History of Joseph Smith*, pp. 127-29.)

In a later revelation, the Lord gave some hint of the extent of the suffering and the continuing agony Joseph and Martin both endured for several weeks following. Referring to the great suffering that will come upon the unrepentant, the Lord said: "Wherefore, I command you again to repent, lest I humble you with my almighty power; and that you confess your sins, lest you suffer these punishments of which I have spoken, of which in the smallest, yea, even in the least degree you have tasted at the time I withdrew my Spirit." (D&C 19:20.)

How did God cause Joseph and Martin to suffer as they did? Although the intensity of their suffering did not approach the suffering of Christ, the principle by which they suffered was the same. Elder Marion G. Romney described it in this way:

"The Father's plan for proving his children did not exempt the Savior himself. The suffering he undertook to endure, and which he did endure, equaled the combined suffering of all men. Eighteen hundred years after he had endured it, he spoke of it as being so intense that it 'caused myself, even God, the greatest of all, to tremble because of pain, and to bleed at every pore, and to suffer both body and spirit. . . .'

"President Brigham Young pointed out that the intensity of Christ's suffering was induced by the withdrawal from him of the Father's Spirit. And I quote from Brother Young:

" ' . . . at the very moment . . . when the crisis came . . . the Father withdrew . . . His Spirit, and cast a veil over him. That is what made him sweat blood. . . . he then plead with the Father not to forsake him. "No," says the Father "you must have your trials, as well as others." '
(*Journal of Discourses*, Vol. 3, p. 206.)

"The severity of the suffering incident to the withdrawal of the Father's Spirit is intimated in the Lord's statement, through the prophet, to Martin Harris, in which he said:

" ' . . . repent . . . lest you suffer these punishments of which I have spoken, of which in the smallest, yea, even in the least degree you have tasted at the time I withdrew my Spirit.' (D&C 19:20.)" (CR, Oct. 1969, pp. 57-58.)

(4-5) Joseph's Mother Said She Would Never Forget the Suffering of That Occasion

"I well remember that day of darkness, both within and without. To us, at least, the heavens seemed clothed with blackness, and the earth shrouded with gloom. I have often said within myself, that if a continual punishment, as severe as that which we experienced on that occasion, were to be inflicted upon the most wicked characters who ever stood upon the footstool of the Almighty—if even their punishment were no greater than that, I should feel to pity their condition." (Smith, *History of Joseph Smith*, p. 132.)

And so to the Lord Joseph went, torn with anguish and shame at his unwillingness to heed counsel—and to face Moroni. At Cumorah the angel had warned the boy prophet that the stewardship was now his. Joseph had failed to follow counsel, and the sacred manuscript had been lost. Back into Moroni's care went the plates; the Urim and Thummim was taken; the Lord's stinging rebuke rang clear: "For although a man may have many revelations, and have power to do many mighty works, yet if he boasts in his own strength, and sets at naught the counsels of

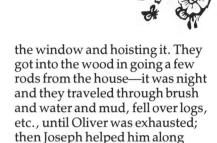

God, and follows after the dictates of his own will and carnal desires [how that must have stung Joseph's sorrowing heart!], he must fall and incur the vengeance of a just God upon him." (D&C 3:4.)

[Read all of Section 3 to see what the Lord said to Joseph at this time.]

Yet even in the rebuke there was hope extended. Joseph's privileges of being prophet and translator were taken only "for a season." (D&C 3:14.) His repentance was deep and sincere, and these privileges were soon restored. The Lord made it clear that it was Satan who lay behind the loss of the manuscript but that God's

"wisdom is greater than the cunning of the devil." (D&C 10:43. Read all of section 10 for the details of the Lord's plan for thwarting the plan to use the stolen manuscript for evil purposes.)

The work went forth, the translation was completed, and the book destined to be the keystone of the restored religion was published. Joseph, committed now to trust not in the arm of flesh, moved on to other divine appointments, other eternal commitments. In May 1829, the ministry of angels continued. The resurrected John the Baptist returned to the earth. He conferred sacred power on Joseph and Oliver, and his visit was soon followed by the return of other holy messengers and by the restoration of the power necessary to establish the kingdom of God upon the earth once more.

[Read Joseph Smith— History 66-75.]

RESTORATION OF THE MELCHIZEDEK PRIESTHOOD TO JOSEPH AND OLIVER

(4-6) The Melchizedek Priesthood Was Restored to Joseph and Oliver While They Were Being Pursued by Their Enemies

" . . . Peter, James and John appeared to him—it was at a period when they were being pursued by their enemies and they had to travel all night, and in the dawn of the coming day when they were weary and worn who should appear to them but Peter, James and John, for the purpose of conferring upon them the Apostleship, the keys of which they themselves had held while upon the earth, which had been bestowed upon them by the Savior." (Erastus Snow in *JD*, 23:183.)

[Read D&C 128:20.]

Joseph apparently related the account of the restoration of the Melchizedek Priesthood to some men in a conversation at Nauvoo a few days before the martyrdom. One man who heard that account reported that Joseph said that "at Cole[s]ville, he and Oliver were under arrest on a charge of deceiving the people. When they were at the justice's house for trial in the evening, all were waiting for Mr. Reid, Joseph's lawyer. . . .

"Mr. Reid came in and said he wanted to speak to his clients in private and that the law allowed him that privilege, he believed. The judge pointed to a door to a room in the back part of the house and told them to step in there. As soon as they got into the room, the lawyer said there was a mob outside in front of the house, 'and if they get hold of you they will perhaps do you bodily injury; and I think the best way for you to get out of this is to get right out there,' pointing to

the window and hoisting it. They got into the wood in going a few rods from the house—it was night and they traveled through brush and water and mud, fell over logs, etc., until Oliver was exhausted; then Joseph helped him along through the mud and water, almost carrying him.

"They traveled all night, and just at the break of day Oliver gave out entirely and exclaimed,

" 'O Lord! Brother Joseph, how long have we got to endure this thing?' They sat down on a log to rest and Joseph said that at the very time Peter, James and John came to them and ordained them to the Apostleship.

"They had sixteen or seventeen miles to go to get back to Mr. Hales, his father-in-law's, but Oliver did not complain any more of fatigue." (Addison Everett, letter to Oliver B. Huntington, 17 February 1881, cited in *Young Women's Journal* 2:75-76 [Nov. 1890].)

(4-7) Peter, James, and John Did Three Things When They Came to Joseph and Oliver

" . . . Peter, James, and John came to Joseph Smith and Oliver Cowdery. When they came they did three things. They conferred upon Joseph and Oliver the Melchizedek Priesthood. This is power and authority. They gave them the keys of the kingdom of God. In other words, they gave them the right to preside in the Melchizedek Priesthood and over the kingdom of God on earth, which is the church of Jesus Christ. Now, it did not exist yet, but they had the right to preside over it. Then Peter, James, and John gave Joseph Smith and Oliver Cowdery what is called the keys of the dispensation of the fulness of times. That means the right to preside over the dispensation and

direct all of the labors in spiritual things of all the people who live in this dispensation of the earth's history." (Bruce R. McConkie, "The Keys of the Kingdom," Address at Wilford Stake priesthood meeting, 21 Feb. 1955.)

And so it was that a few months later, April 6, 1830, the kingdom of God was once again set up upon the earth. The work of the infant Church began under the direction of a man commissioned and instructed by angels, a man with power to lead the kingdom of God through its opening years—yea, even a mighty prophet of God. In the next few years, revelations were received, missionaries were called, and converts were made.

PREPARING THE SAINTS FOR A SPIRITUAL OUTPOURING

(4-8) The Prophet's Heart Yearned to Lighten the Burdens of the Saints

It was June 1833 at Kirtland. The Church was just three years old. Missionaries had been sent out to raise the warning voice, and many converts had been gathered to the infant kingdom at Fayette, Palmyra, Colesville, and other settlements of western New York. Then the Saints were told to move westward to Kirtland, Ohio. Many, fleeing from persecution in New York, came from the East almost daily. The means of established members were taxed to the limit in caring for the bulging Mormon population in Kirtland and the

surrounding counties. The Saints could hardly buy hominy and milk. They were largely a penniless and destitute city of pilgrims. In this period of the Prophet's grave concern for the poverty of the people, the Lord revealed to him a startling requirement: "Organize yourselves; prepare every needful thing; and establish a house, even a house of prayer, a house of fasting, a house of faith, a house of learning, a house of glory, a house of order, a house of God." (D&C 88:119.) That this was a commandment to be taken seriously was made clear by the Lord a short time later.

[Read D&C 95:3-12.]

(4-9) The Prophet's Obedience to God Prompted Him to Require Greater Sacrifice from the Saints

The same day that section 95 was received, a committee was appointed to collect funds from the already suffering Saints. Some may have criticized and thought that the requests for money were too severe. But Joseph knew that far more than the building of a physical facility was involved. He knew that the spiritual survival of the last dispensation depended on the spiritual endowment that God had promised to pour out upon the Saints when the temple was completed. Of Joseph's faithfulness in this, President Brigham Young later declared:

"Soon after, the Church, through our beloved Prophet Joseph, was commanded to build a temple to the Most High, in Kirtland, Ohio. Joseph not only received revelation and commandment to build a temple, but he received a pattern also. . . .

"Without revelation, Joseph could not know what was wanted, any more than any other man, and, without commandment, the

The Kirtland Temple

Church were too few in number, too weak in faith, and too poor in purse, to attempt such a mighty enterprise. But by means of all these stimulants, a mere handful of men, living on air, and a little hominy and milk; and often salt or no salt, when milk could not be had; the great Prophet Joseph, in the stone quarry, quarrying rock with his own hands; and the few then in the Church, following his example of obedience and diligence wherever most needed; with laborers on the walls, holding the sword in one hand to protect themselves from the mob, while they placed the stone and moved the trowel with the other, the Kirtland temple—the second house of the Lord, that we have any published record of on the earth, was so far completed as to be dedicated. And those first Elders who helped to build it, received a portion of their first endowments, or we might say more clearly, some of the first, or introductory, or initiatory ordinances, preparatory to an endowment." (Brigham Young, *Discourses of Brigham Young,* p. 415.)

(4-10) Sacrifice Brought Down Blessings from Heaven

What sacrifices could be too great, however, by either Joseph or the Saints, when weighed against the blessings that were poured out generally upon the brethren when the temple was completed? Joseph's own account records what he saw in vision. Part of what he says is now included in the Pearl of Great Price.

[Read Joseph Smith—Vision of the Celestial Kingdom 1-9.]

In addition, the Prophet wrote:

"I also beheld Elder M'Lellin in the south, standing upon a hill, surrounded by a vast multitude, preaching to them, and a lame man standing before him supported by his crutches; he threw them down at his word and leaped as a hart, by the mighty power of God. Also, I saw Elder Brigham Young standing in a strange land, in the far south and west, in a desert place, upon a rock in the midst of about a dozen men of color, who appeared hostile. He was preaching to them in their own tongue, and the angel of God standing above his head, with a drawn sword in his hand, protecting him, but he did not see it. And I finally saw the Twelve in the celestial kingdom of God. I also beheld the redemption of Zion, and many things which the tongue of man cannot describe in full.

"Many of my brethren who received the ordinance with me saw glorious visions also. Angels ministered unto them as well as to myself, and the power of the Highest rested upon us, the house was filled with the glory of God, and we shouted Hosanna to God and the Lamb. My scribe also received his anointing with us, and saw, in a vision, the armies of heaven protecting the Saints in their return to Zion, and many things which I saw.

"The Bishop of Kirtland with his Counselors, and the Bishop of Zion with his Counselors, were present with us, and received their anointings under the hands of Father Smith, and this was confirmed by the Presidency, and the glories of heaven were unfolded to them also.

"We then invited the High Counsilors of Kirtland and Zion into our room, and President Hyrum Smith anointed the head of the President of the Counsilors in Kirtland, and President David Whitmer the head of the President of the Counsilors of Zion. The President of each quorum then anointed the heads of his colleagues, each in his turn, beginning at the oldest.

"The visions of heaven were opened to them also. Some of them saw the face of the Savior, and others were ministered unto by holy angels, and the spirit of prophecy and revelation was poured out in mighty power; and loud hosannas, and glory to God in the highest, saluted the heavens, for we all communed with the heavenly host. And I saw in my vision all of the Presidency in the celestial kingdom of God, and many others that were present." (Smith, *HC,* 2:381-82.)

(4-11) Would Joseph Have Been Kinder Not to Require the Sacrifice That Built the Kirtland Temple?

The events described above occurred in that temple which the Saints had built at great sacrifice. Joseph had prayed by revelation at its dedication.

[Read D&C 109:5, 12, 13, 79, 80.]

The Prophet described other scenes in the Kirtland Temple by this language:

"We then laid our hands upon Elder Thomas B. Marsh, who is President of the Twelve, and ordained him to the authority of anointing his brethren. I then poured the consecrated oil upon his head, in the name of Jesus Christ, and sealed such blessings upon him as the Lord put into my heart. The rest of the Presidency then laid their hands upon him and blessed him, each in his turn, beginning at the oldest. He then anointed and blessed his brethren from the oldest to the youngest. I also laid my hands upon them, and pronounced many great and glorious things upon their heads. The heavens were opened, and angels ministered unto us.

Sidney Rigdon–counselor to Joseph Smith

"The Twelve then proceeded to anoint and bless the Presidency of the Seventy, and seal upon their heads power and authority to anoint their brethren. . . .

"President Rigdon arose to conclude the services of the evening by invoking the blessing of heaven upon the Lord's anointed, which he did in an eloquent manner; the congregation shouted a long hosanna: the gift of tongues fell upon us in mighty power, angels mingled their voices with ours, while their presence was in our midst, and unceasing praises swelled our bosoms for the space of half-an-hour.

"I then observed to the brethren, that it was time to retire. We accordingly closed our interview and returned home at about two o'clock in the morning, and the Spirit and visions of God attended me through the night. . . .

"When the Twelve and the seven presidents were through with their sealing prayer, I called upon President Sidney Rigdon to seal them with uplifted hands; and when he had done this, and cried hosanna, that all the congregation should join him, and shout hosanna to God and the Lamb, and glory to God in the highest. It was done so, and Elder Roger Orton

saw a mighty angel riding upon a horse of fire, with a flaming sword in his hand, followed by five others, encircle the house, and protect the Saints, even the Lord's anointed, from the power of Satan and a host of evil spirits, which were striving to disturb the Saints.

"President William Smith, one of the Twelve, saw the heavens opened, and the Lord's host protecting the Lord's anointed.

"President Zebedee Coltrin, one of the seven presidents of the Seventy, saw the Savior extended before him, as upon the cross, and a little after, crowned with glory upon his head above the brightness of the sun.

"After these things were over, and a glorious vision, which I saw, had passed, I instructed the seven presidents to proceed and anoint the Seventy, and returned to the room of the High Priests and Elders, and attended to the sealing of what they had done, with up-lifted hands.

"After these quorums were dismissed, I retired to my home, filled with the Spirit, and my soul cried hosanna to God and the Lamb, through the silent watches of the night; and while my eyes were closed in sleep, the visions of the Lord were sweet unto me, and His glory was round about me. Praise the Lord." (Smith, *HC*, 2:382-87.)

(4-12) Foundation Stones More Enduring than Brick and Stone Were Laid in Kirtland

In his final note of the marvelous events that were enjoyed generally, the Prophet wrote:

"Brother George A. Smith arose and began to prophesy, when a noise was heard like the sound of a rushing mighty wind, which filled the Temple, and all the congregation simultaneously

arose, being moved upon by an invisible power; many began to speak in tongues and prophesy; others saw glorious visions; and I beheld the Temple was filled with angels, which fact I declared to the congregation. The people of the neighborhood came running together (hearing an unusual sound within, and seeing a bright light like a pillar of fire resting upon the Temple), and were astonished at what was taking place. This continued until the meeting closed at eleven p.m." (Smith, *HC*, 2:428.)

Why did the Saints need a temple more than they needed bread? Why did the suffering and sacrifice they endured turn out to be a blessing? Realizing as he did the great blessings that could come through the building of the temple, but realizing also that the Saints were poor and on the brink of despair, by what course could the Prophet manifest greater kindness? And what have we to thank the Prophet for? What great blessings came into the Church and into the world because the Prophet had the courage to obey heaven rather than the yearnings of his heart? What is the difference between a prophet and a humanitarian?

JOSEPH REVEALED GREAT KNOWLEDGE FROM THE LORD BUT WAS NOT ALLOWED TO REVEAL ALL THAT HE KNEW

(4-13) Joseph Was Anxious That Every Man Come to a Full Understanding of the Gospel

" . . . God hath not revealed anything to Joseph, but what he will make known unto the Twelve, and even the least Saint may know all things as fast as he is able to bear them. . . . " (Joseph Smith, *Teachings of the Prophet Joseph Smith*, p. 149.)

(4-14) The Prophet Knew Far More Than He Was Permitted to Teach the People

"I am going to take up this subject by virtue of the knowledge of God in me, which I have received from heaven. The opinions of men, so far as I am concerned, are to me as the crackling of thorns under the pot, or the whistling of the wind. I break the ground; I lead the way like Columbus when he was invited to a banquet where he was assigned the most honorable place at the table, and served with the ceremonials which were observed towards sovereigns. A shallow courtier present, who was meanly jealous of him, abruptly asked him whether he thought that in case he had not discovered the Indies, there were not other men in Spain who would have been capable of the enterprise? Columbus made no reply, but took an egg and invited the company to make it stand on end. They all attempted it, but in vain; whereupon he struck it upon the table so as to break one end, and left it standing on the broken part, illustrating that when he had once shown the way to the new world nothing was easier than to follow it.

"Paul ascended into the third heavens, and he could understand the three principal rounds of Jacob's ladder—the telestial, the terrestrial, and the celestial glories or kingdoms, where Paul saw and heard things which were not lawful for him to utter. I could explain a hundred fold more than I ever have of the glories of the kingdoms manifested to me in the vision, were I permitted, and were the people prepared to receive them.

"The Lord deals with this people as a tender parent with a child, communicating light and intelligence and the knowledge of his ways as they can bear it. The inhabitants of the earth are asleep;

they know not the day of their visitation." (Smith, *Teachings*, pp. 304-5.)

This principle of gaining knowledge, that the Prophet is trying to explain to the Saints, is an eternal principle that other prophets have struggled to make clear. "And now Alma began to expound these things unto him, saying: It is given unto many to know the mysteries of God; nevertheless they are laid under a strict command that they shall not impart only according to the portion of his word which he doth grant unto the children of men, according to the heed and diligence which they give unto him.

"And therefore, he that will harden his heart, the same receiveth the lesser portion of the word; and he that will not harden his heart, to him is given the greater portion of the word, until it is given unto him to know the mysteries of God until he know them in full.

"And they that will harden their hearts, to them is given the lesser portion of the word until they know nothing concerning his mysteries; and then they are taken captive by the devil, and led by his will down to destruction. Now this is what is meant by the chains of hell." (Alma 12:10, 11.)

According to these passages, what determines how much a prophet may be permitted to teach the people? How can the people increase the amount a prophet may be permitted to teach them? How serious a matter is it not to prepare to receive more of what a prophet may be permitted to say?

(4-15) Many Cut Themselves Off from Further Light and Knowledge

by their Refusal to Accept the Teachings of the Prophet

"Many men will say, 'I will never forsake you, but will stand by you at all times.' But the moment you teach them some of the mysteries of the kingdom of God that are retained in the heavens and are to be revealed to the children of men when they are prepared for them they will be the first to stone you and put you to death. It was this same principle that crucified the Lord Jesus Christ, and will cause the people to kill the prophets in this generation. . . .

"There are a great many wise men and women too in our midst who are too wise to be taught; therefore they must die in their ignorance, and in the resurrection they will find their mistake. Many seal up the door of heaven by saying, So far God may reveal and I will believe." (Smith, *Teachings*, p. 309.)

(4-16) Many of the Saints Will Endure Trials and Difficulties Valiantly, but Will Still Reject Knowledge

"But there has been a great difficulty in getting anything into the heads of this generation. It has been like splitting hemlock knots with a corn-dodger for a wedge, and a pumpkin for a beetle. Even the Saints are slow to understand.

"I have tried for a number of years to get the minds of the Saints prepared to receive the things of God; but we frequently see some of them, after suffering all they have for the work of God, will fly to pieces like glass as soon as anything comes that is contrary to their traditions: they cannot stand the fire at all. How many will be able to abide a celestial law, and go through and receive their exaltation, I am unable to say, as many are called, but few are chosen." (Smith, *Teachings*, p. 331.)

The Carthage Jail

As the years progressed and the kingdom swelled, the Prophet laid the foundations for a kingdom which he could pass on to others. As he moved toward his destiny, names like Missouri, Haun's Mill, Liberty Jail, Crooked River, and Nauvoo were added to the history of the Church. While it is not the purpose of this study to focus on the detail, through it all Joseph led the Saints. And then, his mission completed, the Lord allowed him to be a martyr for the truth.

The guns at Carthage were silent. Joseph and Hyrum were dead. "From age to age shall their names go down to posterity as gems for the sanctified." (D&C 135:6.)

Who is Joseph Smith? What is his mission? Where is the end of his influence? "The ends of the earth shall inquire after thy name," the Lord had said. (D&C 122:1.) Another prophet testified of Joseph Smith:

" . . . the name of Joseph Smith, the prophet of the nineteenth century, has been, is being, and will be heralded abroad to the nations of the earth, and will be held in honor or contempt by the people of the world. But the honor in which it is now held by a few will by and by be increased that his name shall be held in reverence and honor among the children of men as universally as the name

47

of the Son of God is held today; for he did and is doing the work of the Master. He laid the foundations in this dispensation for the restoration of the principles that were taught by the Son of God, who for these principles lived, and taught, and died, and rose from the dead. Therefore I say, as the name of the Son of God shall be held in reverence and honor, and in the faith and love of men, so will the name of Joseph Smith eventually be held among the children of men, gaining prestige, increasing in honor and commanding respect and reverence, until the world shall say that he was a servant and Prophet of God.'' (Joseph F. Smith, *Gospel Doctrine*, pp. 479-80.)

To an assembly of thousands a few months before his death, Joseph declared:

''You don't know me; you never knew my heart. No man knows my history. I cannot tell it: I shall never undertake it. I don't blame any one for not believing my history. If I had not experienced what I have, I could not have believed it myself. I never did harm any man since I was born in the world. My voice is always for peace.

''I cannot lie down until all my work is finished. I never think any evil, nor do anything to the harm of my fellow-man. When I am called by the trump of the archangel and weighed in the balance, you will all know me then. I add no more.'' (*Teachings*, pp. 361-62.)

When Joseph Smith is called by the trump of the archangel and weighed in the balance, we *shall* all know him. An apostle and counselor in the First

Joseph Smith—Prophet of God

Presidency, who, as a young boy in Nauvoo, had listened to the Prophet's statement noted above, testified:

''He stands at the head. He is a unique character, differing from every other man in this respect, and excelling every other man.

Because he was the head God chose him, and while he was faithful no man could take his place and position. He was faithful, and died faithful. He stands therefore at the head of this dispensation, *and will throughout all eternity, and no man can take that power away from him.*

If any man holds these keys, he holds them subordinate to him. You never heard President Young teach any other doctrine; he always said that Joseph stood at the head of this dispensation; that Joseph holds the keys; that although Joseph had gone behind the veil he stood at the head of this dispensation, and that he himself held the keys subordinate to him. President Taylor teaches the same doctrine, and you will never hear any other doctrine from any of the faithful Apostles or servants of God, who understand the order of the Holy Priesthood. *If we get our salvation we shall have to pass by him; if we enter into our glory it will be through the authority that he has received. We cannot get around him. . . .* '' (George Q. Cannon in *JD,* 23:361. Italics added.)

And that is the end of it, for it is true—we cannot get around him!

CHAPTER 5
APOSTOLIC SUCCESSION AND THE KEYS OF THE PRIESTHOOD

INTRODUCTION

The vicious mob at Carthage had succeeded. The Prophet Joseph Smith was dead. The Patriarch Hyrum Smith was dead. There was no First Presidency over the Twelve. There was no first counselor between Joseph and the Twelve. Brigham Young was the leader of the Church.

But although he was immediately the Lord's mouthpiece on the earth, by virtue of his senior position in the Quorum, Brigham Young still had to be sustained by a competent assembly of members of the Church. The order of apostolic succession that President Joseph Smith had made possible by bestowal of keys still had to be tested.

In an assembly which convened at 2:00 P.M., Thursday, August 8, 1844, the Saints acknowledged the Twelve Apostles as the presiding authority of the Church, with Brigham Young at their head. The following study will explain why. Consider these passages and statements carefully and ponder upon the significance of the message they contain.

JOSEPH DID NOT WANT HYRUM TO GO TO CARTHAGE, BECAUSE HE KNEW WHAT THE END WOULD BE

(5-1) Hyrum Knew They Would Be Murdered If They Surrendered to the Mob

" . . . Joseph called Hyrum, Willard Richards, John Taylor, William W. Phelps, A. C. Hodge, John L. Butler, Alpheus Cutler, William Marks and some others, into his upper room and said, 'Brethren, here is a letter from the

Governor which I wish to have read.' After it was read through Joseph remarked, 'There is no mercy—no mercy here.' Hyrum said, 'No; just as sure as we fall into their hands we are dead men.' " (Joseph Smith, *History of the Church*, 6:545.)

(5-2) Joseph Wanted Hyrum to Be Preserved

"I was but a boy at the time, but I remember it very distinctly. He evidently wanted his brother Hyrum also to be preserved, and for some time before his martyrdom talked about him as the Prophet. But Hyrum, as you know, was not desirous to live away from Joseph; if he was to be exposed to death, he was resolved to be with him." (George Q. Cannon in *JD*, 23:363.)

(5-3) Joseph Suggested That Hyrum Go to Cincinnati Where He Would Be Safe, but Hyrum Would Not

"I advised my brother Hyrum to take his family on the next steamboat and go to Cincinnati. Hyrum replied, 'Joseph, I can't leave you.' Whereupon I said to the company present, 'I wish I could get Hyrum out of the way, so that he may live to avenge my blood, and I will stay with you and see it out.' " (Smith, *History of the Church*, 6:520.)

(5-4) Hyrum Would Have Stood in Joseph's Place Had He Not Been Killed

"It is the test of our fellowship to believe and confess that Joseph lived and died a prophet of God in good standing; and I dont [sic] want any one to fellowship the Twelve who says that Joseph is fallen. If you dont [sic] know whose right it is to give revelations, I will tell you. It is I. There never has a man stood between Joseph and the Twelve, and unless we apostatize there never will. If Hyrum had lived he would not have stood between Joseph and the Twelve but he would have stood for Joseph.—Did Joseph ordain any man to take his place? He did. Who was it? It was Hyrum, but Hyrum fell a martyr before Joseph did." (Brigham Young in *Times and Seasons*, vol. 5, no. 19, 15 Oct. 1844, pp. 683-84.)

(5-5) The Divine Law of Witnesses Required That Hyrum Be Taken with Joseph

" . . . if Hyrum Smith had hearkened to the Prophet and taken his family to Cincinnati, there would have been a President of the Church and it would not have been Brigham Young. Brigham Young was President of the Council of the Twelve, and Hyrum Smith would have been President of the Church by virtue of his ordination, holding the place held by Oliver Cowdery.

" . . . he would have remained as President of the Church had he not died a martyr.

"But here is another point. He had to die. Why? Because we read in the scriptures that the testimony is not of force without the death of

the testator—that is, in his particular case, and in the case of Christ. *It was just as necessary that Hyrum Smith lay down his life a martyr for this cause as a witness for God as it was for Joseph Smith, so the Lord permitted them both to be taken in that way and both sealed their testimony with their blood.* Both of them held the keys of the dispensation of the fulness of times jointly, and they will through all the ages of eternity. Then naturally the Council of the Twelve came into its place, and *by right* Brigham Young became President of the Church." (Joseph Fielding Smith, *Doctrines of Salvation*, 1:220-21.)

BRIGHAM YOUNG AND THE OTHER MEMBERS OF THE TWELVE RECEIVED ALL THE KEYS AND POWERS WHICH JOSEPH AND HYRUM HAD HELD, THOUGH JOSEPH STILL CONTINUES AS HEAD OF THIS DISPENSATION.

(5-6) Joseph Knew That He Would Be Taken and Was Anxious to Prepare the Twelve to Lead the Church

"This great and good man was led, before his death, to call the Twelve together, from time to time, and to instruct them in all things pertaining to the kingdom, ordinances, and government of God. He often observed that he was laying the foundation, but it would remain for the Twelve to complete the building. Said he, 'I know not why; but for some reason I am constrained to hasten my preparations, and to confer upon the Twelve all the ordinances, keys, covenants, endowments, and sealing ordinances of the priesthood, and so set before them a pattern in all things pertaining to the sanctuary and the endowment therein.'

"Having done this, he rejoiced exceedingly; for, said he, the Lord is about to lay the burden on your

Hyrum Smith—martyr

shoulders and let me rest awhile; and if they kill me, continued he, the kingdom of God will roll on, as I have now finished the work which was laid upon me, by committing to you all things for the building up of the kingdom according to the heavenly vision, and the pattern shown me from heaven. With many conversations like this, he comforted the minds of the Twelve, and prepared them for what was soon to follow." (Parley P. Pratt in *Millennial Star*, vol. 5, no. 5, Mar. 1845, p. 151.)

" . . . the mob murdered both Joseph and his brother Hyrum, in the jail. That was to be so. I heard Joseph say many a time, 'I shall not live until I am forty years of age.' " (Brigham Young, *Discourses of Brigham Young*, p. 467.)

(5-7) Joseph Learned by Revelation That Hyrum Would Also Be Taken

Elder Orson Hyde reported that in the early spring of 1844, "we were in council with Brother Joseph almost every day for weeks, says Brother Joseph in one of those councils there is something going to happen; I dont know what it is, but the Lord bids me to hasten and give you your endowment before the temple is finished. He conducted us through every ordinance of the holy priesthood, and when he had gone through with all the ordinances he rejoiced very much, and says, now if they kill me you have got all the keys, and all the ordinances and you can confer them upon others, and the hosts of Satan will not be able to tear down the kingdom, as fast as you will be

able to build it up; and now says he on your shoulders will the responsibility of leading this people rest, for the Lord is gong to let me rest a while. Now why did he say to the Twelve on YOUR shoulders will this responsibility rest, why did he not mention Brother Hyrum? The spirit knew that Hyrum would be taken with him, and hence he did not mention his name. . . . '' (*Times and Seasons*, vol. 5, no. 17, 15 Sept. 1844, p. 651.)

Wilford Woodruff

(5-8) Joseph Conferred All the Keys and Powers upon Each Member of the Quorum of the Twelve

Elder Wilford Woodruff reported that each member of the Quorum ''received their endowment and actually received the keys of the kingdom of God, and oracles of God, keys of revelation, and the pattern of heavenly things; and thus addressing the Twelve, [the Prophet] exclaimed, 'upon your shoulders the kingdom rests, and you must round up your shoulders, and bear it; for I have had to do it until now. But now the responsibility rests upon you. It mattereth not what becomes of me.' '' (*Times and Seasons*, vol. 5, no. 20, 1 Nov. 1844, p. 698.)

On another occasion President Woodruff declared:

''I bear my testimony that Joseph Smith was a true prophet of God, ordained of God to lay the foundation of his church and kingdom in the last dispensation and fulness of times. I bear my testimony that in the early spring of 1844 in Nauvoo, the Prophet Joseph Smith called the Twelve Apostles together, and he delivered unto them the ordinances of the Church and kingdom of God; and all of the keys and powers that God had bestowed upon him, he sealed upon our heads. He told us we must round up our shoulders and bear off this kingdom or we would be damned. I am the only man now living in the flesh who heard that testimony from his mouth, and I know it is true by the power of God manifest through him. At that meeting he began to speak about three hours upon the subject of the kingdom. His face was as clear as amber, and he was covered with a power that I had never seen in the flesh before. In all his testimony to us, the power of God was visibly manifest in the Prophet Joseph.'' (*New Era*, Jan. 1972, p. 66.)

(5-9) The prophet Made It Clear That Brigham Young Was to Preside in the Event of His Death

''He proceeded to confer on elder Young, the President of the Twelve, the keys of the sealing power, as conferred in the last days by the spirit and power of Elijah, in order to seal the hearts of the fathers to the children, and the hearts of the children to the fathers, lest the whole earth should be smitten with a curse.

''This last key of the priesthood is the most sacred of all, and pertains exclusively to the first presidency of the church, without whose

sanction and approval or authority, no sealing blessing shall be administered pertaining to things of the ressurection [*sic*] and the life to come.

''After giving them a very short charge to do all things according to the pattern, he quietly surrendered his liberty and his life into the hands of his blood-thirsty enemies, and all this to save the people for whom he had so long laboured from threatened vengeance.

''Thus nobly fell our worthy founder and leader in the very bloom of life; and thus the responsibility of bearing off the kingdom triumphantly now rests upon the Twelve.'' (Parley P. Pratt, in *Millennial Star*, vol. 5, no. 5, Mar. 1845, p. 151.)

WHEN HYRUM AND JOSEPH DIED AT CARTHAGE, THE RIGHT OF PRESIDENCY IMMEDIATELY FELL ON THE SHOULDERS OF THE TWELVE, WITH BRIGHAM YOUNG AT THEIR HEAD

The crisis is here. The Prophet is dead. The Saints are like sheep without a shepherd. They are, many of them, confused, uncertain—who is to lead the Church? Wolves are prowling about the Saints; several men are attempting to step into the seeming void the Prophet left. Who *is* to lead the Church? Did the Prophet appoint someone to succeed him? How can anyone know for sure?

Suppose you are in Nauvoo. You have heard no explanation of succession in the priesthood. The death of a president of the Church has never occurred before. There appear to be many claims about succession, but you do not understand them. How can you be sure that you will make the right decision? If you

follow the wrong leader, you may go into apostasy and lose the blessings of the gospel. You have no earthly criterion upon which to base your decision.

And the crisis comes so suddenly. You do not realize as you attend the meeting this morning that your experience here will be so important to your destiny in the gospel. Sidney Rigdon is speaking now. In a moment he will stop, and Brigham Young will speak for only a few minutes. Some will know immediately by the revelations of the Holy Ghost that Brigham Young is to lead. Will you? Have you paid the price? Have you followed the counsel of the leaders in the Church before? Are you clean and worthy to have the still, small voice of the Spirit whisper which course you should take? Will you be able to recognize the voice of authority, or will this meeting pass with your not even being aware that God has manifest his will?

Sidney Rigdon has finished. Brigham Young is just now standing up. This instant is the most critical moment of all your years of membership. Are you ready?

(5-10) By Ordination, by Procedure, and by a Manifestation of the Will of Heaven, Brigham Young Is to Lead

"After the martyrdom of the Prophet the Twelve soon returned to Nauvoo, and learned of the aspirations of Sidney Rigdon. He had claimed that the Church needed a guardian. He had appointed the day for the guardian to be selected, and of course was present at the meeting, which was held in the open air. The wind was blowing toward the stand so

Brigham Young appeared as Joseph

strongly at the time that an improvised stand was made out of a wagon, which was drawn up at the back part of the congregation, and which he, William Marks, and some others occupied. He attempted to speak, but was much embarrassed. He had been the orator of the Church; but, on this occasion his oratory failed him, and his talk fell very flat. In the meantime President Young and some of his brethren came and entered the stand. The wind by this time had ceased to blow. After Sidney Rigdon had spoken, President Young arose and addressed the congregation, which faced around to see and hear him, turning their backs towards the wagon occupied by Sidney. Now it is probable that there are some here today who were present on that

occasion, and they, I doubt not, could, if necessary, bear witness that the power of God was manifested at that time, to the joy and satisfaction of the Saints. It was necessary that there should be some manifestation of the power of God, because the people were divided. There was considerable of doubt as to who should lead the Church. . . . But no sooner did President Young arise than the power of God rested down upon him in the face of the people. It did not appear to be Brigham Young; it appeared to be Joseph Smith that spoke to the people—Joseph in his looks, in his manner, and in his voice; even his figure was transformed so that it looked like that of Joseph, and everybody present, who had the Spirit of God, saw that he was the man whom

God had chosen to hold the keys now that the Prophet Joseph had gone behind the veil, and that he had given him power to exercise them. And from that time forward, . . . God has borne testimony to the acts and teachings of His servant Brigham, and those of his servants, the Apostles, who received the keys in connection with him. God sustained him and upheld him, and he blessed all those that listened to his counsel." (George Q. Cannon in *JD*, 23:363-64.)

BRIGHAM YOUNG LED THE CHURCH FOR THREE YEARS AS PRESIDENT OF THE TWELVE

(5-11) At the Death of Joseph and Hyrum, Only One Man Could Hold the Keys Actively

"[The Church] is governed by men who hold the keys of the Apostleship, who have the right and authority. Any one of them, should an emergency arise, can act as President of the Church, with all the powers, with all the authority, with all the keys, and with every endowment necessary to obtain revelation from God, and to lead and guide this people in the path that leads to the celestial glory; but there is only one man at a time who can hold the keys, who can dictate, who can guide, who can give revelation to the Church. The rest must acquiesce in his action, the rest must be governed by his counsels, the rest must receive his doctrines. It was so with Joseph. Others held the Apostleship—Oliver received the Apostleship at the same time that Joseph did, but Joseph held the keys, although Oliver held precisely the same authority. There was only one who could exercise it in its fullness and power among the people. So also at Joseph's death, there was only one man who could exercise that authority and hold

these keys, and that man was President Brigham Young, the President of the Quorum of the Twelve whom God had singled out, who by extraordinary providence had been brought to the front. . . . " (George Q. Cannon in *JD*, 19:234.)

(5-12) During the Interval Between the Death of the President and the Reorganization of the First Presidency, the President of the Quorum of the Twelve Is the President of the Church

"With reference to this subject, the fourth President of the Church, Wilford Woodruff, made a few observations in a letter to President Heber J. Grant, then a member of the Twelve, under date of March 28, 1887. I quote from that letter: ' . . . when the President of the Church dies, who then is the Presiding Authority of the Church? It is the Quorum of the Twelve Apostles (ordained and organized by the revelations of God and none else). Then while these Twelve Apostles preside over the Church, who is the President of the Church [?] It is the President of the Twelve Apostles. And he is virtually as much the President of the Church while presiding over Twelve men as he is when organized as the Presidency of the Church, and presiding over two men.' " (Harold B. Lee in *CR*, Apr. 1970, p. 124.)

(5-13) In Death, the Presidency of the Church Passes from One Man to His Successor in a Heartbeat

"When President Lee passed he was attended by President Marion G. Romney, his second counselor, and President Spencer W. Kimball, the President of the Council of the Twelve. President N. Eldon Tanner was in Arizona at the time. Brother Romney, as the representative of and counselor to President Lee,

was in complete and total charge at the hospital. He gave President Lee a blessing. He felt the spirit of peace and satisfaction, the calm assurance that whatever eventuated would be right. He did not promise President Lee that he would be healed. The President had become ill very rapidly, just in a matter of hours or moments. Shortly after this blessing, he passed away. At the moment he passed, Brother Romney, in harmony with the system and the established tradition and custom of the Church, stepped aside, and President Spencer W. Kimball was then in complete charge and had total direction. President Kimball was at that moment the senior apostle of God on earth. And as the last heart-beat of President Lee ceased, the mantle of leadership passed to President Kimball, whose next heartbeat was that of the living oracle and presiding authority of God on earth. From that moment the Church continued under the direction of President Kimball." (Bruce R. McConkie, "Succession in the Presidency," *Speeches of the Year*, 8 Jan. 1974, p. 19.)

(5-14) The Apostolic Presidency of the Church, with the President of the Twelve at Their Head, Proceed at Once to Reorganize the First Presidency

"There is always a head in the Church, and if the presidency of the Church are removed by death or other cause, then the next head of the Church is the twelve apostles, until a presidency is again organized of three presiding high priests who have the right to hold the office of first presidency over the Church; and, according to the doctrine laid down by President Wilford Woodruff, who saw the necessity for it, and that of President Lorenzo Snow, if the

President should die, his counselors are then released from that presidency, and it is the duty of the twelve apostles to proceed at once, in the manner that has been pointed out, to see that the First presidency is reorganized, so that there may be no deficiency in the working and order of the priesthood in the Church." (Joseph F. Smith in *CR*, Apr. 1913, pp. 4-5.)

(5-15) When the First Presidency of the Church Was First Reorganized in 1847, Brigham Young Assumed His Rightful Place as President of the Church

"In the month of February, 1848, the Twelve Apostles met at Hyde Park, Pottawattamie County, Iowa, where a small Branch of the Church was established. . . . We were in prayer and council, communing together; and what took place on that occasion? The voice of God came from on high, and spake to the Council. Every latent feeling was aroused, and every heart melted. What did it say unto us? 'Let my servant Brigham step forth and receive the full power of the presiding Priesthood in my Church and kingdom.' This was the voice of the Almighty unto us. . . . I am one that was present, and there are others here that were also present on that occasion, and did hear and feel the voice from heaven, and we were filled with the power of God. . . .

"We said nothing about the matter in those times, but kept it still. . . . Men, women, and children came running together where we were, and asked us what was the matter. They said that their houses shook, and the ground trembled, and they did not know but that there was an earthquake. We told them that there was nothing the matter—not to be alarmed; the Lord was only

Brigham Young as a young Apostle

whispering to us a little and that he was probably not very far off. We felt no shaking of the earth or of the house, but were filled with the exceeding power and goodness of God. We knew and realized that we had the testimony of God within us. . . .

"Some persons say that Brigham does not give revelations as did Joseph Smith. But let me tell you, that Brigham's voice has been the voice of God from the time he was chosen to preside, and even before. Who that has heard him speak, or that has read his testimonies, or that is acquainted with his instructions, does not know that God is with him? Who does not know, Jew or Gentile, that has come in contact with his policy, that he possesses a power with which they are unable to compete. He possesses skill, wisdom, and power that trouble wise men and

rulers. God will make him a greater terror to nations than he ever has been.'' (Orson Hyde in *JD*, 8:233-34.)

EACH APOSTLE ORDAINED TODAY RECEIVES A FULNESS OF THE KEYS AND POWERS OF THE PRESIDENCY, WHICH HE HOLDS DORMANT UNLESS HE BECOMES THE PRESIDENT OF THE CHURCH

(5-16) Each Member of the Quroum of the Twelve Moves Toward the Prsidency by Seniority

President Spencer W. Kimball described how, after the death of President David O. McKay, Elder Joseph Fielding Smith assumed the right of presidency. The reorganization occurred in the Salt Lake Temple.

''When these 14 men emerge from the holy edifice later in the morning, a transcendently vital event has occurred—a short interregnum ends, and the government of the kingdom shifts back again from the Quorum of the Twelve Apostles to a new prophet, an individual leader, the Lord's earthly representative, who has unostentatiously been moving toward this lofty calling for 60 years. He now presides over the Church.

''Not because of his name, however, did he accede to this high place, but because when he was a very young man, he was called of the Lord, through the then living prophet, to be an apostle—member of the Quorum—and was given the precious, vital keys to hold in

suspension pending a time when he might become the senior apostle and the President.'' (*CR*, Apr. 1970, p. 118.)

(5-17) Each Member of the Quorum Receives All the Keys, but They Lie Dormant Until the Seniority of the Man Who Bears Them Calls Them into Use

''Now, this is the pattern; this is the system. Succession in the presidency happens in an orderly and systematized way, because the Lord has conferred upon the members of the Council of the Twelve all of the keys and powers and authorities that have ever been held in any dispensation or any age of the past. Every key is given to each apostle who is set apart a member of the Council of the

The Salt Lake Temple under construction

Twelve. But because keys are the right of presidency, they lie dormant, as it were, in each man unless and until he becomes the senior apostle and is thus in a position of presidency to direct the labors and the work of all others. Therefore succession occurs, as it were, automatically." (McConkie, "Succession in the Presidency," p. 25.)

(5-18) The Order of Apostolic Succession Could Be Changed Only by Revelation

At the stand in Nauvoo, that windy day in August 1844, God revealed his mind and will as to who should lead the Church in the event of a president's death. He did not reveal the order at the time—it had been revealed and fully established by Joseph Smith months before. But when Sidney Rigdon had finished speaking and Brigham Young rose in his stead to make a few brief remarks, the Lord poured out his Spirit upon Brigham Young and upon all the faithful Saints there to confirm that the order of succession which had been established was proper and had power and was binding upon the Saints.

A few years later, in a council meeting of the Twelve on the plains of Iowa, the voice of God spoke and directed that Brigham Young be appointed President of the Church. That was done and later accepted by a general conference of the Saints. Now, nearly a century and a half later, the preparation and order and authority and power are the same. As President Wilford Woodruff said,

"As far as I am concerned it would require . . . a revelation from the same God who had organized the church and guided it by inspiration in the channel in which it has travelled . . . before I could give my vote or influence to depart from

The First Presidency and the Quorum of the Twelve Apostles

the paths followed by the Apostles since the organization of the church and followed by the inspiration of Almighty God. . . . " (Cited by Harold B. Lee in *CR*, Apr. 1970, p. 124.)

The order of succession was set and is certain. God controls that order totally, but he does it in such a way that any knowledgeable Saint may

understand and be sure.

And thus from prophet to succeeding prophet, the fulness of keys and powers will continue without a break to the dawn of Jesus' millennial reign. The lights will never go out again. Apostasy shall never triumph. Wickedness shall spend its strength and fall like shattered glass before the certain course of this "stone . . . cut out of the mountain without hands." (Daniel 2:45.) There will be an uninterrupted succession of prophets, each building on the ministry of those who have gone before.

Now, what of you? Can you sustain them? Can you honor their appointment? Can you be obedient to all that God shall require of you through them?

The Church will continue. Prophets will continue. Revelation shall continue. Truth and light shall continue, until "the earth shall be full of the knowledge of the Lord, as the waters cover the sea." (Isaiah 11:9.)

But, will you continue? The destiny of the Church is certain, but the salvation of individuals depends upon their faithfulness. Succession does not replace but, rather, extends. As Elder Parley P. Pratt wrote after the martyrdom of the Prophet Joseph Smith,

"He has organized the kingdom of God.—We will extend its dominion.

"He has restored the fulness of the Gospel.—We will spread it abroad. . . .

"He has laid the foundation of the Temple.—We will bring up the top-stone with shouting.

"He has kindled a fire.—We will fan the flame.

"He has kindled up the dawn of a day of glory.—We will bring it to its meridian splendour.

"He was a 'little one,' and became a thousand. We are a small one, and will become a strong nation.

"In short, he quarried the stone from the mountain; we will cause it to become a great mountain and fill the whole earth."

(*Millennial Star*, vol. 5, no. 5, Mar. 1845, pp. 151-52.)

UNIT THREE
BRIGHAM YOUNG
Second President of the Church

OVERVIEW

Four years before Lucy Mack Smith would bring into the world the first prophet of the final dispensation, another frontier mother labored to bring forth the second. She would not live long enough to see the ninth of her eleven children become a prophet, seer, and revelator, but such Brigham Young was foreordained to be. The family knew work, hardship, and privation. At age fourteen Brigham was an apprentice to a furniture maker and house painter. He excelled at the craft. By twenty-four, he married. At twenty-five he knew the joys of parenthood.

He was moral, hardworking, and honest. He moved to Mendon, New York, which was fifteen miles from the home of Joseph Smith. There his second daughter was born and his wife contracted tuberculosis, which gradually weakened her. Loving, thoughtful, tender—each day before work Brigham saw to his wife's comfort and his children's care. Each night he cooked, cleaned house, bathed the children, kissed them all, and tucked them into bed. It was in Mendon he buried his first wife, Miriam Works.

The two of them had joined the Church after two years of cautious, sincere study. An honest, practical man, Brigham would not be railroaded into anything. His conversion was genuine, sincere, total. After the death of his wife, he gave away all he possessed so as to be unencumbered by the things of the world and served mission after mission. (During this time Heber C. and Vilate Kimball helped him care for his daughters.) Many cities in the United States and Canada were to hear his voice before other calls sent him to England. He had the gifts of the Spirit: revelation, prophecy, and speaking in tongues. Even so, preaching did not come easily; his first attempts were painful. Yet the Spirit burned, and he became a master in declaring the mind and will of God.

Strong, intelligent, and resourceful, he was given leadership responsibilities early, and they increased continually: a captain in Zion's Camp, confidant of Joseph Smith, apostle, organizer of the Missouri exodus, president of the Twelve, and presiding elder of the English Mission. Devoted and trusted, his loyalty to the Prophet was complete. Hardship and trials were the schoolmasters which mellowed him into the controlled, compassionate giant he became. But during the dark days of Kirtland, when apostasy ran rampant even in the high circles of Church leadership, it was Brigham Young's unyielding firmness that became a strength to the loyal Saints. His powerful leadership led the Church during the dark days of the Missouri persecutions while Joseph and Hyrum were languishing in the Liberty Jail. He led the Twelve 300 miles into hostile, even murderous, Missouri so that they could leave on their mission to England from the place where the Lord's servant said they should.

The Twelve struggled under continual pressure from men, nature, and Satan himself. Through it, all was overshadowed by the powerful figure of Brigham Young. He assisted Wilford Woodruff in the mass conversions of Herefordshire, preached in London, spoke in tongues, healed the sick and lame, compiled a book of hymns, published the Book of Mormon and indexed it, established on a firm foundation this first mission across the seas, and organized a system of transporting thousands of converts to America, all the while molding the Quorum of the Twelve into a unified, smooth-working body.

Later, in Nauvoo, under the direction of the First Presidency, he presided over meetings and councils. Yet there was no self-seeking, vainglory, or self-aggrandizement in the man. He was dedicated to supporting with all his heart the Prophet he was drawn to and loved. But then came the day of

infamy—Joseph and Hyrum dead, usurpers and traitors trying to pull the Church apart. Humbly but firmly, Brigham took the head. The mantle fell upon him with power before thousands, and he spoke with the authority of God. With that authority he led the Saints west, directed the exploration and settlement of vast areas, founded towns and cities, and made peace with the Indians; he started schools and established roadways, transportation systems, telegraph lines, irrigation, farming, industry, and mercantile institutions; he directed the ever-expanding missionary system and presided as the first territorial governor of Utah. To the end of his life he worked with such perfect confidence and astonishing elan that many remarked with awe that "Brother Brigham" seemed to know exactly what he was doing from the start. And he did! This master craftsman and builder had been given the perfect blueprints from which to work—nothing less than the heavenly order of the kingdom of God and Zion.

But it was not his executive ability that endeared him to his family and the Saints. Frank, kind, and concerned, he was as a father among them. Working alongside them, he chopped wood, cut timber, made bridges, cleared land, and built roads. During the exodus he was the first up in the morning and the last to retire at night, always making the rounds to see that all were as comfortable as possible. But above all, he was the prophet of God. He could rebuke, yet love and inspire; demand, yet give; lead always, yet follow. And the courage and humor with which he faced trials served as an anchor and a model for the persecution-weary Saints.

For twenty-nine years he led the Church. He knew the divinity and destiny of the work. From this base he continued to build the kingdom that would go forth to encompass the world and eventually transform the world into Zion.

CHAPTER 6

BEHOLD A DISCIPLE INDEED

INTRODUCTION

As Joseph Smith labored up the side of the Hill Cumorah, September 22, 1827, cosmic battle swirled and rampaged. This battle between the forces of light and darkness had raged from the first foundations of this tremendously important world. But now, with the Book of Mormon, the keystone of the Lord's revealed religion, about to come forth, it took on new fury and intensity. Why? Because the coming forth of the book signaled clearly the beginning of the end of the kingdom of hell. Babylon the great was about to fall—but not without an earnest, world-wrenching contest. Lucifer was unleashing all his forces. In full fury, the legions of the adversary would try to thwart the purposes of God. And so the armies of light and darkness marched.

As Joseph toiled and armies marshaled, the world slept in ignorance of the book and the battle. But only a few miles away, within hours after Joseph secured the plates of the book, a man (Brigham Young) saw the angels of light descend in preparation for the battle of the King of kings. Though it would be over four years before he would comprehend the meaning of what he was seeing, yet the veil was taken from his eyes; and in the nighttime's western sky, toward Cumorah, he saw a bright light. Calling his wife excitedly to his side, they watched in amazement as for two hours the shimmering light formed itself into marching armies. (Unpublished minutes

of the Young-Richards Family Meeting, Nauvoo, 18 Jan. 1845, Church Library Archives.)

Little did Brigham know that the vision came in accord with divine foreordination. But such was the case, for soon he would lead the people of God and the forces of righteousness as prophet, seer, and revelator. But on the night of September 22, all he could do was wonder at the great sign that had been given.

AS A YOUTH, BRIGHAM YOUNG LEARNED WELL AND PROSPERED FROM THE LESSONS OF FRONTIER LIVING

(6-1) Brigham Young Knew the Rigors of Frontier Life

"At an early age I labored with my father, assisting him to clear off new land and cultivate his farm, passing through many hardships and privations incident to settling a new country." (Brigham Young, cited in Elden Jay Watson, *Manuscript History of Brigham Young, 1801-1844*, p. 1.)

(6-2) These Taught Him the Value of Hard Work

"Brother Heber and I never went to school until we got into

'Mormonism'; that was the first of our schooling. We never had the opportunity of letters in our youth, but we had the privilege of picking up brush, chopping down trees, rolling logs, and working amongst the roots and getting our shins, feet and toes bruised. The uncle of Brother Merrell, who now sits in the congregation, made the first hat that my father ever bought me; and I was then about eleven years of age. I did not go bareheaded previous to that time, neither did I call on my father to buy me a five-dollar hat every few months, as some of my boys do. My sisters would make me what was called a Jo Johnson cap for winter, and in the summer I wore a straw hat which I frequently braided for myself. I learned how to make bread, wash the dishes, milk the cows and make butter; and can make butter and beat most of the women in this community at housekeeping. Those are about all the advantages I gained in my youth. I know how to economize, for my father had to do it." (Brigham Young, cited in Preston Nibley, *Brigham Young, the Man and His Work*, pp. 1-2.)

(6-3) By These He Was Strengthened Against Hardship

"Instead of crying over our sufferings, as some seem inclined to do, I would rather tell a good story, and leave the crying to others. I do not know that I have ever suffered; I do not realize it. Have I not gone without eating and not half clad? Yes, but that was not suffering. I was used to that in my youth. I used to work in the woods logging and driving team, summer and winter, not half clad, and with insufficient food until my stomach

would ache, so that I am used to all this, and have had no suffering. As I said to the brethren the other night, the only suffering I ever realized in this Church was to preserve my temper towards my enemies. But I have even got pretty much over this.'' (Brigham Young in *JD*, 12:287.)

(6-4) *From His Mother, Brigham Young Learned to Love and Reverence the Bible*

''Of my mother—she that bore me—I can say, no better woman ever lived in the world than she was. . . . My mother, while she lived, taught her children all the time to honor the name of the Father and Son, and to reverence the Holy Book. She said, 'Read it, observe its precepts and apply them to your lives as far as you can. Do everything that is good; do nothing that is evil; and if you see any persons in distress, administer to their wants; never suffer anger to arise in your bosoms, for if you do, you may be overcome by evil. ' '' (Brigham Young, cited in Nibley, *Brigham Young*, p. 2.)

(6-5) *As a Young Adult, He Excelled as a Craftsman*

'' . . . he established himself as the skilled artisan who is famous in this city for the beauty of his stairwell decorations, fanlight doorways, door frames, stair rails, louvered attic windows and above all—fireplace mantels.'' (Mary Van Sickle Wait, *Brigham Young in Cayuga County, 1813-1829*, p. 24.)

'' . . . he excelled when the interiors were planned and finished. He also had a keen feeling for inner decorations of a chaste and substantial nature. He had that care for detail, that appreciation for form and proportion that gave a classic touch to simple models. His mantels, fireplaces, doorways, stairs and cupboards . . . are

worthy of the study of trained architects to-day.'' (Susa Young Gates and Leah D. Widtsoe, *The Life Story of Brigham Young*, p. 227.)

(6-6) *Brigham Was a Devoted Husband and Father*

'' . . . after marriage he worked for half a crown a day when he could not get more; got breakfast for his wife, himself, and the little girls, dressed the children, cleaned up the house, carried his wife to the rocking-chair by the fireplace and left her there until he could return in the evening. When he came home he cooked his own and the family's supper, put his wife back to bed and finished up the day's domestic labours.'' (Gates and Widtsoe, *Brigham Young*, p. 5.)

EARLY IN HIS LIFE, BRIGHAM YOUNG'S HEART YEARNED TOWARD GOD, AND HE SOUGHT SPIRITUAL FULFILLMENT

One becomes great in God's kingdom by becoming loyal to those whom the Lord appoints as his mouthpiece. As you read these few selected incidents from the life of Brigham Young, answer this question: What does each one teach me about loyalty and how can I be a disciplined follower of the Master?

(6-7) *As a Young Man, Brigham Young Searched for Spiritual Fulfillment but Could Not Find It Among the Sectarian Churches*

''Priests had urged me to pray before I was eight years old. On this subject I had but one prevailing feeling in my mind—Lord, preserve me until I am old enough to have sound judgment, and a discreet mind ripened upon a good solid foundation of common sense.'' (Brigham Young in *JD*, 8:37.)

''Before I embraced the Gospel, I

understood pretty well what the different sects preached, but I was called an infidel because I could not embrace their dogmas. . . . there were some things they preached I could believe, and some I could not. . . . As far as their teachings were in accordance with the Bible, I could believe them, and no further.'' (Brigham Young in *JD*, 18:247.)

''I recollect when I was young going to hear Lorenzo Dow preach. He was esteemed a very great man by the religious folks. I, although young in years and lacking experience, had thought a great many times that I would like to hear some man who could tell me something, when he opened the Bible, about the Son of God, the will of God, what the ancients did and received, saw and heard and knew pertaining to God and heaven. So I went to hear Lorenzo Dow. He stood up some of the time, and he sat down some of the time; he was in this position and in that position, and talked two or three hours, and when he got through I asked myself, 'What have you learned from Lorenzo Dow?' and my answer was, 'Nothing, nothing but morals.' He could tell the people they should not work on the Sabbath day; they should not lie, swear, steal, commit adultery, &c., but when he came to teaching the things of God he was as dark as midnight. . . .

''I would as lief go into a swamp at midnight to learn how to paint a picture and then define its colors when there is neither moon nor stars visible and profound darkness prevails, as to go to the religious world to learn about God, heaven, hell or the faith of a Christian. But they can explain our duty as rational, moral beings, and that is good, excellent as far as it goes.'' (Brigham Young in *JD*, 14:197-98.)

"I have often prayed, If there is a God in heaven save me, that I may know all and not be fooled. I saw them get religion all around me—men were rolling and hollering and bawling and thumping but had no effect on me. I wanted to know the truth that I might not be fooled." (Brigham Young, as recorded in the minutes of a Young and Richards family meeting in Nauvoo, 8 Jan. 1845. Church Archives, Church Historian's Office. Spelling and punctuation standardized.)

(6-8) Characteristically, He Investigated the Claims of "Mormonism" with a Patient Caution and Reserve

Here was an honest man seeking earnestly for truth. Brigham would not be pushed. His criteria for judging the Church was straightforward and sound. "I watched," he said, "to see whether good common sense was manifest; and if they had that, I wanted them to present it in accordance with the Scriptures." (*JD*, 8:38.) Therefore, when he received the Book of Mormon his feelings were, " 'Wait a little while; what is the doctrine of the book, and of the revelations the Lord has given? Let me apply my heart to them.' . . . I wished time sufficient to prove all things for myself." (*JD*, 3:91.) This was not procrastination, but the caution of a man who, upon finding truth, would dedicate his whole life to it. "I could not more honestly and earnestly have prepared myself to go into eternity than I did to come into this Church; and when I had ripened everything in my mind, I drank it in, and not till then." (*JD*, 8:38.)

(6-9) Brigham Young's Conversion Came Not by Logic or Reasoning, but by the Divine Witness of the Holy Ghost

"If all the talent, tact, wisdom and

Brigham Young as a Church leader

refinement of the world had been sent to me with the Book of Mormon and had declared in the most exalted of earthly eloquence the truth of it, undertaking to prove it by learning and worldly wisdom, they would have been to me like the smoke which arises, only to vanish away. But when I saw a man without eloquence, or talents for public speaking who could only say, 'I know by the power of the Holy Ghost, that the Book of Mormon is true, that Joseph Smith is a Prophet of the Lord,' the Holy Ghost proceeding from that individual illuminated my understanding, and light, glory and immortality were before me. I was encircled by them, filled with them, and I knew for myself that the testimony was true." (Brigham Young, cited in Nibley, *Brigham Young*, p. 6.)

He was deeply touched at his baptism, for "before my clothes were dry on my back [Brother

Eleazer Miller] laid his hands on me and ordained me an Elder, at which I marvelled. According to the words of the Savior, I felt a humble, child-like spirit, witnessing unto me that my sins wre forgiven." (Watson, *Manuscript History, 1801-1844*, p. 3.)

(6-10) Brigham Young's Conversion Brought with It Total Dedication

(See Matthew 10:37.)

"I felt, yes, I can leave my father, my brothers and sisters and wife and children, if they will not serve the Lord and go with me. . . .

"When I went to Kirtland I had not a coat in the world, for previous to this I had given away everything I possessed that I might be free to go forth and proclaim the plan of salvation to the inhabitants of the earth." (Brigham Young, cited in Nibley, *Brigham Young*, pp. 9-10.)

(6-11) His Conversion Brought the Gifts of the Spirit Also

"A few weeks after my baptism I was at Brother Kimball's house one morning, and while family prayer was being offered up, Brother Alpheus Gifford commenced speaking in tongues. Soon the Spirit came on me, and I spoke in tongues, and we thought only of the day of Pentecost, when the Apostles were clothed upon with cloven tongues of fire." (Brigham Young, cited in Nibley, *Brigham Young*, p. 9.)

(6-12) One of Brigham Young's Greatest Challenges Was Public Speaking, but So Powerful Was the Effect of the Spirit upon Him That He Could Not Be Still

"When I began to speak in public I was about as destitute of language as a man could well be. . . . How I have had the headache when I have had ideas to lay before the people, and not words to express them; but I was so gritty that I always tried my best." (Brigham Young, cited in Nibley, *Brigham Young*, p. 13.)

"When I first commenced preaching, I made up my mind to declare the things that I understood, fearless of friends and threats, and regardless of caresses. They were nothing to me, for if it was my duty to rise before a congregation of strangers and say that the Lord lives, that He has revealed Himself in this our day, that He has given to us a Prophet . . . and if that was all I could say, I must be just as satisfied as though I could get up and talk for hours. . . . had it not been for this feeling, nothing could have induced me to have become a public speaker." (Brigham Young in *JD*, 4:21.)

(6-13) The Spirit of the Lord Was with Him As He Met the Challenges

" . . . one week [after baptism] I had the pleasure of meeting with and preaching to a large congregation. I think there were present on that occasion four experienced Elders, formerly of the Methodist and Baptist persuasions, who had received the Gospel and had been numbered with us. I expected to hear them address the people on the principles that we had just received through the servants of the Lord. They said that the Spirit of the Lord was not upon them to speak to the people, yet they had been preachers for years. I was but a child, so far as public speaking and a knowledge of the world was concerned; but the Spirit of the Lord was upon me, and I felt as though my bones would consume within me unless I spoke to the people and told them what I had seen, heard and learned—what I had experienced and rejoiced in; and the first discourse I ever delivered I occupied over an hour. I opened my mouth and the Lord filled it. . . . " (Brigham Young in *JD*, 13:211.)

(6-14) At Their First Meeting, Prophetic Power Rested upon Both Joseph Smith and Brigham Young Such That Each Understood the Greatness of the Other

"Brother Heber C. Kimball took his horse and wagon, Brother Joseph Young and myself accompanying him, and started for Kirtland to see the Prophet Joseph. We visited many friends on the way and some branches of the Church. We exhorted them and prayed with them and I spoke in tongues. . . .

"We proceeded to Kirtland and stopped at John P. Greene's who had just arrived there with his family. We rested a few minutes, took some refreshments and started to see the Prophet. We went to his father's house and learned that he was in the woods chopping. We immediately went to the woods, where we found the Prophet and two or three of his brothers, chopping and hauling wood. Here my joy was full at the privilege of shaking the hand of the Prophet of God, and I received the sure testimony, by the spirit of prophecy, that he was all that any man could believe him to be, as a true Prophet. He was happy to see us and made us welcome. We soon returned to his house, he accompanying us." (Brigham Young, cited in Nibley, *Brigham Young*, pp. 10-11.)

"In the evening a few of the brethren came in and we conversed together upon the things of the Kingdom. He (Joseph) called upon me to pray; in my prayer I spoke in tongues. As soon as we arose from our knees the brethren flocked around him, and asked his opinion concerning the gift of tongues that was upon me. He told them it was the pure Adamic language. Some

said to him they expected he would condemn the gift brother Brigham had, but he said, 'No, it is of God, and the time will come when Brother Brigham Young will preside over this Church.' The latter part of this conversation was in my absence.'' (Brigham Young, cited in Nibley, *Brigham Young*, p. 11.)

BRIGHAM YOUNG DEVELOPED LOVE FOR THE PROPHET JOSEPH SMITH AND WAS INSTRUCTED IN DEPTH BY HIM

(6-15) He Rejoiced That He Knew a Living Prophet

''I feel like shouting hallelujah all the time when I think that I ever knew Joseph Smith, the Prophet whom the Lord raised up and ordained, and to whom he gave the keys and power to build up the Kingdom of God on earth and sustain it.'' (Brigham Young, *Discourses of Brigham Young*, p. 458.)

(6-16) The Application of the Prophet's Words Became the Key to His Success

''In my experience I never did let an opportunity pass of getting with the Prophet Joseph and of hearing him speak in public or in private, so that I might draw understanding from the fountain from which he spoke, that I might have it and bring it forth when it was needed. My own experience tells me that the great success with which the Lord has crowned my labors is owing to the fact of applying my heart to wisdom. . . . In the days of the Prophet Joseph, such moments were more precious to me than all the wealth of the world. No matter how great my poverty—if I had to borrow meal to feed my wife and children, I never let an opportunity pass of learning what the Prophet had to impart. This is the secret of the success of

your humble servant.'' (Brigham Young in *JD*, 12:269-70.)

(6-17) Because of His Faithfulness, He Became Great in the Kingdom

Joseph Smith recognized early the greatness of Brigham Young, and over the course of the years the hearts of these two giants of the Restoration were knit together. Brigham Young listened to the

Prophet preach and teach, not only in session with others but also privately. The future president of the Church was taught the mysteries of godliness, was given keys and powers of administration, and was trusted with sacred teachings shared initially by few others. He knew how to receive the mind and will of the Lord, was taught truth upon truth, received

Brigham Young was firm and faithful

revelation upon revelation and ordinance upon ordinance, until all was given which was necessary for him to preside among the brethren and eventually over the whole Church.

BRIGHAM YOUNG EXERCISED GREAT FAITH IN THE LORD AND HAD MANY SPIRITUAL EXPERIENCES THEREBY

(6-18) An Example of His Faith Was Exhibited During the Period of His Mission Service

In 1839 Brigham Young sailed for England and two years of missionary service. During the trip a storm arose which stopped the progress of the ship. "I went up on deck and felt impressed in spirit to pray to the Father in the name of Jesus for forgiveness of all my sins, and then I felt to command the winds to cease and let us go safe on our journey. The winds abated and glory and honor and praise be to that God that rules all things." (Brigham Young's Diary, 1837-40. Spelling and punctuation standardized.)

On board ship returning from England, again very bad weather hindered all progress. "When the winds were contrary, the Twelve agreed to humble themselves before the Lord and ask him to calm the seas and give us a fair wind. We did so and the wind immediately changed, and from that time to this it has blown in our favor." (Brigham Young's Diary, 1840-44. Spelling and punctuation standardized.)

AFTER THE DEATH OF JOSEPH SMITH, BRIGHAM YOUNG LED THE SAINTS BY PRECEPT AND EXAMPLE

(6-19) Brigham Young's Sense of Humor, Courage, and Faith Were Examples for the Saints and Inspired Them to Face Their Own

Trials, Tasks, and Dangers with Courage

After the death of Joseph Smith, Brigham Young became the target of harassing lawsuits and arrests. He met the challenges with restraint and humor.

"Hans C. Hanson, the doorkeeper [of the Nauvoo Temple in November 1845] reported that there were two officers waiting at the foot of the stairs for me. I told the brethren that I could bear to tarry here where it was warm as long as they could stay in the cold waiting for me." (Brigham Young in B. H. Roberts, ed. *HC*, 7:535.)

On another occasion Brigham was informed that federal officials were watching the temple so that they might arrest him. He had his coachman bring his carriage around to the front of the temple. William Miller then put on Brigham's cap and Heber C. Kimball's cloak, left the temple,

The Lion House—Brigham Young's home

and acted as though he were going to get into the carriage. The law officers ran up and arrested him. He protested loudly that they had the wrong man, and that he was not guilty of the charges they brought against him. Believing they had Brigham Young, they carted him off to Carthage; all the while he continued to protest and claim his innocence.

Once they arrived in Carthage, word soon spread that the marshal had brought in Brigham Young. There was great excitement until one man recognized William Miller. He called the marshal out, and after the marshal returned he asked Miller if his name was Young.

" . . . he answered, 'I never told you my name was Young, did I?' 'No,' replied the marshal, 'but one of my men professed to be acquainted with Mr. Young, and pointed you out to me to be him.' William Backenstos was called in and he told them William Miller was not Brigham Young. Another man came, and said he could swear Miller was not Brigham Young. The marshal said he was sorry, and asked Miller his name, he replied, 'it is William Miller'.

"The marshal left the room and soon returned accompanied by Edmonds who was laughing heartily at him." (Roberts, ed., *HC*, 7:550-51.)

(6-20) After Joseph Was Taken, Brigham Young Had to Carry the Burden of Care for the Whole Church

In a letter to Wilford Woodruff, Brigham Young reported:

"There are many good buildings erecting in different parts of the city, there is not much sickness in the place, and there never was a more prosperous time, in general, amongst the saints, since the work

commenced. Nauvoo, or, more properly, the 'City of Joseph', looks like a paradise. All the lots and land, which have heretofore been vacant and unoccupied, were enclosed in the spring, and planted with grain and vegetables, which makes it look more like a garden of gardens than a city; and the season has been so favorable, the prospect is, there will be enough raised within the limits of the corporation to supply the inhabitants with corn, potatoes, and other vegetables. Hundreds of acres of prairie land have also been enclosed, and are now under good cultivation, blooming with corn, wheat, potatoes, and other necessaries of life. Many strangers are pouring in to view the Temple and the city. They express their astonishment and surprise to see the rapid progress of the Temple, and the beauty and grandeur of Mormon looks. Many brethren are coming from abroad, who seem highly delighted with the place and all its appendages." (Roberts, ed., *HC*, 7:431.)

(6-21) When It Came Time to Move, Brigham Young Willingly Left His Home to Lead the People Where God Dictated

"It is a matter of doubt about any of the Twelve returning to Nauvoo very soon. It is not the place for me any more until this nation is scourged by the hand of the Almighty who rules in the heavens. . . . Do not think, brother Joseph, that I hate to leave my house and home. Far from that. I am so free from bondage at this time that Nauvoo looks like a prison house to me. It looks pleasant ahead, but dark to look back." (Brigham Young, cited in Nibley, *Brigham Young*, p. 74.)

BRIGHAM YOUNG WAS A TOTALLY DEDICATED DISCIPLE OF THE LORD AND OF THE LORD'S PROPHET

Have you ever been in a position where a friend complained about the bishop or branch president? What did you do?

Consider that which made Brigham Young great in the sight of God. You might focus on his suffering and sacrifices or on his great energy or his practical wisdom. But others were practical and energetic, and others had suffered and sacrificed, some as much as Brigham had. Some had lost wives, husbands, or children; a few endured beatings; and many had been driven. But many others did not exhibit the faithful endurance and profound courage to stand up for the Lord's chosen leaders and follow their counsel and guidance.

What does it mean to be a disciple? Brigham Young once said he was a disciple of Joseph Smith. Could you say you are a disciple of your ecclesiastical leaders and of the present prophet of the Church? Discipleship is shown by action. That means sustaining, upholding, and even defending. Next time someone complains about your leaders, what will you do?

(6-22) During the Great Apostasy at Kirtland, Brigham Young Demonstrated That Loyalty Which Was Characteristic of His Entire Ministry

"During this siege of darkness I stood close by Joseph, and, with all the wisdom and power God bestowed upon me, put forth my utmost energies to sustain the servant of God and unite the Quorums of the Church." (Brigham Young, cited in the *Millennial Star*, vol. 25, no. 31, 1 Aug. 1863, p. 487.)

"On a certain occasion several of

the Twelve, the witnesses to the Book of Mormon, and others of the Authorities of the Church, held a council in the upper room of the Temple. The question before them was to ascertain how the Prophet Joseph could be deposed, and David Whitmer appointed President of the Church. Father John Smith, brother Heber C. Kimball and others were present, who were opposed to such measures. I rose up, and in a plain and forcible manner told them that Joseph was a Prophet, and I knew it, and that they might rail and slander him as much as they pleased, they could not destroy the appointment of the Prophet of God, they could only destroy their own authority, cut the thread that bound them to the Prophet and to God and sink themselves to hell. Many were highly enraged at my decided opposition to their measures, and Jacob Bump (an old pugilist) was so exasperated that he could not be still. Some of the brethren near him put their hands on him, and requested him to be quiet; but he writhed and twisted his arms and body saying, 'How can I keep my hands off that man?' I told him if he thought it would give him any relief he might lay them on. This meeting was broken up without the apostates being able to unite on any decided measures of opposition. This was a crisis when earth and hell seemed leagued to overthrow the Prophet and Church of God. The knees of many of the strongest men in the Church faltered.'' (Brigham Young, cited in Watson, *Manuscript History, 1801-1844*, pp. 15-16.)

(6-23) Such Discipleship Brought Persecution from Others

"On the morning of December 22nd [1837], I left Kirtland in consequence of the fury of the mob and the spirit that prevailed in the apostates, who had threatened to destroy me because I would proclaim, publicly and privately, that I knew, by the power of the Holy Ghost, that Joseph Smith was a Prophet of the Most High God, and had not transgressed and fallen as the apostates declared.'' (Brigham Young, cited in Nibley, *Brigham Young*, p. 20.)

The cost of discipleship is often high, but so are the rewards. Ponder the meaning of the Lord's words when he said,

President and colonizer

"Blessed are they which are persecuted for righteousness' sake.'' (Matthew 5:10.) How do they apply to you as a modern disciple? Why is testimony so essential to discipleship? Can you see how Brigham Young relied on his testimony? Consider this statement of the prophet Brigham:

"I attended prayer meeting in the Assembly Room. President Joseph Smith being absent I presided and instructed the brethren upon the necessity of following our file leader, and our Savior, in all his laws and commandments, without asking any questions why they were so.'' (Cited in Nibley, *Brigham Young*, p. 51.)

Can you see the real testimony needed to voice such faith and confidence in our leaders? Brigham Young could do it because he knew.

The next two readings (**6-24** and **6-25**) are taken from an address he gave. As you read and ponder what this means to you, keep in mind that he is sharing the philosophy and insight which made him one of the greatest of the Lord's disciples.

(6-24) Brigham Young Understood the Basis of True Discipleship

"It is folly in the extreme for persons to say that they love God, when they do not love their brethren; and it is of no use for them to say that they have confidence in God, when they have none in righteous men, for they do not know anything about God. It is reasonable for the Elders of Israel to be very sanguine and strenuous on this point. And were I to be asked whether I have any experience in this matter, I can tell the people that once in my life I felt

a want of confidence in brother Joseph Smith, soon after I became acquainted with him. It was not concerning religious matters—it was not about his revelations—but it was in relation to his financiering—to his managing the temporal affairs which he undertook. A feeling came over me that Joseph was not right in his financial management, though I presume the feeling did not last sixty seconds, and perhaps not thirty. But that feeling came on me once and once only, from the time I first knew him to the day of his death. It gave me sorrow of heart, and I clearly saw and understood, by the spirit of revelation manifested to me, that if I was to harbor a thought in my heart that Joseph could be wrong in anything, I would begin to lose confidence in him, and that feeling would grow from step to step, and from one degree to another, until at last I would have the same lack of confidence in his being the mouthpiece for the Almighty. . . . '' (JD, 4:297.)

What is the ultimate danger in finding fault with any of the Lord's anointed?

(6-25) He Knew That the Prophet Was Responsible Not to Men but to God

"Though I admitted in my feelings and knew all the time that Joseph was a human being and subject to err, still it was none of my business to look after his faults.

"I repented of my unbelief, and that too, very suddenly; I repented about as quickly as I committed the error. It was not for me to question whether Joseph was dictated by the Lord at all times and under all circumstances or not. I never had the feeling for one moment, to believe that any man or set of men or beings upon the face of the

Brigham Young's birthplace marker

whole earth had anything to do with him, for he was superior to them all, and held the keys of salvation over them. Had I not thoroughly understood this and believed it, I much doubt whether I should ever have embraced what is called 'Mormonism.' '' (JD, 4:297.)

"It was not my prerogative to call him in question with regard to any act of his life. He was God's servant, and not mine. He did not belong to the people but to the Lord, and was doing the work of the Lord. . . . That was my faith, and it is my faith still.

"If we have any lack of confidence in those whom the Lord has appointed to lead the people, how can we have confidence in a being whom we know nothing about? . . .

"How are we going to obtain

implicit confidence in all the words and doings of Joseph? By one principle alone, that is, to live so that the voice of the Spirit will testify to us all the time that he is the servant of the Most High; so that we can realize as it were the Lord's declaring that 'Joseph is my servant, I lead him day by day whithersoever I will, and dictate him to do whatever I will; he is my mouth to the people. . . . '

"That is the preaching which you hear all the time, viz.—to live so that the voice of God's Spirit will always be with you, and then you know that what you hear from the heads of the people is right." (JD, 4:297-98.)

What must you do to become a devoted follower of the Lord? Surely the legacy left by Brigham Young should be both an example and a strength to you. He knew Joseph was a prophet, and therefore his knees never faltered; and Joseph himself testified that Brigham had never lifted a heel against him. In Brigham's calling as an apostle, and later as president of the Twelve, he was able to more fully demonstrate his loyalty. His defense of Joseph in Kirtland, his fulfillment of a mission to England against overwhelming opposition, and his essential leadership of the Church after the death of the Prophet bear added testimony to his fervent discipleship.

The Savior taught, "If ye continue in my word [which is spoken by the prophets], then are ye my disciples indeed." (John 8:31.) As it was with Brigham Young, so it can be with you as you increase your testimony and as you become obedient to and exercise loyalty toward the Lord and his anointed.

CHAPTER 7
ESTABLISHING THE MOUNTAIN OF THE LORD'S HOUSE

INTRODUCTION

The ground trembled for a few moments, and houses perceptibly shook. Yet the Saints seemed to sense that the source of power was not within the earth but within a log cabin where the Twelve were met in council. Men, women, and children came running to that spot, wondering what was the matter. They were quickly reassured that all was well, that what they felt was the power of the Lord who was directing and inspiring his leaders.

And indeed he was, for as the council met and deliberated and prayed that the Lord's will might be known as to the reorganization of the First Presidency, not organized since the death of the Prophet Joseph, the voice of God came. There also came the assuring power. Brigham Young was to be the prophet, seer, and revelator. The First Presidency was to be organized immediately. (See item 5-15.)

And so, called by the direct voice of God to the Twelve and sustained at a conference held December 7, 1847, Brigham Young became the second president of the Church, with Heber C. Kimball and Willard Richards as his counselors. Though the first colony of Saints was already placed securely in the valley of the Great Salt Lake, to these three men would fall the awesome responsibility of yet gathering more than 140,000 Saints there. Moreover, they would direct the taming of the wilderness, the colonization of the Great Basin, the establishment of over three

hundred cities, and the transforming of men and women into the children of God. And later, when Brigham Young was released through death, the kingdom of God would be firmly established in the tops of the mountains in preparation for its great work of the latter days.

BRIGHAM YOUNG WAS A TREMENDOUS LEADER, BOTH SPIRITUALLY AND TEMPORALLY, CALLED OF GOD

(7-1) Many, Including Non-Mormons, Recognized His Great Leadership Ability

One non-Mormon, visiting Brigham Young in later life, described him thus:

"I had expected to see a venerable-looking old man. Scarcely a grey thread appears in his hair. . . . His manner is at once affable and impressive, simple and courteous. . . . He shows no sign of dogmatism, bigotry, or fanaticism. . . . He impresses a stranger with a certain sense of power: his followers are, of course, wholly fascinated by his superior strength of brain. It is commonly said that there is one chief in Great Salt Lake City, and that is

'Brigham.' His temper is even and placid . . . and when occasion requires he can use the weapons of ridicule to direful effect, and 'speak a bit of his mind' in a style which no one forgets. He often reproves his erring followers in purposely violent language, making the terrors of a scolding the punishment in lieu of hanging for a stolen horse or cow. His powers of observation are intuitively strong, and his friends declare him to be gifted with an excellent memory and a perfect judgment of character. If he dislikes a stranger at the first interview, he never sees him again. . . . He assumes no airs of sanctimoniousness, and had the plain, simple manner of honesty. His followers deem him an angel of light, his foes, a goblin damned; he is, I presume, neither one nor the other. . . . He has been called hypocrite, swindler, forger, murderer—no one looks it less. . . . Finally, there is a total absence of pretension in his manner, and he has been so long used to power that he cares nothing for its display. The arts by which he rules the heterogeneous mass of conflicting elements are indomitable will, profound secrecy, and uncommon astuteness.

"Such is His Excellency President Brigham Young, 'painter and glazier'—his earliest craft—prophet, revelator, translator, and seer; the man who is revered as king or kaiser, pope or pontiff never was; . . . who, governing as well as reigning, long stood up to fight with the sword of the Lord, and with his few hundred guerillas, against the then mighty power of the United States; who has outwitted all diplomacy

opposed to him; and, finally, who made a treaty of peace with the President of the Great Republic as though he had wielded the combined power of France, Russia, and England." (Richard Francis Burton, cited in Milton R. Hunter, *Brigham Young, the Colonizer*, p. 16.)

(7-2) Brigham Young Was a Reluctant Leader, Never Wanting More Than to Associate with and Take Direction from His Beloved Prophet and Friend, Joseph Smith

Early in his career, responsibility fell to Brigham Young, from being a captain in Zion's Camp to presiding over the Quorum of the Twelve and becoming the presiding elder in the British Mission. Yet he did not seek such positions. His desire was only to proclaim the message of the restored gospel and to be schooled in the mysteries of godliness by the Prophet of the Lord. Always for him, his greatest joy was being at home with his family. When united at last with his wife and children at Nauvoo after his long mission to England, he tenderly confided in his diary, "This evening I am home with my wife alone, by my fireside for the first time in years. We enjoy it and feel to praise the Lord." (Diary, 1837-1845. Spelling and punctuation standardized.)

From your insight into the implications of the above two readings, how would you react to those who accused Brigham Young of seeking power for his own ends and of constantly aspiring to positions of leadership? Would you say the feelings expressed below by President Spencer W. Kimball at the death of President Lee reflect accurately Brigham's feelings at the death of Joseph?

"We prayed it would never happen, our prayers were for

President Harold B. Lee. Night and morning every day, we prayed for a long life and the general welfare of President Lee. I knew the responsibility could fall to me, but I did not seek it. Now I will do my best." (*Church News*, 5 Jan. 1974, p. 4.)

Can you see that prophets do not become prophets by possessing a desire to have dominion over people? Can you see that Brigham was more than content to withdraw from the center of leadership where he had stood for nearly a year while Joseph was imprisoned in Missouri?

And, finally, can you see the sincerity of his remarks when the leadership of the Church was thrust upon him?

"I do not care who leads the church, even though it were Ann Lee; but one thing I must know, and that is what God says about it. I have the keys and the means of obtaining the mind of God on the subject. . . .

"My private feelings would be to let the affairs of men and women alone [including Church leadership], only go and preach and baptize them into the kingdom of God; yet, whatever duty God places upon me, in his strength I intend to fulfill it." (Brigham Young, cited in B. H. Roberts, ed., *HC*, 7:230.)

(7-3) At the Time Brigham Young Assumed the Leadership of the Church, He Knew He Had the Power of the Prophets

After the death of the Prophet Joseph, several men stepped forward as would-be leaders of the Church. Many members were confused as to whom to follow. But at a critical meeting held August 8, 1844, the power of the prophets

was upon Brigham Young. He recorded in his diary: "I arose and spoke to the people, my heart was swollen with compassion toward them and by the power of the Holy Ghost, *even the spirit of the prophets*, I was enabled to comfort the hearts of the Saints." (Diary, 8 Aug. 1844.)

(7-4) The Mantle of the Prophet Fell on Brigham Young So That the Saints Could Tell That He Was the Shepherd

At the meeting mentioned above, after some had tried to persuade the people away from the leadership of the Twelve, Brigham Young arose to speak. At that moment, a vision was opened to many. The following are a few testimonies of those who were there.

"It was the voice of Joseph himself; and not only was it the voice of Joseph which was heard; but it seemed in the eyes of the people as though it was the very person of Joseph which stood before them. . . . They both saw and heard with their natural eyes and ears, and then the words which were uttered came, accompanied by the convincing power of God, to their hearts, and they were filled with the Spirit and with great joy." (*Juvenile Instructor*, 29 Oct. 1870, pp. 174-75.)

"If I had not seen him with my own eyes, there is no one that could have convinced me that it was not Joseph Smith, and anyone can testify to this who was acquainted with these two men." (Wilford Woodruff, cited in Roberts, ed., *HC*, 7:236.)

Benjamin F. Johnson testified that "as soon as [Brigham Young] spoke I jumped upon my feet, for in every possible degree it was Joseph's voice, and his person, in look, attitude, dress and appearance was Joseph himself, personified; and I knew in a moment the spirit and

mantle of Joseph was upon him." (*My Life's Review*, p. 104.)

(7-5) The Voice of the Lord Called for the Reorganization of the First Presidency, with Brigham Young as the Head of the Church

For over three years after the above-mentioned event, the Church was led by the Quorum of the Twelve. Then came the voice of the Lord during the winter of 1847-48, instructing these men to reorganize the First Presidency. (A full account of what took place is recorded in item 5-15 of this manual.)

THROUGH THE INSPIRED LEADERSHIP OF BRIGHAM YOUNG, THE SAINTS BECAME SECURE IN THE TOPS OF THE MOUNTAINS

(7-6) In Brigham Young, One Finds a Perfect Blend of the Practical and the Spiritual

Brigham, like Joseph, was both practical and visionary. Though his practicality is most often stressed, one must always keep in mind that it was grounded firmly on the vision of the Restoration, of the kingdom of God, of Zion, and of celestial glory. He said of his younger days, "I wanted to thunder and roar out the Gospel to the nations. It burned in my bones like fire pent up. . . . nothing would satisfy me but to cry abroad in the world, what the Lord was doing in the latter days." (*JD,* 1:313.) As the prophet, seer, and revelator, his desire continued to burn with perhaps even more intensity. He was determined to do everything possible to bring to fruition all that the Lord wanted done in the last days. Joseph Smith had laid the foundation of the kingdom of God in the last days; others would rear the superstructure.

"I know that he was called of God,

and this I know by the revelations of Jesus Christ to me, and by the testimony of the Holy Ghost. Had I not so learned this truth, I should never have been what is called a 'Mormon,' neither should I be here to-day." (*JD,* 9:364-65.) Because of this revelation from the Lord, the second latter-day prophet knew the Saints could rear the superstructure of the kingdom. And this was the only practical thing they could do.

Knowing this helps one understand why Brigham Young did some things that must have seemed to many as very impractical. An example of this occurred prior to the time the Saints left Nauvoo, Illinois, when Brigham insisted on continuing the expenditure of time, money, and talent in completing the Nauvoo Temple when it was apparent that the Saints would not be able to enjoy it long. But in Brigham's view it was a very practical thing, for from that house, even if used only briefly, would come the power necessary for the Saints to make the sacrifices and endure the hardships they would be called upon to endure during the exodus. Surely in this one man is demonstrated the balance and blend of the practical, the spiritual, and the perspective of the eternal.

(7-7) The Combining of the Practical with the Spiritual Was a Key to the Power of Brigham Young's Leadership

"There were those, of course, who criticized Brigham Young's intimate involvement with secular and temporal pursuits—his concern with fencing farms, with negotiating contracts for selling grain, his mobilizing workers to build the transcontinental railroad—but his point of view was that temporal and spiritual concerns were indissoluble. In wearing many different

hats—prophet, businessman, governor, and family patriarch—he saw his task and goal to be to promote the temporal *and* spiritual welfare of his people. In his view, he was the Lord's steward in using all human resources—public and private, church and state—to create an economic and social order where all God's children under his care might live in peace and prosperity. . . .

"Contemporary observers whom we have a right to respect—persons of education and experience and standing who traveled to Utah to observe him—emphasized three characteristics: his self-confidence, his sincerity, and his good common sense. Fitz Hugh Ludlow, a nationally known writer and artistic critic, found that Brigham Young had 'absolute certainty of himself and his own opinions.' Governor Young, he wrote, was convinced that he was doing God's work, and that if he and other mortals did all they could to establish the kingdom, God would see to the rest. This helps us to understand the governor's firmness, his calmness, and his unshakeable optimism in the face of seemingly impossible circumstances." (Leonard J. Arrington and Ronald K. Esplin, "Building a Commonweath: The Secular Leadership of Brigham Young," *Utah Historical Quarterly,* vol. 45, no. 3 [Summer 1977], pp. 219-20.)

(7-8) Under the Direction of This Prophet-Leader, the Saints Successfully Met the Challenges of Colonizing the Arid West

"The Great Basin, with its many Rocky Mountain valleys, was the place selected by their prophet-leader, Brigham Young. 'The country to which they went

was one inhabited by roving tribes of Indians; it was so desolate and forbidding that Daniel Webster had declared it unfit for any use except for wild animals.'

"Yet, this desert country served as an ideal laboratory for the Mormons to put into effect their theories of empire building. The unusual success at colonization of those pioneer builders will stand in history as one of the noble accomplishments of a group of God-fearing people. In the words of Dr. Thomas Nixon Carver:

" 'I have been interested in the Mormon policy. It is one of the most interesting and instructive experiments in the world. It throws a great deal of light on the art of nation building. It therefore furnishes a laboratory for the study of the science of statesmanship. . . . The great statesman of the Golden Age of Greece "boasted that he could make a small city into a great and glorious one;" but the Mormon leaders did even better than that. They did not have a small city to start with. They started with nothing and built a great and glorious commonwealth. It was necessary for the Mormon Church to train its own people. They not only began with desert land and had to put everything on it, even water; they also had to start with relatively uneducated people. This double task of developing both land and people could never have been performed except by economizing to the nth degree. The results were a marvel of statesmanship. It may have been a bond of a common religion, it may have been superior intelligence and insight. Whatever the source, the result was good.' [*The Westerner*, 9 Apr. 1930.]

"The rugged mountains and the hot, barren desert, coupled with

The Great Salt Lake as it may have looked when pioneers first arrived

the strenuous conditions of frontier life in the Great West, produced marvelous qualities of leadership in many of the Church members. The desert, the majestic mountains, and the frontier life, however, contributed only their share to the development of leadership. Most important was the religion which these people had espoused which they sincerely believed was the true Church of Jesus Christ and the only church which could assure men exaltation in the kingdom of God." (Hunter, *Brigham Young, the Colonizer*, pp. 350-51.)

(7-9) Within Ten Years After Their Arrival, the Saints Had Colonized Nearly 800,000 Square Miles of Territory

"While the Mormon outposts were being established, numerous towns were springing up on favorable sites on the canyon streams adjacent to Salt Lake Valley. Gradually one valley after another received its portion of

colonists, the growth being mainly southward during the first period, as the climate in that direction was thought to be more favorable for agriculture than that northward. Consequently, in 1857 the community farthest north, excepting Lemhi, was only seventy-five miles from the parent colony. During the first ten years in the Basin, 100 towns were established. The settlements clustered mainly east and south of the Great Salt Lake, of the Jordan River, and of Utah Lake, with a line of communities running in a southwest direction from Juab County to the southwest corner of Utah. Besides these main groups of colonies, a number of Mormons were living in Sanpete County and in the outposts already discussed.

"Thus within ten years after the Saints had arrived in the Great West, they had opened colonization activities in a frontier country extending 1,000 miles from north to south and 800 miles from east to west. Brigham Young's plan

The Salt Lake Temple was envisioned by Brigham Young, who began its construction

of preempting the West was being realized." (Hunter, *Brigham Young, the Colonizer*, pp. 354-55.)

(7-10) As a Colonizer, Brigham Young Has No Peer in All of American History

"During the thirty years of his residence in the Basin, the Mormon leader, Brigham Young, successfully founded and witnessed the development of communities in almost every valley of the present state of Utah, as well as many in southern Idaho, Arizona, and Nevada. Most of the towns built by the Mormons were within a rectangular district 500 miles long by 400 miles wide, omitting the Arizona settlements. However, some were as distant as 1,000 miles east of Salt Lake City in Iowa and Nebraska; San Bernardino was about 750 miles southwest of the parent colony, while Fort Lemhi was located in northern Idaho. The total Mormon population at the time of Brigham's

death (1877) was approximately 140,000.

"The magnitude of this achievement can best be understood by making a comparison between the accomplishments of Brigham Young and his people and those of Spain—one of the most successful of European colonizing countries during the early American colonial period. . . .

"Lopez de Velasco, official geographer of New Spain, described the Spanish colonization achievement in his report of 1574. 'At that time there were in North and South America about 200 Spanish towns and cities, besides numerous mining camps, haciendas, and stock ranches. The Spanish population was 32,000 families, or perhaps from 160,000 to 200,000 persons.' Besides the Spanish population there were 40,000 negro slaves and approximately 5,000,000 Indians." (Hunter, *Brigham Young, the Colonizer*, pp. 357-58.)

(7-11) Brigham Young Also Led the Saints in Appreciating the Finer Things of Life

"While building homes, developing farms and establishing themselves a government, the Mormon colonists did not neglect the finer side of life. Education, religion, art, drama, and music were fostered for the social development of the people. The Saints built their own theatres and trained their children in the various sciences and in music. Simultaneously with the erection of private dwellings, each group of colonists through cooperative effort constructed a public hall which was used as a church house, a school house, and a place in which dances and dramas were conducted. In October, 1847, the first pioneer group opened a school in an old military tent. Even while these frontiersmen were struggling to construct their first shelters in the Salt Lake Valley, this school was conducted daily. Only two years elapsed before Governor Young signed an act, passed by the first legislative Assembly of the State of Deseret, incorporating a university, later known as the University of Utah.

"As early as 1850 the Salt Lake Musical and Dramatic Association was formed, conducting its earlier performances in the Temple Square Bowery. Later, 1852, the Social Hall was built. It was one of the first theatres erected west of the Missouri River." (Hunter, *Brigham Young, the Colonizer*, pp. 359-60.)

(7-12) In the West the Saints Became Secure; and Under the Able Direction of Their Prophet, They Were Fused into a Harmonious, Social Unit

"Brigham Young led a persecuted, disheartened group of devout religionists into the center of an

uninviting desert country which no other group of people would at that time consider occupying. There, with the helpful cooperation of his sturdy pioneer associates, he colonized an extensive territory. He sent out exploring parties to select favorable sites for the new colonies and often chose the sites himself. He sent balanced groups of industrial and agricultural workers to found these new communities. Brigham personally supervised the laying out of many of the towns into surveyed square blocks with wide streets and the alloting of farming lands and city lots to the Saints.

"While he was founding colonies he also provided his followers with civil government, with social institutions for their education and enjoyment, and with the necessary equipment for their economic independence and prosperity. On March 12, 1849, he was elected the Provisional Governor of the 'State of Deseret.' The following year, September 28, 1850, Utah was made a territory with Brigham as the governor. This position he held until 1858, when he was replaced by Alfred Cumming. While acting as governor, as well as throughout his entire career in Utah as President of the Mormon Church, Brigham Young deserves much credit for the success of federal Indian agents, federal surveys across the Basin, the building of the transcontinental railway, and the construction of the telegraph.

"All of the Mormon colonization accomplishments were made possible partially by adding thousands of colonists to his ranks which he did by sending missionaries to various parts of the United States as well as to Europe, Canada, Hispanic America, India, Australia, and the Islands of the Pacific. He was able to fuse this heterogenous mass of humanity, representing several different races, into a harmonious social unit." (Hunter, *Brigham Young, the Colonizer,* pp. 358-59.)

As we review the hardships of the Saints and their leaders, it is a temptation to wish that the Lord had made it easier for them. But ponder these questions:

1. Is not the success of this dispensation a miracle that inspires testimony?

2. Would the purposes of mortal testing be fulfilled if building the kingdom and establishing Zion were easy?

Main Street in early Salt Lake City

3. Will not the struggles of the early Saints and their prophets serve as a testimony to the poorer Saints of today in many nations that with the Lord's help, they too can fill missions and build temples?

THROUGHOUT HIS LONG AND ABLE ADMINISTRATION, BRIGHAM YOUNG WAS INSPIRED OF THE LORD

(7-13) Before Leaving Nauvoo, He Saw in Vision the Valley to Which the Saints Would Go

As the Saints prepared to leave Nauvoo for the wilderness of western America, Brigham Young related a dream to Willard Richards and others, accurately describing not only the valley of the Great Salt Lake, but also the hill which later became known as Ensign Peak. (Willard Richard's Diary, pp. 288-89; see also *JD*, 13:85-86.)

(7-14) As He Arrived in the Valley of the Great Salt Lake, He Saw in Vision That Which He Would Assist to Come to Pass

The last of the journey into the Valley was very hard on Brigham Young because of illness. Anxious that the Saints get into the Valley as soon as possible, he had sent one contingent ahead. On July 23, 1847, the rear elements, traveling slowly for the sake of the prophet, crossed over the last of the mountains that obstructed their view of the Valley. Upon hearing that it could now be seen, Brigham asked that the carriage in which he was lying be turned that he might see the view.

He was struck with joy. "The spirit of light rested upon me and hovered over the valley, and I felt that there the Saints would find protection and safety." (Elden Jay Watson, *Manuscript History of Brigham Young*, 1846-47, p. 564.)

By mid-morning of the next day, the last units of the pioneer company were just a few miles from the Valley floor. Again the prophet asked that the carriage be stopped that he might look. Wilford Woodruff, who attended the president, said he "was enwrapped in vision for several minutes. He had seen the valley before in vision, and upon this occasion he saw the future glory of Zion and of Israel, as they would be, planted in the valleys of these mountains." (Dale L. Morgan, *The Great Salt Lake*, p. 199.)

The building years of Brigham Young

(7-15) Through the Force of His Personality and Character, Brigham Young Motivated the Saints to Do That Which They Were to Do

The prophet Brigham Young knew how to motivate people. Wit, sarcasm, poignant and impassioned speeches, and outright threats were all tools he used to motivate his people to become saints of God. But it was his sense of humor that endeared him to his followers. For example, he dictated a letter to a disgruntled sister who had asked that her name be removed from the records of the Church: "Madam . . . I have this day examined the records of baptism for the remission of sins in the Church . . . and not being able to find [your name] recorded therein, I was saved the necessity of erasing your name therefrom. You may therefore consider that your sins have not been remitted you and you can enjoy the benefits thereof." (Letter of Brigham Young to Elizabeth Green, 28 Dec. 1851.) To a woman who called upon him complaining that her husband had told her to go to hell, "he replied, simply, 'Sister, don't go, don't go!' " (Arrington and Esplin, "Building a Commonwealth," p. 224.)

When his sons were caught donating some props (without permission) for a play written by their friends, Brigham Young said to the theater manager, "These boys have a play. They call it 'The Robbers of the Rocky Mountains.' I don't know much about the mountains, but they certainly made a clean job of my old barn. Give them a date at the Theater." (Clarissa Young Spencer with Mabel Harmer, *Brigham Young at Home*, p. 160.)

The quality which made the Saints honor and revere him was the love which showed in his concern for each one of them, even from the early days of his leadership. On the plains, at a stopping place named Hickory Grove, he was out in the rain all day arranging wagons, helping to pitch tents, chopping wood, and in every way seeing that all were comfortable. Later, in

The President and the Quorum of the Twelve (1868)

Utah, he insisted in meeting every wagon train or handcart company he could, and he would not leave until every soul had a place to stay and a job assignment by which he could be secure for the present.

FOLLOWING THE PROPHET NOT ONLY PROTECTS THE CHURCH AND MAKES IT SECURE, BUT DOES THE SAME THING FOR THE INDIVIDUAL

What is the role of the prophet in bringing peace, security, and protection from evil and designing forces against the Church and against you as an individual? To expand your answer, read carefully D&C 21:4-6. According to verse 4, what two things are required of the Saints?

In verse 6, what three blessings are promised? What is the significance to you of these three promises? Do you know what it means when the Lord says that—

1. "The gates of hell shall not prevail against you"? Consider your answer in light of D&C 17:8.
2. "The Lord God will disperse the powers of darkness from before you"? For insights, see D&C 98:12, 13 and D&C 11:7.
3. He will "cause the heavens to shake for your good"? A clue to the importance of this promise is found in D&C 29:23-25.

Can you see that the three promises are interrelated and actually point to one great promise? What is the promise given to you if you walk in holiness and give heed unto the words of the prophets? Could God promise any greater thing?

You might ask, The promise of eternal blessings is great, but what about me right here and right now? Is there a way I can feel secure now? The answer is yes. Turn to section 103 in the Doctrine and Covenants and ponder the implication of verses 5-7. What is your key to prevailing against the enemies you face, enemies such as false philosophy or theology, the doctrines of men and devils, indecision, and insecurity?

Now read this statement by Brigham Young, and consider its implications in your life.

"There is no doubt, if a person lives according to the revelations given to God's people, he may have the Spirit of the Lord to signify to him his will, and to guide and to direct him in the discharge of his duties, in his temporal as well as his spiritual exercises. I am satisfied, however, that in this respect, we live far beneath our privileges. If this is true, it is necessary that we become more fervent in the service of God—in living our religion—and more truthful and honest with one another, that we be not slack in the performance of any duty, but labor with a right good will for God and truth. If this people, called Latter-day Saints, live beneath their privileges in the holy Gospel of the Son of God, are they justified in every respect before him? They are not. If we do not live in the lively exercise of faith in the Lord Jesus, possessing his Spirit always, how can we know when he speaks to us through his servants whom he had placed to lead us?" (Brigham Young, *Discourses of Brigham Young*, pp. 32-33.)

You may wish to reverse the last question. What will happen in your life as you exercise faith in the Lord, become fervent in your duties, and possess his Spirit?

UNIT FOUR
JOHN TAYLOR
Third President of the Church

OVERVIEW

John Taylor received his first lessons and probation in the realms of light and was distinguished among his fellows by his accomplishments in that world before. In the divine design of the Eternal Father, John Taylor entered the mortal world at the appointed time and place.

John Taylor was born in England. The family moved frequently during the years of his childhood. At age fourteen he was apprenticed to a barrel maker. John then left home to learn the art of working with a wood lathe. He pursued and mastered that occupation from his fifteenth to his twentieth year. Pure in his nature, holy in his daily walk and talk, he instructed by the inspiration of the Almighty to go to America.

Two years later he came to Canada, where he practiced his craft again, studied the Bible, married Leonora Cannon and commenced his family.

Then it happened! A Mormon apostle came to Canada and proclaimed the restoration of Christ's ancient church. John studied, compared, reflected, challenged, and then he sought the inspiration of heaven. He was baptized and became a disciple of Jesus Christ.

At the age of twenty-eight he was made the presiding elder of the Church in Canada. He visited briefly in Kirtland during the dark days of apostasy and defended Joseph Smith by testimony before gatherings of apostates who threatened death to anyone who spoke for Joseph. He then returned to Canada, where he labored zealously to preach and set in order the branches of the Church. At age twenty-nine he received a summons from the Prophet to join the Saints in Missouri. Those were dark days; the faithful had been driven from Ohio, and when he arrived in Missouri after an arduous journey of nearly two thousand miles, they were

driven from Missouri as well.

He was ordained an apostle at Far West in December 1838, at the age of thirty. He assisted Brigham Young in settling the exiled Church in Nauvoo; then, with Brigham and others, he made his way back through Missouri so they could leave for their mission to England.

John Taylor traveled over the whole of his assigned area in England, raising the warning voice. Thousands flocked to the standard of truth he helped to hold aloft. He published and defended the faith in England and then returned to Nauvoo, where he was appointed to petition Congress for redress of the wrongs heaped upon his people. He was judge advocate and colonel in the Nauvoo Legion, a member of the Nauvoo City Council, and a regent of the University of Nauvoo; he served as editor of the *Times and Seasons,* which was the official newspaper of the Church, and editor of the *Nauvoo Neighbor,* another paper. He was fearless in his ministry. He nominated Joseph to be a candidate for president of the United States. When Joseph went to Carthage, John Taylor went with him. He slept in the same cell, offered support and comfort, refused to leave the jail when the opportunity for liberty and life was extended, sang a hymn which embodied the highest principles of his own and Joseph's sacrifice, parried away the guns at the door of the cell, and, failing in that effort, received the fire himself. Escape was impossible; John Taylor was wounded in a savage manner, receiving four bullets, as did Joseph and Hyrum; but he lived.

He lived to sustain Brigham Young and help him in the exodus of the Saints to the great west. He lived to assist in organizing the Mormon Battalion at Winter Quarters, to serve another mission to England, to lead a large company of pioneers to the Salt Lake Valley, and to serve as an associate

justice of the Supreme Court of the provisional state of Deseret. He lived to serve missions to France and Germany and to publish the Book of Mormon and newspapers in both countries, to publish his masterful *Government of God,* to serve briefly in the Utah Territorial Legislature, and then to preside over the Eastern States Mission from New York, where he published another newspaper, *The Mormon.* He lived to serve again in the territorial legislature, to preside as probate judge of Utah County, and to labor as territorial superintendent of schools in Utah. He lived to become president of the Council of the Twelve, and, at the death of Brigham Young, to preside over the whole Church. He lived to open missions in the Northwest, Mexico, Pakistan, Turkey, and the Indian Territory. He lived to organize the Primary Association and to complete the organization of the other auxiliaries. Still carrying some of the bullets in his body, John Taylor lived to publish the inspired *Mediation and Atonement of Our Lord and Savior.*

He lived to urge obedience to the law by his people but to denounce and resist with an astounding strength improper interpretations of the law and the excesses of enforcement which were common in the territory. He lived to dedicate the Logan Temple and to go into voluntary exile. He lived to administer the affairs of God's kingdom from hiding, to mourn the decline and death of his wife and be forbidden by the circumstances of his exile to look upon her face even at her interment. He lived to finally die in exile, in perhaps the darkest hour of the Church's struggle to survive, as a martyr to the principles of loyalty and integrity, as a martyr to freedom of religion, as a martry to the divinity and witness inherent in his own apostolic calling, as a martyr to the restoration of the true church of Jesus Christ, and as a martyr to the reality of Jesus himself, whose servant he was.

CHAPTER 8
COURAGEOUS CHAMPION OF LIBERTY

INTRODUCTION

John Taylor was the only president of the Church who was not a native-born American. He was born in Milnthorpe, Westmoreland, England, in 1808, one of ten children. Although they were not wealthy, the Taylor family was close-knit and religious and taught their children the value of hard work. John labored on a farm on the family estate, and later he mastered the woodturner's trade.

Although baptized as an infant, John cared little for the creeds of his parent's faith. As a youth he was instructed by dreams and visions.

" 'Often when alone,' he writes, 'and sometimes in company, I heard sweet, soft, melodious music, as if performed by angelic or supernatural beings.' When but a small boy he saw, in vision, an angel in the heavens, holding a trumpet to his mouth, sounding a message to the nations. The import of this vision he did not understand until later in life." (B. H. Roberts, *The Life of John Taylor*, pp. 27-28.)

While in his mid-teens, John Taylor joined the Methodist Church and actively labored to involve his friends in prayer and other religious activities. His zeal and native abilities of expression made such an impression upon church leaders that he was appointed a lay preacher at the age of seventeen. While walking to an appointment, he was overcome by a powerful influence. He turned to his companion and said, "I have a strong impression

on my mind, that I have to go to America to preach the gospel!" (Roberts, *Life of John Taylor*, p. 28.)

In 1832 the way opened up for him to migrate to America. While yet in the English Channel, his ship encountered weather so severe that several vessels around it were wrecked in the storm. The officers and crew expected their own ship to sink at any time. He remained unshaken.

"The voice of the Spirit was still saying within him, 'You must yet go to America and preach the gospel.' 'So confident was I of my destiny,' he remarks, 'that I went on deck at midnight, and amidst the raging elements felt as calm as though I was sitting in a parlor at home. I believed I should reach America and perform my work.' " (Roberts, *Life of John Taylor*, p. 29.)

What was the work that impelled him on? Hardly did he realize that indeed the Lord was with him, but for purposes far more significant than he could have guessed.

JOHN TAYLOR'S SEARCH FOR TRUTH BROUGHT AN APOSTLE TO CANADA WITH THE GOSPEL

(8-1) An Intensive Study of the Scriptures Began His Search for the Church of Jesus Christ

John Taylor settled in Canada to be near his parents. Aligning himself with the local Methodist Church, he was soon occupied as a class teacher and itinerant preacher. He and a few close friends soon discovered from their studies that their faith differed significantly from the New Testament church and teachings of the Master. Of this experience he said:

"Not being then acquainted with this Church [LDS], a number of us met together for the purpose of searching the Scriptures; and we found that certain doctrines were taught by Jesus and the Apostles, which neither the Methodists, Baptists, Presbyterians, Episcopalians, nor any of the religious sects taught; and we concluded that if the Bible was true, the doctrines of modern Christendom were not true; or if they were true, the Bible was false. . . . In addition . . . we prayed and fasted before God; and the substance of our prayers was, that if he had a people upon the earth anywhere, and ministers who were authorized to preach the Gospel, that he would send us one. This was the condition we were in." (*Journal of Discourses*, 23:30.)

(8-2) Parley P. Pratt Had the Answer to John Taylor's Prayer of Faith

"About this time [May, 1836] Parley P. Pratt called on me with a letter of introduction from a merchant of my acquaintance. I had peculiar feelings on seeing him. I had heard a great many stories of a similar kind to those that you have heard, and I must say

John Taylor's birthplace–Milnthorpe, England

that I thought my friend had imposed upon me a little in sending a man of this persuasion to me. I, however, received him courteously. . . . I told him, however, plainly, my feelings, and that in our researches I wanted no fables; I wished him to confine himself to the scriptures. We talked for three hours or upwards, and he bound me as close to the scriptures as I desired, proving everything he said therefrom. I afterwards wrote down eight sermons that he preached, in order that I might compare them with the word of God. I found nothing contrary. . . . A number of others and myself were baptized [on May 9, 1836]. . . . '' (John Taylor, *Three Nights' Public Discussion . . . ,* pp. 17-18

DISAFFECTED SAINTS CAUSED JOHN TAYLOR TO BEGIN HIS LIFELONG DEFENSE OF THE FAITH

(8-3) A Visit to Kirtland, Ohio, Brought John Taylor a Testimony and a Challenge

Following his conversion to the Church, nearly a year passed before John Taylor had the

opportunity to meet Joseph Smith. When they had clasped hands and had spent some time together, the spirit which radiated from the Prophet, together with his teachings and explanations of the gospel, greatly strengthened John's testimony of the restored church. Soon afterward, however, he met some members of the Church whose faith was failing and who had begun to be critical of the Prophet. Among their number was Parley P. Pratt, who made it a point to lay his complaints and criticisms before Elder Taylor. To this the English convert replied:

"I am surprised to hear you speak so, Brother Parley. Before you left Canada you bore a strong testimony to Joseph Smith being a Prophet of God, and to the truth of the work he has inaugurated; and you said you knew these things by revelation, and the gift of the Holy Ghost. You gave to me a strict charge to the effect that though you or an angel from heaven was to declare anything else I was not to believe it. Now Brother Parley, it is not man that I am following, but the Lord. The principles you taught me led me to Him, and I now have

the same testimony that you then rejoiced in. If the work was true six months ago, it is true today; if Joseph Smith was then a prophet, he is now a prophet." (Cited in Roberts, *Life of John Taylor,* p. 40.)

Elder Taylor, commenting later on this experience, said of Elder Pratt:

"He with many others . . . were passing under a dark cloud; he soon made all right with the Prophet Joseph, and was restored to full fellowship." (Cited in Roberts, *Life of John Taylor,* p. 40.)

During these dark days in Kirtland, a meeting was convened at which the apostates sought to be heard. In the course of this assembly, a man spoke who was full of lies and who lashed out viciously against the character of the Prophet Joseph Smith, who was not present. Elder Taylor stood it as long as he could, then sought and received permission to address the group. He began by recalling the rebellion of ancient Israel against the Lord and his prophet Moses. He then asked the audience to identify the source of their present knowledge of the kingdom of God and of all spiritual matters. To his own question John replied:

"It was Joseph Smith, under the Almighty, who developed the first principles, and to him we must look for further instructions. If the spirit which he manifests does not bring blessings, I am very much afraid that the one manifested by those who have spoken, will not be very likely to secure them. The children of Israel, formerly, after seeing the power of God manifested in their midst, fell into rebellion and idolatry, and there is certainly very great danger of us doing the same thing." (Cited in Roberts, *Life of John Taylor,* p. 41.)

These incidents in Kirtland established John Taylor's

reputation as one of great courage and eloquence in defending in the gospel. It was under different circumstances, however, that he became known as the "Champion of Liberty." As Elder Taylor was called upon to defend the rights of the Church and its members against her enemies, this Englishman quickly learned to appreciate the constitutional freedoms guaranteed by law to everyone living in America.

FULFILLING A MISSION CALL TO GREAT BRITAIN WAS A SUPREME ACT OF FAITH

(8-4) The Work Pressed Forward in Spite of Trials and Hardships

After the Saints had been driven from Missouri and had found refuge in Illinois, the Prophet Joseph called the Quorum of the Twelve to preach the gospel in Europe. Elder Taylor had been called to the apostleship in the fall of 1837 and was ordained at Far West a few days after his thirtieth birthday.

The brethren who went on these missions left their families in poverty and illness. Elder Taylor wrote of his mixed feelings at the time of his departing for England:

"The thought of the hardships they had just endured, . . . the uncertainty of their continuing in the house they then occupied— and that only a solitary room—the prevalence of disease, the poverty of the brethren, their insecurity from mobs, together with the uncertainty of what might take place during my absence, produced feelings of no ordinary character. . . . But the thought of going forth at the command of the God of Israel to revisit my native land, to unfold the principles of eternal truth and make known the things that God had revealed for the salvation of the world, overcame every other feeling." (Cited in Roberts, *Life of John Taylor*, pp. 67-68.)

Elder Taylor himself was penniless and in very poor health. Yet, like his companions, he felt that their trials were but for a small moment, and he knew that the Lord would provide for their needs.

(8-5) Success in Liverpool

After an arduous journey, Elder Taylor and his companion arrived in England and were assigned to labor in the port city of Liverpool. There they met with a Protestant congregation who were seeking for the restoration of the Holy Ghost and the coming of Christ's kingdom.

Speaking of the group, Elder Taylor bore a powerful testimony of the restoration of the gifts and blessings they sought. He said:

"Brethren and friends, we are the humble followers of Jesus Christ and are from America. I lately arrived in this place, and have

John Taylor, a defender of the prophets

come five thousand miles without purse or scrip, and I testify to you, my brethren, that the Lord has revealed Himself from heaven and put us in possession of these things you are so anxiously looking for and praying that you may receive. ('Glory be to God,' was shouted by many present, and great emotion manifested.)

"That thing has taken place which is spoken of by John in the Revelations, where he says: 'I saw another angel fly in the midst of heaven, having the everlasting gospel to preach unto them that dwell upon the earth, and to every nation and kindred and tongue and people, saying with a loud voice, Fear God and give glory to him, for the hour of his judgment is come.' Brethren, we the servants of God are come to this place to warn the inhabitants of their approaching danger, and to call upon them to repent and be baptized in the name of Jesus Christ, and they shall receive the gift of the Holy Ghost.

"I feel an anxious desire to deliver this testimony. I feel the word of the Lord like fire in my bones and am desirous to have an opportunity of proclaiming to you those blessings that you are looking for, that you may rejoice with us in those glorious things which God has revealed for the salvation of the world in the last days." (Cited in Roberts, *Life of John Taylor,* pp. 77-78.)

It was fitting that in his first sermon in England, Elder John Taylor should bear witness of the vision of an angel with a trumpet that he had seen many years before he had joined the Church. That vision had been fulfilled. The angel had come and the gospel had been restored. Through his efforts, ten of those present received baptism. From this initial beginning, the work moved ahead so rapidly that a large

branch of the Church was soon established.

(8-6) Opposition in the Isle of Man

While serving as a missionary in the British Isles, Elder Taylor labored for a period of time on the beautiful little Isle of Man in the Irish Sea, the birthplace and girlhood home of his wife, Leonora.

In nearly every area of his mission he was challenged by the local clergy to defend the restored gospel. On the Isle of Man, four ministers challenged him. Reverend Robert Heys strongly opposed the Church's claim to have been founded on new revelation. Reverend Heys based his claim on three passages from the Bible which appeared to forbid new revelation to be added to the scriptures. To this argument Elder Taylor replied:

"It is true, he quotes three passages—one from Deuteronomy, one from Proverbs, and another from Revelation; but not one of them contains the decree! That in Deuteronomy refers exclusively to the Book of the Law. If they declared the revelation of God to be *complete,* the other scriptures could never have been written. That in Proverbs refers to the portion of the sacred writings then in existence. If it declared the Holy Scriptures were *complete,* there would not have been afterwards a continued written revelation. That in the Revelation refers to the Apocalypse alone, it being, when written, a separate book, unconnected with the other books of the New Testament which were not then collected; it could not, therefore, have reference to any other book or books of the Holy Scriptures. According to his own interpretation of the above scriptures, in quoting from Proverbs, he would reject the New

Testament and all the prophets that prophesied after Solomon's day; and in his quotation from Deuteronomy, he would reject all the Bible but the five books of Moses. But let Mr. [Heys] take care that he himself is not incurring the curse by altering the meaning of the words of the very books to which the prohibition positively and particularly refers!" (Cited in Roberts, *Life of John Taylor,* pp. 94-95.)

The Lord can use adversity and opposition to his advantage in building the kingdom of God. A case in point is the opposition which Elder Taylor faced on the Isle of Man. Many people were drawn to the debates and found that John Taylor's message contained answers to their questions. Elder Taylor and his companion founded a thriving branch of the Church on the island before returning to England. John Taylor had left England several years before, saying that he felt strongly he should go to America and preach the gospel. Ironically, he went to America and *found* the gospel, then was called back to England to *preach* the gospel. Have you ever felt promptings that, when followed, resulted in events far different from those you expected? This too is part of the courage of John Taylor. He made the commitment to find answers through the Spirit. But as is often the case, the Spirit gives answers and also makes new demands. Through following the promptings of the Spirit, even though such action may require great moral courage, new vistas and opportunities can be opened up. And even now, what you think are the new vistas may be only preparation for even greater things. John Taylor could easily

John Taylor, an early Apostle

(8-7) The Spirit of Gathering Moved upon the Saints

Because of problems attendant to resettling the Missouri Saints in Illinois, the apostles had been instructed by the Prophet to say nothing, as yet, to the European Saints about immigrating to Nauvoo. However, once people were baptized, many of them had experiences where they dreamed of the Saints traveling to distant places. "I find it difficult to keep anything from the Saints," wrote Elder Taylor, "for the Spirit of God reveals it to them." (Roberts, *Life of John Taylor*, p. 96.) After the troubles in Missouri had been ended by the exodus of the Church to Illinois, and after the Prophet had communicated with the apostles in England that immigration could commence, John Taylor then assisted in the founding of a permanent shipping agency in Liverpool and helped over eight hundred converts to immigrate to America.

(8-8) John Taylor's Mission Report to the British Saints

Prior to departing for Nauvoo with the other apostles in the early part of 1841, Elder Taylor gave this report of his labors to the Saints:

"I feel to rejoice before God that He has blessed my humble endeavors to promote His cause and Kingdom and for all the blessings I have received from this island; for although I have traveled 5,000 miles without purse or scrip, besides traveling so far in this country on railroads, coaches, steamboats, wagons, on horseback, and almost every way, and been amongst strangers and in strange lands, I have never for once been at a loss for either money, clothes, friends or a home, from that day until now; neither have I ever asked a person for a farthing. Thus I have proved the Lord, and I

have thought, "Now I see why I went to America, so I could bring the truth to my native land." But now we see that that too was only the next step to a greater threshhold of endeavor.

know that He is according to His word. And now as I am going away, I bear testimony that this work is of God—that He has spoken from the heavens—that Joseph Smith is a Prophet of the Lord—that the Book of Mormon is true; and I know that this work will roll on until 'the kingdoms of this world become the Kingdoms of our God and His Christ.' " (Cited in Preston Nibley, *The Presidents of the Church*, p. 74.)

"YE RECEIVE NO WITNESS UNTIL AFTER THE TRIAL OF YOUR FAITH"

(8-9) A New Order of Marriage

Returning to Nauvoo, the Twelve were confronted with a challenge unlike any they had ever faced in their missionary labors. The Prophet Joseph taught them the need for the restoration of celestial marriage, including the doctrine of plural wives. It was most difficult for them to face. Of his feelings, Elder Taylor wrote:

"I had always entertained strict ideas of virtue, and I felt as a married man that this was to me, outside of this principle, an appalling thing to do. The idea of going and asking a young lady to be married to me when I had already a wife! It was a thing calculated to stir up feelings from the innermost depths of the human soul. I had always entertained the strictest regard of chastity. . . . Hence, with the feelings I had entertained, nothing but a knowledge of God, and the revelations of God, and the truth of them, could have induced me to embrace such a principle as this." (Cited in Roberts, *Life of John Taylor*, p. 100.)

Obedient to the Prophet's counsel, and with Leonora's consent, Elder Taylor eventually entered into plural marriage and became one of

President John Taylor

the Church's chief spokesmen in its defense throughout the remainder of his life.

Plural marriage was perhaps the most difficult of God's laws that some of the early Saints were called upon to live. But, among other things, it served a useful purpose; it was a timely test of their faith in the Lord and of their obedience to his mouthpiece on the earth.

Today plural marriage is no longer practiced. In 1890, acting under revelation from the Lord, the Church ceased to contract plural marriages. However, the challenge to live the gospel remains the same. The prophet continues to call upon the Saints to live certain principles or to avoid certain practices. Often this counsel runs counter to the prevailing philosophies and attitudes of the world, and we may be tempted to ask, Is this really true? Is this really required of me?

We may not fully understand why the Lord asks the Saints to do what he desires of them. Moroni explains why it must often be this way: " . . . I would show unto the world that faith is things which are hoped for and not seen; wherefore, dispute not because ye see not, for ye receive no witness until after the trial of your faith." (Ether 12:6.)

Those who are willing to walk by faith and obedience in all that the Lord may ask of them are promised a special blessing: "Wherefore, if ye shall be obedient to the commandments, and endure to the end, ye shall be saved at the last day." (1 Nephi 22:31.)

"I, THE LORD, JUSTIFY YOU . . . IN BEFRIENDING . . . THE CONSTITUTIONAL LAW OF THE LAND"

(8-10) John Taylor Nominated Joseph Smith for the Office of President of the United States

In February of 1842, John Taylor became the associate editor (later the editor) of the Church publication *Times and Seasons*. A year later he also assumed the editorial post for the *Nauvoo Neighbor*, a weekly newspaper. Elder Taylor's columns soon became noted for their powerful and forthright spirit.

The year 1844 was a presidential election year. The Saints had strong objections to the candidates of both national parties. Both of the major parties had been contacted, but neither would promise to give any help in preserving the constitutional rights of the Saints. There were even strong indications that plans would be laid to persecute the Saints further after the election had been held.

The Saints comprised a substantial voting block—perhaps the strongest in Illinois. Acting as spokesman for the Saints, and also for concerned civic and church leaders, Elder Taylor nominated Joseph Smith for president of the United States in a *Nauvoo Neighbor* editorial. He then explained some of the reasons for so doing:

"One great reason that we have for pursuing our present course is that at every election we have been made a political target for the filthy demagogues in the country to shoot their loathsome arrows at. And every story has been put into circulation to blast our fame, from the old fabrication of 'walk on the water' down to the 'murder of Governor Boggs.' The journals have teemed with this filthy trash, and even men who ought to have more respect for themselves—men contending for the gubernatorial chair—have made use of terms so degrading, so mean, so humiliating, that a Billingsgate fisherwoman would have considered herself disgraced with. We refuse any longer to be thus bedaubed for either party; we tell all such to let their filth flow in its own legitimate channel, for we are sick of the loathsome smell. . . . Under existing circumstances we have no other alternative [than that of withdrawing from both political parties,] and if we can accomplish our object, well; if not we shall have the satisfaction of knowing we have acted conscientiously and have used our best judgment; and if we have to throw away our votes, we had better do so upon a worthy, rather than upon an unworthy individual, who might make use of the weapon we put in his hand to

destroy us." (Cited in Roberts, *Life of John Taylor*, pp. 104-5.)

The Church never seeks to dictate the votes of its people, but it certainly does urge that where the Saints are allowed a voice in choosing those by whom they will be governed, they elect responsible, moral individuals who will seek to uphold the sovereign rights and freedoms due mankind, those who will respond to the righteous will of the people. Latter-day Saints would do well to emulate John Taylor's example of boldly speaking out on issues which have such a vital effect on the well being of their nation and its citizens. Certainly we have been blessed with a rare insight into the true purpose for laws and governments. (See D&C 101:77-80 as an example.) In an editorial, Elder Taylor explained from personal experience why it is essential that our voices be heard:

"Certainly if any person ought to interfere in political matters, it should be those whose minds and judgments are influenced by correct principles—religious as well as political; *otherwise those persons professing religion would have to be governed by those who make no professions; be subject to their rule; have the law and word of God trampled under foot, and become as wicked as Sodom and as corrupt as Gomorrah, and be prepared for final destruction.* We are told 'when the wicked rule the people mourn.' [D&C 98:9.] This we have abundantly proved in the state of Missouri, and having had our fingers once

burned, we dread the fire. The cause of humanity, the cause of justice, the cause of freedom, the cause of patriotism, and the cause of God requires us to use our endeavors to put in righteous rulers. Our revelations tell us to *seek diligently* for good and for wise men. [D&C 98:10.]

"Let every man then that hates oppression, and loves the cause of right, not only vote himself but use his influence to obtain the votes of others, that we may by every legal means support that man whose election will secure the greatest amount of good to the nation at large." (*Times and Seasons,* vol. 3, no. 4, 15 Mar. 1844, pp. 470-71.)

Such courage was typical of John Taylor and serves as a model for us to follow. Perhaps in your case the challenge may not be a political one. It may come in your family, in your interaction with friends, or in your occupation. Most Saints will not be called on to endure the persecutions of Missouri or the years of plural marriage. Most will never be the prophet and president of the Church. But that is not the point we learn from John Taylor's life. He serves as an example for us to follow in how he responded to the challenges of life and the calls from the Lord. Our calls will almost certainly differ greatly from his. But in his courage and faithfulness we see *how* to respond, we learn how to be faithful, we find how to become our own defender of the faith and a champion of liberty.

CHAPTER 9

HIS BLOOD WAS MINGLED WITH THE BLOOD OF MARTYRS

INTRODUCTION

It was shortly after 5:00 P.M. on the hot afternoon of June 27, 1844. The mob had fled in panic once their evil purpose had been accomplished. The Prophet Joseph lay outside near the well, where he had plunged from the window. His older brother, Hyrum, lay dead on the floor of the room in which they had taken refuge. John Taylor lay under the bed where he had been hastily covered by Willard Richards to hide him from the murderers. Joseph, the Prophet, called to head the last and greatest dispensation, was dead, shot four times. So, likewise, was his beloved brother. By all rights, the same fate should have been true of John Taylor, because he too had been hit four times. But the Lord decreed otherwise. There were yet missions unfulfilled, callings to come.

Forty years later, referring to the martyrdom, President Taylor said, "Was there anything surprising in all this? No. If they killed Jesus in former times, would not the same feeling and influence bring about the same results in these times? I had counted the cost when I first started out, and stood prepared to meet it." (JD, 25:92.)

Elder Taylor had, indeed, counted the cost. On another occasion he stated: "I do not believe in a religion that cannot have all my affections, . . . but I believe in a religion that I can live for, or die for." (B. H. Roberts, *The Life of John Taylor*, p. 423.)

There is a principle involved for those who are martyred. Speaking of Christ, Paul taught:

"For where a testament is, there must also of necessity be the death of the testator.

"For a testament is of force after men are dead: otherwise it is of no strength at all while the testator liveth.

"Whereupon neither the first testament was dedicated without blood." (Hebrews 9:16-18.)

As mediator of the new covenant, Christ died that those who seek salvation might have the hope of eternal life. (See Hebrews 9:15.) Joseph and Hyrum Smith died as ordained witnesses of the risen Lord and his restored kingdom. John Taylor shed his blood as a witness that the gospel was restored through Joseph Smith and that Joseph lived and died a prophet in good standing. His eloquent witness and courageous defense of these truths served to strengthen and sustain the Saints through all the difficult trials that faced the Church in the nineteenth century.

Today there are undoubtedly many persons who are willing to die for the Lord's kingdom. More often, the Lord needs those who are totally committed to live and serve in its behalf. Are you committed to the truth of the Church? Are you willing to live for the Lord's church as well as die for it?

(9-1) John Taylor Rebuked Those Who Believed the Church Would Fall with Joseph's Death

The deaths of Joseph and Hyrum Smith caused many enemies of the Church—and some within the Church—to feel that the Church would fall. In a *Times and Seasons* editorial, John Taylor contended otherwise. It was, he said, the Lord's church—not man's.

"The idea of the Church being disorganized and broken up because of the Prophet and the Patriarch being slain, is preposterous. This Church has the seeds of immortality in its midst. It is not of man, nor by man,—it is the offspring of Deity: it is organized after the pattern of heavenly things, through the principles of revelation; by the opening of the heavens, by the ministering of angels, and the revelations of Jehovah. It is not affected by the death of one or two, or fifty individuals. It possesses a priesthood after the order of Melchizedec [*sic*], having the power of an endless life, 'without beginning of days, or end of years.' It is organized for the purpose of saving this generation, and generations that are past; it exists in time and will exist in eternity. This church fail? No! Times and seasons may change, revolution may succeed revolution, thrones may be cast down, and empires be dissolved, earthquakes may rend the earth from center to circumference, the mountains may be hurled out of their places, and

This watch saved John Taylor's life

Warren, to protest their inaction. In turn, Major Warren upbraided the Saints for resisting the law. Elder Taylor replied:

"You talk, sir, about 'the majesty of the law, . . . ' why sir, the law to us is a mere farce. For years past the law has been made use of only as an engine of oppression. We have received no protection from it. . . .

" . . . What has become of those murderers [of the Prophet and his brother]? Have they been hung or shot, or in any way punished? No, sir, you know they have not. . . . They are still burning houses under your supervision . . . men have been kidnapped, cattle stolen, our brethren abused and robbed. . . . Are we to stand still and let marauders and houseburners come into our city . . . and yet offer no resistance to their nefarious deeds? Are we to be held still by you, sir, while they thrust the hot iron rod into us? I tell you plainly for one I will not do it. . . . I will not stand it. . . . and there is not a patriot in the world but would bear me out. . . . " (Cited in Roberts, *Life of John Taylor*, pp. 163-65.)

Months later the Saints were encamped at Council Bluffs, Iowa, when they were approached by Captain Allen, an officer of the United States Army. Captain Allen had come to seek the enlistment of 500 Mormon men to assist in the Mexican War. Feelings of loyalty and patriotism were somewhat strained among the Saints. In a speech, Elder Taylor recognized this when he said:

"Many have felt something like rebelling against the government of the United States. I have myself felt swearing mad at the government for the treatment

the mighty ocean be moved from its bed; but amidst the crash of worlds and the crack of matter, truth, eternal truth, must remain unchanged, and those principles which God has revealed to his Saints be unscathed amidst the warring elements, and remain as firm as the throne of Jehovah." (vol. 5, no. 23, 15 Dec. 1844, p. 744.)

(9-2) John Taylor Vigorously Defended the Rights of the Saints in Nauvoo

Following the martyrdom, enemies of the Church began to circulate false statements about the Church and its members as a basis upon

which to drive the Saints out of Nauvoo. Raiding parties burned homes, stole cattle, murdered men, and drove women and children out of their homes.

Civil authorities offered no protection, so a state military militia was sent to maintain order so that the Saints could have a season of peace in which to prepare to move West. This militia did not defend the rights of the Saints at all, but sat idly by while the mobs further outraged the privacy and property of the Saints. Angered by this callous disregard for the rights of the Saints, Elder Taylor met with the militia commander, Major

we have received at the hands of those in authority, although I don't know that I ever swore much. We have had cause to feel as we have, and any man having a spark of the love of liberty in him would have felt likewise." (Cited in Roberts, *Life of John Taylor*, p. 173.)

In spite of those legitimate feelings, Elder Taylor then made a motion to trust the government and raise the battalion. His motion carried. This "Champion of Liberty" was as concerned with supporting his country as he was with fighting for the constitutional rights of the Saints.

It would generally be the natural reaction for people to seek to "get even" when they have been repeatedly wronged, especially if they have been deprived of their rights as the Saints had been. Yet here were men who were near enough to the mind and heart of the Savior to follow the proper course of action. In Matthew 5:43-48, the Lord sets the celestial standard. Will you strive to rise above the world and follow the Master's teachings?

JOHN TAYLOR DEFENDED THE FAITH WHILE SERVING ON MISSIONS AT HOME AND ABROAD

(9-3) Three Protestant Ministers Attacked the Character of Joseph Smith

In October of 1849, John Taylor was called on a mission to France. While laboring in Boulogne, he was challenged to a debate by three ministers. In the course of the debate, these three ministers attacked the Prophet Joseph Smith. In defense of the Prophet, Elder Taylor said:

"I testify that I was acquainted with Joseph Smith for years. I have traveled with him; I have been with him in private and in public; I have associated with him in councils of all kinds; I have listened hundreds of times to his public teachings, and his advice to his friends and associates of a more private nature. I have been at his house and seen his deportment in his family. I have seen him arraigned before the courts of his country, and seen him honorably acquitted, and delivered from the pernicious breath of slander, and the machinations and falsehoods of wicked and corrupt men. I was with him living, and with him when he died; when he was murdered in Carthage jail by a ruthless mob with their faces painted, and headed by a Methodist minister, named Williams—I was there, and was myself wounded. I, at that time, received four balls in my body. I have seen him, then, under these

various circumstances, and I testify before God, angels and men, that he was a good, honorable, virtuous man—that his doctrines were good, scriptural and wholesome—that his precepts were such as became a man of God—that his private and public character was unimpeachable—and that he lived and died as a man of God and a gentleman. This is my testimony; if it is disputed bring me a person authorized to receive an affidavit, and I will make one to this effect." (Cited in Roberts, *Life of John Taylor*, pp. 213-14.)

(9-4) A Printer's Mission to New York City

In 1852 the doctrine of plural marriage was publicly announced. However, based on the reports of corrupt apostates, gross misrepresentations of the practice were described in the nation's press.

John Taylor supported polygamy as it was revealed

As printer and editor, he defended the faith

In order to stem the tide of prejudice, Elder Taylor and four other brethren were called upon to publish newspapers across America in defense of the Church. Elder Taylor chose to open the offices of *The Mormon* squarely between the offices of the *New York Herald* and the *New York Tribune*, the two newspapers most critical of the Church. In the maiden issue of February 17th, 1855, Elder Taylor wrote:

"We are Mormon . . . inside and outside; at home or abroad, in public and private—everywhere. We are so, however, from principle. We are such, not because we believe it to be the most popular, lucrative, or honorable (as the world has it); but because we believe it to be true, and more reasonable and scriptural, moral and philosophic; because we conscientiously believe it is more

calculated to promote the happiness and well-being of humanity, in time and throughout all eternity, than any other system which we have met with." (Cited in Roberts, *Life of John Taylor*, p. 249.)

But Elder Taylor was not intimidated by the other media giants. A few issues later he issued this challenge:

"We have said before and say now, that we defy all the editors and writers in the United States to prove that Mormonism is less moral, scriptural, philosophical; or that there is less patriotism in Utah than in any other part of the United States. We call for proof; bring on your reasons, gentlemen, if you have any; we shrink not from the investigation, and dare you to the encounter. If you don't do it, and you publish any more of your stuff, we shall brand you as poor, mean,

cowardly liars; as men publishing falsehoods knowing them to be so, and shrinking from the light of truth and investigation." (Cited in Roberts, *Life of John Taylor*, p. 249.)

It took courage of a kind few men possess to defend the Church in the same bold and forthright manner that Elder Taylor defended it. Of his labors, President Young said:

"With regard to the labors of Brother Taylor in editing the paper called *The Mormon*, published in the city of New York, I have heard many remarks concerning the editorials in that paper, not only from the Saints, but from those who do not profess to believe the religion we have embraced; and it is probably one of the strongest edited papers that is now published." (Cited in Roberts, *Life of John Taylor*, p. 271.)

(9-5) President Buchanan Heard the Voice of the Saints

In a step toward statehood, Utah received territorial status in 1850. Brigham Young was appointed its first governor by President Millard Fillmore, but many other positions were filled by government appointees from other areas of the country. Some of these officials were not honorable men. Nearly all lacked familiarity with and sensitivity to the standards, ideals, and goals of the Church.

In 1857 President Buchanan received reports from one corrupt territorial judge charging that the Mormons had destroyed federal court records, resisted all federal laws, were disloyal to the country, and were obedient only to Brigham Young. The accusations were purely ludicrous, and without further investigation Buchanan appointed Alfred Cumming of Georgia as the new governor of Utah and sent a force of

twenty-five hundred troops to escort him to Utah and resolve the so-called "Utah rebellion." Further, he made no attempt to notify Governor Young of his plans. Thus, when scattered reports of the "Utah Expedition" reached the Saints, they feared the worst and prepared for war.

Called home from his New York mission, John Taylor prepared a memorandum to the President and the Congress of the United States, which read, in part:

"We appeal to you as American citizens who have been wronged, insulted, abused and persecuted; driven before our relentless foes from city to city—from state to state—until we were finally expelled from the confines of civilization to seek a shelter in a barren, inhospitable clime, amid the wild, savage tribes of the desert plains. We claim to be a portion of the people, and as such have rights that must be respected, and which we have a right to demand. We claim that in a republican form of government, such as our fathers established, and such as ours still professes to be, the officers are and should be the servants of the people—not their masters, dictators or tyrants.

"To the numerous charges of our enemies we plead not guilty, and challenge the world before any just tribunal to the proof. . . . Treat us as friends—as citizens entitled to and possessing equal rights with our fellows—and not as alien enemies, lest you make us such. . . . The administration have been imposed upon by false, designing men; their acts have been precipitate and hasty, perhaps through lack of due consideration. Please to let us know what you want of us before you prepare your halters to hang, or 'apply the knife to cut out the loathsome, disgusting ulcer.' Do

you wish us to deny our God and renounce our religion? That we shall not do. . . . Withdraw your troops, give us our Constitutional rights and we are at home." (Cited in Roberts, *Life of John Taylor,* pp. 294-95.)

(9-6) John Taylor Saw the Lord's Hand in Preserving the Saints from Unrighteous Oppression

Although the Saints were prepared to resist the army if necessary, they did all they could to avoid such a confrontation. The new governor was welcomed into the territory and negotiations began to successfully resolve the misunderstandings. Through the wisdom of Brigham Young and the help of the Lord, the Saints succeeded in holding the army itself out of the Salt Lake Valley until the spring of 1858. When the army was permitted to enter on a promise of good behavior, they found the Saints ready to set fire to their homes rather than submit to

unlawful oppression. Speaking in the Salt Lake Tabernacle, John Taylor said:

"I do not remember having read in any history . . . where an army has been subjugated so easily, and their power wasted away so effectually without bloodshed, as this in our borders. If this is not the manifestation of the power of God to us, I do not know what is. Has any man's life been lost in it? No—not one. . . .

"Suppose Uncle Sam should rise up . . . and send 50,000 men here . . . —who of us can tell the result? . . .

"What if we should be driven to the mountains? Let us be driven. What if we have to burn our houses? Why, set fire to them with a good grace, and dance a jig round them while they are burning. What do I care about these things? We are in the hands of God, and all is right. . . . " (*JD,* 6:112-13.)

Early Salt Lake City street scene

(9-7) John Taylor Defended the Church in a Debate with a Vice-President of the United States

In October 1869, Schuyler Colfax, Vice-President of the United States, delivered a speech in Utah in which he claimed that plural marriage was not a legitimate part of the religious beliefs of the Church.

"I have no strictures to utter as to your creed on any really religious question. Our land is a land of civil and religious liberty, and the faith of every man is a matter between himself and God alone. You have as much right to worship the Creator through a President and twelve apostles of your church organization, as I have through the ministers and elders and creed of mine. And this right I would defend for you with as much zeal as the right of every other denomination throughout the land.

"But our country is governed by law, and no assumed revelation justifies any one in trampling on the law. If it did, every wrong-doer would use that argument to protect himself in his disobedience to it." (Cited in Roberts, *Life of John Taylor*, p. 301.)

Mr. Colfax's remarks were eventually reported in various eastern newspapers. Elder Taylor, in Boston at the time, replied to the Vice-President through an article in the *New York Tribune*:

"That our country is governed by law all admit; but when it is said that 'no assumed revelation justifies anyone in trampling on the law,' I should respectfully ask, What! not if it interferes with my religious faith, which you state 'is a matter between God and myself alone?' Allow me, sir, here to state that the assumed revelation referred to is one of the most vital parts of our religious faith; it emanated from God and cannot be legislated away; it is part of the 'Everlasting Covenant' which God has given to man. Our marriages are solemnized by proper authority; a woman is sealed unto a man for time and for eternity, by the power of which Jesus speaks, which 'seals on earth and it is sealed in heaven.' With us it is 'Celestial Marriage;' take this from us and you rob us of our hopes and associations in the resurrection of the just. This not our religion? You do not see things as we do. . . . I make these remarks to show that it is considered, by us, a part of our religious faith, which I have no doubt, did you understand it as we do, you would defend, as you state, 'with as much zeal as the right of every other denomination throughout the land.' Permit me here to say, however, that it was the revelation (I will not say assumed) that Joseph and Mary had, which made them look upon Jesus as the Messiah; which made them flee from the wrath of Herod, who was seeking the young child's life. This they did in contravention of law which was his decree. Did they do wrong in protecting Jesus from the law? But Herod was a tyrant. That makes no difference; it was the law of the land, and I have yet to learn the difference between a tyrannical king and a tyrannical Congress. . . .

" . . . I might ask, who constituted Mr. Colfax a judge of my religious faith? I think he has stated that 'The faith of every man *is a matter between himself and God alone.*'

"Mr. Colfax has a perfect right to state and feel that he does not believe in the revelation on which my religious faith is based, nor in my faith at all; but has he the right to *dictate* my religious faith? I think not; he does not consider it religion, but it is nevertheless mine." (Cited in Roberts, *Life of John Taylor*, pp. 302-3.)

JOHN TAYLOR WAS CALLED TO LEAD THE CHURCH THROUGH AN ANGUISHED DECADE OF INTENSE PERSECUTION

L. to R.: Joseph F. Smith, President John Taylor, and George Q. Cannon (1880)

The Perpetual Immigration Fund aided migrating Saints

(9-8) The Second Apostolic Presidency, 1877-1880

At the death of President Young on August 29, 1877, the Quorum of the Twelve became the presiding quorum of the Church. Formally sustained on September 4, 1877, the Twelve, with John Taylor as quorum president, stood in place of the First Presidency until the First Presidency was formally reorganized on October 10, 1880. (The first apostolic presidency had served from the death of Joseph Smith in 1844 until Brigham Young was sustained as President of the Church on December 27, 1847.)

(9-9) John Taylor's Life Had Been Preserved for a Wise Purpose in the Lord

John Taylor was preserved from death in the Carthage Jail so that he could lead the Church through a decade of great crises. In January of 1880 the Lord confirmed this special mission in a revelation which was recorded by Wilford Woodruff: "I the Lord have raised up unto you my servant, John Taylor, to preside over you and to be a lawgiver unto my Church. He has mingled his blood with that of the martyred prophets. Nevertheless, while I have taken my servants Joseph and Hyrum Smith unto myself, I have preserved my servant John Taylor for a wise purpose in me." (*Journal of Wilford Woodruff*, undated entry following his synopsis of 1880, p. 8, Church Historical Library. Punctuation, capitalization, and spelling standardized.)

It soon became clear that, indeed, President Taylor had a special mission to fulfill. During the twenty-fourth of July Pioneer celebration of 1880, he prophetically stated:

"There are events in the future, and not very far ahead, that will require all our faith, all our energy, all our confidence, all our trust in God, to enable us to withstand the influences that will be brought against us. . . . We cannot trust in our intelligence; we cannot trust in our wealth; we cannot trust to any surrounding circumstances with which we are enveloped; we must trust alone in the living God to guide us, to direct us, to lead us, to teach us and to instruct us. And there never was a time when we needed to be more humble and more prayerful; there never was a time when we needed more fidelity, self-denial, and adherence to the principles of truth, than we do this day." (Cited in Joseph Fielding Smith, *Essentials in Church History*, p. 479.)

(9-10) "Ye Shall Hallow the Fiftieth Year, and Proclaim Liberty Throughout All the Land" (Leviticus 25:10.)

Although storm clouds were on the horizon, there was an air of general rejoicing among the Saints in 1880. It was the fiftieth anniversary of the restoration of the Church. In ancient Israel every fiftieth year had a jubilee—a time to forgive indebtedness and to bless the poor. President Taylor resolved that this should be the theme:

"It occurred to me that we ought to do something, as they did in former times, to relieve those that are oppressed with debt, to assist those that are needy, to break off the yoke of those that may feel themselves crowded upon, and to make it a time of general rejoicing." (Cited in Roberts, *Life of John Taylor*, p. 333.)

The Church canceled the debts of many who had received money from the Perpetual Emigration Fund to help them move to Utah and, who, after having arrived, had experienced failure and hardship to the extent that they were not able to repay their debt to the fund. To the wealthy, President Taylor offered these words of advice:

"The rich . . . have a fitting opportunity for remembering the Lord's poor. If you are holding their notes and they are unable to pay, forgive the interest and the principal, or as much thereof as you might desire them to forgive were their and your circumstances reversed, thus doing unto others as you would that others should do unto you. For upon this hang the law and the prophets. If you have mortgages upon the homes of your brethren and sisters who are poor, worthy and honest, and who desire to pay you but cannot, free them in whole or in part. Extend to them a jubilee, if you can consistently. You will have their faith and prayers and confidence, which may be worth more than money." (Cited in Roberts, *Life of John Taylor,* pp. 336-37.)

(9-11) The Fulfillment of a Sober Prophecy

Dense clouds and heavy rains marked the April general conference of 1882. The weather seemed prophetic of the days ahead. Nineteen months had passed since President Taylor had warned of influences which would gather against the Church. Now those influences began to make themselves felt. In the fall of 1881, ministers of religion began clamoring for stricter laws relating to the practice of plural marriage. On March 22, 1882, the president of the United States signed into law the Edmunds Bill, which disfranchised the entire Church and fined or imprisoned all male members who believed in or practiced plural marriage.

President Taylor advised the Saints to turn up their collars and weather it through:

"We do not wish to place ourselves in a state of antagonism, nor to act defiantly, towards this

President George Q. Cannon (in doorway) and other brethren imprisoned on charges of polygamy

government. We will fulfil the letter, so far as practicable, of that unjust, inhuman, oppressive and unconstitutional law, so far as we can without violating principle; but we cannot sacrifice every principle of human right at the behest of corrupt, unreasoning and unprincipled men; we cannot violate the highest and noblest principles of human nature and make pariahs and outcasts of high-minded, virtuous and honorable women, nor sacrifice at the shrine of popular clamor the highest and noblest principles of humanity!

"We shall abide all constitutional law, as we always have done; but while we are Godfearing and law-abiding, and respect all honorable men and officers, we are no craven serfs, and have not learned to lick the feet of oppressors, nor to bow in base submission to unreasoning clamor. We will contend, inch by inch, legally and constitutionally, for our rights as American citizens, and for the universal rights of universal man. We stand proudly erect in the

consciousness of our rights as American citizens, and plant ourselves firmly on the sacred guarantes of the Constitution; and that instrument, while it defines the powers and privileges of the President, Congress and the judiciary, also directly provides that 'the powers not delegated to the United States by the Constitution, nor prohibited by it to the States, are reserved to the States respectively or to the people.' " (JD, 23:67.)

(9-12) The Full Fury of the Storm Strikes at the Saints

Persecution once again began to plague the Saints. Houses were broken into and ransacked, innocent persons were compelled to accompany federal marshals to places of inquisition, and men were fined and hounded far beyond the legal limits. In the south many missionaries were mobbed and beaten, and some were killed.

Having heard of the great abuse heaped upon the Saints by government officers in Arizona, President Taylor paid them a visit

and recommended that they establish temporary homes in Mexico. Giving heed to the prophet's counsel, over three thousand members eventually relocated in the state of Chihuahua, founding the Mormon Colony cities of Colonia Juarez, Colonia Dublan, and Colonia Diaz. (See Roberts, *Life of John Taylor,* pp. 380-83.)

President Taylor later advised Saints in Cache Valley, Utah, to emigrate to Canada for similar reasons. Many parts of the province of Alberta were settled by Church members.

(9-13) President Taylor Voluntarily Withdrew from Public View

Learning of plans prepared for their arrest, and knowing that their imprisonment might provoke members of the Church to retaliate in such a way as to give the courts and officers of the government a pretext upon which to destroy the Church, the First Presidency elected to withdraw from public view and continue their sacred labors. In his last public address, President Taylor said:

"It is for us to do what is right, to fear God, to observe His laws, and keep His commandments, and the Lord will manage all the rest. But no breaking of heads, no bloodshed, no rendering evil for evil. Let us try and cultivate the spirit of the Gospel, and adhere to the principles of truth. Let us honor our God, and be true to those eternal principles which God has given us to hold sacred. Keep them as sacredly as you would the apple of your eye. And while other men are seeking to trample the Constitution under foot, we will try to maintain it." (*JD,* 26:156.)

(9-14) John Taylor Died July 25, 1887: A Double Martyr for the Truth

Denied his regular exercise, separated from his loved ones, and under great strain from the Church's struggles for its Constitutional rights, President Taylor's health failed and he died at the age of seventy-eight in Kaysville, Utah. Following his passing, his counselors, George Q. Cannon and Joseph F. Smith, issued a lengthy tribute which read, in part:

"Steadfast to and immovable in the truth, few men have ever lived who have manifested such integrity and such unflinching moral and

The temple was nearing completion at President Taylor's death

physical courage as our beloved President who has just gone from us. He never knew the feeling of fear connected with the work of God. But in the face of angry mobs, and at other times when in imminent danger of personal violence from those who threatened his life, and upon occasions when the people were menaced with public peril, he never blenched—his knees never trembled, his hand never shook. Every Latter-day Saint always knew beforehand, on occasions when firmness and courage were needed, where President John Taylor would be found and what his tone would be. He met every issue squarely, boldly and in a way to call forth the admiration of all who saw and heard him. Undaunted courage, unyielding firmness were among his most prominent characteristics, giving him distinction among men who were distinguished for the same qualities. With these were combined an intense love of freedom and hatred of oppression. He was a man whom all could trust, and throughout his life he enjoyed, to an extent surpassed by none, the implicit confidence of the Prophets Joseph, Hyrum and Brigham and all the leading men and members of the Church. The title of 'Champion of Liberty,' which he received at Nauvoo, was always felt to be most appropriate for him to bear. . . .

"By the miraculous power of God, President John Taylor escaped the death which the assassins of Carthage jail assigned for him. His blood was then mingled with the blood of the martyred Prophet and Patriarch. He has stood since then as a living martyr for the truth." (Cited in Roberts, *Life of John Taylor*, pp. 410-11, 413-14.)

President John Taylor championed truth and liberty

You will recall that when John Taylor was a young man sailing toward an unknown destiny in America, his ship passed through a storm so severe that the captain feared the vessel would sink. Yet John was calm and unafraid. He took little notice of the winds and waves. He knew his life was in the hands of God. He was prepared to do whatever the Lord desired of him. Other storms came as his mission unfolded—storms of men and nature. Yet he did not rail against them; he remained calm and serene. He once said:

"So far as I am concerned, I say, let everything come as God has ordained it. I do not desire trials; I do not desire affliction. . . . But if the earthquake bellows, the lightnings flash, the thunders roll, and the powers of darkness are let loose, and the spirit of evil is permitted to rage, and an evil influence is brought to bear upon the Saints, and my life, with theirs, is put to the test; let it come, for we are the Saints of the most High God, and all is well, all is peace, all is right, and will be, both in time and in eternity." (*JD*, 5:114-15.)

Consider the counsel given by Elder Boyd K. Packer, another special witness well acquainted with storms:

"You are participants—more than witnesses—in the trying and important events in the history of the world and the history of the Church in our day. Thank God that you are born in this era. . . . I do not doubt that we are sailing into troubled waters. There are storms to ride out; there are reefs and shoals to negotiate ere we reach port; but we have been through them before and have found safe passage. Consider this verse of scripture: ' . . . the heavens shall be darkened, and a veil of darkness shall cover the earth; the heavens shall shake, and also the earth; and great tribulation shall be among the children of men, but my people will I preserve.' (Moses 7:61.)

Steady as she goes. Our craft has weathered the storm before. It is seaworthy. What a glorious time to be alive; what a marvelous age in which to live! Thank the Lord for the privilege of living in an adventuresome day of challenge. . . . [Never forget that] there is a celestial radar—revelation from God guiding us and guiding you. There is an inspired captain—a prophet of God.

"I bear witness to you that The Church of Jesus Christ of Latter-day Saints is . . . the only true and living Church upon the face of the whole earth. I bear witness that Jesus is the Christ, and that the Church was formulated for strength in difficult times. Steady as she goes. Now I leave for your contemplation these words about another storm at another time:

" 'And there arose a great storm of wind, and the waves beat into the ship, so that it was now full . . . and they awake him, and say unto him [as many say in our day], Master, carest thou not that we perish?

" 'And he arose, and rebuked the wind, and said unto the sea, Peace, be still. *And the wind ceased, and there was a great calm.*' (Mark 4:37-39. Italics added.)"

("To Those Who Teach in Troubled Times," Address to Seminary and Institute personnel, Brigham Young University, July 1970; see the attachment for the *Growing Edge*, vol. 5, no. 3, Nov. 1972, p. 6.)

Be assured that the Lord loves you, that you are never alone. In your moments of storm and trouble, he will see you through and you too will find a great calm.

UNIT FIVE

WILFORD WOODRUFF

Fourth President of the Church

OVERVIEW

Wilford Woodruff, the fourth presiding prophet of The Church of Jesus Christ of Latter-day Saints, was, as are all of the Lord's anointed, foreordained to be one of those who would move the cause of Zion in mighty power. His life extended through almost the total length of the nineteenth century; and from his conversion in 1833 until his death in 1898, he was caught up in the development of the growing kingdom of God.

Wilford Woodruff was born in 1807 in Farmington, Connecticut. His early years were marked by many difficulties and accidents; and though his life was often imperiled, through the grace of God he was preserved. He learned in his youth the value of work, and with his father, he labored in the Farmington grist mills.

While young, Wilford hungered after righteousness. He was an avid student of the scriptures and pondered deeply over their meaning. Robert Mason, a godly man who had great influence on him as a youth, predicted that he would live not only to witness but to participate in the restored church of Jesus Christ. When he heard the witness of two Mormon missionaries on December 29, 1832, he was quick to recognize the truth and was baptized just two days later. From this point on, there was no turning back.

At the age of twenty-seven Wilford Woodruff joined Zion's Camp, and through this experience of marching with the Prophet Joseph he was further honed and sharpened—prepared for greater service in the cause of the Master. By mid 1834 this young man's desire to be a missionary had become so intense that in many prayers he pleaded with the Lord for that privilege. He filled his first mission to the southern states, testified that he had the ministration of angels and that never had he been more blessed than as a priest in the Aaronic Priesthood

fulfilling an honorable mission. Without purse or scrip and walking as far as sixty miles in a single day, the young Wilford went forth.

In 1838 he was called to the apostleship and subsequently served as a special witness of Christ for over half a century. A year later Elder Woodruff commenced his momentous mission to England. Like Paul of old, being led by the Spirit, this faithful man ranged over the earth, bringing literally thousands of souls unto Christ. President Heber J. Grant was later to testify that "no other man who ever walked the face of the earth was a greater converter of souls to the gospel."[1]

As the years sped by, Elder Woodruff came to greater and greater prominence in the Church. He became a member of the Nauvoo City Council in 1841, worked on the Nauvoo Temple in 1842, and labored as business manager for the *Times and Seasons*. He was present when Joseph Smith conferred the full keys of the kingdom upon the Quorum of the Twelve.

After the death of the Prophet, Wilford Woodruff saw the mantle of Joseph fall upon Brigham Young. He was in the pioneer company that entered Salt Lake Valley on July 24, 1847. Wilford was an active participant in the early establishment of the territory of Deseret. He struggled through difficult days serving on the legislature.

In 1856 Wilford Woodruff began his official career as a Church Historian, but from the beginning of his life in the Church he felt that he had a special stewardship to record the important happenings, speeches, places, people, and events of the Restoration. His extensive journals are the basis of much of the early Church history.

To Wilford Woodruff, one of the most precious principles of the gospel was the work for the dead. He became the first president of the St. George Temple, and later he was instrumental

in organizing the Genealogical Society to facilitate the work of salvation for those beyond the veil.

As General Superintendent of the Young Men's Mutual Improvement Association, Elder Woodruff expressed his great love for the youth. He pleaded with God that they might carry off the kingdom, and through revelation he was promised that they would.[2]

Finally, after eighty-two years of rich experience, learning, growing, and polishing, Wilford Woodruff was honored in receiving, in his own words, "the highest office ever conferred upon any man in the flesh."[3] On April 7, 1889, he became President of the Church. During his presidency, all the talents given him of God and polished in the crucible of life's adversity were brought to the fore. He guided the Church through the last of the polygamy persecutions and through revelation issued the Manifesto. He warned the world of the great judgments to come and moved the work for the dead forward with zeal. During his administration the Salt Lake Temple was completed and dedicated. He presided over a growing missionary effort. His example of individual righteousness and submission to the Spirit blessed the Saints. His family life exemplified the central gospel principles that success at home is of highest priority.

Here was a man who in his early youth dreamed of some day seeing an apostle of the Lord Jesus Christ, and he lived to walk himself in the way of the prophets and even finally to preside among the Saints. It was President Woodruff's wish that he remain faithful in all things to the end of his life, and when he died on September 2, 1898, that hope found fulfillment.

Joseph Smith had called him "Wilford the Faithful."[4] In an early revelation the Lord called him "my servant."[5] What greater an epitaph for any son of God?

CHAPTER 10

SEEING AFAR OFF

INTRODUCTION

In 1815 the Treaty of Vienna reshaped the destiny of Europe after the abdication of Napoleon. In 1825 the first railway was established. Revolution shook much of the world in 1830 and again in 1848 as kings were toppled and republics established. The industrial revolution advanced, and in England Queen Victoria presided over an empire upon which the sun never set. Men such as Karl Marx and Charles Darwin were to influence the course of worldly thought. In 1861 the United States entered into its Civil War, changing the nature of warfare forever. These are some of the world events Wilford Woodruff was to witness during his life. However, he was to take a major role in things of far grander influence than these—God's great work of restoration, which would be the marvel of the ages. Though few grasped the significance of the little stone cut out of the mountain without hands, the Lord raised up seers who saw (see Hebrews 11:13) and in a measure comprehended the purposes of the Almighty, not only for their time but for all times. Wilford Woodruff was one of these.

"This is the only dispensation which God has ever established that was foreordained, before the world was made, not to be overcome by wicked men and devils. . . . The prophet asked the Lord whether there would ever be a time when the earth should rest; and the Lord answered that in the dispensation of the fulness of times the earth would fill the measure of its days, and then it would rest from wickedness and abominations, for in that day he would establish his kingdom upon it, to be thrown down no more for ever. Then a reign of righteousness would commence and the honest and meek of the earth would be gathered together to serve the Lord, and upon them would rest power to build up the great Zion of God in the Latter-days. . . .

"This dispensation is one that all the patriarchs and prophets had their eye upon, and the Lord has commenced it, and has carried it on. . . .

"The work that is to be so marvelous in the eyes of men has already commenced, and is assuming shape and proportion; but they cannot see it. It will consist in preaching the gospel to all the world, gathering the Saints from the midst of all those nations who reject it; building up the Zion of God; establishing permanently in the earth his kingdom; preparing for the work of the gathering of the Jews and the events that will follow their settlement in their own lands, and in preparing for ourselves holy places in which to stand when the judgments of God shall overtake the nations. This

is truly a good work; and it is a marvel. . . . " (Wilford Woodruff, *The Discourses of Wilford Woodruff*, pp. 109-11.)

As you study the life of this seer, ponder the things which qualified him to perceive those things which were of greatest spiritual significance, both present and future.

WILFORD WOODRUFF WAS AMONG THE GREAT IN PRE-EARTH LIFE

(10-1) Wilford Woodruff, Among Others, Was Foreordained to Labor in the Earth for the Salvation of Men's Souls

"The Prophet Joseph Smith, and . . . Hyrum Smith, Brigham Young, John Taylor, Wilford Woodruff, and other choice spirits who were reserved to come forth in the fulness of times to take part in laying the foundations of the great Latter-day work, . . . were also among the noble and great ones who were chosen in the beginning to be rulers in the Church of God. Even before they were born, they, with many others, received their first lessons in the world of spirits, and were prepared to come forth in the due time of the Lord to labor in his vineyard for the salvation of the souls of men." (Joseph F. Smith, *Gospel Doctrine*, p. 475.)

(10-2) Wilford Woodruff Was Blessed to Have an Important Part in Building Up the Kingdom of God

One who had significant influence on Wilford Woodruff even before he heard of the Restoration was Robert Mason, a godly man who yearned for the full gospel of Christ. The Lord had mercy upon him, and by a vision he was enlightened concerning that which

would soon be accomplished on the earth. Though he himself would not live to participate in the marvelous work, the vision made clear to him that Wilford Woodruff would.

"When Father Mason had finished relating the vision and its interpretation, he said, calling me by my Christian name: 'Wilford, I shall never partake of this fruit in the flesh, but you will and you will become a conspicuous actor in the new kingdom.' He then turned and left me. These were the last words he ever spoke to me upon the earth. To me this was a very striking circumstance. I had passed many days during a period of twenty years with this old Father Mason. He had never mentioned this vision to me before. On this occasion he said he felt impelled by the Spirit of the Lord to relate it to me.

"The vision was given to him about the year 1800. He related it to me in 1830, the spring in which the Church was organized. Three years later when I was baptized into the Church of Jesus Christ of Latter-day Saints, almost the first person I thought of was this prophet, Robert Mason. Upon my arrival in Missouri with Zion's Camp, I wrote him a long letter in which I informed him that I had found the true gospel with all its blessings; that the authority of the Church of Christ had been restored to the earth as he had told me it would be; that I had received the ordinances of baptism and the laying on of hands; that I knew for myself that God had established through Joseph Smith, the Prophet, the Church of Christ upon the earth.

"He received my letter with great joy and had it read over to him many times. . . . He was very aged and soon died without having the privilege of receiving the ordinances of the gospel at the hands of an elder of the Church.

"The first opportunity I had after the truth of baptism for the dead was revealed, I went forth and was baptized for him in the temple font at Nauvoo." (Wilford Woodruff, cited in Matthias F. Cowley, *Wilford Woodruff*, pp. 17-18.)

Note Jeremiah 1:4, 5. How could these verses be applied to Wilford Woodruff? Is there an application for you? How might a patriarchal blessing compare to the vision of Robert Mason? Peter (2 Peter 1:9) and Paul (Hebrews 11:13) both spoke of promises enabling men and women to "see afar off." Could your patriarchal blessing give you an opportunity to see afar off? How? And is "seeing" enough? What more is required?

IN HIS YOUTH, WILFORD WOODRUFF SAW AFAR OFF AND MADE STRATEGIC PREPARATIONS

(10-3) The Young Wilford's Philosophy of Life

A great part of the wisdom of Wilford Woodruff was his perception of the real purpose of his life. Notice what he decided was the key to happiness.

"I was twenty-three years of age; and in reflecting upon the past, I became sincerely convinced that there was no real peace of mind or true happiness except in the service of God and in doing those things which would meet His approval. As far as my imagination would enable me, I brought before my mind all the honor, glory, and happiness of the whole world. I thought of the gold and the wealth of the rich, of the glory, grandeur, and power of kings, presidents, princes, and rulers. I thought of the military renown of Alexander, Napoleon, and other great generals. I cast my mind over the innumerable paths through which the giddy world travels in search of pleasure and happiness. In summing up the whole matter in the vision of my mind, I had to exclaim with Solomon: 'All is vanity of vanities sayeth the preacher.'

"I could see that within a few years all would end alike in the grave. I was convinced that no man could enjoy true happiness and obtain that which would feed the immortal soul, except God was his friend and Jesus Christ his advocate. I was convinced that man became their friend by doing the will of the Father, and by keeping His commandments. I made a firm resolution that from then I would seek the Lord to know His will, to keep His commandments, and to follow the dictates of His Holy Spirit. Upon this ground I was determined to stand and to spend my future life in the maintenance of these convictions." (Cited in Cowley, *Wilford Woodruff*, pp. 26-27.)

(10-4) Wilford Woodruff Was a Seeker of Truth

The gospel did not come to the young Wilford in a vacuum. Energetic preparations paved the way.

" . . . I got up prayer meetings in our village and prayed for light and knowledge. It was my desire to receive the ordinances of the gospel, as I could plainly see by reading the Bible that baptism by immersion was a sacred ordinance. In my eagerness, yet being ignorant of the holy priesthood and of the true authority to officiate in the ordinances of eternal life, I requested the Baptist minister to baptize me. At first he refused because I told him I would not join his church as it did not harmonize

with the apostolic church which our Savior established. Finally after several conversations, he baptized me on the 5th of May, 1831. He also baptized my brother Asahel. This was the first and only gospel ordinance I sought for until I joined the Church of Jesus Christ of Latter-day Saints. . . .

"On one occasion, after praying most earnestly to know about the people of the Lord, if any such there were on earth, he says: 'The Spirit of the Lord said unto me: "Go to my Word and I will there show thee my will and answer thy prayer." I opened the Bible promiscuously, praying the Lord to direct me to that portion of his Word which would answer my prayer. I opened to the 56th Chapter of Isaiah. I was satisfied it was in response to my prayer. I felt that the salvation of God was about to be revealed and His righteousness come forth. I was also satisfied that I should live to see the people of God gathered. From this time on until the gospel found me I was contented and felt that I should trouble myself no more about the churches and the ministers.' " (Cited in Cowley, *Wilford Woodruff*, p. 29.)

Thus we see in Wilford Woodruff an example of one who prepared while young, one who was early in catching the vision of his great mission in life. He later counseled young people:

"I feel to exhort and counsel you, my young friends, to listen to the voice of God and obey it while young, as Samuel did, that you may be great, good, and useful, and the beloved of the Lord and your parents and by all good men. Obey your parents and honor them, for by doing this you will obtain those great

blessings which God has promised you. . . .

" . . . You are now laying a foundation in the bloom and beauty of youth and in the morning of your days to step forth upon the stage of life to act a conspicuous part in the midst of the most important dispensation and generation in which man has ever lived. And I can say in truth and safety that the result of your future lives, the influence which you will exert among man, and finally your eternal destiny for time and eternity, will in a great measure depend upon the foundation which you lay in the days of your youth, the manner in which you store your mind and cultivate while young." (Woodruff, *Discourses of Wilford Woodruff*, pp. 265-66.)

Read Alma 37:35. According to this scripture, what makes youth such a critical time for "laying a foundation"?

WILFORD WOODRUFF'S CONVERSION AND EARLY LABORS IN THE CHURCH BROUGHT FULFILLMENT TO HIS LIFE AND HELPED PREPARE HIM FOR BROADER SERVICE IN THE KINGDOM

(10-5) On December 31, 1833, Wilford Woodruff Joined the Church

The day one enters the Church should be a rebirth into the kingdom of God. It was for Wilford Woodruff.

"I felt that I could truly exclaim with the prophet of God, 'I had rather be a door-keeper in the house of my God than to dwell in the tents of wickedness.' The fulness of the everlasting gospel had come at last. It filled my heart with great joy. It laid the foundation of a greater and more

glorious work than I ever expected to see in this life. I pray God in the name of Jesus Christ to guide my future life, that I may live to His honor and glory, and be a blessing to my fellowmen, and in the end be saved in His celestial kingdom, even so, Amen." (Cited in Cowley, *Wilford Woodruff*, p. 36.)

(10-6) As a Priest, Wilford Woodruff Experienced the Ministering of Angels and Began His Great Missionary Service

"I had the administration of angels while holding the office of a priest. I had visions and revelations. I traveled thousands of miles. I baptized men, though I could not confirm them because I had not the authority to do it.

"I speak of these things to show that a man should not be ashamed of any portion of the priesthood. Our young men, if they are deacons, should labor to fulfil that office. If they do that, they may then be called to the office of a teacher, whose duty it is to teach the people, visit the Saints and see that there is no evil or iniquity carried on. God has no respect for persons in this priesthood any further than as they magnify their callings and do their duty." (Woodruff, *Discourses of Wilford Woodruff*, p. 298.)

(10-7) Zion's Camp Was an Education for Wilford Woodruff

By revelation in 1833, the Lord called upon the faithful priesthood of his church to travel from Kirtland, Ohio, to Missouri to regain the land of Zion. (See D&C 101.) They were to be led by the Prophet Joseph. Wilford Woodruff was among the approximately two hundred who went. When the camp left, he had been a member of the Church less than half a year.

"We were young men, and were called upon in that early day to go

up and redeem Zion, and what we had to do we had to do by faith. We assembled together from the various States at Kirtland and went up to redeem Zion, in fulfilment of the commandment of God unto us. God accepted our works as He did the works of Abraham. We accomplished a great deal, though apostates and unbelievers many times asked the question, 'What have you done?' We gained an experience that we never could have gained in any other way. We had the privilege of beholding the face of the prophet, and we had the privilege of travelling a thousand miles with him, and seeing the workings of the Spirit of God with him, and the revelations of Jesus Christ unto him and the fulfilment of those revelations. And he gathered some two hundred Elders from throughout the nation in that early day and sent us broadcast into the world to preach the Gospel of Jesus Christ. Had I not gone up with Zion's Camp I should not have been here to-day, and I presume that would have been the case with many others in this Territory.'' (Wilford Woodruff in JD, 13:158.)

IN FULFILLING A STEWARDSHIP AS A PROPHETIC HISTORIAN, WILFORD WOODRUFF REACHED OUT TO FUTURE TIMES AND GENERATIONS

(10-8) Wilford Woodruff Followed the Counsel of Joseph Smith

In the archives of the Church Historian's Office there are stored some seven thousand pages of the journals of Wilford Woodruff. The record he kept was invaluable for himself, for his family, and now for the whole Church.

"There is one subject I wish to speak upon and that is the keeping of a journal with respect to the dealings of God with us. I have

many times thought the Quorum of the Twelve and others considered me rather enthusiastic upon this subject; but when the Prophet Joseph organized the Quorum of the Twelve, he counseled them to keep a history of their lives, and gave his reasons why they should do so. I have had this spirit and calling upon me since I first entered this Church. I made a record from the first

sermon I heard, and from that day until now I have kept a daily journal. Whenever I heard Joseph Smith preach, teach, or prophesy, I always felt it my duty to write it; I felt uneasy and could not eat, drink, or sleep until I did write; and my mind has been so exercised upon this subject that when I heard Joseph Smith teach and had no pencil or paper, I would go home and sit down and write the whole

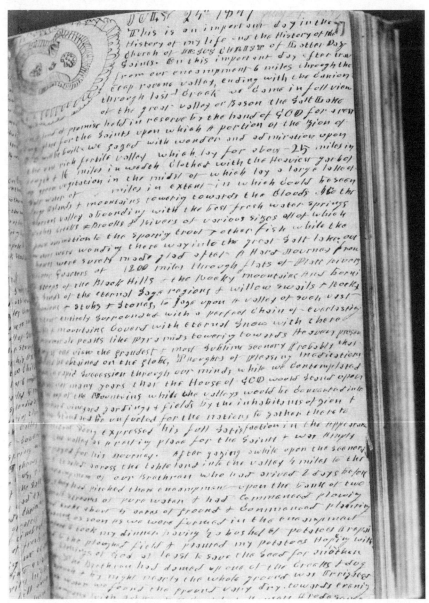

A page from Wilford Woodruff's ample journal

sermon, almost word for word and sentence by sentence as it was delivered, and when I had written it it was taken from me, I remembered it no more. This was the gift of God to me.

"The devil has sought to take away my life from the day I was born until now, more so even than the lives of other men. I seem to be a marked victim of the adversary. I can find but one reason for this: the devil knew if I got into the Church of Jesus Christ of Latter-day Saints, I would write the history of that Church and leave on record the works and teachings of the prophets, of the apostles and elders. (Cited in Cowley, *Wilford Woodruff*, pp. 476-77.)

(10-9) Wilford Woodruff Chronicled Events Past, Present, and Future

"I will here say that God has inspired me to keep a journal and write the history of this Church, and I warn the future historians to give credence to my history; for my testimony is true, and the truth of its record will be manifest in the world to come. All the words of the Lord will be fulfilled upon the nations, which are written in this book. . . .

" . . . Our nation is in the hands of God. He holds its destiny. He holds the destinies of all men. I will say to the Latter-day Saints, as an Elder in Israel and as an Apostle of the Lord Jesus Christ, we are approaching some of the most tremendous judgments God ever poured out upon the world. You watch the signs of the times, the signs of the coming of the Son of Man. They are beginning to be made manifest both in heaven and on earth." (Cited in Cowley, *Wilford Woodruff*, pp. 500, 571.)

Beginning with father Adam, the great of the earth have kept records of their proceedings in their day. (Note Moses 6:5, 46; 1 Nephi 1:1.) The counsel of the Lord today is that the saints of God should do the same. Why? Do you think that Church history was all that Wilford Woodruff had on his mind as he kept a record of his life? Will there be important events ahead for all to record?

"I have never spent any of my time more profitably for the benefit of mankind than in my journal writing. . . . Some of the most glorious gospel sermons, truths, and revelations that were given from God to this people through the mouth of the Prophets Joseph, Brigham, Heber, and the Twelve could not be found upon the earth on record only in my journals, and they are compiled in the Church History and transmitted to the saints of God in all future generations. Does not this pay me for my trouble? It does. . . . We are not apt to think of the importance of events as they transpire with us, but we feel the importance of them afterward. We are living in one of the most important generations that man ever lived on earth, and we should write an account of those important transactions which are taking place before our eyes in fulfillment of the prophecies and the revelation of God. There is a great flood of revelations fulfilling in our day, and as they are transpiring before our eyes we want a record made of them." (*Journal of Wilford Woodruff*, 17 Mar. 1857. Church Historical Library. Punctuation, capitalization, and spelling standardized.)

In general conference of April 1978, President Spencer W. Kimball called on all Church members to keep a journal. He said:

"On the bookshelves in my office at home there are thirty-three large, well-filled journal books. In my journal, a year for each book, I have written daily and filed in this library. It records the trips to many of the nations in the world and all around the world and meetings held, people contacted, marriages performed, and all things of interest to my family, and, I hope, someday to the Church.

"I urge all of the people of this church to give serious attention to their family histories, to encourage their parents and grandparents to write their journals, and let no family go into eternity without having left their memoirs for their children, their grandchildren, and their posterity. This is a duty and a responsibility, and I urge every

George Q. Cannon, Wilford Woodruff, Joseph F. Smith

The First Presidency (1889)

person to start the children out writing a personal history and journal.'' (''The True Way of Life and Salvation,'' *Ensign*, May 1978, p.4.)

To fully appreciate this counsel, one need only ponder three questions: How valuable to our understanding of the Church's history are the journals of the early Saints? How important are the events facing the Church in your lifetime? How will the Saints of the millennial era view the journals of those who lived in the days of judgment which brought the Millennium forth?

WILFORD WOODRUFF WAS MAGNIFIED, AND HIS INFLUENCE WAS EXPANDED TO THOSE BEYOND THE VEIL

(10-10) The Ministry of Wilford Woodruff Extended to His Family

''On the 1st of July, 1838, there occurred one of the most interesting events of my whole life in the ministry. When Father Joseph Smith gave me my patriarchal blessing, among the many wonderful things he promised me was that I should bring my father's household into the Kingdom of God; and I felt that if I ever obtained that blessing, the time therefor had come. By the help of God I preached the gospel faithfully to my father's household and to all who were with him, as well as to my other relatives. . . .

'' . . . I led six of my friends into the river and baptized them for the remission of their sins. All of my father's household were included in this number, as the patriarch had promised. . . .

'' . . . 'O Lord, protect my father's house, and bring them to Zion!' '' (Cited in Cowley, *Wilford Woodruff*, pp. 91-92.)

(10-11) Wilford Woodruff Furthered the Work for the Dead–for His Own Progenitors and Others

'' . . . I prayed the Lord to open the way for the redemption of my dead. The spirit of the Lord rested upon me and gave me the following testimony: 'Let My servant Wilford call upon the daughters and mothers in Zion, and let them enter into My holy Temple on the 1st day of March, the day that My servant Wilford shall see the time allotted to man, three score years and ten. There let them receive their endowments for his dead kindred, and this shall be acceptable unto me, saith the Lord. The dead relatives of My servant shall be redeemed in the spirit world and be prepared to meet My servant at the time of his coming, which shall be at the time appointed unto him, yet not revealed to man in the flesh. Now, go to and perform this work and all shall be accomplished according to the desires of thy heart.' '' (Cited in Cowley, *Wilford Woodruff*, p. 496.)

'' . . . it is our duty to rise up and build these temples. I look upon this portion of our ministry as a mission of as much importance as preaching to the living; the dead will hear the voice of the servants of God in the spirit world, and they cannot come forth in the morning of the resurrection, unless certain ordinances are performed, for, and in their behalf, in temples built to the name of God. It takes just as much to save a dead man as a living man.'' (Woodruff, *Discourses of Wilford Woodruff*, p. 160.)

(10-12) Wilford Woodruff Received the Full Keys of Apostleship and Saw the Vast Work Yet to Be Done Through Those Keys

''When the Lord gave the keys of the kingdom of God, the keys of the Melchizedek Priesthood, of the apostleship, and sealed them upon the head of Joseph Smith, he sealed them upon his head to stay here upon the earth until the coming of the Son of Man. Well might Brigham Young say, 'The keys of the kingdom of God are here.' They were with him to the day of his death. They then rested upon the head of another man—

Salt Lake City in 1890

President John Taylor. He held those keys to the hour of his death. They then fell by turn, or in the providence of God, upon Wilford Woodruff.

"I say to the Latter-day Saints, the keys of the kingdom of God are here, and they are going to stay here, too, until the coming of the Son of Man. Let all Israel understand that. They may not rest upon my head but a short time, but they will then rest on the head of another apostle, and another after him, and so continue until the coming of the Lord Jesus Christ in the clouds of heaven to 'reward every man according to the deeds done in the body.' . . .

"It is a day in which the gospel is to be preached to every nation, tongue and people for a witness of what shall follow; a day in which the Israel of God who receive it in their dispersed and scattered condition are to gather together. . . .

"I thank God that the day is at hand when the Jews will be restored. I have felt to pray for them; I feel interested in their behalf. . . .

" . . . Zion is bound to rise and flourish. The Lamanites will blossom as the rose on the mountains. I am willing to say here that, though I believe this, when I see the power of the nation destroying them from the face of the earth, the fulfilment of that prophecy is perhaps harder for me to believe than any revelation of God that I ever read. It looks as though there would not be enough left to receive the gospel; but notwithstanding this dark picture, every word that God has ever said of them will have its fulfilment, and they, by and by, will receive the gospel. It will be a day of God's power among them, and a nation will be born in a day. Their chiefs will be filled with the power of God

Wilford Woodruff as an Apostle

and receive the gospel. . . . " (Woodruff, *Discourses of Wilford Woodruff*, pp. 73, 110, 117-18, 121.)

"Again, here are the ten tribes of Israel; we know nothing about them only what the Lord has said by his prophets. There are

prophets among them, and by and by, they will come along, and they will smite the rocks, and the mountains of ice will flow down at their presence, and a highway will be cast up before them, and they will come to Zion, receive their endowments, and be crowned

under the hands of the children of Ephraim. . . . '' (Woodruff, *Discourses of Wilford Woodruff*, p. 119.)

(10-13) By Revelation, Wilford Woodruff Extended the Temple Work for Great Men and Women of the Past

'' . . . two weeks before I left St. George, the spirits of the dead gathered around me, wanting to know why we did not redeem them. Said they, 'You have had the use of the Endowment House for a number of years, and yet nothing has ever been done for us. We laid the foundation of the government you now enjoy, and we never apostatized from it, but we remained true to it and were faithful to God.' These were the signers of the Declaration of Independence, and they waited on me for two days and two nights. I thought it very singular, that notwithstanding so much work had been done, and yet nothing had been done for them. The thought never entered my heart, from the fact, I suppose, that heretofore our minds were reaching after our more immediate friends and relatives. I straightway went into the baptismal font and called upon brother McCallister to baptize me for the signers of the Declaration of Independence, and fifty other eminent men, making one hundred in all, including John Wesley, Columbus, and others; I then baptized him for every President of the United States, except three; and when their cause is just, somebody will do the work for them.'' (Wilford Woodruff in *JD*, 19:229.)

(10-14) The Perspective of a Prophet

''The God of heaven has put into our hands the Gospel, the Priesthood, the keys of his kingdom, and the power to redeem the earth from the dominion of sin and wickedness under which it has groaned for centuries, and under which it groans to-day. Let us lay these things to heart, and try to live our religion; so that when we get through we may look back on our lives, and feel that we have done what was required of us, individually and collectively.'' (Wilford Woodruff in *JD*, 14:6.)

And so in Wilford Woodruff we see one who caught the vision of life and was then faithful to it throughout the whole of his life. His is a superb example. What are some of the things that keep many from ''seeing afar off''? Note these words of President Woodruff:

''What will it profit a man to gain the whole world and lose his own soul? Not much. What will a man give in exchange for his soul, when he gets on the other side of the veil? I marvel very

Wilford Woodruff, after being sustained as President

much at the little interest manifested by the inhabitants of the earth generally in their future state. There is not a person here today but what is going to live on the other side of the veil as long as his Creator—to the endless ages of eternity, and the eternal destiny of every individual depends upon the manner in which the few short years of the life in the flesh are spent. I ask, in the name of the Lord, what is popularity to you or me? What is gold or silver, or this world's goods to any of us, any further than to enable us to obtain what we need to eat, drink, and wear, and to build up the kingdom of God. And for us to stop praying, and to become crazy after the riches of the world, is the very height of foolishness and folly. To see the way that some people act, you might suppose that they are going to live here eternally, and that their eternal destiny depends upon the number of dollars they have. I sometimes ask the Latter-day Saints, how much we had when we came here? How much did we bring, and where did it come from? I do not think any one of us brought a wife or a brick house; I do not think that any of us were born on horseback or in a carriage, or that we brought railroad scrip and cattle and houses with us, but we were born naked as Job, and I think that we shall leave here as naked as he did.'' (Woodruff, *Discourses of Wilford Woodruff*, pp. 243-44.)

CHAPTER 11

BEING LED IN THE WAY OF THE LORD

INTRODUCTION

It was a time of grave crisis for the Church when President Wilford Woodruff began to preside among the Saints in 1887. President Taylor had died in exile, and most of the prominent Church leaders were in prison or were unable to lead effectively. The federal laws not only made it unlawful to practice plural marriage but also prohibited those who did so from voting or running for public office. Utah's admission as a state seemed hopelessly deadlocked. There was legislation that sought to disenfranchise all members of the Church. The Church, as an institution, was disincorporated, tithing funds were seized, and Temple Square and other Church properties were transferred to the United States Government. There was a serious attempt by many to actually destroy the entity of The Church of Jesus Christ of Latter-day Saints. Missionary work for the living and temple work for the dead were greatly threatened.

But the Lord is able to do his own work. Each man who has presided over the Lord's people has been empowered to pursue a steady course by being a willing servant. Because this is so, the Lord will totally fulfill his purposes.

His Saints will finally rejoice, and those who have stood at the forefront will be honored among the people because they have heard the voice of the Shepherd and have done his work. But before a man of God, obstacles melt like frost before the burning sun. In 1890, after earnest pleading with the Lord, Wilford Woodruff received the answer. The Church had proven itself. Plural marriage was rescinded with the issuance of the Manifesto, and the kingdom rolled on.

In his eighty-sixth year, on April 6, 1892, Wilford Woodruff stepped forward and said, "Attention, all ye House of Israel, and all ye nations of the earth. We will now lay the top stone of the Temple of our God. . . . " And the people shouted, "Hosanna! Hosanna! Hosanna! to God and the Lamb! Amen! Amen! and Amen!" (Cited in B. H. Roberts, *A Comprehensive History of The Church of Jesus Christ of Latter-day Saints,* 6:233.) And so it was that a prophet of God, being led by the Lord against seemingly insurmountable opposition, once again moved the cause of Zion.

WILFORD WOODRUFF, LIKE OTHERS OF THE LORD'S SERVANTS, WAS LED BY THE SPIRIT OF REVELATION

(11-1) Wilford Woodruff's Life Was Preserved by Revelation

"What is revelation? The testimony of the Father and Son. How many of you have had revelation? How many of you have had the Spirit of God whisper unto you—the still small voice? I would have been in the spirit world a great many years ago if I had not followed the promptings of the still small voice. These were the revelations of Jesus Christ, the strongest testimony a man or a woman can have. I have had many testimonies since I have been connected with this Church and kingdom. I have been blessed at times with certain gifts and graces, certain revelations and ministrations; but with them all I have never found anything that I could place more dependency upon than the still small voice of the Holy Ghost." (Wilford Woodruff, *The Discourses of Wilford Woodruff,* p. 45.)

(11-2) Revelation Was a Key to Wilford Woodruff's Missionary Service in England

"Before I rose to speak to the people, the Spirit of the Lord said to me, 'This is the last meeting you will hold with this people for many days.' I told the congregation when I arose what the Spirit of the Lord had manifested to me. They were as much surprised as I was. I did not know what the Lord wanted, but I saw the purpose of God afterwards. The Spirit of the Lord said to me, 'Go south.' I traveled eighty miles; went into the south of England. As soon as I arrived, I met John Benbow. It was clearly made manifest to me why I had been called thither. I had left a good field, where I was baptizing every night in the week. When I got to

this place, I found a people—some 600 of them. . . . I found that they were praying for light and truth and that they had gone about as far as they could go. I saw that the Lord had sent me to them. I went to work amongst them and ultimately baptized their superintendent, forty preachers and some 600 members. . . . Altogether some 1800 were baptized in that field of labor. . . . I name these things to show how we have to be governed and led by the revelations of God day by day. Without this we can do nothing." (Woodruff, *Discourses of Wilford Woodruff*, p. 60.)

(11-3) Another Typical Instance of Revelation

For the date of January 26, 1880 Wilford Woodruff's journal records the following:

"I went to bed filled with prayer and meditation. I fell asleep and remained in slumber until about midnight, when I awoke. The Lord then poured out His spirit upon me and opened the vision of my mind so that I could comprehend in a great measure the mind and will of God concerning the nation and concerning the inhabitants of Zion. I saw the wickedness of the nation, its abominations and corruptions and the judgments of God and the destruction that awaited it. Then I also comprehended the great responsibility which rested upon the Quorum of the Apostles. My head became a fountain of tears, and my pillow was wet with the dews of heaven. Sleep departed from me. The Lord revealed unto me the duty of the Apostles and of all the faithful elders of Israel. The revelation was submitted to the Quorum of the Twelve Apostles just prior to the April conference of that year." (Cited in Matthias F. Cowley, *Wilford Woodruff*, pp. 530-31.)

(11-4) His Humble Reflections at Becoming President of the Church

"This 7th day of April, 1889, is one of the most important days in my life, for I was made President of the Church of Jesus Christ of Latter-day Saints by the unanimous vote of ten thousand of them. The vote was first taken by quorums and then by the entire congregation as in the case of President John Taylor. This is the highest office ever conferred upon any man in the flesh. It came to me in the eighty-third year of my life. I pray God to protect me and give me power to magnify my calling to the end of my days. The Lord has watched over me until the present time. (Cited in Cowley, *Wilford Woodruff*, pp. 564-65.)

(11-5) The President Is to Have Power and Fellowship with God

"It is my duty to have fellowship with God, as weak an instrument as I am in the hands of God. It is my duty to have power with God. And when I have this, then my counselors should stand by me and with me. We should be of one heart and mind in all matters, temporal and spiritual, that come before us in the labor of the Church and kingdom of God. And I am thankful to say that this has been the case since I have been called to this position, or since the organization of the Presidency of the Church." (Woodruff, *Discourses of Wilford Woodruff*, p. 89.)

(11-6) Revelation Is Always the Rock Foundation upon Which the Lord's Church Is Built

"Where are the revelations of President Young? Do you find them on record? Only a few; but the Holy Ghost and the revelations of God were with Brigham Young from the day that he received this gospel until the day that he laid

down his life and his tabernacle was carried to the grave. There was no necessity particularly for Brigham Young to give written revelation, only in a few instances. So with John Taylor. So with Wilford Woodruff. And so in a great measure probably with all who may follow us, until the coming of the Son of man. . . .

"The Lord would not permit me to occupy this position one day of my life, unless I was susceptible to the Holy Spirit and to the revelations of God. It is too late in the day for this Church to stand without revelation." (Woodruff, *Discourses of Wilford Woodruff*, pp. 55, 57.)

You have just read how critical revelation was in the life of Wilford Woodruff and that it is the essential foundation upon which the Lord's church is built. Is it important to you as an individual? Why? Does the Church generally need revelation any more than you do personally? What gift do you possess that entitles you to revelation? (Read D&C 8:2-5.) President Woodruff has testified:

"It is this preknowledge which God has given concerning his work . . . which is one of the chief causes of the strength possessed by the Latter-day Saints. It is the principle of revelation from the head of the church to the church itself—a principle which in its operation is not confined to one man, or to three men, or to twelve men; but is extended to every individual in the Church, in greater or less degree, as each one chooses to avail himself of it. There is an appointed way, however, in which revelation from the Lord for the government of his church is received. There is but one man on the earth, at a time, who

holds this power. But every individual member has the privilege of receiving revelation from the Lord for his guidance in his own affairs. . . ." (Woodruff, *Discourses of Wilford Woodruff,* p. 54.)

What, then, is the order of revelation in the Lord's church? Why must it be this way?

WILFORD WOODRUFF'S INSPIRED WISDOM GUIDED AND REGULATED THE AFFAIRS OF THE LORD'S CHURCH DURING DIFFICULT DAYS

(11-7) Satan Strove to Halt the Work of the Lord

In a letter written to President John Taylor dated September 15, 1879, President Woodruff stated:

"The devil is making a hard struggle to stop the building of temples, and the work of God, and the wicked are helping him, but, brethren, God reigns and will stand by you to the end. . . . That God may bless you and give you the victory, is the earnest prayer of Your brother in the gospel,

WILFORD WOODRUFF."

(Cited in Cowley, *Wilford Woodruff,* p. 528.)

(11-8) The Deepening Crisis of 1884

By 1884 the forces of the Federal government were being mobilized, not only to confront the popular issue of so-called polygamy, but to threaten the very lives of the Latter-day Saint people and the existence of the Church as an institution among men. The temper of the times is in part reflected by the following statement of a Latter-day Saint newspaper editor, John Nicholson, to a federal judge:

" . . . my purpose is fixed and, I

hope, unalterable. . . . I shall stand by my allegiance to God, fidelity to my family, and what I conceive to be my duty to the Constitution . . . which guarantees the fullest religious liberty to the citizen. . . . " The judge replied, " . . . If you do not submit to it of course you must take the consequences; but the will of the American people . . . and this law will go on and grind you and your institution to powder." (*Deseret News* [Weekly], 21 Oct. 1885, p. 1.)

(11-9) The Year 1890 Was to Be Significant for the Saints and the United States

"Thus ends the year 1889. And the word of the Prophet Joseph Smith is beginning to be fulfilled that the whole nation would turn against Zion and make war upon the Saints. The nation has never been filled so full of lies against the Saints as today. 1890 will be an important year with the Latter-day Saints and the American nation." (*Journal of Wilford Woodruff,* 31 Dec. 1889. Church Historical Library. Punctuation, capitalization, and spelling standardized.)

(11-10) Wilford Woodruff's Issuance of the Manifesto, Through Revelation, Disarmed the Enemies of the Church and Allowed the Work to Go On

The Manifesto on plural marriage made clear the will of the Lord. After years of sacrifice and proving, the Lord saw fit to move upon his servant:

" 'And whatsoever they shall speak when moved upon by the Holy Ghost shall be scripture, shall be the will of the Lord, shall be the mind of the Lord, shall be the word of the Lord, shall be the voice of the Lord, and the power of God unto salvation.' [D&C 68:4]

"It is by that power that we have

led Israel; by that power President Young presided over and led the Church. By the same power, President John Taylor presided over and led the Church. And that is the way I have acted according to the best of my ability in that capacity. I do not want the Latter-day Saints to understand that the Lord is not with us, and that he is not giving revelations to us; for He is giving us revelation, and will give us revelation until the scene is wound up.

"I have had some revelations of late and very important ones to me and I will tell you what the Lord has said to me. Let me bring your minds to what is termed the Manifesto. . . .

"Since I received that revelation, I have heard of many who are tried in these things. . . . the Lord showed me by a vision and revelation exactly what would take place if we did not stop this practice. . . . the Lord is with him [Wilford Woodruff] and with this people. He has told me exactly what to do and what the result would be if we did not do it. . . . I went before the Lord, and I wrote what the Lord told me to write. I laid it before my brethren, such strong men as George Q. Cannon, Brother Joseph F. Smith and the Twelve Apostles . . . these men agreed with me and ten thousand Latter-day Saints agreed with me. Why? Because they were moved upon by the spirit of God and by the revelations of Jesus Christ to do it. . . . (*Deseret News,* November 7, 1891.)" (Cited in Spencer W. Kimball, *Faith Precedes the Miracle,* p. 42.)

Read the Manifesto of Wilford Woodruff as given in the Doctrine and Covenants, pages 256-57. Why is this statement "binding on the Saints"? What is

Lights for the new temple

the significance of President Lorenzo Snow's statement that follows the Manifesto? Is there any possibility that the Saints will ever be led astray by the presiding prophet? Why is it fundamentally wrong to cut oneself off from the president of the Church? How significant is the following testimony of President Wilford Woodruff?

"There are men today, there will be men till the coming of the Son of Man, I expect, who feel as though they ought to lead the Church, as though it is not going on right—that this, that, and the other is wrong. I say to all Israel at this day, I say to the whole world, that the God of Israel, who organized this Church and kingdom, never ordained any President or Presidency to lead it astray. Hear it, ye Israel, no man who has ever breathed the breath of life can hold these keys of the kingdom of God and lead the people astray." (Woodruff, *Discourses of Wilford Woodruff*, p. 74.)

(11-11) Wilford Woodruff Received Revelations Furthering the Work for the Dead

President Woodruff was always very concerned with the work for the dead. In 1894 the Genealogical Society was organized under his direction. In that same year, the Lord revealed important matters of procedure relating to family sealings:

"We want the Latter-day Saints from this time to trace their genealogies as far as they can, and to be sealed to their fathers and mothers. Have children sealed to their parents, and run this chain through as far as you can get it. . . . This is the will of the Lord to this people, and I think when you come to reflect upon it you will find it to be true. . . .

" . . . Save your fathers, and stand at the head of your father's house, as saviors upon Mount Zion, and God will bless you in this. This is what I want to say, and what I want carried out in our temples. . . . I have had a great anxiety over this matter. I have had a great desire that I might live to deliver these principles to the Latter-day Saints, for they are true. They are one step forward in the work of the ministry and in the work of the endowments in these temples of our God. . . .

" . . . I have gone to work with the assistance of my friends and redeemed my father's and my mother's house. When I inquired of the Lord how I could redeem my dead, while I was in St. George, not having any of my family there, the Lord told me to call upon the Saints in St. George and let them officiate for me in that temple, and it should be acceptable unto him. . . . This is a revelation to us. We can help one another in these matters." (Woodruff, *Discourses of Wilford Woodruff,* pp. 157-59.)

(11-12) Policy, Principle, and the Law of the Fast

In 1896, under the direction of President Woodruff, the policy of having "fast day" on the first Thursday of the month was changed to the present observance of the first Sunday of the month. Along with this change eternal principles were reiterated.

"In some places the custom has arisen to consider it a fast to omit eating breakfast. This is not in accordance with the views and practice of the past. When fasts were observed in the early days, it was the rule to not partake of food from the previous day until after the meeting in the afternoon of the fast day. In making donations to the poor also it has been the understanding that the food that would be necessary for the two

Temple Square in 1892

Salt Lake City from the top of the new temple (1892)

meals should be donated to the poor, and as much more as those who are liberally inclined, and have the means, may feel disposed to give." (Cited in Roberts, *A Comprehensive History of the Church,* 6:348-49.)

(11-13) The Good Ship Zion Moves Steadily Onward–It Does Not Drift

And so throughout President Woodruff's administration, as in past years and in all time to come, the work of the Lord went forward.

"So many things have occurred which are entirely different to preconceived notions as to the course that would be taken in building up Zion that each one needs to have a knowledge that God is leading us in the path which we are now pursuing. To some who are inclined to despond and to take a gloomy view of affairs, the ship Zion may, perhaps, appear to be drifting away from its old moorings because things are being done or movements consented to which, to their eyes, portend disaster to us and to the work of God.

"There has always been a few among us who have been filled with evil forebodings, and who have failed to see the wisdom of God in the steps which his people have been led to take. They have questioned and found fault with the counsel that has been given and the measures which have been adopted and have asserted that revelation had ceased and the Saints were no longer guided by men to whom God made known his will. . . . Experience has proved that in all such cases those who make these accusations are themselves in the dark.

"But the faithful people—those who have lived strictly in accordance with their profession as Saints and with the requirements of the gospel—have not been assailed by doubts of this character. There might be many things which they could not fully understand, the reasons for which might not be be fully apparent to them at the time; but possessing the Spirit of God, and being led by it, they trusted in the Lord and felt satisfied to leave the management of his kingdom and its affairs to his supreme wisdom. Time developed to their minds the correctness of the course which the Church had been led to adopt. This has occurred so frequently in our career that the instances will readily suggest themselves to those familiar with our history. In this way, however, the faith of the people has been constantly tested." (Woodruff, *Discourses of Wilford Woodruff,* pp. 141-42.)

According to that which you have just read, what great challenge faces the Saints as they continue to see changes and regulations in the Church?

George Q. Cannon, President Woodruff, and Joseph F. Smith in 1894

What is the significance of D&C 21:4-6 in this context? Note these words from President Woodruff:

"Joseph Smith visited me a great deal after his death, and taught me many important principles. . . . Among other things, he told me to get the Spirit of God; that all of us needed it. . . .

" . . . He said, 'I want you to teach the people to get the Spirit of God. You cannot build up the Kingdom of God without that.' . . .

" . . . But how is it with the Holy Ghost? The Holy Ghost does not leave me if I do my duty. It does not leave any man who does his duty. We have known this all the way through. Joseph Smith told Brother John Taylor on one occasion to labor to get the Spirit of God, and to follow its dictation, and it would become a principle of revelation within him. God has blessed me with that, and everything I have done since I have been in this Church has been done upon that principle. The Spirit of God has told me what to do, and I have had to follow that." (*Deseret News* [Weekly], 7 Nov. 1896.)

What, then, is the critical imperative in every Saint's life? According to President Woodruff, what is a key to keeping the companionship of the Holy Ghost?

(11-14) Wilford Woodruff, a Man Devoted

"One of the most important events of President Woodruff's long life was the celebration of his 90th birthday on March 1st, 1897. On that occasion thousands of Latter-day Saints gathered in the Salt Lake Tabernacle to do him honor. Appropriate remarks were made by his counselors, and others of the general authorities. A silver mounted cane was presented to him by temple workers. The vast congregation sang 'We Thank Thee, O God, for a Prophet.' On returning to his home President Woodruff recorded his impressions of the day in his journal. 'The scene completely overpowered me. The events of my childhood and early manhood came to my mind. I remembered vividly how I prayed to the Lord that I might live to see a Prophet or an Apostle who would teach me the gospel of Christ. Here I stood in the great Tabernacle filled with ten thousand children, with Prophets, Apostles and Saints. My head was a fountain of tears. Still I addressed the mighty congregation.' " (Preston Nibley, *The Presidents of the Church*, p. 166-67.)

When President Woodruff's great heart ceased to beat on September 2, 1898, the Saints of God had reason to mourn, for a noble life had been removed from their midst. It was a noble life because it had been consecrated to the furtherance of the cause of Zion. An example of this we find written in his journal years earlier:

"Be it known that I, Wilford Woodruff, do freely covenant myself, unto the Lord, for the purpose of assisting in the building up of His Kingdom and His Zion upon the earth, that I may keep His law. I lay all before the Bishop of His Church, that I may be [a] lawful heir to the Celestial Kingdom of God." (Cited in Nibley, *Presidents of the Church*, p. 137.)

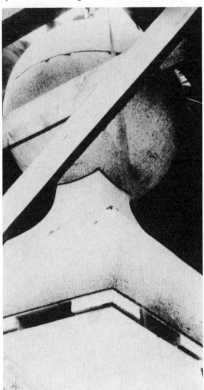

The capstone set in place

124

OVERVIEW

As a spirit son, he dwelt with the Father, saw his face, heard his voice, and what is more important than all else, believed his word and kept his law. Lorenzo Snow kept his first estate, retained the foreordination he had received *there* by his obedience and faithfulness *here,* and ascended to wield in this world the sceptre that had been appointed to him before.

He was a farm boy, matured on the frontier of nineteenth century America, in Ohio. Felling trees, clearing fields, overseeing in his father's frequent absence, ferrying produce downriver to New Orleans—he was the oldest son in a large family and did not know what it meant to be idle. They developed bonds of love and trust and mutual help that were set to endure. Tolerant, broadminded, sympathetic, he would always bear kind feelings for the opposing view and, as his father before him, never approach religion in a narrow, dogmatic way. He would regard Mormonism as an army which carried a banner of peace, as a hospital station on the field of the world to offer healing solace to injured, diseased souls. Resolute in his kindness, decisive in his gentleness, he was ever the steady hand. He sought and obtained formal education, excelled in his military ambitions, and commanded the respect of his family and townspeople. At the invitation of his older sister, Eliza Roxey Snow, he attended the Mormon Hebrew school in Kirtland, studied the religion cautiously, listened to the Prophet Joseph's public discourses, and conversed with him privately. He befriended the Prophet's father, who said to him, Lorenzo, "You will soon be convinced of the truth of the latter-day work, and be baptized, and you will become as great as you can possibly wish—even as great as God, and you cannot wish to be greater."[1] He marveled, he was astonished, he pondered, he believed, he was baptized and was then converted in a marvelous manner. His life changed—he could no longer seek to serve himself, but others. He sought ordination to be an elder, and into the mission field he went.

He preached to his father's family in Ohio, then walked on foot to preach in Missouri, Illinois, and Kentucky—he could not rest. Pure, determined, he sought for knowledge and obtained revelation and promise about the ultimate destiny of man. But his missions continued. He arrived in England in 1840. He would preach and administer throughout Great Britain. Like Wilford Woodruff and John Taylor, Lorenzo Snow would bring thousands into the Church and would bear witness before queens and princes.

School master, campaigner, husband, father, temple builder, superintendent of schools, temple officiator, branch president, pioneer, and apostle. As a member of the Quorum of the Twelve, he sat in council, administering the business of the Church, guided in his ministry by dreams and revelations, managing the Perpetual Immigration Fund, founding the Italian Mission, supervising the translation of the Book of Mormon into new languages, preparing and publishing tracts, reaching, straining—he preached in Malta but was called home to urgent business while planning to preach in Corinth, Bombay, and Calcutta and then returned to Utah via China and the Pacific. He served as regent of a university, as territorial legislator, as founder and preeminent spirit of philosophical and scientific societies; he was ever the worker, behind the scenes. Austere, as some would say, devoted and selfless—he was not laboring for Lorenzo Snow but for the Master, whose servant he was.

He was called to preside among the Saints in Box Elder, Utah, which was later called Brigham City. He would interrupt that assignment numerous times, to serve in the Utah War, to fill missions to Hawaii and the Holy Land, and to counsel with the Brethren in Salt Lake. But always he would return to Brigham City, where finally a cooperative enterprise flowered. Though the cooperative was dissolved under the federal pressure of plural marriage of the late 1870s, a historian

observed that if the accomplishments of that order were known abroad, Lorenzo Snow would be ranked as one of the foremost social reformers of the age.

He dedicated the Manti Temple, served a mission to the Lamanites, and in 1886 was charged and convicted of violating the Edmund's law. Appeal of the plural marriage cases beyond territorial courts to the United States Supreme Court could not be scheduled unless the defendant was in durance; and so for scores of his brethren Lorenzo Snow volunteered himself for prison. He served a term of eleven months, during which time he organized a school and did other worthy things. Patient in bonds, undaunted by abuse, he was like Paul, and testified: "Where is the man among you having once burst the veil and gazed upon this purity, the glory, the might, majesty, and dominion of a perfected man, in celestial glory, in eternity, will not cheerfully resign life, suffer the most excruciating tortures, let limb be torn from limb sooner than dishonor or resign his priesthood?"[2]

He was a counselor to the First Presidency under Brigham Young, served for nine years as President of the Twelve, and at the great age of eighty-four years, assumed the presidency. Vigorously, and for a duration of three years, he struggled mightily to wrest the Church from the financial difficulties occasioned by the decades of persecution. "Before I die," he declared, "I hope to see the Church cleared of debt and in a commanding position financially."[3] He succeeded in seeing the Church well on its way to complete solvency and then went on to contemplate again the vision of his first apostolic years—to establish missions throughout the earth. He sent missionaries to Japan and spoke of sending the gospel to all nations. The destiny of Zion, he taught, was a world destiny—Zion would eventually spread over the whole earth. He urged, he pressed, he sought to purify, and then he fell asleep, secure in the promise of his lifelong precept: "The destiny of man is to be like his Father—a god in eternity."[4]

CHAPTER 12

SACRIFICE BRINGS FORTH THE BLESSINGS OF HEAVEN

INTRODUCTION

Suppose you were a young Mormon elder visiting at the door of a home in Europe. Suppose it is October 1901, just a few days after you had received word that President Lorenzo Snow had passed away.

The man at the door is speaking. He is dressed well and has a rather bemused disdain for you and your companion as he speaks. "Lorenzo Snow! Who is Lorenzo Snow? You say he is a prophet. Well, I have heard of Peter and Paul and many others, but I have never heard of Lorenzo Snow."

"But he is a prophet," you say earnestly. "He traveled thousands of miles for the gospel's sake. He helped with the immigration of thousands of Saints, and he established probably the most successful cooperative enterprise the world has ever known in modern times, at Brigham City, Utah."

The man at the door interrupts, "What can possibly be so great about this place and this man I have never heard of?"

"He was a gentle, kindly man who loved the truth. He was a pure man, and holy—pure enough to see the Lord and holy enough to talk with angels."

"Oh, was he now?" the man says, his voice rising. "And I say that you are a fool and that this Lorenzo Snow was not ever a prophet!"

"He was," you insist patiently. "He was a prophet, and we know it!"

"Well, you can't prove it to me now, for he is dead, as you say.

We shall just have to wait until the glorious judgment to see if you tell the truth about this Lorenzo Snow. Then we shall see."

"Oh, stubborn heart," you think to yourself, "What we could teach you if only you would listen. What you could learn from Lorenzo Snow if only you would study his life and read his sermons. He could teach you so much about your possible destiny! But he is dead now. Soon you will be dead, too. All of us who live now will follow someday, and then there will be that glorious judgment that you so irreverently speak about. And as you say, then we shall see."

LORENZO SNOW'S EARLY LIFE SERVED TO PREPARE HIM FOR THE MISSION HE WAS TO PERFORM

(12-1) He Was Born to a Prosperous Farming Family in Ohio

Oliver and Rosetta Snow were natives of New England and had been married there. After some years and the birth of two daughters, they moved from New England to Ohio, where they had five other children, two more girls and three boys. Lorenzo was the

fifth child but the oldest boy. His parents established themselves as farmers and were soon joined in Portage County, Ohio, by relatives and former friends from New England. As the years rolled along, the Snow family became prosperous and influential. Mantua was an island of easterners in a sea of frontiersmen and westerners—Lorenzo's parents and relatives and many other townspeople were educated, cultured, and cosmopolitan, and they encouraged their children in the pursuit of intellectual honor and social accomplishment. In his turn, Lorenzo received this same encouragement and struggled determinedly to satisfy the expectations of those around him.

(12-2) He Was Decisive, Responsible, and Sound in Judgment When Still a Child

Lorenzo's father was frequently away from home on private and public business. Although Lorenzo was only a child, on such occasions as this he would be left in charge. The responsibilities of a large and prosperous farm seemed no serious obstacle to him. In carrying these early burdens, he was punctual, resolute, energetic, and decisive. As he grew older he would superintend the shipment of farm produce downriver to New Orleans; and although such excursions would require months, he appears to have been ever responsible and equal to the task.

(12-3) As a Child, He Was Taught to Be Sympathetic, Broad-Minded, and Tolerant

His parents were Baptists; but as his sister Eliza Roxey Snow Smith later wrote, "Not of the rigid, iron-bedstead order; their house

was a resort for the good and intelligent of all denominations, and their hospitality was proverbial." (*Biography and Family Record of Lorenzo Snow,* p. 2.) Discussions at home were never allowed to become bigoted or narrow, and Lorenzo, along with his brothers and sisters, was encouraged to form broad acquaintance with people and views representing all locations and levels of society. His frequent shipping excursions to New Orleans gave him much practical opportunity to observe a variety of situations and people.

(12-4) Lorenzo Preferred Books to Other Amusements Normal in Youth

Books were his constant companion. When his attention was not demanded by the responsibilities of the farm, he would take a book and go off where he would not be disturbed. He read widely and became acquainted with history, geography, and literature, both classics and contemporary. It was perhaps due partly to his interest in history that he developed the determination to be a military man.

(12-5) Lorenzo Was Determined to Be a Military Man

He progressed through his secondary studies and his military training. Shortly after his twenty-first birthday, he completed his secondary studies and had won a lieutenant's commission by appointment from the governor of Ohio. His sister recalled, "At length he must have a first class military suit, and no one could make it so precisely to his liking as his sister; she had made his 'freedom suit' (at the time referred to he had passed his twenty-first year), which everyone admired—it fitted him exactly, and

now this most important of all mortal habiliments should be entrusted to no other. I made the suit—it was beautiful, magnificent, and my brother donned it with as much, if not of military pride, of self-satisfaction as ever Napoleon won a battle, but it proved of short duration, for he soon felt that his ambition could not be satisfied without a collegiate education." (Smith, *Biography,* p. 3-4.) Feeling that college would brighten his military prospects, he temporarily laid his military training aside, sold his share of his father's estate, and moved to Oberlin, Ohio, where the Presbyterians had established a widely acclaimed college just a few years before.

(12-6) He Apparently Became Interested in Formal Religion at Oberlin

Lorenzo stayed a year at Oberlin. Although by training and nature he was able to cherish tender regards for the people, he had never been particularly attracted to institutionalized religion, and he said near the end of his term, "If there is nothing better than is to be found here in Oberlin College, goodbye to all religions." (Smith, *Biography,* p. 5.) First his mother and another sister joined the Church, and then his sister Eliza. Lorenzo had deep respect for Eliza's opinions and judgment. He wrote to her at Kirtland and asked many questions about the newly revealed religion. She responded to his questions and also requested that he come to Kirtland and study with Professor Seixas, who had been engaged by the leaders of the Church to teach Hebrew. In the spring of 1836 Lorenzo left Oberlin and moved to Kirtland. He would never be the same.

LORENZO SNOW RECEIVED A WITNESS, CERTAIN AND TRUE

(12-7) He Was Anxious to Know the Prophet Joseph

Not long after Lorenzo had arrived in Kirtland, he was talking with his sister on the street when "Joseph passed by, seemingly in a big hurry. He paused just long enough to be introduced to Lorenzo and to say to Eliza: 'Eliza, bring your brother over to the house to dinner.' She was then boarding at the home of the Prophet and teaching his private school. Lorenzo watched the stranger as far as he could see him, and then remarked to his sister: 'Joseph Smith is a most remarkable man. I want to get better acquainted with him. Perhaps, after all, there is something more to Joseph Smith and to Mormonism than I have ever dreamed.' " (Thomas C. Romney, *The Life of Lorenzo Snow,* p. 23.)

(12-8) Through Study and Faith, Lorenzo Snow Decided He Would Accept Baptism

Lorenzo observed the members of the Church and was astonished with the testimonies of the elders, that they could be so plain and positive about heavenly things. He was astonished at the obviously divine power as it was manifest through the administrations of Patriarch Joseph Smith, Sr.

"Being present at a 'Blessing Meeting,' in the Temple, previous to his baptism into the Church; after listening to several patriarchal blessings pronounced upon the heads of different individuals with whose history he was acquainted, and of whom he knew the Patriarch was entirely ignorant; he was struck with astonishment to hear the peculiarities of those persons positively and plainly referred to in their blessings. And, as he afterwards expressed, he was convinced that an influence, superior to human prescience,

"The manifestation did not immediately follow my baptism, as I had expected, but, although the time was deferred, when I did receive it, its realization was more perfect, tangible and miraculous than even my strongest hopes had led me to anticipate.

"Some two or three weeks after I was baptized, one day while engaged in my studies, I began to reflect upon the fact that I had not obtained a *knowledge* of the truth of the work—that I had not realized the fulfilment of the promise 'he that doeth my will shall know of the doctrine,' and I began to feel very uneasy. I laid aside my books, left the house, and wandered around through the fields under the oppressive influence of a gloomy, disconsolate spirit, while an indescribable cloud of darkness seemed to envelop me. I had been accustomed, at the close of the day, to retire for secret prayer, to a grove a short distance from my lodgings, but at this time I felt no inclination to do so. The spirit of prayer had departed and the heavens seemed like brass over my head. At length, realizing that the usual time had come for secret prayer, I concluded I would not forego my evening service, and, as a matter of formality, knelt as I was in the habit of doing, and in my accustomed retired place, but not feeling as I was wont to feel.

"I had no sooner opened my lips in an effort to pray, than I heard a sound, just above my head, like the rustling of silken robes, and immediately the Spirit of God descended upon me, completely enveloping my whole person, filling me, from the crown of my head to the soles of my feet, and O, the joy and happiness I felt! No

His sister, Eliza R. Snow, introduced him to the Church

dictated the words of the one who officiated." (Smith, *Biography*, p. 9.)

He also studied and diligently compared the claims of Mormonism with ancient Christianity. He recalled:

"Previous to accepting the ordinance of baptism, in my investigations of the principles taught by the Latter-day Saints, which I proved, by comparison, to be the same as those mentioned in the New Testament taught by

Christ and His Apostles, I was thoroughly convinced that obedience to those principles would impart miraculous powers, manifestations and revelations. With sanguine expectation of this result, I received baptism and the ordinance of laying on of hands by one who professed to have divine authority; and, having thus yielded obedience to these ordinances, I was in constant expectation of the fulfilment of the promise of the reception of the Holy Ghost." (Smith, *Biography*, p. 7.)

language can describe the almost instantaneous transition from a dense cloud of mental and spiritual darkness into a refulgence of light and knowledge, as it was at that time imparted to my understanding. I then received a perfect knowledge that God lives, that Jesus Christ is the Son of God, and of the restoration of the holy Priesthood, and the fulness of the Gospel. It was a complete baptism—a tangible immersion in the heavenly principle or element, the Holy Ghost and even more real and physical in its effects upon every part of my system than the immersion by water; dispelling forever, so long as reason and memory last, all possibility of doubt or fear in relation to the fact handed down to us historically, that the 'Babe of Bethlehem' is truly the Son of God; also the fact that He is now being revealed to the children of men, and communicating knowledge, the same as in the Apostolic times. I was perfectly satisfied, as well I might be, for my expectations were more than realized, I think I may safely say in an infinite degree.

"I cannot tell how long I remained in the full flow of the blissful enjoyment and divine enlightenment, but it was several minutes before the celestial element which filled and surrounded me began gradually to withdraw. On arising from my kneeling posture, with my heart swelling with gratitude to God, beyond the power of expression, I felt—I *knew* that He had conferred on me what only an omnipotent being can confer—that which is of greater value than all the wealth and honors worlds can bestow. That night, as I retired to rest, the same wonderful manifestations were repeated, and continued to be for several successive nights. The sweet remembrance of those

Lorenzo Snow as an Apostle

glorious experiences, from that time to the present, bring them fresh before me, imparting an inspiring influence which pervades my whole being, and I trust will to the close of my earthly existence." (Smith, *Biography*, pp. 7-9.)

LORENZO SNOW WANTED TO BE OUT IN FRONT AMONG THOSE WHO SERVE GOD, THOUGH SUCH SERVICE CALLED FOR GREAT SACRIFICE

(12-10) He Wanted to Become an Elder So That He Could Go on a Mission

Throughout the fall of 1836, as the elders returned from their missions, they would bear testimony of the experiences they had enjoyed and of the marvelous things they had seen. Lorenzo Snow listened to these testimonies and wanted to serve as they were serving. At this same time the First Presidency issued a statement desiring that any who wished to be

ordained elders should make their feelings known to the Presidency. Consequently, Lorenzo Snow submitted his name, was found worthy, and was ordained. Within a few weeks he started on the first of many missions that he would serve to spread the truth.

(12-11) It Tried His Natural Integrity to Travel Without "Purse or Scrip"

" . . . I shouldered my valise and started out like the ancient missionaries, 'without purse or scrip,' on foot and alone, to proclaim the restoration of the fulness of the Gospel of the Son of God, and to bear witness of what I had seen and heard, and of the knowledge I had received by the inspiration of the Holy Ghost.

"It was, however, a severe trial to my natural feelings of independence to go without purse or scrip—especially the purse; for, from the time I was old enough to work, the feeling that I 'paid my way' always seemed a necessary adjunct to self respect, and nothing but a positive knowledge that God required it now, as He did anciently of His servants, the Disciples of Jesus, could induce me to go forth dependent on my fellow creatures for the common necessaries of life. But my duty in this respect was clearly made known to me, and I determined to do it." (Smith, *Biography,* p. 15.)

(12-12) He Had Never Thought of Himself as a Preacher, and It Was with Great Difficulty That He Faced His First Congregation

"The first meeting I held was in the neighborhood of my uncle, by the name of Goddard, near the county seat of Medina County, Ohio. The people were notified and a respectable congregation assembled. It was a sore trial to face that audience in the capacity of a preacher, but I believed and felt an assurance that a Spirit of inspiration would prompt and give me utterance. I had sought by prayer and fasting—I had humbled myself before the Lord, calling on Him in mighty prayer to impart the power and inspiration of the holy Priesthood; and when I stood before that congregation, although I knew not one word I could say, as soon as I opened my mouth to speak, the Holy Ghost rested mightily upon me, filling my mind with light and communicating ideas and proper language by which to impart them. The people were astonished and requested another meeting." (Smith, *Biography,* p. 16.)

(12-13) He Would Go to the Ends of the Earth to Serve People Because He Loved Them

"As I pursued my journey, in company with my brethren, many conflicting feelings occupied my bosom—the gardens and fields around our beloved city were exchanged for the vast wilderness which lay spread out before us for a thousand miles. If my mind still glanced onward, there was the stormy main, and, in the far distant perspective, a land of strangers—the field of my mission. We were hastening further, and still further from the mighty magnet—Home! but we knew that the work in which we were engaged was to carry light to those who sat in darkness, and in the Valley of the Shadow of Death, and our bosoms glowed with love and our tears were wiped away." (Letter to Eliza R. Snow, cited in *Tullidge's Quarterly Magazine,* vol. 2, no. 111 [Jan. 1833], p. 381.)

On one of his missionary journeys, Elder Snow left Salt Lake and traveled to England. There another elder was selected to accompany him to Italy. As he watched this elder take painful farewell of his family, Lorenzo was reminded of the tearful goodbyes he had said in Utah nearly six months before. He later said to his new companion: "Did the people of Italy but *know* the heart-rending sacrifices we have made for their sakes, they could have no heart to persecute." (Letter to Brigham Young, cited in *Tullidge's Quarterly Magazine,* 2:384.)

(12-14) Even the Expectations of Martyrdom Could Not Discourage Him from the Missions to Which He Had Been Appointed

As was mentioned in the preceding quote, Lorenzo Snow was called to serve a mission in Italy in 1850. This was the fountainhead of Catholicism, and the people there remained hostile toward any missionary activity of other churches. Laws against proselyting were extant throughout the whole Italian nation and imposed the strictest penalties. From his many letters and statements during the course of this mission, it appears that Lorenzo Snow fully expected persecution and had seriously contemplated the thought that he might suffer worse than persecution. In Rome, on June 27, 1851, he observed a feast day honoring Saint Peter. In a letter written that day to President Brigham Young, Elder Snow commented on the irony of the circumstances. The ancestors of these people had crucified Peter. Now they had built a mighty church in monument to his name and honored him with feasting and celebration—this even as they rejected and persecuted living apostles in their midst. Such an attitude reminded Elder Snow of what Jesus said about the Jewish leaders of his day:

"Woe unto you, scribes and Pharisees, hypocrites! because ye build the tombs of the prophets, and garnish the sepulchres of the righteous,

"And say, If we had been in the days of our fathers, we would not have been partakers with them in the blood of the prophets.

"Wherefore ye be witnesses unto yourselves, that ye are the children of them which killed the prophets." (Matthew 23:29-31.)

Elder Snow must have pondered what the ultimate outcome of such an attitude would mean for him and his companion, for his next words to President Young were these:

"Pleasing reflections—*starvation!—bonds! imprisonment! —and martyrdom!* and subsequent generations paying us divine honors." (Cited in *Tullidge's Quarterly Magazine,* 2:384.)

(12-15) In Addition to His Willingness to Sacrifice, Lorenzo Snow Had Perfect Faith That God Would Protect Him and Help Him in the Course of His Ministry

"One day, as we were taking our noon-tide meal, and our horses were quietly grazing on the prairies, the following scene occurred: A startling shout resounded through our little camp—*To arms! To arms! The Indians are upon us!* We looked and beheld a spectacle, grand, imposing and fearful. Two hundred warriors upon their furious steeds, painted, armed and clothed with all the horrors of war, rushing towards us like a mighty torrent. In a moment we placed ourselves in an attitude of defence [*sic*]. But could we expect with thirty men to withstand this powerful host? Onward came the savage band with accelerated speed, as a mighty rock, loosed from the mountain's brow, rushes impetuously downward, sweeping, overturning, and burying everything in its course. We saw it was their intention to crush us beneath the feet of their foaming

chargers. Now they were within a few paces, and in another moment we should be overwhelmed, when, lo! an alarm like an electric shock struck through their ranks and stayed their career, as an avalanche, sweeping down the mountain side, stops in the midst of its course by the power of a hand unseen—the Lord had said, *Touch not mine anointed and do my prophets no harm!*

"Many incidents occurred which often called forth the remark, that in our past experience, the hand of the Lord had never been more visibly manifested. When we arrived on the banks of the great Missouri, her waters immediately congealed for the first time during the season, thus forming a bridge over which we passed to the other side: this was no sooner accomplished than the torrent ran as before." (Letter to Eliza R. Snow, cited in *Tullidge's Quarterly Magazine,* 2:381.)

It was quiet in the mission home in Hong Kong. The mission president, his assistants, and a number of elders whose mission service had ended were assembled. Those who were leaving had been invited by the president to stand in turn and bear testimony. Elder Kenneth Ching had been serving the Lord. He spoke softly when his turn came. "I am so grateful to see the light of the gospel going to so many of our brothers and sisters here in Hong Kong. I am grateful the Lord has given me the chance to come here and see his love for these people." Then he paused, and with that deep sincerity born of actually doing what he said, concluded, "My only desire in the Lord's service here and in all the years that lay before me, is to be out in front among the workers."
Lorenzo Snow possessed that

same desire—never for the honor, but for the service instead; seldom in the headlines but always in the front lines—to be out in front among the workers. Now, what about you?

"SACRIFICE BRINGS FORTH THE BLESSINGS OF HEAVEN"

(12-16) Lorenzo Snow Established a Cooperative Commonwealth That Was a Unique Social Order and a Successful Demonstration of the Blending of Temporal and Spiritual Affairs

"His first step in the co-operative movement was in the mercantile line. In 1863-64 he commenced by establishing a co-operative store," with stock in shares of $5.00, thus making it possible for people of very moderate circumstances to become shareholders.

"Many difficulties occurred in the start, and the progress was slow, but it steadily gained in the confidence of the people, the stockholders realizing from twenty to twenty-five per cent per annum in merchandise, and in five years it was an acknowledged success. Then, aided by the profits from the mercantile department, an extensive tannery was erected at a cost of $10,000, the people having the privilege of putting in labor as capital; and soon after these departments were in succesful operation, a woolen factory, at a cost of nearly forty thousand dollars, was brought into working order, again taking labor as stock.

"A co-operative sheep-herd, for supplying the factory, was soon added—then co-operative farms, and to these a cheese dairy. Thus one department of industry after another was established, until between thirty and forty departments were combined—all working harmoniously like the wheels of a grand piece of

machinery.'' (Eliza R. Snow, as cited in the *Historical Record*, vol. 6, no. 2 [Feb. 1887], pp. 142-43.)

Those who knew him attributed his great success at Brigham City to his spiritual nature. Said one: ''President Snow's spirituality was highly developed. It was the predominating trait of his character. All other traits were simply adjuncts and accessories clustering around this one great dictator, obedience to its will and assisting to accomplish its aim. For years he preached about and labored in the affairs of this world, but things temporal were only the means to things spiritual. The financier was at all times subservient to the Apostle.'' (Leslie Woodruff Snow, ''President Lorenzo Snow,'' *Young Woman's Journal*, vol. 14, no. 9 [Sept. 1903], p. 392.)

(12-17) During the Persecution That Preceded the Manifesto, the Saints Had Become Neglectful of the Law of Sacrifice

The Edmunds Act of 1862 and the Edmunds Tucker Bill of 1887 were enforced during three decades prior to the issuing of the Manifesto in 1890. During that time the property of the Church was impounded and either sold or the Church was required to pay rent upon it in order to use their own buildings and lands. Because the major properties of the Church were confiscated, it seemed to many members that to pay tithing and other offerings was simply to give means away to be used by the enemies of the Church. The people were not wealthy, and so many of them unwisely decided that they would not pay tithing.

(12-18) President Wilford Woodruff Was Considerably Affected by the Heavy Financial Conditions of the Church

Through almost the whole decade of his administration, President

Woodruff repeatedly noted his sorrow at the financial burdens of the Church. The following entries from his journal are instructive:

''August 8, 1894 'I don't sleep nights and am weary by day. As trustees in trust and the presidency of the church we have taken such a load upon us it is difficult to carry it.'

''August 9, 1894 'There is a heavy load resting upon us in church affairs, our debts are very heavy.'

''December 30, 1896 'The presidency of the church are so overwhelmed in financial matters it seems as though we shall never live to get through with it unless the Lord opens the way in a marvelous manner. It looks as though we shall never pay our debts.'

''April 7, 1897 'I spoke of this financial condition of the church, explained the action of the government officials in starting our debts. I did not want to die until the church and myself as trustee-in-trust are out of debt.' '' (James R. Clark, comp. *Messages of the First Presidency of The Church of Jesus Christ of Latter-day Saints*, 3:304.)

But President Woodruff had done his work, and it remained for his successor to go forward, directed by revelation, and launch the course that would clear the Church of debt. President Woodruff died September 2, 1898, and was succeeded by Lorenzo Snow.

(12-19) In Answer to His Pleas for Guidance in Solving the Financial Crisis, President Snow Was Told by Revelation to Go to St. George, Utah

In early May, 1899, the Lord revealed to President Snow that he and others of the leading brethren should go to St. George (a

settlement in southern Utah) and hold a conference. The Lord did not reveal at that time the purpose of their visit, but merely that they should go and then conduct a series of special conferences in all of the settlements on their return from St. George to Salt Lake City. On Monday, May 15, the party departed by rail for Milford, Utah, and arrived late that night. Early on Tuesday, May 16, they continued their journey by rail to Modena, Utah, where they were met by President McArthur, the stake president of St. George Stake, and they continued on to St. George by carriage, a distance of about thirty miles.

(12-20) As President Snow Was Addressing the Congregation in St. George, the Lord Revealed to Him That the Saints Must Obey the Law of Sacrifice

The first session of the conference in St. George was held May 17, 1899. President Snow's first statement, after the session opened, was this:

''My brethren and sisters, we are in your midst because the Lord directed me to come; but the purpose of our coming is not clearly known at the present, but this will be made known to me during our sojourn among you.'' (Cited in Romney, *Life of Lorenzo Snow*, p. 456.)

In a subsequent session of that same conference, President Snow was speaking and his son later recalled:

''I was sitting at a table reporting the proceedings, when all at once father paused in his discourse, complete stillness filled the room. When he commenced to speak again his voice strengthened and the inspiration of God seemed suddenly to come over him, as well as over the entire assembly.''

(Cited in Romney, *Life of Lorenzo Snow*, p. 456.)

(12-21) The Lord Revealed to President Snow That He Was Extremely Displeased That the Saints Had Neglected the Law of Sacrifice

"Then he revealed to the Latter-day Saints the vision that was before him. God manifested to him there and then the purpose of the call to visit the Saints in the south. He told them that he could see, as he had never realized before, how the law of tithing had been neglected by the people, also that the Saints, themselves, were heavily in debt, as well as the Church, and now through strict obedience to this law—the paying of a full and honest tithing—not only would the Church be relieved of its great indebtedness, but through the blessings of the Lord this would also be the means of freeing the Latter-day Saints from their individual obligations, and they would become a prosperous people." (*Church News*, 20 Jan. 1934, p. 4.)

(12-22) By Paying Tithes and Offerings, the Saints Had the Power to Bring Blessings to the Church and to the Land

There had been drought in southern Utah for eighteen months prior to President Snow's visit, such severe drought that many of the wells and streams had dried up and the situation was critical. President Snow prophesied that if the Saints would obey the law of sacrifice, the drought would be removed and the earth would yield her strength once again. He had been speaking about the ultimate destiny of man, but after he had paused and the Lord had revealed to him the purpose of his visit, his language was plain and revelatory:

"But the Lord requires me to say

something to you, and since I commenced to labor in His interest, I have never failed, thank the Lord, to do that which He has required at my hands; and I shall not do it today, nor any other day, the Lord being my helper. The word of the Lord to you is not anything new; it is simply this: THE TIME HAS NOW COME FOR EVERY LATTER-DAY SAINT, WHO CALCULATES TO BE PREPARED FOR THE FUTURE AND TO HOLD HIS FEET STRONG UPON A PROPER FOUNDATION, TO DO THE WILL OF THE LORD AND PAY HIS TITHING IN FULL. That is the word of the Lord to you, and it will be the word of the Lord to every settlement throughout the land of Zion. . . . the time has come when every man should stand up and pay his tithing in full. The Lord has blessed us and has had mercy upon us in the past; but there are times coming when the Lord requires us to stand up and do that which He has commanded and not leave it any longer. What I say to you in this Stake of Zion I will say to every Stake of Zion that has been organized. There is no man or woman that now hears what I am saying who will feel satisfied if he or she fails to pay a full tithing." (Clark, *Messages of the First Presidency*, 3:312.)

(12-23) President Snow Declared That the Temporal Security of the Saints Depended upon Their Obedience

"You are capable of understanding a proposition when it is presented. . . . I understand all this, but there are certain times when the most simple thing is required to be presented to the Latter-day Saints that does not require great education to understand, it requires only the Spirit of the Lord; that, you certainly possess. . . .

" . . . We wish you to consult yourselves and the Spirit of the Lord in reference to this principle. People who have never paid a cent tithing go into the temples. This law of tithing is one which if it is not kept, the land shall not be sanctified unto those who disobey it, and it shall not be a land of Zion unto them. This is a plain and simple statement and can be understood by the most ignorant. Here we have been getting into debt to the Lord. . . . Many poor people pay tithing and it goes to support the temples, while the other people who pay no tithing at all are permitted to receive the same blessings. What do you suppose the Lord thinks of this? And how far does this go to sanctify and preserve us here in this land? President Young came here and knelt down and sanctified the land and dedicated it to God, and here come thousands of people and ignore that law, which if kept, will preserve us; and if not observed, we will have to leave here, or some general calamity will come upon us." (Clark, *Messages of the First Presidency*, 3:314-16.)

(12-24) He Taught That in Emphasizing the Revelation on Sacrifice, They Were Laying a Foundation in Temporal Matters That Would Endure Forever

"This revelation that was given to me in regard to this matter of tithing that we have talked about in the different settlements, was given me just as fully and I know it just as clearly as any manifestation the Lord ever gave me. . . . The Lord requires it of us now to go to and perform those sacred duties that He required of us in the beginning. He has not urged it upon us in the past as He has some revelations, perhaps, but he requires it now of us. This visit of ours, there is something marvelous about it, from the day we

commenced to talk upon this matter in St. George throughout all the settlements. This will be a matter of record that will go down to generations to come; it will be eternal and everlasting. Everyone of you that has been a member of this company will have this matter renewed to you, and you will see it clearly; and you will see one of the greatest revolutions that has ever been made since this Church was organized, in this matter. There are things connected with it that I can see in the future. . . . '' (Cited in Romney, *Life of Lorenzo Snow*, pp. 462-63.)

THE LIFE OF LORENZO SNOW DEMONSTRATES THE POWER THAT COMES WHEN ONE LIVES THE LAW OF SACRIFICE, SERVING GOD IN WHATEVER WAY HE REQUIRES

(12-25) Though Lorenzo Snow Lived to an Old Age, His Strength, Vitality, and Clarity of Mind Were Unabated

Many people expressed fear that a man of Lorenzo Snow's age would not be capable of standing up under the strains and challenges of the presidency. He was not a large man physically. He was slight of build and appeared deceptively frail and weak, weighing about 125 pounds. But he quickly dispelled such fears. He was erect, strong, active, and full of inspiration up to the time of his last illness at the age of eighty-seven. His clarity of mind was demonstrated again and again as he spoke to the Saints, directed the Church, and moved the kingdom forward toward its destiny. His youngest daughter, born when he was eighty-two, recalled that he was accustomed to carrying her up the stairs on his back up until the last year of his life. More importantly, however, the Lord seemed unconcerned about President Snow's advanced age,

for He it was who called this eighty-four-year-old giant to be His prophet.

(12-26) When President Snow Was Eighty-Five Years Old, He Beat Joseph F. Smith in a Carriage Race

After the conference in St. George, where the revelation on tithing had been received, President Snow and his party made their way by carriage from St. George through as many settlements as possible on their way back to Salt Lake City, preaching at every stop. As the party was traveling between Cove Fort and Fillmore, President Snow's buggy led the procession. The day was clear, and everyone was in good spirits.

"As a rule the party had some difficulty in maintaining the pace, but upon this occasion the President's carriage was jogging along at a most comfortable rate. President Joseph F. Smith, who was second in line, drove along side the President and suggested, 'Perhaps it would be as well to go a

trifle faster over these good roads, President Snow.'

'' 'Very well,' was the answer, 'just follow us.' President Snow gave his teamster a knowing nudge and in another minute both teams were on a forty-mile gait, over sage brush and ditches, and those behind saw only a cloud of dust, with now and then a glimpse of something resembling a buggy top. On and on the horses dashed, and the excitement of the occupants increased with every leap. It was invigorating. The horses had traveled neck and neck for two miles or more. The eyes of the aged leader flashed like diamonds as he rose in his seat and watched the progress of the race.

'' 'Go on, go on!' he shouted, 'never mind the ruts. We'll get beat. Go!' and the driver did so. President Smith's team was slightly outclassed, and the other managed to maintain the lead. Clumps of sage brush and five-foot washouts were as pebbles to these venerable leaders, now thoroughly enshrouded in their boyhood days. Up in the air and down, touching only the high places here and there, the contest lasted for fifteen miles, and President Snow loves to relate how his team came out victorious, though the honors are disputed by President Smith.'' (Cited in Romney, *Life of Lorenzo Snow*, pp. 453, 455.)

(12-27) Because of His Willingness to Serve God, Lorenzo Snow Was Called to Lead the Church at an Age When Many Men Have Retired from Service and Active Living

For eighty-four years Lorenzo Snow's life had been one of preparation and service. He had demonstrated again and again his willingness to fulfill whatever purpose the Lord had asked of him. On the plains of the pioneer trek, through the persecutions of

Italy, in decades of apostleship and leadership, he had shown his commitment to what he had been given shortly after his baptism. Here was a man who could call on the Saints to sacrifice because his life had been a living testimony of his willingness to do the same. It is not surprising, then, to find the Lord unwilling to let him retire at the age of eighty-four. What matters the age of a man to the Lord? And so it was, that even as he prayed earnestly that Wilford Woodruff would outlive him, Lorenzo Snow discovered that the Lord had yet other service to ask of him. And with the call came an accompanying witness of the Lord's acceptance of a noble life of sacrifice.

(12-28) Lorenzo Snow Received a Personal Visitation from the Savior

"For some time President Woodruff's health had been failing. Nearly every evening President Lorenzo Snow visited him at his home. This particular evening the doctors said that President Woodruff could not live much longer, that he was becoming weaker every day. President Snow was greatly worried. We cannot realize today what a terrible financial condition the Church was in at that time—owing millions of dollars and not being able to pay even the interest on its indebtedness.

"My father went to his room in the Salt Lake Temple, dressed in his robes of the Priesthood, knelt at the sacred altar in the Holy of Holies in the House of the Lord and there plead to the Lord to spare President Woodruff's life, that President Woodruff might outlive him and that the great responsibility of Church leadership would not fall upon his shoulders. Yet he promised the Lord that he would devotedly perform any duty

required at his hands. At this time he was in his eighty-sixth year. . . .

[On September 2, 1898, after receiving word of the death of Wilford Woodruff, President Snow went to the temple.]

"President Snow put on his holy temple robes, repaired again to the same sacred altar, offered up the signs of the Priesthood and poured out his heart to the Lord. He reminded the Lord how he plead for President Woodruff's life to be spared, that President Woodruff's days would be lengthened beyond his own; that he might never be called upon to bear the heavy burdens and responsibilities of the Church. 'Nevertheless,' he said, 'Thy will be done. I have not sought this responsibility but if it be Thy will, I now present myself before Thee for Thy guidance and instruction. I ask that Thou show me what Thou wouldst have me do.'

"After finishing his prayer he expected a reply, some special manifestation from the Lord. So he waited,—and waited—and waited. There was no reply, no voice, no visitation, no manifestation. He left the altar and the room in great disappointment. Passing through the Celestial room and out into the large corridor a glorious manifestation was given President Snow which I relate in the words of his grand-daughter, Allie Young Pond. . . .

"'One evening while I was visiting grandpa Snow in his room in the Salt Lake Temple, I remained until the door keepers had gone and the night-watchmen had not yet come in, so grand-pa said he would take me to the main front entrance and let me out that way. He got his bunch of keys from his dresser. After we left his room and while we were still in the large corridor leading into the celestial room, I

was walking several steps ahead of grand-pa when he stopped me and said: "Wait a moment, Allie, I want to tell you something. It was right here that the Lord Jesus Christ appeared to me at the time of the death of President Woodruff. He instructed me to go right ahead and reorganize the First Presidency of the Church at once and not wait as had been done after the death of the previous presidents, and that I was to succeed President Woodruff."

"'Then grand-pa came a step nearer and held out his left hand and said: "He stood right here, about three feet above the floor. It looked as though He stood on a plate of solid gold."

"'Grand-pa told me what a glorious personage the Savior is and described His hands, feet, countenance and beautiful white robes, all of which were of such a glory of whiteness and brightness that he could hardly gaze upon Him.

"'Then he came another step nearer and put his right hand on my head and said: "Now, grand-daughter, I want you to remember that this is the testimony of your grand-father, that he told you with his own lips that he actually saw the Savior, here in the Temple, and talked with Him face to face." ' " (LeRoi C. Snow, "An Experience of My Father's," *Improvement Era*, Sept. 1933, p. 677.)

By revelation, Lorenzo Snow called on the Saints to be obedient to the law of tithing. Obedience of the Saints to that call eventually brought the Church out of debt (in Joseph F. Smith's administration) and established a firm temporal foundation for the kingdom of

God. Much of today's growth of chapels and Church programs around the world is the direct result of the temporal prosperity of the Church that came, and still comes, as the result of Saints living the law of tithing.

But was that the only purpose for the revelation given that day in St. George? If it were merely a matter of financing the kingdom, there were surely more direct ways the Lord could have used. A revelation about the location of some fabulously valuable vein of gold could have removed the debts of the Church in one fell swoop. Notice again the words of the revelation given to the Saints:

"THE TIME HAS NOW COME FOR EVERY LATTER-DAY SAINT, WHO CALCULATES TO BE PREPARED FOR THE FUTURE AND TO HOLD HIS FEET STRONG UPON A PROPER FOUNDATION, TO DO THE WILL OF THE LORD AND PAY HIS TITHING IN FULL." (Cited in Clark, *Messages of the First Presidency*, 3:312.)

Preparation for the future. Feet planted strong on a proper foundation. Obviously the Lord was thinking of more than just financial matters. Principles of spiritual power are revealed here, and they go far beyond the law of tithing. "Do the will of the Lord"—that is the key to preparing for the future and

building a firm foundation. Whether His will is to pay tithing or to give Church service or to serve as a missionary or to do a thousand other things, the principle is the same. Joseph Smith said:

"Let us here observe, that a religion that does not require the sacrifice of all things never has power sufficient to produce the faith necessary unto life and salvation; for, from the first existence of man, the faith necessary unto the enjoyment of life and salvation never could be obtained without the sacrifice of all earthly things. It was through this sacrifice, and this only, that God has ordained that men should enjoy eternal life; and it is through the medium of the sacrifice of all earthly things that men do actually know that they are doing the things that are well pleasing in the sight of God. When a man has offered in sacrifice all that he has for the truth's sake, not even withholding his life, and believing before God that he has been called to make this sacrifice because he seeks to do his will, he does know, most assuredly, that God does and will accept his sacrifice and offering, and that he has not, nor will not seek his face in vain. Under these circumstances, then, he can obtain the faith necessary for him to lay hold on eternal life." (N. B. Lundwall, comp., *A Compilation Containing the*

Lectures on Faith, Lecture Sixth, vs. 7, p. 58.)

In the life of Lorenzo Snow you have a model of commitment to sacrifice and a promise of the power that flows to a person when that commitment to sacrifice is exercised. Do you long for more spiritual power in your own life? Then rejoice when the Lord gives you opportunity to sacrifice. Be it tithing, offerings, welfare service, a full-time mission, or the quiet determination to live a gospel principle in the face of social pressure or personal weakness, the promise is the same. Power will flow into your life when you do the will of the Lord, just as it flowed into the life of Lorenzo Snow. That is one of the great lessons of his life. As one of our hymns explains, "Sacrifice brings forth the blessings of heaven." Here are President Snow's own words:

"It is well for us, once in a while to look away ahead and see what will be the result of all the sacrifices and labors that we endure and perform in this life. . . . Our future is glorious. . . . Those who endure unto the end shall sit upon thrones. . . . All things shall be given unto such men and women. . . . In view of these prospects, what should we not be willing to sacrifice when duty requires?" (Lorenzo Snow in *CR*, Oct. 1898, pp. 55-56. See 13-12 for the full quote.)

CHAPTER 13

AS GOD IS, MAN MAY BE

LORENZO SNOW LEARNED THAT A MAN COULD BECOME AS HIS FATHER IN HEAVEN

INTRODUCTION

"But what is the purpose of it all?" Frank blurted out to his father. "Why do we do all the things we are supposed to do? Yes, I know the Church is true and that we will be judged in eternity for how well we do here. But the requirements here are so precise. And the promises about future blessings are so vague. What are we seeking, really?"

Have you ever felt like Frank? Is it easy for us to sometimes forget the actual objective that we have in the Church? Is it easy for us to begin to think of the Church as an end in itself? Do we ever get so busy paying tithing, holding home evenings, doing home teaching, and all the rest that God requires, that we sometimes forget why we are doing it? If the farmer sees only the plowing, the sowing, the labor of preparation, and loses sight of the harvest, he may become discouraged.

Mortality is a great and glorious opportunity, but it is only a stage of preparation—one tiny aspect of a more grand and glorious eternity. Why is the law so precise, the requirements so high? Perfection sometimes seems so unreachable. Why must we be perfect?

President Lorenzo Snow knew the answers to these questions. He saw things in their eternal perspective and expounded in great detail about the end for which we strive. Once you catch this same vision—the real purpose of mortality—of the Church, of its programs, and of obedience, the need for perfection becomes clear.

(13-1) The Father of the Prophet Joseph Smith Was the First to Speak to Lorenzo About How Great Man May Become

When Lorenzo Snow was in Kirtland attending the Hebrew school, he was in the temple one day to witness a meeting where patriarchal blessings were being given. The Patriarch, Joseph Smith, Sr., was giving blessings to a number of people, some of whose lives Lorenzo was thoroughly familiar with and whom, Lorenzo was certain, Father Smith was not. Lorenzo was astonished to note how Father Smith referred to peculiar and personal qualities of several of the people without having any previous acquaintance with them whatsoever. After the meeting, Lorenzo asked to be introduced to Father Smith, and when this occurred Father Smith said to him: "You will soon be convinced of the truth of the latter-day work, and be baptized. And you will become as great as you can possibly wish—EVEN AS GREAT AS GOD, and you cannot wish to be greater." (Eliza R. Snow Smith, *Biography and Family Record*

of Lorenzo Snow, p. 10.) This was perfectly astonishing to Lorenzo. He thought of his aspirations to make a name for himself scholastically and in a military career. That, he had thought, would make him great. But to be as great as God . . . of this he thought:

"The old gentleman's prediction, that I should ere long be baptized, was strange to me, for I had not cherished a thought of becoming a member of the 'Mormon' Church; but when he uttered the last clause, I was confounded. That, to me, was a big saying, and, I then thought, approaching almost to blasphemy. And why not? After years of study and diligent search after knowledge, in that which most intimately concerned me—'From whence came I?' 'Why am I here?' 'What is my future destiny?' In all this, I was profoundly ignorant. As yet I had received no key that could unlock those mysteries—that could make known, to my satisfaction, my relationship to Him who controls the universe.

"I looked at Father Smith, and silently asked myself the question: Can that man be a deceiver? His every appearance answered in the negative. At first sight, his presence impressed me with feelings of love and reverence. I

had never seen age so prepossessing. Father Joseph Smith, the Patriarch, was indeed a noble specimen of aged manhood.

"But with all my favorable impressions of the Patriarch, that *big saying* was a dark parable." (Smith, *Biography*, p. 10.)

(13-2) By Direct, Personal Revelation, He Received the Knowledge of Man's Possible Destiny

About four years after his baptism, four years during which he had labored zealously and tirelessly on missions throughout several states, Lorenzo was back again in Nauvoo. He had received a call to serve a mission to England and would depart within a few days. He had accepted an invitation to spend an evening in the home of his friend Henry G. Sherwood, and during that evening, while listening to Brother Sherwood's explanation of the parable of the Husbandman in Matthew 22, he later recalled that "the Spirit of the Lord rested mightily upon me—the eyes of my understanding were opened, and I saw as clear as the sun at noon-day, with wonder and astonishment, the pathway of God and man. I formed the following couplet which expresses the revelation, as it was shown to me, and explains Father Smith's dark saying to me at a blessing meeting in the Kirtland temple, prior to my baptism, as previously mentioned in my first interview with the Patriarch:

> As man now is, God once was:
> As God now is, man may be.

I felt this to be a sacred communication which I related to no one except my sister Eliza, until I reached England, when in a confidential, private conversation with President Brigham Young, in Manchester, I related to him this extraordinary manifestation." (Cited in LeRoi C. Snow, "Devotion to a Divine Inspiration," *Improvement Era*, June 1919, p. 656.)

(13-3) Joseph Smith Confirmed and Explained the Revelation Given to Lorenzo Snow

Some three years later, shortly after returning from his mission to England, he related to the Prophet Joseph what he had learned about man's divine potential and how that revelation had affected him. The Prophet assured him: "Brother Snow, that is true doctrine, and it is a revelation from God to you." (*Improvement Era*, June 1919, p. 656.)

The principle had long before been revealed to Joseph Smith and his father. In fact, it was the statement made by the Patriarch four years before his personal revelation, that first awakened the thought in Lorenzo Snow's mind. However, the doctrine was not publically taught until 1844. Lorenzo Snow was present during that April conference in which the Prophet preached a general funeral sermon for an elder in the Church, King Follet, significant paragraphs of which are cited here.

"God himself was once as we are now, and is an exalted man, and sits enthroned in yonder heavens! That is the great secret. If the veil were rent today, and the great God who holds this world in its orbit, and who upholds all worlds and all things by his power, was to make himself visible,—I say, if you were to see him today, you would see him like a man in form—like yourselves in all the person, image, and very form as a man; for Adam was created in the very fashion, image and likeness of God, and received instruction from, and walked, talked and conversed with him, as one man talks and communes with another. . . .

" . . . It is the first principle of the Gospel to know for a certainty the Character of God, and to know that we may converse with him as one man converses with another, and that he was once a man like us; yea, that God himself, the Father of us all, dwelt on an earth, the same as Jesus Christ himself did; and I will show it from the Bible. . . . (Teachings, pp. 345-46.)

(13-4) This Doctrine Became One of the Major Themes of President Snow's Sermons

On May 14, 1971, President Joseph Fielding Smith visited the campus of Snow College in Central Utah and paid tribute to the Snow family, for whom the college was named, by summarizing this doctrine so loved by President Snow. In that address he said:

"I think I can pay no greater tribute . . . than to preach again a glorious doctrine which they taught and which was one of the favorite themes, particularly of President Lorenzo Snow.

"It has been said that one of his favorite passages of scripture was the statement of the Risen Lord to the Beloved John:

" 'To him that overcometh will I grant to sit with me in my throne, even as I also overcame, and am set down with my Father in his throne.'

"The Lord taught this same doctrine to the Nephites, when he said to some of them:

" 'Ye shall have fulness of joy; and ye shall sit down in the kingdom of my Father; yea, your joy shall be full, even as the Father hath given me fulness of joy; and ye shall be even as I am, and I am even as the Father; and the Father and I are one.'

"The teaching here involved is that men may be perfect even as their Father in heaven is perfect. It is that the Father is a glorified, exalted, and perfected Man, who has all power, all might, and all dominion, and who lives in the family unit.

"It is that Christ our Exemplar 'received a fulness of the glory of the Father,' and that we too may advance and progress until we become like them and have

exaltation with them in the celestial kingdom.

"We have been promised by the Lord that if we know how to worship, and know what we worship, we may come unto the Father in his name, and in due time receive of his fulness. We have the promise that if we keep his commandments, we shall receive of his fulness and be glorified in him as he is in the Father.

"This is a doctrine which delighted President Snow, as it does all of us. Early in his ministry he received by direct, personal revelation the knowledge that (in the Prophet Joseph Smith's language), 'God himself was once as we are now, and is an exalted man, and sits enthroned in yonder heavens,' and that men 'have got to learn how to be Gods . . . the same as all Gods have done before.'

"After this doctrine had been taught by the Prophet, President Snow felt free to teach it also, and he summarized it in one of the best known couplets in the Church in these words:

'As man now is, God once was;
'As God now is, man may be.

"This same doctrine has of course been known to the prophets of all the ages. . . .

"Now I hold this glorious hope out to you as the goal toward which all members of the Church should strive. Our whole purpose in life should be to do those things which will enable us to gain eternal life, and eternal life is the name of the kind of life possessed by the Father and the Son; it is exaltation in the eternal realms." (Joseph Fielding Smith, address at Snow College on Snow Day, 14 May 1971, pp. 1-7.)

(13-5) "As Now God Is, So Man May Be—Which Doth Unfold Man's Destiny"

President Snow: "As man now is, God once was"

In later life, Lorenzo Snow wrote a poetic summary of this doctrine. He addressed the poem to the apostle Paul in response to Paul's epistle to the Philippians, especially Philippians 2:5, 6. In the poem he also referred to some of the teachings of the apostle John. (See 1 John 3:2.)

Man's Destiny

"Let this mind be in you, which was also in Christ Jesus, who, being in the form of God, thought it not robbery to be equal with God" (Philippians 2:5, 6).

"Dear Brother:

Hast thou not been unwisely bold,
Man's destiny to thus unfold?
To raise, promote such high desire,
Such vast ambition thus inspire?

Still, 'tis no phantom that we trace
Man's ultimatum in life's race;
This royal path has long been trod
By righteous men, each now a God:

As Abra'm, Isaac, Jacob, too,
First babes, then men—to gods they grew.

As man now is, our God once was;
As now God is, so man may be,—
Which doth unfold man's destiny.

For John declares: When Christ we
see
Like unto him we'll try to be.
And he who has this hope within,
Will purify himself from sin.

Who keep this object grand in
view,
To folly, sin, will bid adieu,
Nor wallow in the mire anew;

Nor ever seek to carve his name
High on the shaft of worldly fame;
But here his ultimatum trace:
The head of all his spirit-race.

Ah, well: that taught by you, dear
Paul,
'Though much amazed, we see it
all;
Our Father God, has ope'd our
eyes,
We cannot view it otherwise.

The boy, like to his father grown,
Has but attained unto his own;
To grow to sire from state of son,
Is not 'gainst Nature's course to
run.

A son of God, like God to be,
Would not be robbing Deity;
And he who has this hope within,
Will purify himself from sin.

You're right, St. John, supremely
right:
Whoe're essays to climb this
height,
Will cleanse himself of sin entire—
Or else 'twere needless to aspire."

(*Improvement Era,* June, 1919, pp.
660-61.)

LORENZO SNOW TAUGHT HOW IT IS THAT MAN MAY BECOME LIKE GOD

(13-6) As an Infant Can Grow to Be a King, So Man Can Grow to Be as God

"As an illustration, here is an infant
upon its mother's breast. It is
without power or knowledge to
feed and clothe itself. It is so
helpless that it has to be fed by its
mother. But see its possibilities!
This infant has a father and a
mother, though it knows scarcely
anything about them. Who is its
father? Who is its mother? Why, its
father is an emperor, its mother is
an empress, and they sit upon a
throne, governing an empire. This
little infant will some day, in all
probability, sit upon his father's
throne, and govern and control the
empire, just as King Edward of
England now sits upon the throne
of his mother. We should have this
in mind; for we are the sons of God,
as much so and more, if possible,
than we are the sons of our earthly
fathers.

"You sisters, I suppose, have read
that poem which my sister, Eliza R.
Snow Smith, composed, years ago,
and which is sung quite frequently
now in our meetings. It tells us that
we not only have a Father in 'that
high and glorious place.' but that
we have a Mother, too; and you
sisters will become as great as your
Mother, if you are faithful."
(Lorenzo Snow, cited in Snow,
"Devotion to a Divine Inspiration,"
p. 658.)

(13-7) They Shall Organize Worlds and Rule Over Them as Gods

"Only a short time before his
death, President Snow visited the
Brigham Young University, at
Provo. President Brimhall escorted
the party through one of the
buildings; he wanted to reach the
assembly room as soon as possible,
as the students had already
gathered. They were going
through one of the kindergarten
rooms; President Brimhall had
reached the door and was about to
open it and go on when President
Snow said: 'Wait a moment,
President Brimhall, I want to see
these children at work; what are
they doing?' Brother Brimhall
replied that they were making clay
spheres. 'That is very interesting,'
the President said. 'I want to watch
them.' He quietly watched the
children for several minutes and
then lifted a little girl, perhaps six
years of age, and stood her on a
table. He then took the clay sphere
from her hand, and, turning to
Brother Brimhall, said:

" 'President Brimhall, these
children are now at play, making
mud worlds, the time will come
when some of these boys, through
their faithfulness to the gospel, will
progress and develop in
knowledge, intelligence and
power, in future eternities, until
they shall be able to go out into
space where there is unorganized
matter and call together the
necessary elements, and through
their knowledge of and control
over the laws and powers of
nature, to organize matter into
worlds on which their posterity
may dwell, and over which they
shall rule as gods.' " (Snow,
"Devotion to a Divine Inspiration,"
pp. 658-59.)

PRESIDENT SNOW STRESSED THAT GOSPEL OBEDIENCE IS THE ONLY PATH TO GODHOOD

(13-8) You Have Got to Learn How to Be Gods Yourselves

From Joseph Smith, Lorenzo Snow
learned the necessity of
progressing in righteousness to
become as God. In the April
Conference of 1844 mentioned
earlier, the Prophet said:

"Here, then, is eternal life—to
know the only wise and true God;
and you have got to learn how to be
Gods yourselves, and to be kings
and priests to God, the same as all
Gods have done before you,
namely, by going from one small
degree to another, and from a small
capacity to a great one; from grace

to grace, from exaltation to exaltation, until you attain to the resurrection of the dead, and are able to dwell in everlasting burnings, and to sit in glory, as do those who sit enthroned in everlasting power." (Smith, *Teachings*, pp. 345-47.)

(13-9) Because We Are His Children, We Have the Seeds of His Divinity Within Ourselves

" . . . we may look forward far away into the spirit-land, with full assurance that when reaching that happy clime, we shall be crowned with the sons and daughters of God, and possess the wealth and glory of a Celestial kingdom. . . .

"We are the offspring of God, begotten by Him in the spirit world, where we partook of His nature as children here partake of the likeness of their parents. Our trials and sufferings give us experience, and establish within us principles of godliness." (Lorenzo Snow in *JD*, 26:368.)

(13-10) The Trial of Mortality Is the School of Perfection

"Deity is within us, our spiritual organization is Deity—the child of God, begotten in his image. . . . "We are here that we may be educated in a school of suffering and of fiery trials, which school was necessary for Jesus our elder brother, who, the scriptures tell us, was made perfect through suffering. It is necessary we suffer in all things, that we may be qualified and worthy to rule and govern all things, even as our Father in heaven and his eldest son Jesus. . . .

"And now, where is the man among you having once burst the veil and gazed upon this purity, the glory, the might, majesty, and dominion of a perfected man, in celestial glory, in eternity, will not cheerfully resign life, suffer the

President Lorenzo Snow

most excruciating tortures, let limb be torn from limb sooner than dishonor or resign his priesthood. . . .

. . . "Your hearts, your thoughts and feelings, are no longer associated with those Babylonish schemes which chain thought and reason, making it blasphemy for man to dare speak of the nobility of his birth, and true being of his Father in Heaven. . . . " (Lorenzo

Snow, cited in Thomas C. Romney, *The Life of Lorenzo Snow*, p. 135.)

(13-11) We Should Keep the Promises We Have Received Ever Before Us

"I cannot imagine anything that is so vastly important as to work for and obtain one's own individual exaltation and glory. That undoubtedly is one great purpose for which we came into the world. . . . Paul said, he pressed

Elder Snow as an Apostle

forward toward the mark in the high calling of God in Christ Jesus. Now this is a very good principle for us to keep constantly before us day by day, month by month and year by year. We should labor for perfection so far as possible, and seek to go onward.'' (Lorenzo Snow in *CR*, Apr. 1898, p. 12.)

(13-12) We Should Be Willing to Sacrifice Whatever May Be Necessary

''It is well for us, once in a while to look away ahead and see what will be the result of all the sacrifices and labors that we endure and perform in this life. This existence is but a moment; but the other life is continuous from eternity to eternity. . . . Our future is glorious. We could not desire more for our happiness than has been prepared for us. Those who endure unto the end shall sit upon thrones, as Jesus hath overcome and sat down upon His Father's throne. All things shall be given unto such men and women, so we are told in the revelations we have received. In view of these prospects, what should we not be willing to sacrifice when duty requires? . . . The glory that is before us is open to every man and every woman, through this Gospel, which is the power of God unto salvation, glory and exaltation, in the fulness thereof. We have learned some things that are more valuable to us than a gold mine of the highest richness could possibly be. We are the offspring of God, He is our Father, and we have a mother in the other life as well. These women that are sealed to us for time and eternity will, with our children be ours in the other life, going on in honor and glory. The Lord has revealed this to us, and we know it is so.'' (Lorenzo Snow in *CR*, Oct. 1898, pp. 55-56.)

(13-13) We Should Work Earnestly to Receive the Blessings Conditioned upon Our Obedience

''There is great enjoyment to be had in having done right in the past and meditating upon the fact, and feeling that we are doing right now, because it is the privilege of every Latter-day Saint to know when he is doing that which pertains to the things of the Lord. If our past conduct has been such, and our present conduct is such that we will be entitled to receive glory and exaltation, and have our bodies free from disease and death, and be crowned with immortal glory in the midst of our wives, children and friends, worlds without end, these are contemplations which cause us to enjoy ourselves. This is the way Latter-day Saints should live. . . . There is this privilege that every Latter-day Saint should seek to enjoy, to know positively that his work is accepted of God. I am afraid Latter-day Saints are not much better and perhaps they are worse than other people if they do not have this knowledge and seek to do right. . . .

''Every man having this hope in him purifies himself. There then naturally arises a determination to work for that high and noble position, to work for those wonderful promises made. There

The General Authorities (Sept. 1898)
Back, L. to R.: M. F. Cowley, A. O. Smoot, Geo. Teasdale, F. M. Lyman, J. H. Smith, H. J. Grant, J. W. Taylor, and M. W. Merrill
Front: Brigham Young, Jr.; Franklin D. Richards; President Lorenzo Snow; George Q. Cannon; Joseph F. Smith; and A. H. Lund

is an inducement to pursue a course of righteousness.'' (Lorenzo Snow in *CR*, Apr. 1898, p. 13.)

(13-14) We Should Try to Be Better Today Than We Were Yesterday

''We ought to improve ourselves and move faster toward the point of perfection. It is said that we cannot be perfect. Jesus has commanded us to be perfect even as God, the Father, is perfect. It is our duty to try to be perfect, and it is our duty to improve each day, and look upon our course last week and do things better this week; do things better today than we did

them yesterday, and go on and on from one degree of righteousness to another. Jesus will come by and by, and appear in our midst, as He appeared in the day when upon the earth among the Jews, and He will eat and drink with us and talk to us, and explain the mysteries of the Kingdom, and tell us things that are not lawful to talk about now.'' (Lorenzo Snow in *CR*, Apr. 1898, pp. 13-14.)

(13-15) We Require Divine Assistance to Overcome the World

''We are dependent upon the Spirit of the Lord to aid us and to

manifest to us from time to time what is necessary for us to accomplish under the peculiar circumstances that may surround us. It is the privilege of Latter-day Saints, when they get into difficulties, to have supernatural power of God, and in faith, day by day; to secure from the circumstances which may surround us that which will be beneficial and advance us in the principles of holiness and sanctification, that we may as far as possible be like our Father. It certainly is possible to advance ourselves toward the perfections of

the Almighty to a very considerable extent, to say the least. In fact, we are commanded to be perfect, even as our Father in heaven is perfect. From everything that arises, whether it be of a disagreeable nature or of a pleasant character, we should derive information and secure power to serve ourselves in the path of exaltation and glory over which we are moving.'' (Lorenzo Snow in *CR,* Oct. 1898, p. 2.)

What is the ultimate destiny of righteous men and women, sealed together and exalted by their faithfulness and obedience on the earth? The resurrected Jesus said to the beloved apostle John:

[Read Revelation 3:21.]

How is Christ the example? What shall be the status of those who overcome the world and become one with Christ? To others, Jesus gave this reassurance:

[Read 3 Nephi 28:10.]

What is Jesus expressing to these men? What does eternity hold in store for them? Is God jealous of his station to the extent that he is loath to see his children rise up to the perfection of glory, knowledge, and power that he has obtained? Is it wrong to strive to be like him?

[Read Philippians 2:5-12.]

What is the significance of these passages? When Jesus lived in the world, was his glory manifested publicly for all to see, or was it tabernacled within him? Will his personal glory be manifest to the world someday? Will the personal glory of his followers be manifest someday? Study these verses carefully and ponder the significance of the message they contain:

[1 John 2:27, 28; 3:1-3
D&C 130:18-21
D&C 50:24
D&C 93:19, 20, 27, 28]

These passages were those cited most often by Lorenzo Snow in his sermons about the destiny of righteous men. It was his desire that the Saints understand who and what God is and who and what they are. Has your reading of his words given you a sense of what is your own great potential? God is a perfected, glorified and exalted man who has all power, dominion, and might, and because you, too, are man, of the same race as he, you can become what he is as you obey the same law.

LORENZO SNOW TAUGHT THAT MAN MAY RECEIVE ASSURANCE HERE OF THE DESTINY THAT AWAITS THEM THERE

(13-16) He Knew What Would Happen to the Faithful

''I devoted myself to be worthy to receive something that no mortal man can receive except through the spirit and power of the Holy Ghost, and the Lord has shown me things and made me to understand them as clearly as the sun at noonday in regard to what shall be the outcome of those Latter-day Saints that are faithful to their callings. . . .

''There are many Scriptures bearing upon this point. I believe in this. I believe that we are the sons and daughters of God, and that He has bestowed upon us the capacity for infinite wisdom and knowledge, because He has given us a portion of Himself.'' (Lorenzo Snow in *CR,* Apr. 1898, pp. 62-63.)

(13-17) He Taught That We Too Have a Right to This Understanding

'' . . . as we advance in years and come nearer to what we generally consider as the time of our departure into the other life we are more inclined to devote our thoughts and reflections upon those things that we anticipate we may receive in the next life. . . . We have a perfect right to understand something of what we may receive in the other life. We have to suffer almost everything in accomplishing the duties that are imposed upon us in moving along in this line that we have chosen. . . . It has proved very truly with the Latter-day Saints what Jesus said on a certain occasion, when He compared the kingdom of God to a man seeking pearls. Having found one of very great value, he went and sold all that he possessed that he might secure that pearl. Then again He compared it unto a man that found a treasure in a field, which, having found, he went and sold everything that he possessed in order that he might come in possession of that treasure. That has been the case with the Latter-day Saints. We have been called to suffer and to sacrifice that which was more dear to ourselves than our lives, and some have been called to sacrifice their mortal existence, having been placed in circumstances that they could not avoid suffering the loss of their lives. We are called upon daily to make sacrifices. The Lord requiring this at our hands, and we as a general thing having complied, it is our privilege to know something in regard to the future—what will be the result of this sacrifice, what will be the result of traveling upon this path. Indeed a Latter-day Saint can hardly sustain himself in the Church of God unless he does get some knowledge of this kind, that cannot be unfolded by common wisdom. We are no better than

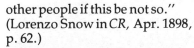

other people if this be not so."
(Lorenzo Snow in *CR*, Apr. 1898,
p. 62.)

He walked among other men throughout an extended life. He was subject in this world to all that other men received. But his mind comprehended eternity and his eye penetrated to see where most men do not. His religion was not obedience for the sake of obedience. The progress of the Church on the earth was only incidental to the cause of his hope and assurance. He saw the end of the gospel, its object and purpose, to a degree that was majestic in its simplicity. Lorenzo Snow did not worship the gospel, but he used the gospel to worship God, to seek God, and to seek to become like God. And he sought diligently to teach the Saints to do the same.

And now what of you? For you have the same gospel and the same ordinances. As now God is, so you may be as well, if only you will.

St. George Tabernacle, where he received his revelation on sacrifice

UNIT SEVEN
JOSEPH F. SMITH
Sixth President of the Church

OVERVIEW

Joseph F. Smith was enveloped in a storm even before he was old enough to understand. Faithfulness and valor had earned for him a trusted foreordination in the eternal worlds. From the peace and glory of the celestial realms, on November 13, 1838, he was born into the midst of severe persecution of the saints of God. His father, Hyrum Smith, along with his uncle, the Prophet Joseph, were imprisoned. His mother, Mary Fielding, ill from physical and emotional strain, had to have help taking care of him and the five other children of Hyrum. Indeed it was as though he had been born in a storm and would not find relief therefrom until his death seventy-eight years later.

The youth of Joseph F. Smith was unusually strenuous. It served to mature him beyond his years. He lost his father to the assassins of Carthage when he was six, drove an ox team over two hundred miles from Nauvoo to Winter Quarters at the age of eight, and became a responsible herd boy at the age of nine. Sober and trustworthy, he saved the pioneers' cattle from an Indian attack, worked with his family to prepare for the trek west, and again drove his own team of oxen over one thousand miles to Salt lake City. Tender and caring, he would throw his arms about the necks of his animals and cry when they lowed from strain, fatigue, and thirst.

In the Valley, at the age of ten, he was again placed in charge of the family herd, but he added to that labor plowing, canyon work, farming, and harvesting. He was untiring, dependable, robust. He never lost an animal that was in his care.

When he was fourteen his mother died. At fifteen he was ordained an elder and began a three-year mission in Hawaii; he overcame fatigue, severe illness and material loss by flood and fire; he learned the native tongue in a mere 100 days; and he preached, healed the sick,

cast out devils, and presided over numerous branches of the Church. Faith filled, dedicated, hard working, he was ordained a seventy when he returned and then a year later was made a high priest and a stake high councilor. He joined the militia, helped intercept Johnston's Army, took part in Indian expeditions. At age twenty-one he married, at twenty-two he served his second mission—this time to Great Britain, where he presided over a number of districts. After being home again for only five months, he was called back to Hawaii on a third mission, where he served as an assistant to two apostles.

Home again, he was employed in the Church Historian's Office and acted as recorder and officiator in the Endowment House. He was called to practice plural marriage and received five wives over a period of years. Thoughtful and kind, he deeply loved his wives and children. "The riches of all my earthly joys is in my precious children."[1]

The Spirit whispered, the call came, and he was ordained an apostle of the Lord. While holding this office, he served as European Mission President, as a counselor in the MIA, a counselor in the First Presidency, a councilman on both the Salt Lake City and Provo City councils, and as a member of the territorial legislature; he also presided over the state constitutional convention of 1882. Fearless and articulate, he was a powerful preacher and writer. As a tool of the Holy Spirit, he could make tears well, joy distill, and men and women forget the fatigue of a long journey. Once a veteran newsman became so enthralled with his talk that he forgot to take notes. Joseph F. Smith turned these gifts to the defense of the kingdom—denouncing its enemies, defending its truths—until he became known as the fighting apostle.[2] Obedient, respectful, one of the greatest trials of his life was leaving his family for years, but under the direction of John Taylor he did so to

avoid arrest during the so-called Mormon Crusade in which the Church was persecuted for plural marriage. Much of that time he spent in Hawaii directing the work there. Far away, powerless, indignant, and suffering from the most acute illness of his life, he heard about the harrassment of the Saints, his family's forced abandonment of their home, the death of a child. Determined, unfaltering, he wrote, "Trials are necessary to the perfection of mankind, as friction is necessary to separate the dross of human judgment from the pure gold of divine wisdom."[3] Finally the day of amnesty came, and the home found joy as its father returned.

At the death of President Lorenzo Snow in 1901, the office of president of the Church fell upon the shoulders of Joseph F. Smith. But this had been foretold. Two inspired prophets had before said it would be.[4] As prophet, he continued the emphasis on tithing begun by President Snow and finally saw the Church completely free from debt. He issued doctrinal statements and was a great instrument in turning away hatred, bigotry, and persecution, but not before he was put under one of the greatest trials he ever endured. An anti-Mormon faction, its leader filled with almost murderous hate, launched a verbal attack against President Smith. vilified and lampooned in newspapers, maliciously lied about, the "fighting apostle" would not so much as write a letter in his own defense. He insisted all must be forgiven. Truth would eventually dominate. Indeed it did. Upon his death many of those who had been bitter enemies, enlightened by the purity and strictness of his life, wrote words of sorrow and praise.

In greatness he had led the Church. He refused to let the abuse canker his soul or diminish his love. With humble endurance came power; the veil drew thin, and he was permitted to see the Savior, the spirit world, and the things of God. To the end he bore a fervent witness of Christ, whose servant he was.

CHAPTER 14

PREPARING THE SAINTS FOR THE CHALLENGES OF THE TWENTIETH CENTURY

INTRODUCTION

Members of the mob-militia gathered outside the Far West home of Hyrum Smith. The voice of Reverend Bogart, a fiery preacher who had been a major force in inspiring mob hatred toward the Saints, could be heard. Inside, Mary Fielding Smith lay sick in bed. Her sister, Mercy Thompson, concerned that Mary might not recover from her illness, tried to quiet her own fears and reassure her sister.

Mary's serious condition had been aggravated emotionally when her husband was yanked away from his home under bayonet point; a fiendish guard told Mary to say her last farewell to Hyrum, for she need not suppose she would see him alive again. And she had suffered physically, for not two weeks later, already weak, she gave birth to her first child. She named him after her beloved brother, Joseph Fielding. So taxed had she been that she did not have sufficient strength even to nurse her little son. And so Mercy, whose husband had been forced to flee to save his life, moved in with Mary to care for her and nurse her child.

Though members of the militia had forced their way into many homes on the pretext of searching for arms (but in reality had used the opportunity to plunder and abuse the Saints), up to this hour the two sisters had not been molested. In a moment the ruffians were within their home. Not caring for anyone's condition, the mobbers forced all but the baby Joseph into one area of the house

and then began to loot and pillage. They broke into a trunk and helped themselves to its contents. Others in another room picked up a bed made on the floor and threw it on top of another bed during their frantic search for loot. In their disregard for life they had totally buried the infant Joseph beneath the suffocating weight of the bedding.

Having taken what they wanted, the mobbers departed as swiftly as they had come. It took some moments for the household to recover from their fright. Suddenly Joseph F. was remembered. In great anxiety the quilts and blankets were pulled from the bed and the small baby recovered. Though buried for some time and blue from lack of oxygen, he had been spared from death. Mary held the tiny infant in her arms, grateful that he had survived.

Little did she realize on that cold December day in 1838 that in her arms was one who, with profound vision and inspiration, would help to prepare the members of the kingdom of God for the challenges and

tribulations of the twentieth century. And although those challenges would be different from those experienced by Church members that winter in Missouri, they would be a great threat to the Saints in a future day.

JOSEPH F. SMITH WAS RECOGNIZED EARLY AS ONE WHO WOULD LEAD THE CHURCH OF JESUS CHRIST

(14-1) The Lord Knew Him and Protected Him from the Adversary and His Servants

"I believe that the Lord knew him before he ever came here, and I believe that when Joseph F. Smith was born in Missouri that God knew him, and I believe that Lucifer, the 'son of the morning,' knew him, and that he, the adversary of all good, sought to destroy him. Perhaps it is not generally known, but Lucifer knows it, that, at Far West, Missouri, in the fall of 1838, when he was but a few weeks old the mob tried to destroy him. The leader of that mob, a minister of the gospel, in ransacking the home of the mother of President Smith and trying to find valuables for which he sought, found the child lying upon a bed, a helpless infant, and threw the bedding over him, and the infant, now our President, was nearly smothered when he was discovered. I believe that he was recognized by Lucifer, that he was to become a great leader in Israel." (Samuel O. Bennion in *CR*, Oct. 1917, p. 121.)

(14-2) The Spirit Directed His Call to the Apostleship

"July 1, 1866, Joseph F. Smith met with President Brigham Young and

a number of the Apostles in the upper room in the Historian's Office, in a council and prayer meeting according to the custom of the presiding brethren; Joseph F. was the secretary of this council. After the close of the prayer circle, President Brigham Young suddenly turned to his brethren and said, 'Hold on, shall I do as I feel lead? I always feel well to do as the Spirit constrains me. It is my mind to ordain Brother Joseph F. Smith to the Apostleship, and to be one of my counselors.' He then called upon each of the brethren present for an expression of their feelings, and each responded individually stating that such action met with their hearty approval. The brethren then laid their hands upon the head of Joseph F. . . . '' (Joseph Fielding Smith, comp., *Life of Joseph F. Smith*, pp. 226-27.)

(14-3) The Call of Joseph F. Smith to the Presidency Had Been Predicted on Several Occasions by Leading Brethren in the Church

"Interestingly, both Presidents Wilford Woodruff and Lorenzo Snow had prophesied that Joseph F. Smith would sometime become president of the Church. Thirty-seven years earlier in the Hawaiian Islands when President Snow, then a member of the Council of Twelve, nearly lost his life by drowning, he declared that the Lord made known to him 'that this young man, Joseph F. Smith . . . would some day be the Prophet of God on the earth.' President Woodruff was once relating to a group of children some incidents in the life of the Prophet Joseph Smith. 'He turned to Elder Joseph F. Smith and asked him to arise to his feet. Elder Smith complied. ''Look at him, children,'' Wilford Woodruff said, ''for he resembles the Prophet Joseph more than any man living. He will

become the President of The Church of Jesus Christ of Latter-day Saints. I want everyone of you to remember what I have told you this morning.'' ' After President Woodruff's death, President Snow told Joseph F. Smith that the spirit of God whispered to him that he, Joseph, would succeed him, Lorenzo, as president of the Church.'' (Joseph Fielding Smith, Jr., and John J Stewart, *The Life of Joseph Fielding Smith*, p. 124.)

Joseph F. Smith, an Apostle at age 27

(14-4) Through Complete Dedication to the Savior, He Lived to Fulfill His Divinely Appointed Mission

Elder Melvin J. Ballard, an apostle closely associated with President Smith, stated:

"I recall my early recollections of President Smith with a good deal of pleasure—because I admired him, he was to me my ideal, I tried in my life, as I became acquainted with him, to be as he was. I knew as a

child, for the Lord revealed it unto me, that President Smith would some day preside over this Church; and in connection with that I saw many things that President Smith would do; and when, last October, he stood before the congregations of the Saints, . . . I knew that all that the Lord had for President Smith to do had been done. That which I saw as a child was fulfilled, finished, completed." (*CR*, Apr. 1919, p. 68.)

AS PRESIDENT OF THE CHURCH, JOSEPH F. SMITH CONTINUED TO PREPARE THE SAINTS FOR THE ASSAULTS OF THE ADVERSARY WHICH WOULD BE LAUNCHED THROUGHOUT THE TWENTIETH CENTURY

Do you need the vision and perspective of the angels to understand that the day rapidly approaches when Satan and his kingdom of spiritual Babylon shall crumble and collapse? (See D&C 1:16; 64:24; Revelation 18:1-24.) Many in the world sense the danger signs and the symptoms of deep sickness in our society, and yet they look not to God nor to his servants for solutions and for salvation. They trust in their own wisdom, which ultimately contributes to the problem rather than solves it. And yet those humble men called by God in this last dispensation to offer prophetic guidance continue to see ahead of their time, warning of conditions which will be of the greatest threat to the Saints, often before those conditions have fully developed.

But for those who will trust in God and look to his servants for counsel, the results are clearly foretold: " . . . the day cometh that they who will not hear the voice of the Lord, neither the

voice of his servants, neither give heed to the words of the prophets and apostles, shall be cut off from among the people." (D&C 1:14.)

Think in such terms as you now read of Joseph F. Smith and his exercise of the prophetic calling. With the enlarged perspective given us by time, we can now see the effects of those things which had barely surfaced in his time, but of which he warned us.

(14-5) As a Tool of the Holy Spirit, Light and Power Flowed from President Smith

"As a preacher of righteousness, who could compare with him? He was the greatest that I ever heard—strong, powerful, clear, appealing. It was marvelous how the words of living light and fire flowed from him. He was a born preacher, and yet he did not set himself up to be such. He never thought highly of his own good qualities. Rather, he was simple, plain and unaffected to the last degree; and yet, there was a dignity with it all which enabled anyone and everyone to say: 'He is a man among men!' I ask, as preacher, leader, teacher, husband, father, citizen and man, who among our mighty ones can be likened unto him?" (Charles W. Nibley, cited in Joseph F. Smith, *Gospel Doctrine*, p. 522.)

(14-6) Through the Power of Inspiration, He Identified Three Dangers Which the Church Would Face

"There are at least three dangers that threaten the Church within, and the authorities need to awaken to the fact that the people should be warned unceasingly against them. As I see these, they are flattery of prominent men in the world, false educational ideas, and sexual

impurity." (Smith, *Gospel Doctrine*, pp. 312-13.)

The statement you have just read was issued in 1914. Consider for a moment the prophetic context of President Smith's warning. At that time the Church was still under attack by newspapers and magazines around the world. President Smith was being vilified and lampooned by many men who might have been considered prominent in the world. No one of worldly importance seemed to want to flatter anyone in the Church. False educational ideas, such as those attacking the belief that God created the earth, or even that he existed, had not yet flowered. And although immorality was a concern, the seductive philosophy of the "new morality" had not yet been given its illigitimate birth.

From your perspective in the final quarter of the twentieth century, would you say that the Church has indeed been tried in each of these areas?

(14-7) Joseph F. Smith Stressed the Need for Moral Cleanliness, That the Spirit of Man Might Not Be Robbed of Power and Life

"Not alone is it fundamentally proper and in strict accord with both the spirit and the letter of the Divine Word, but absolutely essential to the stability of the social order that the marriage relation shall be defined and regulated by secular law. Parties to the marriage contract must be definitely invested with the responsibilities of the status they assume; and for fidelity to their obligations they are answerable to each other, to society, and to their God. . . .

"Like many bodily diseases, sexual crime drags with itself a train of other ills. As the physical effects of

drunkenness entail the deterioration of tissue, and disturbance of vital functions, and so render the body receptive to any distemper to which it may be exposed, and at the same time lower the powers of resistance even to fatal deficiency, so does unchastity expose the soul to divers spiritual maladies, and rob it of both resistance and recuperative ability. The adulterous generation of Christ's day were deaf to the voice of truth, and through their diseased state of mind and heart, sought after signs and preferred empty fable to the message of salvation." (Joseph F. Smith, "Unchastity the Dominant Evil of the Age," *Improvement Era*, June 1917, pp. 739-42.)

(14-8) He Taught That the Ideal Home Was the Most Sacred Institution of Heaven and a Fountain of All Righteousness

"There is no substitute for the home. Its foundation is as ancient as the world, and its mission has been ordained of God from the earliest times. . . . The home then is more than a habitation, it is an institution which stands for stability and love in individuals as well as in nations. . . .

"The very foundation of the kingdom of God, of righteousness, of progress, of development, of eternal life and eternal increase in the kingdom of God, is laid in the divinely ordained home; and there should be no difficulty in holding in the highest reverence and exalted thought, the home, if it can be built upon the principles of purity, of true affection, of righteousness and justice. The man and his wife who have perfect confidence in each other, and who determine to follow the laws of God in their lives and fulfil the measure of their mission in the

earth, would not be, and could never be, contented without the home. Their hearts, their feelings, their minds, their desires would naturally trend toward the building of a home and family and of a kingdom of their own; to the laying of the foundation of eternal increase and power, glory, exaltation and dominion, worlds without end." (Smith, *Gospel Doctrine*, pp. 300, 304.)

(14-9) He Emphasized the Need for, and the Blessings That Come to, the Home Where the Patriarchal Order Is Followed

"There is no higher authority in

President Joseph F. Smith

matters relating to the family organization, and especially when that organization is presided over by one holding the higher Priesthood, than that of the father. The authority is time honored, and among the people of God in all dispensations it has been highly respected and often emphasized by the teachings of the prophets who were inspired of God. The patriarchal order is of divine origin and will continue throughout time and eternity. . . . Wives and children should be taught to feel that the patriarchal order in the kingdom of God has been established for a wise and

beneficent purpose, and should sustain the head of the household and encourage him in the discharge of his duties, and do all in their power to aid him in the exercise of the rights and privileges which God has bestowed upon the head of the home. This patriarchal order has its divine spirit and purpose, and those who disregard it under one pretext or another are out of harmony with the spirit of God's laws as they are ordained for recognition in the home. It is not merely a question of who is perhaps the best qualified. Neither is it wholly a question of who is living the most worthy life. It is a question largely of law and order, and its importance is seen often from the fact that the authority remains and is respected long after a man is really unworthy to exercise it." (Smith, *Gospel Doctrine*, pp. 286-87.)

(14-10) The Home: A Fortress in the Satanic Battlefield of the Twentieth Century

With the exception of war, perhaps no other factor characterizes the twentieth century better than the battle against the family. Many forces are at work tearing at the foundations of this God-ordained institution. Loud, strong voices full of seductive appeal cry from all sides. Abortion, alternate forms of marriage, homosexuality, women's so-called liberation, and the limiting of children are all loudly proclaimed with a kind of messianic piety and self-righteousness. The proponents of these insidious movements express loud indignation when any would defend the most noble institution God has revealed to save his children.

Long before any of these were critical issues, the Lord inspired his prophet. President Joseph F. Smith recognized the need to strengthen the homes of the Saints so that they might effectively combat those forces which would try to pull the home apart. An official announcement issued in 1915 urged the Saints to begin a program which would be the basis of a strong and happy home. This announcement read, in part, as follows:

" . . . we advise and urge the inauguration of a 'Home Evening' throughout the Church, at which time fathers and mothers may gather their boys and girls about them in the home and teach them the word of the Lord. They may thus learn more fully the needs and requirements of their families; at the same time familiarizing themselves and their children more thoroughly with the principles of the Gospel of Jesus Christ. This 'Home Evening' should be devoted to prayer, singing hymns, songs, instrumental music, scripture-reading, family topics and specific instruction on the principles of the gospel, and on the ethical problems of life, as well as the duties and obligations of children to parents, the home, the Church, society and the nation. For the smaller children appropriate recitations, songs, stories and games may be introduced. Light refreshments of such a nature as may be largely prepared in the home might be served.

"Formality and stiffness should be studiously avoided, and all the family participate in the exercises.

"These gatherings will furnish opportunities for mutual confidence between parents and children, between brothers and sisters, as well as give opportunity for words of warning, counsel and advice by parents to their boys and girls. They will provide opportunity for the boys and girls

to honor father and mother, and to show their appreciation of the blessings of home so that the promise of the Lord to them may be literally fulfilled and their lives be prolonged and made happy. . . .

"If the Saints obey this counsel, we promise that great blessings will result. Love at home and obedience to parents will increase. Faith will be developed in the hearts of the youth of Israel, and they will gain power to combat the evil influence and temptations which beset them." (The First Presidency [Joseph F. Smith, Anthon H. Lund, Charles W. Penrose], cited in James R. Clark, *Messages of the First Presidency*, 4:338-39.)

What do you think of the promise contained in the last paragraph of this official announcement? Consider now the family of which you are a vital member. Has it had good weekly family home evenings over the past years? If so, what evidences do you see of the fulfillment of these promises? If not, what could you do to help your family realize these blessings?

As you reflect on the above questions, you may wish to take into consideration a few details from the life of Joseph F. Smith. Did you know that he was the father of forty-three children and that he adopted into his home five more? And did you know that they, along with his wives, dearly loved, reverenced, and honored him? Can you feel the sincerity of one of his wives as she reported on how she felt when he asked her hand in marriage?

" . . . I spent quite a good deal of time at [my sister] Julina's [Joseph F. Smith's wife] helping tend the babies, etc. This is where I became acquainted with

my brother-in-law Joseph. When he proposed marrriage to me I was thrilled for I had seen how kind and wonderful he was." (Cited in Smith and Stewart, *Life of Joseph Fielding Smith*, p. 47.)

Did you know that all of his children remained true and faithful to the Church, one following in his footsteps all the way to the office of president? How do you suppose he kept his large family active? It was by practicing throughout his life the ideals he shared with the Saints and admonished them to follow.

Read the following glimpses of his family life. He knew of the strength a good home could have in combating satanic philosophies and worldly temptations.

JOSEPH F. SMITH IMPLEMENTED INTO HIS OWN LIFE THE IDEALS HE ADMONISHED THE SAINTS TO LIVE

(14-11) He Knew the Main Business of His Life Was to Properly Rear His Family

"There can be no genuine happiness separate and apart from the home, and every effort made to sanctify and preserve its influence is uplifting to those who toil and sacrifice for its establishment. Men and women often seek to substitute some other life for that of the home; they would make themselves believe that the home means restraint; that the highest liberty is the fullest opportunity to move about at will. There is no happiness without service, and there is no service greater than that which converts the home into a divine institution, and which promotes and preserves family life." (Smith, *Gospel Doctrine*, p. 300.)

(14-12) He Took Time and Put Effort into Caring for His Children

"I have visited at his home when one of his little children was down sick. I have seen him come home from his work at night tired, as he naturally would be, and yet he would walk the floor for hours with that little one in his arms, petting it and loving it, encouraging it in every way with such tenderness and such a soul of pity and love as not one mother in a thousand would show." (Charles W. Nibley, "Reminiscences of President Joseph F. Smith," *Improvement Era*, Jan. 1919, p. 197.)

(14-13) He Shared with Them His Testimony and Instructed Them in the Things of God

His son, Joseph Fielding Smith, remembering the power of his father's teachings, reported:

" . . . he spent [part of his home time] instructing his children in the principles of the gospel. They one and all rejoiced in his presence and were grateful for the wonderful words of counsel and instruction which he imparted on these occasions in the midst of anxiety. They have never forgotten what they were taught, and the impressions have remained with them and will likely to do so

President Smith as a youth of 19

forever. . . . My father was the most tenderhearted man I ever knew. . . . Among my fondest memories are the hours I have spent by his side discussing principles of the gospel and receiving instruction as only he could give it. In this way the foundation for my own knowledge was laid in truth." (Cited in Smith and Stewart, *Life of Joseph Fielding Smith*, p. 40.)

(14-14) Joseph F. Smith Recognized That Staying True to the Gospel Was More Important Than Life Itself

"God forbid that there should be any of us so unwisely indulgent, so thoughtless and so shallow in our affection for our children that we dare not check them in a wayward course, in wrong-doing and in their foolish love for the things of the world more than for the things of righteousness, for fear of offending them. I want to say this: Some people have grown to possess such unlimited confidence in their children that they do not believe it possible for them to be led astray or to do wrong. . . . The result is, they turn them loose, morning, noon, and night, to attend all kinds of entertainments and amusements, often in company with those whom they know not and do not understand. Some of our children are so innocent that they do not suspect evil, and therefore, they are off their guard and trapped into evil. . . .

"I would rather take one of my children to the grave than I would see him turn away from this Gospel." (Smith, comp., *Life of Joseph F. Smith*, p. 404.)

(14-15) But Most of All, He Loved His Wives and Children with a Pure and Holy Love Seldom Surpassed

" 'It would be difficult to find in any part of the world any family where the members manifested greater love and solicitude for each other than in the family of President Joseph F. Smith,' wrote Joseph Fielding. 'No father ever at any age of the world, we feel confident in saying, had a greater love for wife or wives and children, and was more earnestly concerned for their welfare. . . . Out in the world, where marriage is looked upon too frequently merely as a contract, which on the slightest provocation may be broken; where families are constantly racked by disunity, and where, through the action of the divorce courts, children are deprived of the most sacred right of loving parental affection, there is a general feeling that a family such as that of President Smith's could only be a family of discord and jealous strife and hatred. To the contrary, there was and is no monogamist family which could be more united. To the astonishment of the unbelieving world, the wives loved each other dearly. In times of sickness they tenderly waited upon and nursed each other. When death invaded one of the homes and a child was taken, all wept and mourned together with sincere grief. . . . Two of the wives [Julina and Edna] were skilled and licensed practitioners in obstetrics, and brought many babies into the world. They waited upon the other wives, and when babies came all rejoiced equally with the mother.

" 'The children recognized each other as brothers and sisters, full-fledged not as half, as they would be considered in the world. They defended each and stood by each other no matter which branch of the family was theirs. . . . Joseph F. Smith loved his wives and children with a holy love that is seldom seen, never surpassed.

Like Job of old, he prayed for them night and day and asked the Lord to keep them pure and undefiled in the path of righteousness. . . . ' " (Smith and Stewart, *Life of Joseph Fielding Smith*, pp. 46-47.)

As you read the preceding items, did you see why President Smith could admonish the Saints to strengthen their homes? Do you see the influence a good home has on both the children and the parents therein? And can you look beyond this little example to the wider implications about the prophets of God and the role they play? Can you see that, in reality, counsel and direction come from God and that the prophet is under the same responsibility as the Saints and receives the same promise for obedience?

Why, then, does the real safety of the Saints lie in following the counsel of the living prophets?

J. F. Smith, an ideal family man

CHAPTER 15

HE SHALL CONSECRATE THINE AFFLICTIONS FOR THY GAIN

INTRODUCTION

The chilly wind tugged at the overcoat of President Joseph F. Smith as he mounted the steps to the Senate chambers of the United States Capitol Building. The responsibility he bore was ominous. Assembled in a large committee room were men of tremendous power and influence—senators of the United States. Their expressed purpose for meeting was to examine whether or not Reed Smoot, senator from Utah and apostle of the Church, would be allowed to retain his seat as a member of the Senate. But their real motive was far different.

Some of the senators making up the committee of investigation were bitterly hostile toward the Church. Only one of the fourteen senators who comprised this committee would initially show any sympathy or concern. Most of the others wanted to use their influence to embarrass and defame the Church, its president, and its members.

Before this group, President Smith had been called to testify as first witness. As he continued to climb the long steps he was fully aware of the real issue and its magnitude. It was not Reed Smoot who was on trial, but the Church. Newspapers across the country would carry reports of the hearings as front-page news. Many of these would be anxious to print anything that would put the Church in a bad light. Yet the prophet was confident.

How different was this tall, magnificent man from the boy, who years before as a missionary to the Hawaiian Islands, had felt "as if I was so debased in my condition of poverty, lack of intelligence and knowledge . . . that I hardly dared look a white man in the face." (Joseph F. Smith, *Gospel Doctrine*, p. 542.) What caused the change? What unlocked the power within, such that it became coupled with the power from above? It was not the life of ease but of hardship through which he grew strong in godly ways.

AS A YOUTH, JOSEPH F. SMITH ENDURED TRIALS AND TESTS THROUGH WHICH HE CAME TO UNDERSTAND THE WAYS OF GOD

(15-1) Not Yet Eight Years of Age, He Drove an Ox Team West As the Family Made Its Escape from Mobocracy

"Mary Smith with her family remained in Nauvoo until the summer of 1846. It was only a day or two before the battle of Nauvoo, when, under threats, she hastily loaded her children in a flat boat with such household effects as could be carried, and crossed the Mississippi to a point near Montrose. There under the trees on the bank of the river the family pitched camp that night, and there they experienced the horror of listening to the bombardment of Nauvoo. . . . Although Joseph was not yet eight years of age, he was required to drive one of the ox teams most of the way from Montrose to Winter Quarters. At this place the family sojourned until the spring of 1848, endeavoring in the meantime, by help from friends who were not prepared to continue on the journey, and by constant toil, to gather sufficient teams and necessities to make the journey across the plains." (Joseph Fielding Smith, comp., *Life of Joseph F. Smith*, p. 131.)

(15-2) He Endured the Hardships and Dangers of the Wild Frontier and Evidenced the Bravery, Presence of Mind, and Courage Which Would Mark His Later Years

As an eight-year-old, Joseph F., along with other boys, was assigned to watch the cattle as they were sent out to graze about two miles from the town of Winter Quarters. One morning as the cattle grazed, the boys mounted their horses and amused themselves by running short races and jumping ditches. Suddenly they were attacked by Indians. Joseph F. recalls:

"My first impression, or impulse was to save the cattle from being driven off, for in a most incredible short time, I thought of going to the valley; of our dependence upon our cattle, and the horror of being compelled to remain at Winter Quarters. I suited the action to the thought, and at full speed dashed out to head the cattle and if possible turn them towards home." (Cited in Smith, comp., *Life of Joseph F. Smith*, p. 135.)

While the others ran, Joseph F. reacted differently. Driving the cattle as fast as he could, he was still unable to outrun the Indians. Soon they overtook him. Even so, the little fellow continued to dodge and run until his horse became winded.

" . . . one Indian rode upon the left side and one on the right side of me, and each took me by an arm and leg and lifted me from my horse; they then slackened their speed until my horse run from under me, then they chucked me down with great violence to the ground. Several horses from behind jumped over me, but did not hurt me. My horse was secured by the Indians and without slackening speed they rode on in the direction from whence they had come." (Joseph F. Smith, cited in Smith, comp., *Life of Joseph F. Smith*, p. 136.)

The chase, however, had taken enough time that men came from the fields, discouraging a return of the Indians.

(15-3) In His Youth He Responded to the Great Faith Demonstrated by His Mother Through Which Trials and Hardships Were Overcome

While on a trip to procure provisions for the long trip from Winter Quarters to the Salt Lake Valley, young Joseph saw how trust and faith in God can overcome real obstacles. Camping by a creek one night near some men with a herd of cattle, Joseph turned their oxen out to graze. The next morning the cattle could not be found. Joseph and his uncle searched all morning until they were both disheartened.

" . . . I Joseph was the first to return to our wagons, and as I approached I saw my mother kneeling down in prayer. I halted for a moment and then drew gently near enough to hear her pleading with the Lord not to suffer us to be left in this helpless condition, but to lead us to recover our lost team, that we might continue our travels in safety. When she arose from her knees I was standing nearby. The first expression I caught upon her precious face was a lovely smile, which discouraged as I was, gave me renewed hope and an assurance I had not felt before." (Joseph F. Smith, cited in Smith, comp., *Life of Joseph F. Smith*, p. 132.)

After Joseph and his uncle had returned to camp, Joseph's mother insisted that they eat while she went out to look. Her brother tried to dissuade her, insisting that they had looked everywhere. But she was determined to go and walked some distance toward the river. There she was met by one of the men from the cow herd, who told her he had seen the oxen headed in the opposite direction from the one in which she was walking. She ignored him and kept right on walking. Upon reaching the river, she turned and beckoned her son and brother. Hurrying to her side, they saw their "oxen fastened to a clump of willows growing in the bottom of a deep gulch which had been washed out of the sandy bank of the river by the little spring creek, perfectly concealed from view. We were not long in releasing them from bondage and getting back to our camp, where the other cattle had been fastened to the wagon wheels all the morning, and we were soon on our way home rejoicing. The worthy herdsmen had suddenly departed when they saw mother would not heed them; I hope they went in search of estray honesty, which I trust they found." (Joseph F. Smith, cited in Smith, comp., *Life of Joseph F. Smith*, p. 133.)

Later, during the actual journey west, Joseph F. once again saw the power of faith demonstrated. Having traveled a good share of the way to Zion, one of the overtaxed oxen fell to the ground.

"Producing a bottle of consecrated oil, Widow Smith asked her brother and James Lawson if they would please administer to the ox just as they would do to a sick person, for it was vital to her interest that the ox be restored that she might pursue her journey. Her earnest plea was complied with. These brethren poured oil on the head of the ox and then laid their hands upon it and rebuked the power of the destroyer just as they would have done if the animal had been a human being. Immediately the ox got up and within a very few moments again pulled in the yoke as if nothing had ever happened." (Smith, comp., *Life of Joseph F. Smith*, p. 150.)

(15-4) As a Boy, He Was Responsible and Mature Beyond His Years

From 1848 to 1854, Joseph F.'s principle occupation was that of herd boy, to which he labored diligently. " . . . I cannot recall the loss of a single 'hoof' by death, straying away, or otherwise, from neglect or carelessness on my part during that period," he later recalled. (Ibid., p. 163.) At one time during the winter of 1848, "he saw a wolf chasing a sheep out in the open field. It was a rainy day and the ground was soft. The wool of the sheep was heavy with moisture which retarded its flight. As the wolf was about to seize the sheep Joseph arrived at the rescue and saved the sheep. Although wolves were numerous and bold, Joseph was often out on the range after dark, in cold weather, where he would hear the ferocious howls of the marauders. He had a dog to aid him in his work, but at times the dog would become terrified

The First Presidency (1901-1910): John R. Winder, President Joseph F. Smith, Anthon H. Lund

because of the great number of wolves and would crouch at his feet. This was the nature of the amusement accorded to this faithful boy at an age when most boys like to play and engage in athletic sports." (Smith, comp., *Life of Joseph F. Smith*, p. 164.)

DURING HIS FIRST MISSION, HE SUFFERED GREATLY FROM SICKNESS, FATIGUE, AND MATERIAL LOSS; YET HE BECAME A LEADER AMONG THE PEOPLE IN SPITE OF THESE TRIALS

(15-5) Joseph F. and His Companions Were Beset by Many Difficulties and Trials

The challenges which were overcome by the fifteen-year-old elder were described years later by a close friend.

"On this mission to the Sandwich Island [present-day Hawaii], he encountered severe hardships. I remember on our first trip over to the Islands, and I was over there on four trips with him, that sailing among the different small islands, he would point out to me such and such a place: 'There is where I lived so long in a little straw hut'—which burned down or which was destroyed by flood. Here was another place where he had lain sick and where the good Hawaiian people had ministered to him. This experience, and the other, he would tell as we journeyed along, all of which, if I had time to relate, are faith-promoting and inspiring, and would point out to you the manliness of the young boy—for he was then, as I told you, fifteen or sixteen years of age." (Charles W. Nibley in *CR*, Apr.1919, p. 62.)

(15-6) These Trials Were Overcome by Faith and Fortitude

Shortly after arriving on the island,

Elder Smith became very ill. Kind treatment by friends helped him to recover. Undaunted, he used his convalescent time to study the Hawaiian language. He had been promised by Elder Parley P. Pratt that he would master the language by faith and study. He applied both of these, and within one hundred days he was speaking the language fluently in spite of his illness.

Sometime later he was taken ill again and did not fully recover for three months. Nevertheless, he applied himself to gospel study and to perfecting his language skills. It was during the period of this second illness that the power of the adversary seized the woman of the house, causing her to go through all manner of hideous contortions. Though fearful at first, the boy prayed and found the power by which he successfully rebuked the evil spirit.

(15-7) His Desire Was to Bear a Strong Testimony Under Any Circumstances

In a letter to his relatives in Utah, Elder Smith wrote poignantly of his great desires:

" . . . I know that the work in which I am engaged is the work of the living and true God, and I am ready to bear my testimony of the same, at any time, or at any place, or in whatsoever circumstances I may be placed; and hope and pray that I ever may prove faithful in serving the Lord, my God. I am happy to say that I am ready to go through thick and thin for this cause in which I am engaged; and truly hope and pray that I may prove faithful to the end. These are my feelings. . . .

" . . . I had rather die on this mission, than to disgrace myself or my calling. These are the sentiments of my heart. My prayer is that we may hold out faithful to the end, and eventually be crowned in the kingdom of God, with those that have gone before us." (Cited in Smith, comp., *Life of Joseph F. Smith,* pp. 176-77.)

HE WAS COURAGEOUS AND UNDAUNTED IN DEFENDING TRUTH AND RIGHTEOUSNESS

(15-8) Under No Condition Would He Deny His Testimony or Falter in the Faith

During the last half of the nineteenth century, the Saints continued to receive abuse and hatred. Some extremists went so far as to kill. On his way home from his first mission, Joseph F. and his companions ran into such a group when they camped one evening. The leader of the group swore he would kill anyone who was a Mormon. Pointing his gun at Joseph he demanded, "Are you a Mormon?" Expecting fully for the

gun to discharge, nonetheless he answered, "Yes, siree; dyed in the wool; true blue, through and through." The answer, given boldly and without hesitation, completely disarmed the belligerent man, and in bewilderment all he could do was shake the young lad's hand and praise him for his courage. The men then rode off and did not molest them further. (See Smith, comp., *Life of Joseph F. Smith,* p. 189.)

Three years later Joseph F. again showed that same kind of conviction. This time he was traveling to serve a mission to England. As he and his companions approached Nauvoo, where they had decided to visit for a while, they found a particularly bitter mob spirit and threats of murder. Although Joseph F. and his companions had been evasive about revealing who they were so as to avoid trouble, a Catholic priest pinned them down by asking directly if they were Mormon elders. Joseph F. confessed that at that moment temptation to deny the truth had never been so strong; but resisting, he said they were. The reply satisfied the priest and did not increase the imprecations of the other people. When they arrived at Nauvoo, they found themselves in the same quarters as the priest. Elder Smith stated of this experience, "I had never felt happier than when I saw the minister there, and knew that we had told him the truth about our mission." (Smith, *Gospel Doctrine,* p. 534.)

(15-9) Because of His Firm and Unyielding Defense of the Kingdom, He Became Known As the Fighting Apostle

As a young apostle, Joseph F. decried and condemned the hypocrites who persecuted the

Church. He continually fought for the rights and privileges of the Saints. Elder John A. Widtsoe, one who knew him well, wrote, "The fighting apostle they called him, as he hurled back the untruths about 'Mormonism,' and his relentless watchfulness became a deterrent power among those who planned evil for a good and peaceful people.

"A fighting apostle he has always been—fighting for the cause of truth." (Cited in Smith, *Gospel Doctrine,* p. 511.)

In Romans 1:16 the apostle Paul said: "For I am not ashamed of the gospel of Christ: for it is the power of God unto salvation to every one that believeth. . . . " What made Paul so bold in his declaration? Consider his stand toward the gospel as compared with some others who were seen in vision by Lehi. Read 1 Nephi 8:24, 25. The people saw—actually partook of—the powers of the gospel (as symbolized by the tree and its fruit); but after doing so, how did they react? According to verses 26-28, what was the cause of their reaction? Turn now to Mormon 8:38. Does Mormon verify the conclusion of Lehi?

In what ways might a person show that he is ashamed of the gospel of Christ? Does he have to actually deny it? Can he, instead, merely refrain from ever taking a stand for the Church—just simply be quiet as to what he believes when issues are raised in his presence?

Though Joseph F. Smith and his companions were careful to avoid any problems, how did they demonstrate they were not ashamed of the gospel? Consider the promise in 2 Nephi 7:7, 8. If one is not ashamed of the Lord, can he ever be shamed by the world?

President Smith and his wife Julina Lambson on golden wedding day

(15-10) Though Unyielding in His Beliefs, Joseph F. Smith Was Considerate and Kind to All

"Many of the older people now alive can recall that forty years ago, or even less, he was considered a radical, and many a one of that time shook his head and said, 'What will become of things if that fiery radical ever becomes president of the Church?' But from the time he was made president of the Church, and even before that time, he became one of the most tolerant of men; tolerant of others' opinions, and while he would denounce sin with such righteous wrath as you would seldom see in any man, yet for the poor sinner he had compassion and pity, and even forgiveness, if sincere repentance were shown. None, more ready than he to forgive and forget." (Charles W. Nibley, "Reminiscences of President Joseph F. Smith," *Improvement Era*, Jan. 1919, p. 193.)

DURING HIS APOSTLESHIP AND ADMINISTRATION AS PROPHET, JOSEPH F. SMITH WAS NOT IMMUNE FROM CHALLENGES, HEARTACHE, AND ABUSE

(15-11) He Felt the Grief and Heartache Associated with Losing a Child, and from Being Forced from His Home for Years; yet His Faith in a Loving God Remained Firm

Ten times Joseph F. Smith and his wives passed through sorrow as their children died, children for whom he tenderly and earnestly prayed and helped nurse. Concerning the death of one of these children, he recorded:

" . . . our prayers did not avail!

"At last I took her in my arms and walked the floor with her and helplessly, powerless to aid my darling, dying child, I watched her feeble breath depart to come no more in time, and her glorious intelligence, her bright angelic spirit took her flight to God from whence she came. It was then about 20 minutes to 8 p.m. With her was swept away all our fond hope and love and joy of earth. Oh! how I loved that child! She was intelligent beyond her years; bright, loving, choice and joyous! But she is gone to join the beauteous and glorious spirits of her brothers and sisters, who have gone before!" (Smith, comp., *Life of Joseph F. Smith*, p. 463.)

Because of the "Mormon Crusade" he was forced to be absent when the other children passed away. These were times not only of acute sorrow, but also of bitter separation. The spirit of this great man chaffed under the ordeal; yet he endured the absence away from those he loved, being obedient to the counsel of the prophet of God.

(15-12) As President of the Church, He Came Under Personal Attack and Abuse from the Enemies of the Church

After the crusade against plural marriage cooled down, many men applied for and received amnesty. Joseph F. Smith was one of these men. By the time he assumed the presidency in 1901, the persecutions of the late nineteenth century were a thing of the past. But the trials he would face were not yet through. An anti-Mormon political party was organized in Utah. This party launched a massive verbal attack against the prophet and the Church. The chief organ of this attack was a local newspaper in Salt Lake City.

"During these years [1905 to 1912] this newspaper almost daily cartooned President Joseph F. Smith with a spirit of wicked and malicious villification. These papers were scattered all over the United States, and naturally, appearing day by day and month after month, the people of the nation and even beyond the borders of the United States, reached the conclusion that the President of the Church, Joseph F. Smith, was the lowest and most despicable character in all the world. Missionaries out in the world were made to suffer and were persecuted and insulted in all parts of the earth. Yet during it all the Church continued to grow." (Smith, comp., *Life of Joseph F. Smith*, p. 350.)

(15-13) He Would Not Even Defend Himself from the Daily Abuse, but, Rather, He Showed Forth Love and Concern

"Joseph F. Smith endured persecution, the revilings and ravings of the wicked, false accusations coming from the most contemptible and vilest creatures of the human family, and endured it all without a word of retaliation. . . . He took the stand that if Joseph Smith could endure the abuse and vilification which was heaped upon him; if the Son of God could endure it and not return in kind, then he, too, as the humble servant of the Master, could endure in silence, for his fear was not in the arm of flesh but in the Lord, and the time must come when truth would triumph and the falsifier would sink into oblivion and be forgotten." (Smith, comp., *Life of Joseph F. Smith*, p. 439.)

BY TRIUMPHING OVER THE TRIALS AND DIFFICULTIES OF HIS LIFE, PRESIDENT JOSEPH F. SMITH WAS PREPARED TO BEHOLD THE THINGS OF GOD

(15-14) He Lived in Close Communion with the Spirit of the Lord

"He lived in close communion with the Spirit of the Lord, and his life was so exemplary and chaste that the Lord could easily manifest

himself to his servant. Truly he could say 'Speak Lord, for thy servant heareth.' Not every servant can hear when He speaks. But the heart of President Smith was attuned to the Celestial melodies—he could hear, and did hear." (Nibley, "Reminiscences," pp. 197-98.)

"While he was a hard-headed, successful business man, yet very few in this dispensation have been more gifted with spiritual insight than he. As we were returning from an eastern trip, some years ago, on the train just east of Green River, I saw him go out to the end of the car on the platform, and immediately return and hesitate a moment, and then sit down in the seat just ahead of me. He had just taken his seat when something went wrong with the train. A broken rail had been the means of ditching the engine and had thrown most of the cars off the track. In the sleeper we were shaken up pretty badly, but our car remained on the track.

"The President immediately said to me that he had gone on the platform when he heard a voice saying, 'Go in and sit down.'

"He came in, and I noticed him stand a moment, and he seemed to hestitate, but he sat down.

"He said further that as he came in and stood in the aisle he thought, 'Oh, pshaw, perhaps it is only my imagination;' when he heard the voice again, 'Sit down,' and he immediately took his seat, and the result was as I have stated.

"He, no doubt, would have been very seriously injured had he remained on the platform of that car, as the cars were all jammed up together pretty badly. He said, 'I have heard that voice a good many times in my life, and I have always profited by obeying it.' " (Nibley, "Reminiscences," p. 197.)

(15-15) During His Last Months of Life, He Was in Continuous Communication with the Spirit

As Joseph F. Smith closed his long and able career as a special witness of the Lord, fittingly the veil was very thin. During his last discourse delivered at General Conference, he declared:

"I will not, I dare not, attempt to enter upon many things that are resting upon my mind this morning, and I shall postpone until some future time, the Lord being willing, my attempt to tell you some of the things that are in my mind, and that dwell in my heart. I have not lived alone these five months. I have dwelt in the spirit of prayer, of supplication, of faith and of determination; and I have had my communication with the Spirit of the Lord continuously. . . ." (CR, Oct. 1918, p. 2.)

Indeed, just the day before this conference convened, the heavens were opened and he beheld the vision of the redemption of the dead, wherein he saw the ministry of the Lord in the spirit world. This great revelation is now a part of the Pearl of Great Price. (See Joseph F. Smith—Vision of the Redemption of the Dead.)

For three days President Joseph F. Smith testified before the Senate committee in defense of Reed Smoot. His sincerity, his openness, his candor, greatly affected some of the members of the committee. Misunderstanding and bigotry began to melt under the warm radiance of truth. As the hearing continued, an effect for good was produced across the country. Though there were those of anti-Mormon sentiment who testified against the Church, many of those called to testify truly told the Church's

story. These testimonies were recorded by the press and many, for the first time, read and understood the Church's views and teachings. Everywhere attitudes began to change, and the Church gained acceptance. The confidence President Smith had maintained from the beginning had been justified.

But what was the source of that confidence? It was born years before when a fifteen-year-old missionary—humble, sick, and discouraged—was lifted up by a night vision. Permitted to see Joseph Smith, Hyrum Smith (his father), his mother, and others, he became "a man, though only a boy. There was not anything in the world that I feared. I could meet any man or woman or child and look them in the face. . . .

" . . . when I woke up I felt as if I had been lifted out of a slum, out of despair, out of the wretched condition that I was in; and . . . I was not afraid of any white man nor of anyone else. . . ." (Smith, Gospel Doctrine, pp. 542-43.)

From that point on, his strength was in the Lord. So it was before the Senate committee. So it was when he defended his stand sometime later before a friend:

"I recall one night we were on shipboard returning from Europe, in 1906. It was a bright moonlight night, and we stood there leaning over the railing enjoying the smooth sea and balmy summer night air. The Smoot investigation, which had just occurred a little while before and which had stirred up so much controversy throughout the land was fresh in our minds, and we were talking of it. I took the position that it would be unwise for Reed Smoot to be

Main Street, Salt Lake City (1904)

re-elected to the United States Senate. I was conscientious in my objection, and I had marshaled all the facts, arguments, and logic, that I could; and I was well informed, I thought, on the subject, and had presented them to him in as clear and yet in as adroit a manner as I possibly could. It would take too much space here to go over the arguments, but it seemed to me that I had the best of it. I could see he began to listen with some little impatience, and yet he let me have my say, but he answered in tones and in a way that I shall never forget. Bringing his fist down with some force on the railing between us, he said, in the most forceful and positive manner:

" 'If ever the Spirit of the Lord has manifested to me anything clear and plain and positive, it is this, that Reed Smoot should remain in the United States Senate. He can do more good there than he can anywhere else.'

"Of course, I did not contend further with him, but accepted from that hour his view of the case and made it mine, too. Twelve years have passed since that time, and looking back on it now, I cannot help but think how marvelously and splendidly the inspiration of the Almighty has been vindicated, while my argument, facts and logic have all fallen to the ground." (Nibley, "Reminiscences," p. 195.)

The life of this prophet of God drew to a close on November 19, 1918. But, as you have seen, for him the veil had already become very thin. Indeed, he had truly beheld the things of God. Consider the depth of meaning about the prophet in the testimony of one who himself was a special witness of the Lord:

" . . . I do bear witness to you that Joseph F. Smith was one of the real apostles of the Lord Jesus Christ. I have listened to his ringing words of testimony and warning before the assemblies of thousands, and I have sat with him, on very rare occasions, alone; and on occasions less rare, but still not common, with my brethren and associates, I have heard him preach in conversation, and I have never seen his face so enlightened nor his frame so thrilled with power as when he was bearing testimony of the Christ. He seemed to me to know Jesus Christ as a man knows his friend." (James E. Talmage in *CR*, Apr. 1919, p. 59.)

His life had not been easy, yet his mettle was such that he was not overcome by the trials he faced. Those trials were necessary, that he might behold and reveal those things of the Spirit which the Lord has for his children.

Surely his life demonstrated that the prophets of God are not immune to the sorrows, challenges, and trials of life and that they too must work out their own salvation. But is there another lesson that you might take to heart? Is it not encouraging to know that your own trials may serve to strengthen you, enabling you to have the Spirit in your life and callings? Do you, as President Smith did, have the courage to overcome?

UNIT EIGHT
HEBER J. GRANT
Seventh President of the Church

OVERVIEW

At a time when the Latter-day Saints were held in the lowest esteem that they had ever been, a frail baby boy was born in Salt Lake City, Utah. When he died eighty-eight years later, it was said that "the change in sentiment toward the Mormon people was largely brought about through his own untiring individual efforts.[1] A press preoccupied with sensationalism and a reckless use of its freedom was grinding out commercialized hatred against the "Mormons" when Heber Jeddy Grant was born November 22, 1856. Heber J. Grant learned to walk and talk, and he began to watch the freight wagons go by his home on Main Street, just half a block south of Temple Square.

Because his father, Jedediah M. Grant, a counselor to Brigham Young, was also thin and died at an early age, some predicted that Heber would not survive long. But the Spirit contradicted these dire predictions. A wife of Brigham Young, Eliza R. Snow, prophesied in tongues that Heber would be an apostle. The interpretation was given by "Aunt Zina," another of Brigham Young's wives. Many other blessings and prophecies confirmed this prediction. One such blessing was given by Heber C. Kimball, who sat him on a banquet table and prophesied that he would be an apostle and become a greater man in the Church than his father had been.[2]

The heavens knew he could be trusted as chief steward of the affairs of the kingdom; so he was called, prepared, and placed in the right time and circumstances. A direct revelation to President John Taylor placed Heber J. Grant on the Council of the Twelve one month before his twenty-sixth birthday. Before this calling he had already held many positions in the kingdom, including General Secretary of the YMMIA at the age of twenty-three and president of the Tooele Stake later that same year.

One could say that Heber J. Grant was an important link in the bridge over which the Church crossed from an old world of hate to a new world of guarded respect and some outright admiration and friendliness. He personally knew every president of the church in this dispensation except Joseph Smith. And he knew every apostle of this generation except a few who had passed on before his birth and a few who have been called since his death. Among recent General Authorities who were called by him are President Spencer W. Kimball, President Marion G. Romney, President Ezra Taft Benson, and Elder Mark E. Petersen.

Heber turned down an appointment to the Naval Academy. Instead, he pursued his second love: business. And he pursued it with vigor through good times and bad, through successes and reversals. He walked with such courage and well-earned credentials that not even his comparative youth stood in his way. The great financiers of Wall Street in Chicago and points west came to know that Heber J. Grant would never default and would never take money on terms that were not the best his backers could offer.

Business doors opened other doors. By the time Heber J. became President of the Church he had many friends in the world whose admiration for his ability and integrity was so great that they simply took the position that nothing he had anything to do with could be the least bit dishonest or bad. He took advantage of every opportunity to use his friendship to promote the Church. He was in great demand as a speaker and was honored and feted by important nonmember groups and individuals. His subject was always the same—the story of his Church and people and their principles. And he got standing ovations.

His family was beautiful. He was a most beloved and attentive father and husband. His wives and daughters were treated as queens and princesses. His courtesy, generosity, and fairness were a constant source of joy to them. Yet, because of sickness and death, his family was one of his greatest trials. He lost his only two sons—one as a baby and the other as a small boy. His grief knew no bounds because he so wanted a son. Then untimely death also took two of his three wives—one three years after the Manifesto was issued and the second a few years later. But as great as was his grief, these events brought equally rewarding spiritual experiences which affirmed God's love and will in these losses of loved ones.

And through all the big accomplishments, the less spectacular but equally important things were not neglected. He established at least a score of small businesses in the hopes of fostering home industry. His Church assignments were numerous, including a lifelong commitment to the MIA, in which he held many positions of leadership and helped establish the *Improvement Era*, serving as an editor and contributor from its beginning. And somehow he found the time and means to attend the temple weekly when near one. He usually arranged to have family members accompany him. It was said of him by a head of the Genealogical Society that his name led all the Church in family research accomplished.[3] Besides all this, there were the thousands of books sent with personal messages in his own matchless handwriting to members and nonmembers; there were the endless hours spent in reclaiming the wayward; and there were the widows' mortgages paid off, and other philanthropies.

The Second World War was ending in Europe when his tall, thin frame was laid to rest. Member and nonmember alike honored and eulogized him. Thousands came to view him. At his funeral one of his counselors said of him: "He so lived his life that it had no dark place across which he must draw a curtain. His life had nothing to embarrass, nothing to hide, nothing of which he must be ashamed."[4]

CHAPTER 16

THEN WILL I MAKE WEAK THINGS BECOME STRONG UNTO THEM

INTRODUCTION

The first child born in the Salt Lake Valley to LDS parents was only nine years old when Heber Jeddy Grant was born. By the time Heber himself was nine, the Civil War was over. He would have seen Union soldiers pass by his home half a block south of the Salt Lake temple block. President Abraham Lincoln had established Fort Douglas and had sent troops into Utah on a permanent basis.

A more common sight to Heber would have been the fine horses and carriages of Brigham Young, George Q. Cannon, Daniel H. Wells, and other successful men of Church and business in the bustling frontier town with the wide streets. He also would have watched freighters going north toward Ogden and south toward Provo, pulled by teams made up of multiple pairs of horses, mules, or oxen. There would have been short hikes to Temple Square to check the progress of the construction of the Tabernacle and the temple, and also around the block to look at the new Salt Lake Theater. But much of Heber's time was spent playing in streets and in yards. He often won enough marbles to use as pay to get his friends to do his chores so that he could spend more time practicing the art of pitching a baseball. And, of course, there was school.

His best friends were a son and a grandson of President Brigham Young. Together they ran into the Lion House when the prayer bell was rung and joined in the Young's family prayers. Sometimes young Heber peeked to see if Brigham was talking face to face with his Heavenly Father, because his prayers sounded as though he must have been. In addition to the prayers, Heber sometimes attended Brigham Young's school. And there were long talks with President Young, with Eliza R. Snow, and with her brother Erastus, whom Heber regarded as the ideal of what an apostle should be. They told Heber about Joseph Smith, to whom Eliza R. Snow and his own mother were sealed, and about Jedediah M. Grant, one of the most trusted of the Prophet's friends—his very name opened doors to Heber when he began to travel in business circles. These were potent influences in the life of a gifted child of great destiny. Out of these and other influences was born a great determination to conquer his own flesh and to overcome obstacles that others would have considered insurmountable. He set many goals—hard ones to reach—and reached all of them except those that had to be set aside because of the call of duty to God and family. Even so, his motives were so pure and so in harmony with the right, as a Saint should see the right, that he rarely had to give up a goal.

EVEN THOUGH GIFTED, PRESIDENT GRANT HAD EXPERIENCES WHICH MADE HIM FEEL INADEQUATE

(16-1) Heber J. Grant Depicted Himself as a Person Without Much Promise

Like all prophets who lead the church of God, President Grant was a person of great ability. This was demonstrated over and over in his life. No doubt there were those who recognized this ability early. Yet his own feelings about himself, as revealed in his public statements, showed a sense of deep humility, if not inadequacy. He felt that he measured up to the goals he set only by great determination and constant effort. He lived in a day when leaders quite often expressed appreciation for learning, for artistic talent, for professional success, and for other achievements that depended on what usually is defined as talents or gifts. It was in these areas that he had to struggle the hardest. His talents lay in the field of business and social success. These talents often escape notice even though they may be more important to the welfare of humanity. So even as he spoke about his shortcomings, his strengths carried him over all obstacles.

(16-2) Because of His Frail Appearance, He Was Not Expected to Live Long

"Back in 1856, when Salt Lake City was in its infancy and many of its inhabitants were still living in log cabins and all its business places

faced a wide and often dusty street—in a pioneer home, standing where Z. C. M. I. now stands, a son of promise was born. When this child was nine days old, his father died. His widowed mother was left in poverty. If the delicate infant were to survive, which many doubted he would do, he must have the tenderest care. He survived, and the story of his accomplishments as a boy and a man should, for all time, stir the imaginations of aspiring youth.'' (Bryant S. Hinckley, *Heber J. Grant: Highlights in the Life of a Great Leader*, p. 15.)

(16-3) In His Younger Years, Heber J. Grant Was Taunted with Being a "Sissy," Which Created in Him a Great Determination to Succeed

''Being an only child, my mother reared me very carefully. Indeed, I grew more or less on the principle of a hothouse plant, the growth of which is 'long and lanky' but not substantial. I learned to sweep, and to wash and wipe dishes, but did little stone throwing and little indulging in those sports which are interesting and attractive to boys, and which develop their physical frames. Therefore, when I joined a baseball club, the boys of my own age and a little older played in the first nine; those younger than I played in the second, and those still younger in the third, and I played with them.

''One of the reasons for this was that I could not throw the ball from one base to the other. Another reason was that I lacked physical strength to run or bat well. When I picked up a ball, the boys would generally shout:

'' 'Throw it here, sissy!'

''So much fun was engendered on my account by my youthful companions that I solemnly vowed that I would play baseball in the

Heber J. and his mother, Rachael Ridgeway Ivins Grant

nine that would win the championship of the Territory of Utah.'' (Heber J. Grant, *Gospel Standards*, pp. 342-43.)

(16-4) His School Chums Laughed at His Handwriting

''At the beginning his penmanship was so poor that when two of his chums were looking at it one said to the other, 'That writing looks like hen tracks.' 'No,' said the other, 'it looks as if lightning had struck an ink bottle.' This touched Heber's pride and, bringing his fist down on his desk, he said, 'I'll some day be able to give you fellows lessons in penmanship.' '' (Hinckley, *Life of a Great Leader*, p. 40.)

(16-5) His Childhood Efforts of Learning to Sing Met with Failure

''My mother tried to teach me when I was a small child to sing but failed because of my inability to carry a tune.

''Upon joining a singing class taught by Professor Charles J. Thomas, he tried and tried in vain to teach me when ten years of age to run the scale or carry a simple tune and finally gave up in despair. He said that I could never, in this world, learn to sing. Perhaps he thought I might learn the divine art in another world. Ever since this attempt, I have frequently tried to sing when riding alone many miles from anyone who might hear me, but on such occasions could never succeed in carrying the tune of one of our familiar hymns for a single verse, and quite frequently not for a single line.

''When I was about twenty-five years of age, Professor Sims informed me that I could sing, but added, 'I would like to be at least forty miles away while you are doing it.' '' (Grant, *Gospel Standards*, p. 351.)

PRESIDENT GRANT MET EVERY CHALLENGE HEAD-ON AND CONQUERED IT

(16-6) He Refused to Be Overpowered by His Body

"I have never known a man who exemplified so completely the mastery of mind over matter—whose will could so masterfully bring under subjection physical whims and desires. Perseverance and self-mastery are qualities that will always be connoted with the name of Heber J. Grant." (David O. McKay, "President Heber J. Grant," *Improvement Era*, June 1945, p. 334.)

(16-7) His Determination Was Encouraged by a Wise Mother

"Early in his youth there was developed . . . a spirit of independence and determination that later made him outstanding among his associates. You who have heard President Grant tell about those early days cannot doubt that in the humble surroundings and spiritual atmosphere of his boyhood home were formed those sterling traits of character which in maturity made him so distinguished.

"President Grant always spoke with deference and heartfelt appreciation of his noble inheritance from both his parents.

"God in mere caprice does not give to one child noble, and to another ignoble parents. Spirits come through the lineage for which they have prepared themselves in their pre-existent state. . . .

"Deprived of a father's companionship, President Grant appreciated all the more deeply the transforming power of a mother's love. It was she who changed his timidity to courage; his self-depreciation to self-confidence; impetuousness to

self-control; lack of initiative to perseverance. . . . " (McKay, "President Heber J. Grant," p. 334.)

Heber J. Grant as an Apostle

Have you ever noticed that you must often expose your inadequacies to others in order to overcome them? You cannot learn a new language without letting an expert in that language hear you blunder through your efforts to polish your pronunciation. You cannot learn to swim or ride a bicycle without someone knowing that you are learning. It takes a certain degree of moral courage to accept the fact that the laughter you generate in trying new things is evidence of empathy—not ridicule. Little children have that quality as they learn to walk and talk. They laugh with you. President Grant had this quality to a remarkable degree. At least, he did expose himself to possible ridicule. Imagine how many good-natured jokes were made

about his singing; yet he laughed at himself and persevered. You will see that characteristic as you read the next few items. You will also see that perhaps it was just as hard for him to pay this price for excellence as it would be for you. There is a price—usually a stiff one—for everything worth having.

(16-8) Young Heber Paid a High Price for Excellence as an Athlete

"My mother was keeping boarders . . . for a living, and I shined their boots until I saved a dollar which I invested in a baseball. I spent hours and hours throwing the ball at Bishop Edwin D. Woolley's barn, which caused him to refer to me as the laziest boy in the Thirteenth Ward. Often my arm would ache so that I could scarcely go to sleep at night. But I kept on practicing and finally succeeded in getting into the second nine of our club. Subsequently I joined a better club, and eventually played in the nine that won the championship of the territory and beat the nine that had won the championship for California, Colorado, and Wyoming. Having thus made good my promise to myself, I retired from the baseball arena." (Grant, *Gospel Standards*, p. 343.)

(16-9) After Others Gave Up, Horace S. Ensign Helped Heber Learn to Sing

"One of the leading Church officials, upon hearing me sing, when I first started to practice, remarked that my singing reminded him very much of the late Apostle Orson Pratt's poetry. He said Brother Pratt wrote only one piece of poetry, and this looked as if it had been sawed out of boards, and sawed off straight. . . .

"Upon my recent trip to Arizona, I asked Elders Rudger Clawson and J. Golden Kimball if they had any objections to my singing one hundred hymns that day. They took it as a joke and assured me that they would be delighted. We were on the way back from Holbrook to St. Johns, a distance of about sixty miles. After I had sung about forty tunes, they assured me that if I sang the remaining sixty they would be sure to have nervous prostration. I paid no attention whatever to their appeal, but held them to their bargain and sang the full one hundred. One hundred and fifteen songs in one day, and four hundred in four days, is the largest amount of practicing I ever did.

"Today [1900] my musical deafness is disappearing, and by sitting down to a piano and playing the lead notes, I can learn a song in less than one-tenth the time required when I first commenced to practice." (Grant, *Gospel Standards*, pp. 352, 354.)

(16-10) His Penmanship Went from "Hen Scratches" to the Best in Utah

"One day Heber was playing marbles with some other boys when the bookkeeper from the Wells Fargo Company Bank was walking down the other side of the street. One of the boys remarked, 'That man gets $150.00 a month.' Heber figured to himself that not counting Sundays, that man made $6.00 a day and that at five cents a pair, he would have to black 120 pairs of boots to make $6.00. He there and then resolved that some day he would be a bookkeeper in the Wells Fargo and Company's bank. In those days all the records and accounts of the bank were written with a pen, and one of the requisites of a good bookkeeper was the ability to write well. To learn to write well was his first approach to securing this job and the fulfilment of his resolve; so he set to work to become a penman. . . .

"He secured a position as bookkeeper and policy clerk in an insurance office at fifteen. About this he said: 'I wrote a very nice hand, and that was all that was needed to satisfactorily fill the positon which I then had. Yet I was not fully satisfied but continued to dream and scribble when not otherwise occupied. . . . I learned to write well, so well, that I often made more before and after office hours by writing cards, invitations, and making maps than the amount of my regular salary. At nineteen I was keeping books and acting as policy clerk for Henry Wadsworth, the agent of Wells Fargo and Company. My time was not fully employed, and I was not working for the company but for the agent personally. I did the same as I had done in Mr. White's bank, volunteered to file a lot of bank letters, etc., and kept a set of books for the Sandy Smelting Company, which Mr. Wadsworth was doing personally. My actions so pleased Mr. Wadsworth that he employed me to do the collecting for Wells Fargo and Company and paid me $20.00 a month for this work in addition to my regular compensation of $75.00 from the insurance business. Thus I was in the employ of Wells Fargo and Company and one of my day-dreams had become a reality.' " (Hinckley, *Life of a Great Leader*, pp. 39-42.)

"At one of the territorial fairs in which he had not competed, he noticed the exhibits of four professional penmen. He remarked to the man in charge of the art department that he could write better than that before he was seventeen years of age. The man in charge laughed and said that nobody but a cheeky insurance agent would make such a remark. He handed the gentleman three dollars which was the fee necessary to compete for a diploma and sent for the specimen which he had written before he was seventeen and hung it up with the remark, 'If you judges know good penmanship, when you see it, I will get the diploma.' He walked away with a diploma for the best penmanship in the territory. He encouraged the art of good penmanship among the youth of Zion and offered many prizes for the best specimens." (Hinckley, *Life of a Great Leader*, p. 41.)

"He later became teacher of penmanship and bookkeeping at the University of Deseret (University of Utah)." (Hinckley, *Life of a Great Leader*, p. 40.)

(16-11) His Perseverance Carried Over into Areas of Spiritual Growth As Well

"I can remember very distinctly when Uncle Anthony Ivins, brother of the father of Elder Anthony W. Ivins, said to me and to his son, Anthony C. Ivins:

" 'Heber, Anthony, have you read the Book of Mormon?'

"We answered, 'No.'

"He said, 'I want you to read it. I want you to pledge to me that you will not skip a word, and to the one who reads it first, I will give a pair of ten dollar buckskin gloves with beaver tops.'

"Any boy of fourteen who had a pair of those gloves thought he was 'it.' I remember that my mother had urged me to read systematically the Book of Mormon, but I had not done it. I determined to read the book, say, twenty-five pages a day and get the benefit of its contents. I believed its contents were true because my mother and many others had told

me so; and because of the testimony of the teacher of the class that Richard W. Young and I attended, I thought that to win the gloves I would have to read the book so rapidly that I would get no benefit; and therefore decided to let Anthony win the gloves.

"I met my cousin, Anthony C., the next morning, and he asked, 'How many pages have you read?'

"I said: 'I have read twenty-five pages.'

"He said: 'I have read over one hundred and fifty. I sat up until after midnight.'

"I said: 'Good-bye gloves.'

"I went on reading twenty-five pages a day and occasionally I got so interested that I read fifty or seventy-five pages, and, lo and behold, I got through first and got the gloves. He got such a good start he did not bother to read any more until after I got through with the book." (Grant, *Gospel Standards*, pp. 350-51.)

(16-12) He Added Faith in God to His Great Power of Determination and Thus Overcame His Weaknesses

"Years rolled on, and before I was twenty-four I was made the president of the Tooele Stake of Zion. I announced in a speech that lasted seven and a half minutes that I would ask no man in Tooele to be a more honest tithe payer than I would be; that I would ask no man to give more of his means in proportion to what he had than I would give; I would ask no man to live the Word of Wisdom better than I would live it, and I would give the best that was in me for the benefit of the people in that stake of Zion.

"That night I heard in the dark a man say in a contemptuous way: 'It is a pity if the General Authorities

Heber Jeddy Grant, stake president at 23, Apostle at 25

have to send a man out here to preside, . . . that they could not have sent one with sense enough to talk at least ten minutes; and that they had to send a boy to preside over us.'

"When I heard this, I remember thinking: 'The boy is the only one who has any right to complain.' . . . However, I was

not able during the next three or four Sundays to talk as long as I did the first one. I ran out of ideas in five, six, and six and a half minutes.

"At the lunch table after my first short speech which lasted seven and a half minutes, President Smith said: 'Heber, you said you believe the gospel with all your heart, and propose to live it, but

you did not bear your testimony that you know it is true. Don't you know absolutely that this gospel is true?'

"I answered: 'I do not.'

" 'What, you! a president of a stake?' said President Joseph F. Smith

" 'That is what I said.'

" 'President Taylor, I am in favor of undoing this afternoon what we did this morning. I do not think any man should preside over a stake who has not a perfect and abiding knowledge of the divinity of this work.'

"I said: 'I am not going to complain.'

"Brother Taylor had a habit, when something pleased him excessively, of shaking his body and laughing. He said, 'Joseph, Joseph, Joseph, he knows it just as well as you do. The only thing that he does not know is that he does know it. It will be but a short time until he does know it. He leans over backwards. You do not need to worry.'

"I went to the little town of Vernon in Tooele County, took two others with me to do the preaching, and I got up to say a few words and spoke for forty-five minutes with perfect ease under the inspiration of the Lord. That night I shed tears of gratitude to the Lord for the abiding, perfect, and absolute testimony that came into my life of the divinity of this work.

"The next Sunday after speaking at Vernon, I was at Grantsville. I told the Lord I would like to talk forty-five minutes. I got up to speak and ran out of ideas in five minutes, and I was sweating.

"After the meeting I walked out past the farthest house in the west part of Grantsville, I am sure nearly three miles, and I got down behind

Heber J. Grant, Lewis A. Kalsch, Horace S. Ensign, and Alma D. Taylor dedicated Japan for missionary work Sept. 1, 1901

a haystack and I shed some more tears. But they were tears of humiliation. I made a pledge to God there upon that occasion that never again in my life would I stand up before an audience with the feeling that all I needed to do was just stand up and talk; but that I would get up upon all occasions with a desire to say something that might be of benefit to the people to whom I spoke, and not with the spirit of pride, such as I had that day when I stood up in Grantsville. And I have never failed from that day until now—fifty-odd years ago—to have any desire in my heart when speaking except that I might say or read something that

would be of lasting benefit to those who listened to my voice." (Grant, *Gospel Standards*, pp. 191-93.)

(16-13) His Faith in God Gave Him Great Confidence

"I remember as a young man I had $50.00 in my pocket on one occasion which I intended to deposit in the bank. When I went on Thursday morning to fast meeting—the fast meeting used to be held on Thursdays instead of Sundays—and the bishop made an appeal for a donation, I walked up and handed him the $50.00. He took five of it and put it in the drawer and gave the $45.00 back to me and said that was my full share.

"I said, 'Bishop Woolley, by what right do you rob me of putting the Lord in my debt? Didn't you preach here today that the Lord rewards fourfold? My mother is a widow, and she needs $200.00.'

"He said, 'My boy, do you believe that if I take this other $45.00, you will get your $200.00 quicker?'

"I said: 'Certainly.'

"Well, he took it.

"While walking from fast meeting to the place where I worked, an idea popped into my head. I sent a telegram to a man asking him how many bonds of a certain kind he would buy at a specified price within forty-eight hours and allow me to draw a draft on him through Wells Fargo's Bank. He was a man whom I did not know. I had never spoken to him in my life, but I had seen him a time or two on the streets of Salt Lake.

"He wired back that he wanted as many as I could get. My profit on that transaction was $218.50.

"The next day I walked down to the bishop and said: 'Bishop, I made $218.50 after paying that $50.00 donation the other day and so I owe $21.85 in tithing. I will have to dig up the difference between $21.85 and $18.50. The Lord did not quite give me the tithing in addition to a four to one increase.'

"Someone will say that it would have happened anyway. I do not think it would have happened. I do not think I would have had the idea. I do not think I would have sent the telegram.

"I feel in my heart that we grow financially, spiritually, and in every way, as Latter-day Saints, by doing our duty. When we are obedient to the commandments of the Lord and generous with our time and our means, we grow in the spirit and testimony of the

gospel, and I do not believe that we are ever poorer financially. I am a firm believer that the Lord opens up the windows of heaven when we do our duty financially and pours out upon us blessings of a spiritual nature, which are of far greater value than temporal things. But I believe he also gives us blessings of a temporal nature." (Cited in Hinckley, *Life of a Great Leader*, pp. 98-100.)

HIS PERSEVERANCE AND FAITH PAID OFF, AND AT AN EARLY AGE HEBER J. GRANT WAS DOING THINGS THAT ARE USUALLY DONE BY OLDER MEN

(16-14) By the Age of Twenty-Six, Heber Was Respected by Prominent Men of the World

"I had a letter when I, as a young man, was made an apostle, from a nonmember of the Church. . . . Of prominence in the world so far as business affairs are concerned, he was the manager of a great corporation. . . . He said: 'I never thought very much of the leaders of the Mormon people, in fact I thought they were a very bright, keen, designing lot of fellows, getting rich from the tithes that they gathered in from a lot of ignorant, superstitious, and over-zealous religious people. But now that you are one of the fifteen men at the head of the Mormon Church, I apologize to the other fourteen. I know that if there were anything crooked in the management of the Mormon Church you would give it all away.'" (Grant, *Gospel Standards*, p. 70.)

(16-15) He Was Overwhelmed by His Call to the Apostleship

"I have felt my own lack of ability. In fact when I was called as one of the apostles I arose to my feet to say it was beyond anything I was

worthy of, and as I was rising the thought came to me, 'You know as you know that you live that John Taylor is a prophet of God, and to decline this office when he had received a revelation is equivalent to repudiating the prophet.' I said, 'I will accept the office and do my best.' I remember that it was with difficulty that I took my seat without fainting." (Grant, *Gospel Standards*, p. 194.)

(16-16) A Revelation Was Given to Elder Grant Which Helped Him to Overcome His Sense of Inadequacy in the Office to Which He Had Been Called

"There are two spirits striving with us always, one telling us to continue our labor for good, and one telling us that with the faults and failings of our nature we are unworthy. I can truthfully say that from October, 1882, until February, 1883, that spirit followed me day and night, telling me that I was unworthy to be an apostle of the Church, and that I ought to resign. When I would testify of my knowledge that Jesus is the Christ, the Son of the living God, the Redeemer of mankind, it seemed as though a voice would say to me: 'You lie! You lie! You have never seen Him.'

"While on the Navajo Indian reservation with Brigham Young, Jr., and a number of others, . . . I was riding along with Lot Smith at the rear of that procession. Suddenly the road veered to the left almost straight, but there was a well-beaten path leading ahead. I said: 'Stop, Lot, stop. Where does this trail lead? . . . ' He said, 'It leads to an immense gully just a short distance ahead, that it is impossible to cross with a wagon. . . . '

"I had visited the day before the spot where a Navajo Indian had

asked George A. Smith, Jr., to let him look at his pistol. George A. handed it to him, and the Navajo shot him.

"I said, 'Lot, is there any danger from Indians here?'

" 'None at all.'

" 'I want to be all alone. Go ahead and follow the crowd.' . . .

"As I was riding along to meet them on the other side, I seemed to see, and I seemed to hear, what to me is one of the most real things in all my life. I seemed to hear the words that were spoken. I listened to the discussion with a great deal of interest. The First Presidency and the Quorum of the Twelve Apostles had not been able to agree on two men to fill the vacancies in the Quorum of the Twelve. There had been a vacancy of one for two years, and a vacancy of two for one year, and the conferences had adjourned without the vacancies' being filled. In this council the Savior was present, my father was there, and the Prophet Joseph Smith was there. They discussed the question that a mistake had been made in not filling those two vacancies and that in all probability it would be another six months before the Quorum would be completed. And they discussed as to whom they wanted to occupy those positions, and decided that the way to remedy the mistake that had been made in not filling these vacancies was to send a revelation. It was given to me that the Prophet Joseph Smith and my father mentioned me and requested that I be called to that position. I sat there and wept for joy. It was given to me that I had done nothing to entitle me to that exalted position, except that I had lived a clean, sweet life. It was given to me that because of my father's having practically sacrificed his life in what was known as the great reformation, so

to speak, of the people in early days, having been practically a martyr, that the Prophet Joseph and my father desired me to have that position, and it was because of their faithful labors that I was called, and not because of anything I had done of myself or any great thing that I had accomplished. It was also given to me that that was all these men, the Prophet and my father, could do for me. From that day it depended upon me and upon me alone as to whether I made a success of my life or a failure. . . .

"No man could have been more unhappy than I was from October, 1882, until February, 1883, but from that day I have never been bothered, night or day, with the idea that I was not worthy to stand as an apostle, and I have not been worried since the last words uttered by Joseph F. Smith to me: 'The Lord bless you, my boy, the Lord bless you: you have got a great responsibility. Always remember this is the Lord's work and not man's. The Lord is greater than any man. He knows whom He wants to lead His Church, and never makes any mistake. The Lord bless you.' " (Grant, *Gospel Standards,* pp. 194-96.)

(16-17) Elder Teasdale's Prophecy Was Confirmed by the Spirit to President Grant

"Forty years ago this October conference [1922], I met the late Elder George Teasdale at the south gate of the Tabernacle grounds. He shook hands with me and said: 'Brother Grant, I am delighted to see you. You and I are going to be—' and he stopped suddenly and his face turned red. But the Lord gave me the balance of the sentence. . . . The balance of Brother Teasdale's sentence was—'sustained this afternoon as apostles of the Lord Jesus Christ to

fill the vacancies in the Quorum. And that went through me like a shock of electricity. . . .

"Those of you who were at that conference remember that it adjourned without filling those vacancies. I do not believe that any mortal man ever more humbly supplicated God during the next few days to forgive him for his egotism than I did for thinking I was to be chosen as an apostle. As you are aware, within a week a revelation came to John Taylor calling Brother Teasdale and myself to those positions." (Grant, *Gospel Standards,* pp. 193-94.)

PRESIDENT GRANT'S TEACHINGS REFLECTED A PHILOSOPHY OF SUCCESS FOR THIS LIFE AND FOR ETERNITY

(16-18) He Predicted the Success of the Church Because It Was Based on Truth

"It is not out of place to predict that the people of the Church of Jesus Christ of Latter-day Saints will continue to thrive and prosper, spiritually and temporally, as long as they (1) keep the commandments of God and (2) walk in the way which He shall point out through His inspired servants holding the Holy Priesthood. They are a people whose faith, teachings, thrift, and temporal and spiritual progress will be a blessing and an advantage to the whole nation. A people whom none need to fear, but on the contrary, bless and welcome, because they seek to do the will of the Lord, to treat all people in conformity with the principles of justice and righteousness, themselves loyal and law-abiding, obedient to the rules and regulations of the just governments of the earth, and the vitalizing gospel of Jesus Christ, established and restored through

Heber J. Grant, his wife Emily Wells Grant, and daughters in England (1914)

the instrumentality of Joseph Smith by visitation of God and His Son, Jesus the Christ, who stands at the head of the great and marvelous work in which we are engaged. Their motto is 'Truth and Liberty,' and they would extend these to all mankind, and make all mankind partakers of the influence of peace and righteousness which accompany the true gospel of Jesus Christ—the only means by which peace and the brotherhood of man may be established in all the world.'' (Grant, *Gospel Standards*, pp. 101-2.)

(16-19) Willingness to Sacrifice Was One of the Reasons President Grant Could Stay with His Good Resolutions

''I have never seen the day since I became the president of Tooele Stake of Zion, at the time I was not yet twenty-four years of age, when I did not want to know what the president of the Church wanted, and what the leading officials of the Church wanted me to do, and that I did not want to do whatever they would have me to do, no matter what my personal likes or dislikes

might be. I have sacrificed my own financial prospects to a great extent, among the prospects being the one this dear friend of mine offered me [Colonel A. G. Hawes], a little job of forty thousand dollars a year when the Church was making me an allowance in tithing office orders of three thousand six hundred dollars.'' (Grant, *Gospel Standards*, pp. 200-201.)

(16-20) Section 121 of the Doctrine and Covenants Was One of the Disciplines in His Life

''In talking to the Latter-day Saints,

there is no revelation in all the Doctrine and Covenants that I have quoted from so often as that contained in Section 121 . . . that 'No power or influence can or ought to be maintained by virtue of the Priesthood, only by persuasion, by long-suffering, by gentleness and meekness, and by love unfeigned.'

"There is no danger of a Priesthood of this kind—gentleness, and meekness, and love unfeigned. But when we exercise control, or domination, or compulsion, upon the souls of the children of men, in any degree of unrighteousness, behold, the heavens withdraw themseves. The Spirit of the Lord is grieved. And when it is withdrawn, 'Amen to the Priesthood or the authority of that man.' These are the words of God." (Grant, *Gospel Standards*, p. 68.)

(16-21) There Is Value in Fault-Finding, but Only of Self

"I have given much advice to the Latter-day Saints in my time, and one of the principal items was never to criticize anyone but ourselves. I believe in fault-finding for breakfast, dinner and supper, but only with our own dear selves." (Grant, *Gospel Standards*, p. 47.)

(16-22) His Definition of Success Was Very Simple and Practical

"Not he who merely succeeds in making a fortune, and in so doing blunts the natural affections of the heart, and chases therefrom the love of his fellows, can be said to be truly successful: but he who so lives that those who know him best shall love him most; and that God, who knows not only his deeds, but also the inmost sentiments of his heart, shall love him; of such an one, only—notwithstanding he may die in poverty—can it be said

indeed and of a truth, 'he should be crowned with the wealth of success.' " (Heber J. Grant in *CR*, Oct. 1911, p. 24.)

(16-23) Work Is the Key to Progress

"I assert with confidence that the law of success, here and hereafter, is to have a humble and a prayerful heart, and to work, *work*, WORK.

"The Lord is no respecter of persons, and will give success to all who work for it. If I can only impress upon the minds of the youth of Zion the eloquence, the inexpressible eloquence of work, I shall feel fully repaid.

"I believe in the man who is willing to do the things which the Lord has commanded, and who shows his faith by his works." (Grant, *Gospel Standards*, p. 182.)

(16-24) Living As Best We Know How

"It is by exercise and by practice that we become proficient in any of the vocations or avocations of life, whether it be of a religious or of a secular character. . . .

"The man that grows each day of his life is the man that fills the plain, simple, everyday duties which devolve upon him. . . .

"I do not believe that any man lives up to his ideals, but if we are striving, if we are working, if we are trying, to the best of our ability, to improve day by day, then we are in the line of our duty. If we are seeking to remedy our own defects, if we are so living that we can ask God for light, for knowledge, for intelligence, and above all, for His Spirit, that we may overcome our weaknesses, then, I can tell you, we are in the straight and narrow path that leads to life eternal. Then we need have no fear." (Grant, *Gospel Standards*, pp. 184-85.)

"I have found nothing in the battle

of life that has been of more value to me than to perform the duty of today to the best of my ability. I know that where young men do this, they will be better prepared for the labors of tomorrow." (Grant, *Gospel Standards*, p. 184.)

(16-25) One of the Secrets of Success Is Service

"I am converted to the thought that the way to peace and happiness in life is by giving service. Service is the true key, I believe, to happiness, because when we perform labors like missionary work, all the rest of our lives we can look back upon our accomplishments in the mission field. When we perform any acts of kindness, they bring a feeling of satisfaction and pleasure into our hearts, while ordinary amusements pass away. We can't look back with any particular satisfaction upon having spent an evening just for the privilege of laughing loud and long." (Grant, *Gospel Standards*, p. 187.)

PRESIDENT GRANT SAW THE CHURCH AND THE GOSPEL PRINCIPLES AS THE KEYS TO TRUE SUCCESS

(16-26) We Have a Religion That Is Better Than We Are

"Many have said that the Mormon people were better than their religion. I heard a magnificent talk from this stand a few Sundays ago by Brother Joseph S. Wells, in which he repudiated this statement. He told how utterly impossible it is for a people to be better than the gospel of our Lord and Master Jesus Christ. I don't know that I ever listened to remarks that impressed me more profoundly than his did upon that occasion, and I endorse them with all my heart. No man lives today, in the Church of Jesus Christ of Latter-day Saints, who is fully

living up to the teachings of the gospel of our Lord and Master Jesus Christ. By and with the help of the Lord, we are trying to do it; but there is no man in the Church of Christ who claims infallibility. We acknowledge our weaknesses, but while we acknowledge them we can also proclaim to the world our strength, strength in the knowledge that God lives, that Jesus is the Christ, that Joseph Smith is a prophet of God, and that we have the truth to proclaim to the world." (Grant, *Gospel Standards*, pp. 100-101.)

(16-27) Joseph Smith Is Not a Problem but an Asset

"I have met hundreds of men who have said: 'If it were not for Joseph Smith I could accept your religion.' Any man who does not believe in Joseph Smith as a prophet of the true and the living God has no right to be in this Church. That revelation to Joseph Smith is the foundation stone. If Joseph Smith did not have that interview with God and Jesus Christ, the whole Mormon fabric is a failure and a fraud. It is not worth anything on earth. But God did come, God did introduce His Son; God did inspire that man to organize the Church of Jesus Christ, and all the opposition of the world is not able to withstand the truth. It is flourishing; it is growing, and it will grow more." (Grant, *Gospel Standards*, p. 15.)

(16-28) It Is Obvious That We Can Profit from the Lord's Help

"When I look around and see the mistakes that I have made, and those that my brethren make from time to time; when I realize how many of those who have been wonderfully blessed of the Lord have fallen by the wayside, it fills me with humility. It fills me with the spirit of meekness and with an earnest desire that I may ever seek to know the mind and the will of God and to keep His commandments rather than to follow out my own desires." (Grant, *Gospel Standards*, p. 36.)

(16-29) The Mormons Are a Happy People

"I call to mind that upon one occasion a man ridiculed the Latter-day Saints, saying, 'You people are always happy. If a man hits a Mormon and knocks him down, the Mormon thanks the Lord because he needed a little chastisement; and if you hit at a Mormon and miss him, he thanks the Lord for not getting hit.' " (Grant, *Gospel Standards*, p. 99.)

If faith is dead without good works, then it follows that you can measure your faith by the good you accomplish. Somehow the mountain will be moved. But you have to start. That usually is the hardest part—starting. And each task well done puts something in you that will help you do the next task. And you gradually will get better and better.

Of course, a Latter-day Saint wants to look back and see that much of the good he has done has been in the service of his Master. "For how knoweth a man the master whom he has not served, and who is a stranger unto him, and is far from the thoughts and intents of his heart?" (Mosiah 5:13.)

With the life of Heber J. Grant as one of your examples, perhaps some day you can say something analogous to the following:

"It has been one of the joys of my life, because of the knowledge which I have of the divine mission of the Savior, to bear my testimony in England, Ireland, Scotland, Wales, Germany, France, Belgium, Holland, Switzerland, Italy, Norway, Sweden, Denmark, Czechoslovakia, Canada, Mexico, in most of the states of the American union, in far-off Japan, and in the Hawaiian Islands, and to lift up my voice declaring that our Heavenly Father and His beloved Son have again spoken from the heavens and that God introduced His Son to Joseph Smith and instructed him to hear His Son; and the Savior promised Joseph Smith that he should be the instrument in the hands of God of again establishing the Church of Jesus Christ upon the earth."

—"HEBER J. GRANT, 1938, Christmas Radio Message."

(Cited in Grant, *Gospel Standards*, p. 189.)

Yours Sincerely,
Heber J. Grant

Oct. 21/20.

HARTSOOK
PHOTO
CALIF.

CHAPTER 17

TO BE ACCOUNTABLE AS A STEWARD OVER EARTHLY BLESSINGS

INTRODUCTION

A man named Job lived in Uz. Though no one knows exactly where that was or exactly when Job lived, it is agreed that he was a chieftain or prince of the East, and that he was very wealthy and as righteous as he was rich. Job suffered great afflictions. He lost everything—his family, his wealth, his influence, most of his friends, even his health.

Most people who read and write about Job become so engrossed in his suffering and in the meaning of suffering that they miss some very significant details about Job's character and activities before afflictions. You must remember that the Lord described Job as a perfect man *before* his afflictions. So if you want to know what a perfect man is like, study Job with the intent of finding descriptions of his activities before he climbed upon the ash pile and began to scrape his boils with a potsherd. (The most productive chapters are Job 29 and 31.)

As you read this chapter on the life of President Heber J. Grant, you will see that he was a man who approached perfection and was very much like Job in his feelings and practices. And you will find a pattern you can safely follow in fashioning your own life.

PRESIDENT GRANT'S LIFE PREPARED HIM FOR HIS ROLE IN THE WELFARE PROGRAM OF THE CHURCH

(17-1) Heber J. Grant Was Deeply Affected by the Sacrifices of His Family

"I want to say that I have never heard and never expect to hear, to

the day of my death, my favorite hymn, 'Come, come, ye Saints, no toil nor labor fear, But with joy wend your way,' but I think of the death and the burial of my little baby sister and the wolves digging up her body on the plains. I think of the death of my father's first wife and the bringing of her body here for burial from Echo Canyon. I think of others that I know about, who laid down their lives. I think of that wonderful journey of Brigham Young and his band of Pioneers, those who followed him. And my heart goes out in gratitude beyond all the power with which God has given me to express it, that my father and my mother were among those who were true to God, and who made those sacrifices for the conviction of their hearts because of the knowledge that they had that God lives, that Jesus is the Christ, and that Joseph Smith is His Prophet." (Heber J. Grant, *Gospel Standards*, p. 342.)

(17-2) He Rose from Inconspicuous Poverty to Great Prominence in Both Spiritual and Temporal Things

"Judging from the viewpoint of earthly possessions, President Grant's boyhood, inconspicuous as it was, and sometimes ridiculed, was spent on the borderline of poverty; yet, from humble

circumstances, by force of energy, intellectual brilliance, determination, and persistence, he rose to high honors in business as well as in ecclesiastical realms.

"The presence today of hundreds of you prominent business men bears eloquent testimony of the respect and honor he achieved among you.

"At his death President Grant was president and director of eight financial institutions (several of which he himself was founder), and, until recently, a director of the Union Pacific Railroad. President Grant is nationally recognized for his sound judgment and clear vision on economic questions, and, greatest and most honorable of all, through worthiness and service, became the President of the Church, the chosen representative of the Lord and Savior, Jesus Christ.

"As long as memory and the written word last, the name of this noble man will connote the esteem, honor, and praise that accompany a successful life." (David O. McKay, "President Heber J. Grant," *Improvement Era*, June 1945, p. 334.)

(17-3) President Grant Never Forgot a Childhood Lesson That Taught Him the Sacredness of Independence and Family Responsibility

"Referring to that wonderful mother of mine, I remember that one day we had at least a half dozen, if not more, buckets on the floor catching the rain that came through the roof. It was raining very heavily, and Bishop Edwin D. Woolley came into the house, and he said:

" 'Why, Widow Grant, this will never do. I shall take some of the money from the fast offerings to put a new roof on this house.'

" 'Oh, no, you won't,' said mother. 'No relief money will ever put a roof on my house. I have sewing here.' (She supported herself and me with a needle and thread for many years; later with a Wheeler and Wilcox sewing machine. I had to be mighty careful not to take hold of a thread and pull it, or I might have my clothes fall off; they had not learned how to fasten the stitches of that machine. They later made sewing machines that overcame this difficulty.)

"Mother said, 'When I get through with this sewing that I am now doing, I will buy some shingles and patch the holes, and this house will take care of me until my son gets to be a man and builds a new one for me.'

"The bishop went away and said he was very sorry for Widow Grant, that if she waited for that boy to build a house she would never have one, for he was the laziest boy in the whole Thirteenth Ward. He went on to tell that I wasted my time throwing a ball across the fence behind the house hour after hour, day after day, and week after week, at his adobe barn.

"Thank the Lord for a mother who was a general as well as a Latter-day Saint; who realized that it was a remarkable and splendid thing to encourage a boy to do something besides perhaps milking cows if he was on a farm, if he had ambitions along athletic lines." (Grant, *Gospel Standards*, pp. 343-44.)

(17-4) President Grant's Closest Associates Knew He Was a Generous Man

"President Grant enjoyed making money, but he loved to use it for the benefit of others. On more than one occasion, quietly, usually, forcefully, if necessary, but always unostentatiously, he has protected the good name of his associates, has paid mortgages on widows' homes, has paid expenses of missionaries, given employment to the unemployed, rendered help and succor wherever needed. No mind has been more eager to bless, no heart more tender, no hand more generous than the heart and hand of President Grant. Thus in 'going about doing good' he 'fanned the flame of human love, and raised the standard of civil virtue among mankind.' " (McKay, "President Heber J. Grant," p. 361.)

"No one will ever know how many mortgages on homes of widows he paid out of his own funds. Time and again he would inquire as to his bank balance. He had no special interest in the accumulation of money except for the good he could do with it." (Joseph Anderson, *Prophets I Have Known*, p. 30.)

(17-5) Heber J. Grant Was Personally Acquainted with Financial Success

"As a young man Heber J. Grant proceeded with boldness to play a large role in the economic history of his people. He was a pioneer in industry, second only to Brigham Young. Pioneering in industry requires much the same sturdy qualities that pioneering new lands requires: faith, vision, imagination, patience, and fortitude, backed by a determination that knows no failure. Heber J. Grant had all of these qualities.

"A boyhood associate, Heber M. Wells, said this of him: 'He has probably been instrumental in establishing and furthering the cause of more successful intermountain industries than any other man of his time. His personal credit, his unquestioned integrity, his super-salesmanship brought capital to the aid of the Church, the community, and private enterprises. In times of panic and in times of plenty Heber J. Grant has been able to raise a few dollars or millions where other men have failed to raise any amount. This has been done largely by his personal guarantee and persuasion. He has never repudiated or failed to pay a dollar of obligation for which he was directly or indirectly responsible, legally or morally, and the result is that today, as during all the many decades since he was a young man, he can walk into the offices of executives and directors of great financial institutions in America and be affectionately greeted by men who are proud to know him as a friend and a leader of financial industries.' " (Bryant S. Hinckley, *Heber J. Grant: Highlights in the Life of a Great Leader*, 51-52.)

(17-6) Heber J. Grant Was Personally Acquainted with the Agony of Debt

His daughter Lucy wrote:

"During those lean years which followed the panic of 1893, when to raise a nickel was harder than it had been to give $5.00, Father still helped those in distress. He knew the widow's lot; he had felt the pinch of poverty; he knew the bitterness and bondage of debt. Through all the dark hours of his life there was a shining and secure faith in God and his promises which sustained him. I know in those years the horror of financial obligation was borne into the souls of those of us who were old enough to see him under this great strain which made us feel that debt was like a huge dragon, into whose ugly mouth the very lifeblood of its victims was drawn. No wonder he was constantly crying unto the

people everywhere to keep out of debt. One whose experiences have been such as his, knows the exquisite pain of honor when on the verge of being crushed, and of a good name when near being dragged into the dust." (Cited in Hinckley, *Life of a Great Leader*, p. 206.)

(17-7) With the Lord's Help, President Grant Preserved His Honor as a Man and as a Saint

"If there is any man living who is entitled to say, 'Keep out of debt,' his name is Heber J. Grant. Thank the Lord that I was able to pay it all, and pay it all without asking a dollar discount from anyone.

"I do not believe I ever would have paid it if I had not been absolutely honest with the Lord. When I made any money, the first debt I paid was to the Lord. And I believe beyond a shadow of a doubt, that if the Latter-day Saints as a people, had taken the advice of the prophet of the Lord, and had been efficient tithe payers they would not be in the condition they are today." (Grant, *Gospel Standards*, p. 59.)

PRESIDENT GRANT WAS INSPIRED TO ESTABLISH THE WELFARE PLAN IN HARMONY WITH REVEALED PRINCIPLES

(17-8) The LDS Welfare Plan Was Based on God-Given, Immutable, Moral, and Economic Laws

"Our primary purpose was to set up, in so far as it might be possible, a system under which the curse of idleness would be done away with, the evils of a dole abolished, and independence, industry, thrift, and self-respect be once more established amongst our people. The aim of the Church is to help the people to help themselves. Work is to be re-enthroned as the ruling principle of the lives of our Church membership." (Grant, *Gospel Standards*, pp. 123-24.)

President Grant spoke on the first radio broadcast over KZN in Salt Lake City (1922)

(17-9) The Law of the Fast Is a Temporal and Spiritual Foundation Stone of the Welfare Plan

"Let me promise you here today that if the Latter-day Saints will honestly and conscientiously from this day forth, as a people, keep the monthly fast and pay into the hands of their bishops the actual amount that they would have spent for food for the two meals from which they have refrained; and if in addition to that they will pay their honest tithing, it will solve all of the problems in connection with taking care of the Latter-day Saints. We would have all the money necessary to take care of all the idle and all the poor.

"Every living soul among the Latter-day Saints that fasts two meals once a month will be benefited spiritually and be built up in the faith of the gospel of the Lord Jesus Christ—benefited spiritually in a wonderful way—and sufficient means will be in the hands of the bishops to take care of all the poor." (Grant, *Gospel Standards*, p. 123.)

(17-10) The Covenant of Tithing Is the Law of Financial Success to Church Members

"The law of financial prosperity to the Latter-day Saints, under covenant with God, is to be an honest tithe payer, and not to rob the Lord in tithes and offerings. Prosperity comes to those who observe the law of tithing. When I say prosperity I am not thinking of it in terms of dollars and cents alone, although as a rule the Latter-day Saints who are the best tithe payers are the most prosperous men, financially. But what I count as real prosperity, as the one thing of all others that is of great value to every man and woman living, is the growth in a knowledge of God, and in a testimony, and in the power to live the gospel and to inspire our families to do the same. That is prosperity of the truest kind. . . .

"A man will say, 'I owe my neighbor and must pay him before I can settle my tithing.' Well, I know I owe lots of my neighbors, and they try to collect from me. But I owe God an honest tithing. He has given me a testimony of Jesus and a hope of eternal life, and I intend to pay Him first, and my neighbors afterwards. It is our duty to settle with the Lord first, and I intend to do it, with the help of my Heavenly Father. And I want to say to you, if you will be honest with the Lord, paying your tithing and keeping His commandments, He will not only bless you with the light and inspiration of His holy Spirit, but you will be blessed in dollars and cents; you will be enabled to pay your debts, and the Lord will pour out temporal blessings upon you in great abundance." (Grant, *Gospel Standards*, pp. 58-59.)

(17-11) President Grant Saw the Relationship of Spiritual Laws to Temporal Laws

"In thinking seriously of the economic condition of the world, I am convinced without doubt, that a revelation in the book of Doctrine and Covenants, known as the Word of Wisdom, given by the Lord, the Creator of heaven and earth, to the Prophet Joseph Smith over one hundred years ago, would solve the economic problems not only of our country but of every other country, if it were obeyed by the people of the world." (Heber J. Grant in *CR*, Apr. 1936, p. 48.)

(17-12) The Welfare Plan Expresses a Timeless Concept of Priesthood Responsibility

"The Church Welfare Plan is the expression of a philosophy that is as old as the Church itself, and the Priesthood is the instrumentality through which its aims may be achieved, with auxiliary aid. The

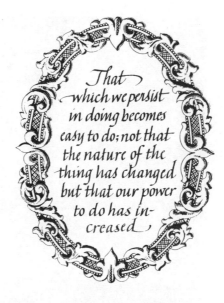

A motto of President Grant's from Ralph Waldo Emerson

Welfare organization which has been called into service since April, 1936, is integral with the Priesthood organization of the Church. . . . in regional, stake, ward, and quorum organizations, the Welfare mechanism is identical with responsible Priesthood authority and organization. Thus the specialized assignments required for the Welfare Program fall directly on the body of the Priesthood. Particularly is this true in the larger objectives of the program, i.e., raising the level of economic and social welfare of all after meeting the emergency relief needs of the worthy poor and the displaced worker. In meeting the basic 'relief' needs of the program, the Church and the Priesthood have been fortunate in the existence of the Relief Society and its intimate knowledge and experience with the fine art of relief administration. Thus this 'aid' to the Priesthood may be fully capable, with Priesthood cooperation, of dealing permanently with the segment of the Welfare problem entailed in

questions of relief. In so marshaling the traditional function of this auxiliary within the objectives of the Plan, the Priesthood is not relieved of administrative responsibility." (John A. Widtsoe, *Priesthood and Church Government*, pp. 284-85.)

(17-13) The Plan Was to Use Voluntary Administration and Voluntary Giving

"As promised at the last April Conference, we inaugurated a Church Security Plan [an early name for the Church Welfare System]. To facilitate the putting into effect of the Plan, we organized a General Committee whose functions were to represent the Presiding Bishopric in the detailed administrative work of coordinating and supervising the labors of the various regularly established Church organizations in their large and important security operations.

"The Security Plan contemplated no new Church machinery for this work, but provided for the use of all the existing Church organizations—the Stake and Ward organizations, the Priesthood quorums, the Relief Society, and the various auxiliary organizations—each of which was to render the maximum service it could furnish in the interest of the general welfare of the Church.

"The announced objective set for the Church under this Program was to provide by October 1, 1936, by a wholly voluntary system of gifts in cash or in kind, sufficient food, fuel, clothing, and bedding to supply through the coming winter, every needy and worthy Church family unable to furnish these for itself, in order that no member of the Church should suffer in these times of stress and emergency." (Heber J. Grant in *CR*, Oct. 1936, pp. 2-3.)

President Heber J. Grant

(17-14) In Introducing the Welfare Plan, President Grant Tied Its Respect for Work and Property to Inspired Men and Documents

"I desire to call attention to a statement by President Brigham Young:

" 'My experience has taught me, and it has become a principle with me, that it is never any benefit to give out and out, to man or woman, money, food, clothing, or anything else, if they are able-bodied and can work and earn what they need, when there is anything on earth for them to do. This is my principle and I try to act upon it. To pursue a contrary course would ruin any community in the world and make them idlers.'

"And what would ruin a community would ruin a state, and I might incidentally remark, a nation also.

" 'The Constitution of the United States is a glorious standard; it is founded in the wisdom of God. It is a heavenly banner; it is, to all those who are privileged with the sweets of liberty, like the cooling shades and refreshing waters of a great rock in a weary and thirsty land. It is like a great tree, under whose branches men from every clime can be shielded from the burning rays of the sun.'—*Joseph Smith*.

"From my childhood days I have understood that we believe absolutely that the Constitution of our country was an inspired instrument, and that God directed those who created it and those who defended the independence of this nation." (Heber J. Grant in *CR*, Oct., 1936, pp. 6-7.)

(17-15) In the Face of Political Opposition President Grant Remained True to a Literal Interpretation of God's Law

"We have on at the present time a great political campaign, and I want to say to the Saints that I hope they will not allow their political affiliations, their regard for political affairs, to cause feelings of ill-will towards one another. I have had some of the most insulting letters that ever came to me, condemning me for not being in favor of the Townsend Plan [a government plan to provide security for the aged] and that I must be ignorant of the Plan. I am not ignorant of the Plan. I have not read every word of it, but I have asked one of my secretaries to read every word of the Plan and to give me the important points, and to my mind it is in direct opposition to everything I have quoted here today from Brigham Young and from the revelations of the Lord. The idea of allowing every man and woman who has reached the age of sixty years and wishes to retire from working to get $200 a month from the government! There is nothing truer than Brigham Young's statement, that we should give nothing to people, unless they are not able to work, without requiring them to do something for it. . . .

"Let every Latter-day Saint who has a farm, farm it, and not try to borrow money to be paid back by the government. Let every man feel that he is the architect and builder of his own life, and that he proposes to make a success of it by working. 'Six days shalt thou labor and do all thy work,' and rest on the seventh, and do not be willing to labor four or five days and then only half labor. Let every Latter-day Saint give value received for everything he gets, whether it be in work, or whatever he does." (Heber J. Grant in *CR*, Oct., 1936, p. 13.)

(17-16) The Welfare Plan Was Old Yet New

"Just a word I desire to say in endorsement of the [Welfare] Plan which has been spoken of at other sessions of this conference, looking after the interests of the members of the Church. Some have said that this is new. I look upon it as a return to that which is old, which is always new when it is true, for that which is true never becomes old, but it is a return to first principles. I hope that it will lead us in love, in the spirit of sympathy, fellowship and brotherly love, to have the interest in our fellowmen that we ought to have, and increase in our hearts a desire to keep the commandments of the Lord and walk in the light as we understand that light, that we may be constantly guided by his Spirit." (Joseph Fielding Smith in *CR*, Oct. 1936, p. 59.)

(17-17) President Lee Bore Testimony of the Foresight That Was Manifested in the Years Before the Plan Was Announced

"For the last five glorious, strenuous years, I have labored, under a call from the First Presidency, with a group of men in the development of and the unfolding of what we have called the Church Welfare Plan. I felt that I should bear my testimony to you concerning that work as I close. It was on April 20th, 1935, when I was called to the office of the First Presidency. That was a year before official announcement of the Welfare Plan was made in this Tabernacle. There, after an entire half day session, at which President Grant and President McKay were present, President Clark then being in the East—they had some communications with him, so that all members of the Presidency were in agreement—I was astounded to learn that for years there had been before them, as a result of their thinking and planning and as the result of the inspiration of Almighty God, the genius of the very plan that is being carried out and was in waiting and in preparation for a time when in their judgment the faith of the Latter-day Saints was such that they were willing to follow the counsel of the men who lead and preside in this Church." (Harold B. Lee in *CR*, Apr. 1941, pp. 120-21.)

ALL THE SAINTS CAN PROFIT FROM THE APPLICATION OF THE WELFARE PRINCIPLES, INCLUDING THE LAW OF SACRIFICE, ADVOCATED BY PRESIDENT GRANT

Some might consider it strange that President Grant included the Word of Wisdom as an important welfare principle. In fact, he mentioned it as a welfare principle almost as often as payment of tithing and the avoidance of debt. But it doesn't take too much thought to recognize the Word of Wisdom as a welfare principle, because welfare is based on caring for oneself and on saving today's resources for use tomorrow. President Grant used to say that if all the Saints obeyed the Word of Wisdom there would be no economic problems among them. Perhaps he was thinking of more than just the money they would save by not buying the harmful things. He also mentioned the money wasted in treating the illnesses that were directly attributable to harmful substances, the loss of employment, the loss of production caused by hangovers and smoking and coffee breaks, and the accidents on the highways caused by drunken drivers and in industry by drunken employees. But he also may have been thinking of the high level of righteousness that inevitably accompanies obedience to the Word of Wisdom.

As you read the following items, see if you can understand why President Grant continually tied personal and Church welfare to principles of obedience that can be obeyed only by a people who look beyond today's needs. For instance, can a person see that tithing will benefit him economically if he cannot see that God has a hand in his temporal blessings?

(17-18) Payment of Tithes and Offerings Helps Overcome Personal Selfishness

"So far as we have investigated in some of the wards—and we have investigated carefully—more than eighty percent of those who are in distress have not lived the law of the Lord (tithing). . . .

"Some people have found it very hard to pay their tithing. The harder it is for an individual to comply with requirements of the Lord in the payment of his tithing, the greater the benefit when he finally does pay it. The Lord loves a generous giver. No man living

upon the earth can pay donations for the poor, can pay for building meetinghouses and temples, academies, and universities, can take of his means and send his boys and girls to proclaim this gospel, without removing selfishness from his soul, no matter how selfish he was when he started in. That is one of the finest things in all the world for men—to get to that point where the selfishness in their natures is cured. When it is eradicated from their dispositions, they are glad and anxious and willing and seeking the opportunity to do good with the means that the Lord places in their hands, instead of trying to get more of it." (Grant, *Gospel Standards*, p. 62.)

(17-19) Avoiding Debt Is a Welfare Principle

"If a person owned what he had and did not have to pay interest, and only bought as he had the money to buy, the majority of people would be in reasonably comfortable circumstances. No matter what the price of potatoes or wheat or anything else was, they would have just as much of it. They would have just as many sacks of flour to take care of themselves, as though the wheat cost more. It has been due to debt, I think, that the main part of this suffering has come. We have mortgaged our future without taking into account the incidents that may happen—sickness, operations, etc." (Grant, *Gospel Standards*, p. 112.)

(17-20) President Grant Subscribed to the Doctrine of Self-Reliance

"Nothing destroys the individuality of a man, a woman, or a child so much as the failure to be self-reliant." (Grant, *Gospel Standards,* p. 184.)

(17-21) Development of Talents Is a Forward-Looking Principle That Aids Personal and Family Welfare

"Developing his own talents was one of his chief objectives and the greatest source of his accomplishments. He never criticized other men's weaknesses but made war on his own. That practice has in it the very essence of personal growth. Self-analysis and self-discipline are the twin virtues that underlie individual development. He engaged in criticism of himself but not of others." (Hinckley, *Life of a Great Leader*, p. 50.)

(17-22) Under Direction of President Grant, a Member of the First Presidency Taught That a Knowledge of Future Calamities Should Encourage Us to Practice Family Welfare

"This prospect gives a new significance to the Church Security [Welfare] Plan and gives the final but unneeded evidence of the inspiration which led President Grant to inaugurate that great and far-reaching movement. If that chaos shall come which these men fear, then those only will survive who shall extend the one to the other a mutual, brotherly, loving, unselfish help. In this view we may not believe we are at the end of the Security [Welfare] Plan; we are only at the beginning. . . .

"Reading together the Scriptures and the signs of the times, and remembering that the measure of time with God is not the measure of time with man, one cannot but consider whether we be not now in the very times foretold by the Savior in his great discourse on the Mount of Olives, and predicted by the prophets from most ancient times. Are not the anti-Christs now walking the earth? . . .

"Let us avoid debt as we would avoid a plague; where we are now in debt let us get out of debt; if not today, then tomorrow.

"Let us straitly and strictly live within our incomes, and save a little.

"Let every head of every household see to it that he has on hand enough food and clothing, and, where possible, fuel also, for at least a year ahead. You of small means put your money in foodstuffs and wearing apparel, not in stocks and bonds; you of large means will think you know how to care for yourselves, but I may venture to suggest that you do not speculate. Let every head of every household aim to own his own home, free from mortgage. Let every man who has a garden spot, garden it; every man who owns a farm, farm it.

"Let us again clothe ourselves with these proved and sterling virtues—honesty, truthfulness, chastity, sobriety, temperance, industry and thrift; let us discard all covetousness and greed.

"We must purge our hearts of the love of ease; we must put out from our lives the curse of idleness. God declared that mortal man should earn his bread by the sweat of his brow. That is the law of this world. In the past it has taxed our economic strength and system to keep the relatively very few idle rich. That task shows us that no great groups can be kept in idleness. It surely is not natural to believe that they may. People have been insufficiently fed and clad with every one working who was able to work. Why delude ourselves into thinking that a third of us may live in idleness and all of us be better off? If a third may be idle, and all be better off than now, then why not a half idle and increase the prosperity; and if half, why not two-thirds, and if two-thirds, then all of us idle and have every man a millionaire, and nobody working.

"Furthermore, to provide by law

A beautifully crafted desk used by President Grant for many years

that a third shall live off the two-thirds, is to set up a legal slavery of the two-thirds who work. As one within the age of the proposed idle class, I protest with all the spirit and strength I possess against the infliction upon me of such a curse. May the Lord forbid that this shall come.

"For the decrepit and infirm, from any cause, I have, we all have, the deepest sympathy, as also for those in distress from causes beyond their control. To all such we owe a sacred duty to help. God's law has always been 'Thou shalt love thy neighbor as thy self.' This we must do. But side by side with this law is that other law, declared from the beginning, that while man can work, he must work. These are the two great laws, the two fundamental principles behind the Church Security Plan. The aim of that plan is to put those two great truths into the lives of all of us." (J. Reuben Clark, Jr., in *CR*, Apr. 1937, pp. 25-27.)

Wisdom is the ability to see the end results of the beliefs you espouse and the acts you commit. The farther you can see, the greater is your wisdom. Everything President Grant did, he did with an eye to the future. As he looked to the future, President Grant maintained a balance. Not all that he did or advocated was for the next world only, although that was ever paramount. His philosophy was a formula for happiness in this life, too. And this brought him to those stations in life which few men achieve. And now he walks with the great in the eternal worlds. Do you plan to walk eternally with such company?

"In the late afternoon, May 14, 1945, President Heber J. Grant, peacefully passed away at his residence in Salt Lake City. He had been ailing for the past five years, but his courage and determination to press on and perform his duty, never deserted him. Each day, up to a short time before his death, he was found at the office attending to duties as much as the physician permitted him to do. His life had been one of great activity. In his early years he appeared frail, was rejected for insurance, because of his

Main Street in Salt Lake City about 1926

physical condition, however, he had been active always, engaging in athletics, one time belonging to the champion baseball team of Utah. His energy was marvelous and his activities never ceased. There was never any compromise on his part with evil. Some of his strongest characteristics the public never realized. He had a tender, sympathetic nature,

loved his friends dearly; was kind to the distressed; assisted the needy scores upon scores of times, the knowledge of which never got into any earthly record. His testimony of the Truth never wavered. His friends were legion outside of the Church, and he was dearly loved by his people." (Joseph Fielding Smith, *Essentials in Church History*, pp. 530-31.)

UNIT NINE

GEORGE ALBERT SMITH

Eighth President of the Church

OVERVIEW

Ulysses S. Grant, Charles Darwin, Alexander Graham Bell—these were some of the names that commanded the attention of the world in 1870. In far-away Utah, a premortal appointment was kept with the birth of an infant who received the earthly name by which he would one day be loved and revered by thousands. It was in Salt Lake City on April 4, and the child was named George Albert Smith.

Like other prophets, his youth was unpretentious. He was a pioneer boy, raised amid the excitement that attended the construction of the now famous Salt Lake Temple. He spent his early youth herding cows, riding horses, studying, and performing—he was a musician. His patriarchal blessing at age thirteen had a profound effect upon his mind and attitudes: " . . . thou shalt become a mighty apostle . . . none of thy father's family shall have more power with God than thou shalt have. . . . "[1]

There were years of preparation, work, service, obedience; years that saw him fill a short-term mission to southern Utah, work for Utah's leading department store, and marry his childhood sweetheart, Lucy Woodruff. These were also years of refinement through suffering—typhoid fever, a severe eye injury, two narrow escapes from death while serving a mission to the Southern States. He was afflicted for five painful years with a serious disease. He feared for his life, but the impression came that his earthly mission was not complete. Suffering brought strength and compassion. A call to apostleship came in 1903—he was just thirty-three. Despite almost continuous physical weakness, he traveled, preached, worked, and prayed. Juvenile delinquents, the displaced and homeless, the blind, "splinter groups" of the Church, the Boy Scout movement—all received his attention.

He was a missionary. In one ten-year period, twelve hundred books and pamphlets were mailed to nonnmembers he met during his travels. Historical sites such as the Hill Cumorah and the Sacred Grove were purchased to further spread the message of salvation. Receiver of public monies for the land office of the state of Utah, president of national congresses, chairman of the boards of directors for many companies, active in the support of social improvement and the arts and sciences—all were done with the major intent to present the Church to the world.

In the face of movements to tear down the government of his country, he was relentless in his efforts to sustain and uphold what he knew to be the divinely inspired Constitution. He had the power to reach the spirit and heart of all people, at all levels. Little children responded to his kindness as he played marbles or skipped rope with them. He served for thirty-one years as general superintendent of the Young Men's Mutual Improvement Association.

His apostolic years were spent defending the faith. As president of the European Mission, he overcame prejudice and hostility through visits to government leaders and newspaper editors. He defended the call of living prophets and prophesied that those who shunned the counsel of the prophets would suffer disastrous results.

Hatred, despair, sorrow; this was the mood of the 1940s. War raged and the hearts of people waxed cold. At this critical period, the Lord called on George Albert Smith to lead His people. Here was a man whose love for others had been forged in the very furnace of affliction, a man who had committed himself to the Lord through long nights of prayer and years of service to others. Now he was God's prophet. Ninety train carloads of food and clothing were sent to the stricken Saints in Europe. A special fast was called and money contributed to aid not only Saints but others. Missions were reopened and new ones created.

The full-time missionary force was raised from its wartime low of 386 in 1945 to over 5,800 in 1951. In vision he saw that the Indian people had been neglected. His love went out to them and missions were organized, relief was sent, and personal visits were made. In a nearby land, a group of Saints had broken away from the Church. For ten long years they remained bitter and hurt. Who could the Church send to bring them back into full fellowship? Counsel was sought; President George Albert Smith went, and 1,200 people rejoined the Church. He dedicated temples, regulated stakes, and raised monuments in honor of those who had given so much to the restoration to the Church in these latter days.

Out of his great love for mankind he could not remain silent about the judgments that would engulf the world if they did not repent. Like Elijah, he spoke with power and authority. "It will not be long until calamities will overtake the human family unless there is speedy repentance."[2] He was as courageous as Abinadi, who, in the face of criticism and slander, prophesied as to the results of such evil. Of those who belittled the Prophet Joseph Smith, he said, "[They] will be forgotten and their remains will go back to mother earth, if they have not already gone, and the odor of their infamy will never die, while the glory and honor and majesty and courage and fidelity manifested by the Prophet Joseph Smith will attach to his name forever."[3]

His days were spent in an unwearying effort to bring people closer to the Master whom he served. Then in 1951, George Albert Smith's health failed rapidly, his energy ebbed away. His life's mission was complete. Prior to his death, he called his family to his bedside. One asked, "Is there not something you would care to say to us before you go"? The reply was, "Yes, simply this, I know that my Redeemer liveth; I know that my Redeemer liveth!"[4]

CHAPTER 18

LIFT UP THE HANDS WHICH HANG DOWN STRENGTHEN THE FEEBLE KNEES

INTRODUCTION

The results of the Second World War were ugly and discouraging. It had lasted for more than five years. More than fifty countries had taken part in the war. An estimated fifty-five million people had lost their lives. It had cost over a trillion dollars. Millions in Europe and Asia were without adequate food, shelter, and clothing. Sorrow, hatred, and despair stalked through nations and homes. In one way or another, World War II had touched the lives of nearly everyone on the earth.

On May 21, 1945, at a time when the full extent of carnage and devastation left behind by the war was just becoming apparent, George Albert Smith was moved from his time of preparation into his foreordained position as President of the Church. President Smith did not presume to declare what his personal mission as prophet, seer, and revelator would be. However, Patriarch Joseph F. Smith, son of Hyrum Mack and grandson of Joseph F. (the sixth president of the Church), uttered this prophetic statement:

"It is frequently said that the Lord has raised up a particular man to perform a particular mission. Everyone of us here has heard that discussed and has heard how the peculiar talents of each of the presidents of the Church have been of a special value during his respective mission. I wish that all the members of the Church could have witnessed the council

meeting wherein the Presidency was reorganized. If ever there was a time when the Spirit of the Lord was indubitably manifest, it was on that occasion. Everyone present thrilled to it. Everyone present was aware, beyond doubt, of the absolute rightness of it.

"It is not for me to say what particular mission President George Albert Smith has ahead of him. This I do know, however, that at this particular time in the world's history, never was the need for love among brethren so desperately needed as it is needed today. Furthermore, I do know this, that there is no man of my acquaintance who loves the human family, collectively and individually, more profoundly than does President George Albert Smith. Those two things coming in conjunction, the need for love, his presidency at this time, have for me at least, peculiar significance." (*CR*, Oct. 1945, pp. 31-32.)

Now, as you study the ministry of President George Albert Smith, you may gain new insights into the admonition

"Lift up the hands which hang down, and strengthen the feeble knees." (D&C 81:5.)

FROM HIS CHILDHOOD, GEORGE ALBERT SMITH RESPONDED KEENLY TO TEACHINGS AND EXAMPLES OF LOVE

(18-1) Personal Experience with Great Leaders

George Albert Smith was raised amid the words and lives of great servants of mankind. He was named after his grandfather, George A. Smith, who had been an apostle and a member of the First Presidency. His father, John Henry Smith, was also an apostle and became a counselor to President Joseph F. Smith. But the key was not just good influences. It was the keen response to these influences which molded George Albert Smith. To illustrate: when George Albert Smith was a boy of five years, his mother sent him to deliver a note to President Brigham Young. As he walked through the massive iron gate that led to the home of Brigham Young, the watchman stopped him and asked what he wanted. The boy replied that he wanted to see President Young. The watchman laughed and said he didn't think Brigham Young had time to see a small boy. At that moment, President Young walked out of his home and asked what was going on. The watchman explained and President Young replied, "Show him in." Recalling this incident, George Albert Smith said:

"President Young took me by the hand and led me into his office, sat down at his desk and lifted me up on his knee and put his arm around

me. In the kindest way one could imagine, he said, 'What do you want of President Young?'

"Just think of it! He was President of a great Church and Governor of a Territory, and with all the duties he had to perform, yet I as a little boy was received with as much dignity, and kindness as if I had come as a governor from an adjoining state." (Cited in Arthur R. Bassett, "George Albert Smith: On Reaching Out to Others," *New Era*, Jan. 1972, p. 51.)

Other boys may have been treated graciously by great men, but did you note how deeply impressed this particular five-year-old was with the graciousness of President Young, how vividly he remembered and cherished it?

"From childhood, I have never been taught to do anything improper, or that would harm one of my heavenly Father's children; but from infancy I have been taught to acquire industry, sobriety, honesty, integrity, and all virtues possessed by men and women whom God delights to honor and bless. I thank my heavenly Father this day that these teachings have come to me from Him through His faithful servants." (George Albert Smith in *CR*, Oct. 1906, pp. 46-47.)

(18-2) The Example and Teachings of His Father

This incident is told by George Albert Smith's daughter:

"One day Father was walking down a street in Salt Lake City with his father, John Henry Smith. A drunkard came up to John Henry and asked for a quarter for a hot meal. Without hesitation, John Henry gave him the money. After this incident, George Albert asked his father why he had given the drunkard the money when it was highly possible that he would spend it on liquor. His father

replied that he would give quarters to ten men he thought might use the money on drink, if there was a chance that just one would use it properly." (From a personal interview with Edith Elliott, daughter of President George Albert Smith.)

President Smith himself said this:

" . . . as I think of my regard and my affection for my Father's family, the human family, I remember something my earthly father said, and I think probably I inherited that in part from him. He said, 'I have never seen a child of God so deep in the gutter that I have not had the impulse to stoop down and lift him up and put him on his feet and start him again.' I would like to say I have never seen one of my Father's children in my life that I have not realized he was my brother and that God loves every one of his children, but he does not love our wickedness and our infidelity." (*Church News*, 16 Feb. 1946, p. 8.)

Suppose you took the time to put in writing a list of your most serious goals and aspirations. What would you list as your most desired achievements and qualities? Whatever they might be, we could say that by reading them we would come to know you very well, for "as [a man] thinketh in his heart, so is he." (Proverbs 23:7.) At the age of thirty-four, George Albert Smith prepared such a list. And it was a crucial time to put in writing just what he wanted to do with the balance of his life, for at this young age he had just been called to apostleship. As you read this list of solemn resolves, remember that you are, as it were, looking into the very soul of a young man of prophetic destiny.

"I would be a friend to the friendless and find joy in ministering to the needs of the poor. I would visit the sick and afflicted and inspire in them a desire for faith to be healed. I would teach the truth to the understanding and blessing of all mankind. I would seek out the erring one and try to win him back to a righteous and a happy life. I would not seek to force people to live up to my ideals but rather love them into doing the thing that is right. I would live with the masses and help to solve their problems that their earth life may be happy. I would avoid the publicity of high positions and discourage the flattery of thoughtless friends. I would not knowingly wound the feeling of any, not even one who may have wronged me, but would seek to do him good and make him my friend. I would overcome the tendency to selfishness and jealousy and rejoice in the successes of all the children of my Heavenly Father. I would not be an enemy to any living soul. Knowing that the Redeemer of mankind has offered to the world the only plan that will fully develop us and make us really happy here and hereafter I feel it not only a duty but a blessed privilege to disseminate this truth." (Cited in Bryant S. Hinckley, "Greatness in Men: Superintendent George Albert Smith," *Improvement Era*, Mar. 1932, p. 295.)

Think over such phrases as

"a friend to the friendless,"
"visit the sick and afflicted,"
"seek out the erring one,"
"rejoice in the successes of all the children of my Heavenly Father."

You may want to consider

George Albert Smith about the time of his marriage

preparing such a list or creed to describe the aspirations of your life. What are the serious resolves of *your* heart?

George Albert Smith wrote his list of personal goals about the year 1904. He was sixty-two years of age when the list was first published. According to those who knew him best, he had literally achieved the lofty goals he had desired earlier. He had not just written something nice on a page. He had strived to live according to his creed in every detail. The things in that creed required of him tremendous sacrifice. His love was sincere and constant. He had shown the ultimate in tolerance, trust, and personal concern toward thousands of our Father's children in his travels and labors. He had come to be a sensitive vessel through whom the love of the Master could be made manifest. And in

the life of George Albert Smith we see that love is no idle feeling. It is action—constant, alert, anxious to serve at any cost.

THROUGHOUT HIS MINISTRY, GEORGE ALBERT SMITH TAUGHT AND LIVED THE PRINCIPLE OF LOVE

(18-3) Love Seeks Out the Sick

"God bless the memory of President George Albert Smith. I am grateful beyond my words of expression for the close association which I have had with him in the last few years. I am grateful that my family has lived in the same ward and has come under the benign influence of his sweet spirit. I shall never cease to be grateful for the visits he made to my home while I was serving as a humble missionary in the nations of war-torn Europe at the end of World War II. Particularly am I thankful for a visit in the still of the

night when our little one lay at death's door. Without any announcement, President Smith found time to come into that home and place his hands upon the head of that little one, held in her mother's arms as she had been for many hours, and promise her complete recovery. This was President Smith, he always had time to help, particularly those who were sick, those who needed him most." (Ezra Taft Benson in *CR*, Apr. 1951, p. 46.)

(18-4) Love Seeks Out the Weary

"During the events of the last few days, many memories have crowded in upon my mind. In a late afternoon of a warm, sultry day in August or September, I sat in my office rather tired after the day's work. The University of Utah had had internal dissensions which had been fanned by enemies into a nationwide scandal. I had been called in to assist others who were trying to return the institution and its work to a normal condition. It was the third time in my life that I had been obliged to serve my state in such a capacity. I was weary. Just then there was a knock upon the door, and in walked George Albert Smith. He said, 'I am on the way home after my day's work. I thought of you and the problems that you are expected to solve. I came in to comfort you and to bless you.'

"That was the way of George Albert Smith. Of the many friends I have throughout the state and beyond, he was the only one, except a few of my intimate friends, who took time to give me the loving help in the work I had to do. Of course I appreciated that; I shall never forget it. We talked together for awhile; we parted, he went home. My heart was lifted. I was weary no longer." (John A. Widtsoe in *CR*, Apr. 1951, p. 99.)

(18-5) Love Is Alert for Any Possibility to Serve

". . . on one occasion he was traveling back from a convention. In his company was the daughter of President Heber J. Grant. She tells of his looking across the aisle and seeing a young mother and her children, surrounded by luggage. He felt a need to talk with her and to inquire after her welfare.

" 'In a few minutes President Smith was over talking to the young mother. He came back to our seat and said, "Yes it is just as I thought. The little mother is going on a long journey; I have looked at her ticket. I can't understand why the man who sold it to her didn't know a better route for her to travel. As it is she will have a long wait in Ogden and again in Chicago. I have her ticket and am going to get off in Ogden and see if I can't get it changed so she can make other connections and not have the long wait in Ogden and Chicago." '

"President Smith was off the train the moment it stopped and set the affairs of the young mother in order, having her ticket changed to afford her greater convenience. Such was the sensitivity for others of this man." (Bassett, "George Albert Smith," p. 52.)

(18-6) Love Finds Time for Others

"On a recent trip to the Middle West, he was rushing to catch a train when a mother with four small youngsters stopped him so that her children might have the opportunity of shaking hands with him. Someone took a picture of the incident, and a copy was sent to President Smith with this notation: 'I am sending you this picture because it is a graphic illustration of the man we believe you are. The reason we treasure it so is because, as busy as you were, in spite of the

The Boy Scout program was always near his heart

fact you were being hurried into your car and then to your waiting train, you still took time out to shake the hand of each child in this family.' " (D. Arthur Haycock, "A Day with the President," *Improvement Era*, Apr. 1950, p. 288.)

As George Albert Smith lived, so he encouraged the rest of us to live. He taught that true happiness was in proportion to service rendered to others and that Latter-day Saints were expected to live every day in such a way as to be sensitive to

distress and want. His sermons were sprinkled liberally with statements of love and kindness—to the gardeners who took care of Temple Square, to the ushers who helped with conference sessions, and to the Saints whom he loved dearly: "Brethren, as one who loves you"; "with love in my heart for all of you"; "I bear my witness to you of the gospel of love."

(18-7) Love Brings Us Near the Lord

"The second great commandment

which was equal to the first, the Master said, 'Love thy neighbor as thyself,' is the key word to the Latter-day Saints, if I may use that term, to bring us near to the Lord, loving his other children as we love ourselves and so doing desirous of bringing to them the knowledge of the truth." (George Albert Smith in *CR*, Apr. 1948, p. 15.)

(18-8) Happiness Is in Proportion to Love and Service

"But do not forget no matter how much you may give in money, no matter how you may desire the things of this world to make yourselves happy, your happiness will be in proportion to your charity and to your kindness and to your love of those with whom you associate here on earth. Our Heavenly Father has said in very plain terms that he who says he loves God and does not love his brother is not truthful." (George Albert Smith, "To the Relief Society," *Relief Society Magazine*, Dec. 1932, p. 709.)

HIS PRESIDENCY WAS A TIME OF REACHING OUT AND LIFTING UP AFTER THE SECOND WORLD WAR

The title of this chapter speaks of hanging hands and feeble knees. How representative of despair and depression are "hands which hang down"! How reminiscent of weariness and weakness are "feeble knees"! And how descriptive of the years immediately following World War II are such words!

One who visited war-torn Europe reported:

"Such scenes cannot be adequately described. They must be witnessed and experienced to be understood and comprehended. But they all bear witness that war is hell!

"Along the way we passed groups of older people and children going to church. Many were in rags and barefooted. At the approach of our car they became frightened—almost to the point of hysteria in some cases—and many ran for the nearest shelter to hide from us. When we blew our horn, it was easy to see the fear and anxiety etched upon their faces. Yet they seemed at times to be so completely unnerved that they just stood transfixed in the roadway, apparently unable to summon the will and the energy to make it to the edge of the road." (Frederick W. Babbel, *On Wings of Faith*, p. 35.)

Like the Master whose servant he was, President George Albert Smith loved these victims of war. He did all in his power to lift up the hands that hung down and to strengthen the feeble knees.

(18-9) Those Outside the Church Were Touched by Him

"When the war was over, I went representing the Church, to see the president of the United States. When I called on him, he received me very graciously—I had met him before—and I said: 'I have just come to ascertain from you, Mr. President, what your attitude will be if the Latter-day Saints are prepared to ship food and clothing and bedding to Europe.'

"He smiled and looked at me, and said: 'Well, what do you want to ship it over there for? Their money isn't any good.'

"I said: 'We don't want their money.' He looked at me and asked: 'You don't mean you are going to give it to them?'

"I said: 'Of course, we would give it to them. They are our brothers and sisters and are in distress. God has blessed us with a surplus, and we will be glad to send it if we can have the co-operation of the government.'

"He said: 'You are on the right track,' and added, 'we will be glad to help you in any way we can.'

"I have thought of that a good many times. After we had sat there a moment or two, he said again: 'How long will it take you to get this ready?'

"I said: 'It's all ready.'

"The government you remember had been destroying food and refusing to plant grain during the war, so I said to him:

" 'Mr. President, while the administration at Washington were advising the destroying of food, we were building elevators and filling them with grain, and increasing our flocks and our herds, and now what we need is the cars and the ships in order to send considerable food, clothing and bedding to the people of Europe who are in distress. We have an organization in the Church that has over two thousand homemade quilts ready.' " (George Albert Smith in *CR*, Oct. 1947, pp. 5-6.)

Of course, his influence upon nonmembers was limited to what contact they would permit him to exercise. So it is with prophets in every age—they are sometimes restricted by a world that knows them not. But that spiritual force which radiated from President Smith could not be hidden; it was remarkable to many who were nonmembers.

"Beverly Nichols, a British novelist, toured the United States on one occasion, studying the American way of life. Later he wrote a very humorous book

entitled *Uncle Samson,* the major tenor of which was a great lampooning of life in the United States. One of his chapters records his visit to Salt Lake City. Like countless other correspondents who confronted life in a Latter-day Saint community for the first time, he found many things rather humorous, but not so his visit with President George Albert Smith, of whom he wrote, 'If ever I met an honest, upstanding, God-fearing man, I met him in President Smith.' '' (Bassett, "George Albert Smith," p. 50.)

"He was a man without guile, a religious man and a spiritual leader, not only in his own Church—in any group. Even alone with him you had a feeling of this man's spirituality. . . .

". . . He loved to talk about the brotherhood of man, his genuine love of all mankind, which after all is the true charity of Christ, deeper than any doctrinal differences, that gift from above that makes for richer, fuller understanding of man's feeling toward man." (John F. Fitzpatrick, cited in Doyle L. Green, "Tributes Paid President George Albert Smith," *Improvement Era,* June 1951, p. 405.)

A woman representing the Society for the Sightless (a group for which President Smith had shown deep concern), overwhelmed by the mixture of greatness, humility, and utter kindness of President Smith, wrote this tribute:

"When life beats hard with
  stormy hands
And bitter teardrops fall,
When friendless winter chills
  my soul

President George Albert Smith and Helen Keller

And empty echoes call,
'Tis then I turn with eager
  steps—
My steps though spent and
  lame—
To find an understanding heart
Where burns a friendly flame,
A heart where gentle wisdom
  dwells
Compassionate and kind,
Whose faith in God and man has
  taught
A like faith to the blind.
I lay my troubles at his feet;
Each trial, each bitter loss,
The burdens of a hundred
  more—
He helps us bear the cross.

Consecrated by our Lord
With apostolic light,
Consecrated in his soul
He makes our darkness bright.
A loving radiance he sheds
That comes from God to man.
And we who walk in life's long
  night
Can see as others can.
Although his tender, loving face
From us is shut apart,
We see the gracious wisdom
Of his understanding heart.
We feel the peace within his
  soul
And know a peace our own,
We hear his silent prayer
And know we do not walk alone.

An early picture of George Albert and a friend

His faith in us will give us
   strength
As unseen paths we plod,
Our souls uplifted by this man
In partnership with God."
(Irene Jones, "A Tribute to
George Albert Smith,"
Improvement Era, June 1951, p.
405.)

(18-10) George Albert Smith's Love and Concern Were Expressed by Sending an Apostle of the Lord

Before the war broke, the
missionaries had been called home
out of many lands. Latter-day
Saints, particularly in European
nations, did not see a

representative of the Church for
years. President Smith was not free
to go to Europe himself after the
war; there were pressing problems
at home for the new prophet. But
he was concerned. How could the
Church help them? How much aid
did they need? President Smith
needed someone to find answers to
these questions. He sent Elder Ezra
Taft Benson, and the great love of
the Savior for his weary Saints
went out from his holy prophet,
through one of his apostles. And
the Saints felt that love. Elder
Benson describes what he saw:

"I will not take time today to
describe the terrors of war, the

worst of which is not the physical
combat but that which follows: the
abandonment of moral and
religious restraints, the increase in
sin, disease; the increase in infant
mortality; and all the suffering
which accompanies famine,
disease, and immorality. We saw
these things on every side. We saw
nations prostrate, flat on their
backs economically. We found it
difficult even to get a telephone call
through from London to many of
our missions on the continent
when we arrived. We could not
even make a telephone call to
Holland, let alone countries like
Poland and Czechoslovakia, and
other nations. Almost the only type
of transportation available was that
under the control of the
military. . . .

"I think I shall never forget those
first meetings with the Saints. They
have suffered much, my brethren
and sisters. We wondered just how
they would receive us, what the
reaction would be. Would their
hearts be filled with bitterness?
Would there be hatred there?
Would they have soured on the
Church? . . . As I looked into their
upturned faces, pale, thin, many of
these Saints dressed in rags, some
of them barefooted, I could see the
light of faith in their eyes as they
bore testimony to the divinity of
this great latter-day work, and
expressed their gratitude for the
blessings of the Lord." (*CR*, Apr.
1947, pp. 153-54.)

Other conditions too needed the
touch of this great man of love.

(18-11) A Prophet's Vision and Compassion Led to Our Present-Day Concern for the Lamanites

"As his great love for his
fellowmen began to grow into a
great compassion, he saw in vision
a certain whole people who went

down from the proverbial Jerusalem to Jericho and they fell among thieves. He saw them stripped of their raiment and sorely wounded. He saw them deserted and deprived. He saw priests come by who saw their plight and passed by on the other side. He saw modern Levites who came and looked and passed by on the other side. President Smith determined it was time to do something constructive for these Indian people who had fallen into misfortune. He determined that it was time to bind up their wounds, and to pour thereon the oil.

"He went to Pres. Heber J. Grant, (President Smith was then in the Council of the Twelve), and asked him for permission to do work among the Indian people which was granted. A committee was organized and the work began in a small way as many programs do." (Spencer W. Kimball in *Church News*, 11 Apr. 1951, p. 11.)

(18-12) His Love Reached Out to Disaffected Groups

President George Albert Smith had a profound concern for people who had become disaffected from the Church, and he sought to show them their error. One incident is representative of this. A large faction had broken away from the Church and established their own church. They were disgruntled with some leaders and presumed to take matters into their own hands. President Smith made a historic visit to this group in 1946. He met with them and shook their hands, spoke to them, and prayed and wept for them. They were touched by his presence. He looked and acted like a prophet. They acknowledged that he was a prophet. Twelve hundred people, feeling the radiant love of Christ reaching out to them through the Lord's anointed, returned to the

His mother, Sarah Farr Smith

safety of the Church from which they had strayed.

THE LIFE AND MINISTRY OF PRESIDENT GEORGE ALBERT SMITH SETS THE EXAMPLE FOR US ON HOW TO LIVE THE LAW OF LOVE

Let it be understood that charity, the pure love of Christ, is infinitely more than ordinary kindness and courtesy. This power fills, blesses, lifts, and heals. Having this, one can serve. Without it service is a hollow gesture. (See 1 Corinthians 13:1-5.) But to obtain it, one must "pray unto the Father with all the energy of heart, that ye may be filled with this love, which he hath bestowed upon all who are true followers of his Son, Jesus Christ." (Moroni 7:48.)

So it is a spiritual matter, this matter of possessing godlike charity. President George Albert Smith possessed this power,

having obtained it by a life of tremendous faith and obedience. It has been so with all the holy men who have presided over The Church of Jesus Christ of Latter-day Saints.

But President Smith's administration radiated this literal power within the Church and even outside the Church. It was sorely needed in that hour of history. Thus, it is not surprising that the following comments were made at his funeral services.

(18-13) His Name Was Love

". . . it has been properly suggested that his real name was Love.

"Throughout our association together which has been close and intimate, and under various and trying circumstances, I have never known him even to indicate that he was impatient, that he had lost his temper, or even that he was under the necessity of controlling it. . . .

". . . Evil slunk away from him at all times. It could not abide the presence of his righteous living. I do not know what more I can say in tribute to him than that.

"There lies before us the worn and wilted suit of clothes he wore here, all that we knew and loved and admired, all that led to his accomplishments, all that inspired his love, all that helped him to live righteously, still lives, and is, and will live throughout the eternities to come; he lives, a great soul who spent his life, his strength at the expense of his health in the service of his master." (J. Reuben Clark, Jr., in *Church News*, 11 Apr. 1951, p. 10.)

(18-14) He Loved His Neighbor as Himself

"He loved everyone because he

George Albert Smith as a missionary about 1891

could see the good within them. He did not look upon sin with the least degree of allowance, but he loved the sinner because he knew that God was love, and that it is God's love that regenerates human souls and may, by that process, transform the sinner into a saint.

"Maybe there are sinners who mistook his love for respect. He didn't respect the sinner, but he loved him. I am sure that love found response in the hearts and in the lives of those whom he loved. . . .

"Men like this never die. He is an eternal being. God attracts the godly, and I am sure that the shortest journey this man of God ever made in all of his travels has been the journey which he has just taken. God is love. George Albert Smith is love. He is godly. God has taken him unto himself." (Matthew Cowley, cited in Green, "Tributes," p. 405.)

(18-15) Could Any Mortal Have Loved More?

"I stand in reverential awe, almost breathless awe, in this auspicious moment in these services of Pres. George Albert Smith.

"A scribe came to the Lord Jesus Christ one day and said, 'Which is the first commandment of all? And Jesus answered him . . . Thou shalt love the Lord thy God with all thy heart, and with all thy soul, and with all thy mind, and with all thy

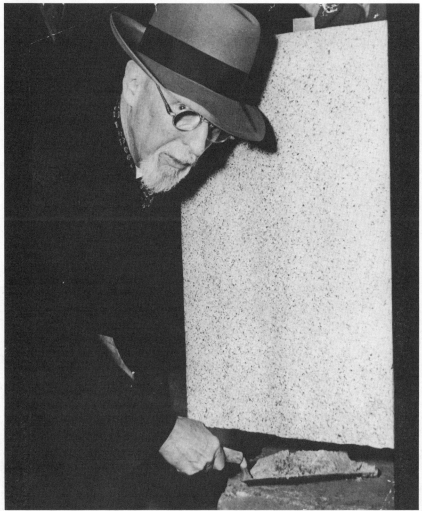

President Smith laying the cornerstone of the Primary Children's Hospital

strength: . . . Thou shalt love thy neighbour as thyself. There is none other commandment greater than these.' And then the scribe added that to love the Lord and to love his neighbour more than himself '. . . is more than all whole burnt offerings and sacrifices.' And then the Lord said, 'Thou art not far from the kingdom of God.'

"Whenever I thought of our beloved President, I have always felt that he was very, very near that kingdom. It seemed to me that every act, every thought of our President would indicate that with all of his heart and soul he loved the Lord, and loved his fellowmen. Is there a mortal being who could have loved them more?" (Spencer W. Kimball in *Church News*, 11 Apr. 1951, p. 11.)

George Albert Smith fulfilled the great command to love God and man. The world did not heed his magnificent life, nor did many give ear to his loving counsels. If they had, imagine what blessings might have since come to the nations of the earth.

But we can heed. We must, for regardless of what other virtues we may have, "if ye have not charity, ye are nothing." (Moroni 7:46.)

Here are three points to consider as you undertake to heed the example of this great servant of God and man:

1. To President George Albert Smith, religion was not theory, not just a beautiful plan to be admired; it was far more than doctrine only. He saw religion in the things a person does, the spirit in which one lives from hour to hour. Saying the kind word, giving a cup of cold water—small things and large, in both word and action. Read James 1:27.

2. President Smith served because he loved. His motives were never hidden in some selfish desire. This is the secret to cheerful sacrifice. Surely if we serve with our own interests in mind, we will not be willing to pay any great price for another person's happiness. We have many accounts of his perfectly sincere love—his influence over the man who was a victim of drink; his tears over the report of a suffering family; his visits to the Primary Children's Hospital where every child received his personal attention—a pat on the head, a small storybook, a blessing; his tireless efforts to help the blind. The list of known examples goes on and on, and what of the unknown ones? None of these things did he do for the sake of impressing us. He sincerely loved.

3. President Smith was enterprising in his serving. His love was active, alert. He

did not wait for invitations and obligations. His list of personal goals used such active verbs as *visit, teach, seek, overcome*.

Remember the parable of the Good Samaritan—his initiative and action in aiding the wounded man? Remember the Savior's command after telling the parable? *"Go,* and *do* thou likewise." (Luke 10:37. Italics added.)

You can learn to love and serve perfectly. Time and effort are required. To obtain this gift called charity should be the desire of each of us. Your happiness will be in proportion to your charity and to your kindness and to your love of those with whom you associate here on earth. As you learn to "lift up the hands which hang down and strengthen the feeble knees," you will find joy beyond expression.

CHAPTER 19
PROPHETIC WARNINGS OF THE LATTER-DAY JUDGMENTS

INTRODUCTION

Chapter 18 emphasized the feeling of love which George Albert Smith possessed for his fellow beings. We saw how President Smith demonstrated the crowning trait of all—charity. But since charity comes by spiritual laws, since it is centered in righteousness, and since it grows out of a genuine love of God, charity is not founded in unrighteousness. As we read in Moroni 7:45, "Charity . . . thinketh no evil, and rejoiceth not in iniquity but rejoiceth in the truth."

It may be asked, Can one really love the souls of men and still hate sin? Indeed! One who loves people and yet considers their sins lightly has not the fulness of love.

Sin breeds sorrow. This is the inevitable and eternal face of the matter. (See Alma 41:10, 11.) A person filled with genuine, intelligent love of others cannot accept the poison of disobedience which limits, cripples, and darkens their lives. Rather, such a person seeks himself to be absolutely obedient, and he sorrows over the ugly blight of sin wherever and whenever he sees it.

Thus, we come to a study of another feature in the personality of President George Albert Smith—his deep and constant concern over wickedness. He had the prophetic discernment to see its spreading presence. He had the vision to see its ultimate consequences for the world. With prophetic wisdom, he knew the cure. With confident

courage, he proclaimed to the Church and to the world the message not only of love, but of repentance. We have read of his inspiring consolation and comfort. We turn now to frank, serious warnings.

THE WORLD IS DANGEROUSLY SICK

(19-1) Many Are Saying to God, in Effect, We Do Not Need You"

"The world is sick. It is not the first time it has been sick. It has had a good many different experiences of that kind. Sometimes nations have had to be wiped out because of the wickedness of the people who live in them. The Lord, all down through the ages, has spoken to his leaders and teachers who are inspired, but when the world refuses to heed after it has been properly taught, it places itself in a position of saying to our Heavenly Father who owns this world—he is our landlord—'We do not need you. We will do just as we please.'

"Unfortunately, people who think that way do not realize how they are shortening their own experiences in life, and setting the stage for the sorrows that may follow." (George Albert Smith in CR, Oct. 1949, p. 167.)

(19-2) The Largest Portion of Mankind Today Is Anti-Christ

"There are many who are anti-Christ, they can believe in anything, almost, that you can think of and produce arguments for believing it, and I want to say to you today, that the largest portion of the population of the world that we live in is anti-Christ, not the followers of Christ at all. And among those who claim to believe in Christianity, comparatively few of them really believe in the divine mission of Jesus Christ." (George Albert Smith in CR, Apr. 1948, p. 179.)

(19-3) Falsehood has Become More Preferred Than Truth

"Someone has said of the people of the world that they would rather believe a lie and be damned than accept the truth. That is rather a severe statement, but I think perhaps it will bear acceptance as fact." (George Albert Smith in CR, Oct. 1949, p. 5.)

(19-4) Our Situation Is Comparable to That of Sodom and Gomorrah

"It seems to me that the world never could have been in any worse condition than it is now, even at the time of the flood, or at the time of the destruction of Sodom and Gomorrah, or the time of the destruction of other places in the world, the destruction in this country at the time of the crucifixion of the Savior. Wickedness was so terrible, and people did not believe in God, apparently; they refused to accept the idea that there was a God; notwithstanding, they were warned in time to repent if they would have done. In the case of Nineveh they did repent and were

not destroyed, but we find so many people today who do not believe in God, do not believe in the divine mission of Jesus Christ—millions of them—and yet, He is the Father of us all." (George Albert Smith in *CR*, Apr. 1948, p. 179.)

If it is surprising to read such statements about the severity of present-day unrighteousness, it may be helpful to study the Lord's own description in a modern revelation. Read D&C 38:10-12.

The Lord loves all mankind more than we can know, but he also sees and understands more than we see and understand. The statements of George Albert Smith, quoted above, were inspired by the Lord in the 1940s. Things had not improved in the hundred years since section 38 of the Doctrine and Covenants was given.

What of the present world situation? Are things getting any better, or are they worsening? For those who intend to endure well through their lives, this is an important question that needs to be answered. How deceiving it would be to think ourselves good only because we seem well when compared to a sick world!

(19-5) Simple, Fundamental Things Are the Cause of the Problem

"What is our trouble? It is that we have sought the creature comforts, we have sought the honors of men, we have sought those things that selfishness puts into our souls. We have sought to set ourselves up and have preferred ourselves to our Father's other children. I am speaking now of the world. We have ignored the commandments that we should honor God and keep his commandments, that we should love our neighbors. We

have failed to pray in the way that we were taught to pray, and men and women have set their judgment up against the teachings of an all-wise Father, and of course we are paying the price." (George Albert Smith in *CR*, Apr. 1932, pp. 44-45.)

WICKEDNESS BRINGS CALAMITY

There are examples from scripture and from secular history that remind us of where a rebelling mankind is headed. Serious sickness, if not cured, brings death. Certainly, prophecies in the standard works which warn against worldwide sin are clear. President Smith's warnings are also clear.

(19-6) World War II Is Only a Beginning

"Unless the people of this world hasten their repentance and turn to the Lord, the conditions that we have recently passed through in this great world war will be intensified in wickedness and sorrow." (George Albert Smith in *CR*, Oct. 1946, p. 4.)

(19-7) A Choice Between Repentance and Calamity

"It will not be long until calamities will overtake the human family unless there is speedy repentance. It will not be long before those who are scattered over the face of the earth by millions will die like flies because of what will come." (George Albert Smith in *CR*, Apr. 1950, p. 169.)

President Smith's excellent radio voice was used to bless the servicemen overseas during World War II

(19-8) It Is Not a Hopeless Situation

"I fear that the time is coming, unless we can find some way not only to prevent the destruction of human life by careless accidents, but also unless we can call the people of this world to repent of their sins and turn from the error of their ways, that the great war that has just passed will be an insignificant thing, as far as calamity is concerned, compared to that which is before us. And we can avoid it if we will; if we will each do our part, it can be prevented." (George Albert Smith in *CR*, Oct. 1946, p. 149.)

AVOIDING CALAMITY: IT MUST BE DONE IN THE LORD'S WAY, NOT IN MAN'S WAY

As armies were returning to their homelands in 1945, leaders of nations were thinking and meeting and talking about treaties, laws, and charters. There were grand hopes for a lasting peace. One national leader said this about the United Nations Charter: "This charter points down the only road to enduring peace. There is no other. Let us not hesitate to join hands with peace-loving peoples of the earth and start down the road—with firm resolve that we can and will reach our goal." (Avery Craven and Walter Johnson, *The U.S. Experiment in Democracy*, p. 826.)

That was the voice of the world—to solve the problems of war by organizing a political entity. In substance this voice echoed itself a million times in a thousand ways. But while the international scurry of reconstruction, legislation, and man-made promises went on, another voice was speaking plainly and certainly. It was the voice of the Lord through his prophet. It was declaring another solution—the only solution.

"We can legislate until doomsday but that will not make men righteous. It will be necessary for people who are in the dark to repent of their sins, correct their lives, and live in such a righteous way that they can enjoy the spirit of our Heavenly Father." (George Albert Smith in *CR*, Oct. 1949, p. 6.)

(19-9) Only with the Spirit of God Could Men Design a Successful Peace

"But this terrible world war that has filled people with hatred for one another, has had its effect on everybody, apparently. And there is no longer the idea among the children of men that they can sit down around a peace table and satisfy all those who are concerned. Why? Because they do not have the Spirit of God; and without it they never will come to an agreement. Now, we know that and the world does not know it." (George Albert Smith in *CR*, Apr. 1948, p. 180.)

As a young boy, George Albert Smith became ill with typhoid fever. The doctor counseled his mother to keep him in bed for three weeks, to give him no solid food, and to have him drink coffee. In later years, President Smith recalled:

"When he went away, I told mother that I didn't want any coffee. I had been taught that the Word of Wisdom, given by the Lord to Joseph Smith, advised us not to use coffee.

"Mother had brought three children into the world and two had died. She was unusually anxious about me.

"I asked her to send for Brother Hawks, one of our ward teachers. He was a worker at the foundry, [a] poor and humble man of great faith in the power of the Lord.

"He came, administered to me and blessed me that I might be healed.

"When the doctor came next morning I was playing outside with other children. He was surprised. He examined me and discovered that my fever had gone and that I seemed to be well.

"I was grateful to the Lord for my recovery. I was sure that he had healed me." (Magazine article in a scrapbook [GAS Collection, U of U, Box 124, Scrapbook 1], p. 4, as cited in Glen R. Stubbs, "A Biography of George Albert Smith, 1870-1951" [Brigham Young University, 1974], p. 12.)

Exactly as the faith of a child has superceded the wisdom of man in conquering typhoid fever, so could a simple childlike faith in God bring answers and astounding blessings to a world otherwise gripped in deadly spiritual disease. Neither typhoid fever nor international disaster with its far-reaching complications, nor any obstacle at all in earth or hell, can stand before true faith in the living God. This principle was proclaimed by George Albert Smith well before the war.

"There is much confusion in the world and there seems to be no way to remove it except by the power of our Heavenly Father. The wisdom of the world is failing, the scripture is fulfilled, and today the wisest of all men are seeking, by means of legislation, to bring about a

better condition and a more wholesome life among the human family. They may strive in that way, but unless men have faith in God, unless they understand the purpose of life, they will not go very far. The people of the world must repent of their sins before the Lord can give to them the peace and happiness desired. No other plan will succeed." (George Albert Smith in *CR*, Apr. 1934, p. 27.)

President Smith received Scouting's highest award, the Silver Buffalo

(19-10) Specific Warnings for America

A burden of accountability before God rests, to some degree, upon each nation. For, as we read in an earlier quote, he indeed "owns this world—he is our landlord." (See 19-1.) But George Albert Smith, as so many prophets before him, raised a warning voice to those who dwell in the land of America. Their position is not only one of opportunity but of jeopardy.

"The Lord raised up men to frame a Constitution for this nation because it was his nation. It was his desire that the people here would be blessed, and there have been no people in all the world who have been more blessed than those who live in the United States of America.

"We have every comfort that you can think of, every blessing that is enjoyed by people in any other nation, and then we have the privilege of worshiping Almighty God according to the dictates of our conscience because the Lord himself made that provision in the Constitution of the United States and in the framing of the laws that govern this nation.

"I wonder if we appreciate that. Do we realize that we can lose it all just as we can lose it with any

epidemic? If an epidemic of some kind, that we did not have a remedy for, was to break out among the people and increase and increase, it would be possible for this entire nation to be wiped out.

"Yet we are trifling with our Heavenly Father and his advice and his counsel. He gave to us his commandments through Moses, anciently, and he gave us advice and counsel in our day through the Prophet Joseph Smith that is intended to keep us in a frame of mind that we would honor God and keep his commandments, that we would love one another.

"It does seem strange how careless we are when we realize we may be destroyed. Think of the atom bomb. If it is all that they say it is, it would be possible to wipe out one of our great cities with its millions of people in just a few moments of time.

"Do we want that kind of thing? Are we going to continue

contending for something of physical power and physical strength or are we going to the Lord and honor him and keep his commandments?" (George Albert Smith in *CR*, Oct. 1949, p. 168.)

(19-11) A Responsibility to Keep the Constitution Where It Started

"I am saying to you that to me the Constitution of the United States of America is just as much from my Heavenly Father as the Ten Commandments. When that is my feeling, I am not going to go very far away from the Constitution, and I am going to try to keep it where the Lord started it." (George Albert Smith in *CR*, Apr. 1948, p. 182.)

"I feel . . . bound to sustain the Constitution of the United States which came from the same source as the Ten Commandments. Unless the people of this great nation can realize these things and repent, they may forfeit the liberty that they now enjoy, and the blessings that are so multiplied

among us." (George Albert Smith in *CR*, Apr. 1949, p. 169.)

(19-12) "How Can He Bless America Until America Repents?"

"What about America? I was in a meeting not very long ago, where a group of Boy Scouts stood and sang, 'God Bless America,' and they sang it beautifully, and all the time they were singing I asked myself the question, 'How can he bless America until America repents?' Every great blessing that we desire is promised us by our Heavenly Father on condition that we honor him and keep his commandments. Praying is not sufficient. Not only must we pray but we must live to be worthy of the blessing." (George Albert Smith in *CR*, Oct. 1948, p. 184.)

Compare these statements from President Smith with typical prophetic utterances from other dispensations about the position of America:
Lehi   2 Nephi 1:7
The brother of Jared   Ether 2:12

What does America stand to lose? Everything! Could it happen? Remember President Smith's warning:

"Do we realize that we can lose it all? . . .

"Yet we are trifling with our Heavenly Father and his advice and his counsel. . . .

"It does seem strange how careless we are when we realize we may be destroyed. . . .

"Do we want that kind of thing?" (George Albert Smith in *CR*, Oct. 1949, p. 168.)

HOW TO HAVE PEACE IN A WORLD OF TUMULT

(19-13) Some Keys for True Peace

We have seen that the teachings of President George Albert Smith are in perfect agreement with the Savior's words to his apostles: "Peace I leave with you, my peace I give unto you: not as the world giveth, give I unto you." (John 14:27.) This message seems to be a constant one in President Smith's sermons, especially during and after the war. A man-made peace is no peace at all—not real peace, not what the Lord calls "my peace." He reserves the right to personally bestow his kind of peace.

President Smith often divided all influences into just two kinds. If we choose the one, there is no safety; if we choose the other, there is perfect safety. His words give the simple key for having peace in a world of tumult:

"There are two influences in the world. The one is the influence of our Heavenly Father and the other is the influence of Satan. We can take our choice which territory we want to live in, that of our Heavenly Father or that of Satan.

"I have many times repeated what my grandfather said. He, too, talked from this stand, and it was he who gave me his name. In advising his family he said, 'There is a line of demarcation, well defined. On one side of the line is the Lord's territory. On the other side of the line is the devil's territory.' And he said, 'If you will stay on the Lord's side of the line, you are perfectly safe, because the adversary of all righteousness can not cross that line.'

"What does that mean? It means to me that those who are living righteous lives, keeping all of the commandments of our Heavenly Father are perfectly safe, but not those who trifle with his advice and counsel." (George Albert Smith in *CR*, Oct. 1949, pp. 5-6.)

(19-14) If We Know Our Lives Are Righteous, We Will Have Unspeakable Peace

"Though the world may be filled with distress, and the heavens gather blackness, and the vivid lightnings flash, and the earth quake from center to circumference, if we know that God lives, and our lives are righteous, we will be happy, there will be peace unspeakable because we know our Father approved our lives." (George Albert Smith in *CR*, Oct. 1915, p. 28.)

Perhaps this lesson was impressed upon George Albert Smith through a dream he had of his grandfather, George A. Smith, who was deceased. In the dream Elder Smith found himself standing facing a great forest.

"I began to explore, and soon I found a trail through the woods which seemed to have been used very little, and which was almost obscured by grass. I followed this trail, and after I had walked for some time and had traveled a considerable distance through the forest, I saw a man coming towards me. I became aware that he was a very large man, and I hurried my steps to reach him, because I recognized him as my grandfather. In mortality he weighed over three hundred pounds, so you may know he was a large man. I remember how happy I was to see him coming. I had been given his name and had always been proud of it.

"When Grandfather came within a few feet of me, he stopped. His stopping was an invitation for me to stop. Then—and this I would like the boys and girls and young people never to forget—he looked at me very earnestly and said:

" 'I would like to know what you have done with my name.'

"Everything I had done passed before me as though it were a flying picture on a screen—everything I had done. Quickly this vivid retrospect came down to the very time I was standing there. My whole life had passed before me. I smiled and looked at my grandfather and said:

" 'I have never done anything with your name of which you need be ashamed.'

"He stepped forward and took me in his arms, and as he did so, I became conscious again of my earthly surroundings. My pillow was wet as though water had been poured on it—wet with tears of gratitude that I could answer unashamed." ("Your Good Name," *Improvement Era*, Mar. 1947, p. 139.)

Isn't that a source of true peace? Each one of us who has been baptized has covenanted to take upon himself the name of our Savior. (See D&C 20:37, 77.) It gives one cause for sobering thought to wonder how we could answer if Jesus should ask us the same question that George Albert Smith's grandfather asked: "I would like to know what you have done with my name." And can you imagine our joy if we could answer as this great prophet answered?

(19-15) Not Only Peace, but Protection

"No matter whether the clouds may gather, no matter how the war drums may beat, no matter what conditions may arise in the world, here in the Church of Jesus Christ of Latter-day Saints, wherever we are honoring and keeping the commandments of God, there will be protection from the powers of evil, and men and women will be permitted to live upon the earth

President Smith loved outdoor life

until their lives are finished in honor and glory if they will keep the commandments of our Heavenly Father." (George Albert Smith in *CR*, Apr. 1942, p. 15.)

(19-16) The Lord Will Fight Our Battles

"Now tonight we are here in peace and quiet. The world is on fire. Everywhere peace has been taken from the earth, and the devil has been given power over his own dominion. God has said if we will honor Him and keep His commandments—if we will observe His laws He will fight our battles and destroy the wicked, and when the time comes He will come down in heaven—not from heaven—but He will bring heaven with Him—and this earth upon which we dwell, will be the celestial kingdom.

"What if all the world knew and believed that? What a change there would be in the conditions among the children of men! What joy would be in the place of sorrow and distress today! It is your duty and mine, having received this information, to impart it to others." (George Albert Smith in *CR*, Oct. 1942, p. 49.)

The perect security of those who obey the Lord, in spite of whatever turmoil may exist around them, is reminiscent of this story from President Smith's childhood:

" . . . we . . . lived in a two story frame house and when the wind blew hard it would rock as if it would topple over. Sometimes I would be too frightened to go to sleep. My bed

was in a little room by itself, and many a night I have climbed out and got down on my knees and asked my Father in Heaven to take care of the house, preserve it that it would not break in pieces and I have got back into my little bed just as sure that I would be safeguarded from evil as if I held my Father's hand." (George Albert Smith, "To the Relief Society," *Relief Society Magazine*, Dec. 1932, pp. 707-8.)

The assurance of George Albert Smith is like that of Lehi:

"Thy throne is high in the heavens, and thy power, and goodness, and mercy are over all the inhabitants of the earth; and, because thou art merciful, thou wilt not suffer those who come unto thee that they shall perish!" (1 Nephi 1:14.)

And it is like that of Nephi:

" . . . the tender mercies of the Lord are over all those whom he hath chosen, because of their faith, to make them mighty even unto the power of deliverance." (1 Nephi 1:20.)

Without any question, distress will be the constant companion of a wicked world. It will be just as the prophets have warned. But the promise of tranquility and watchcare we need to fulfill our work on the earth is also certain. It is a promise founded on the power and kindness of the Almighty. You can live, safeguarded from evil, as if you held your Father's hand.

The great promises and blessings of the Latter-day Saints are, in the Lord's words, "not for your sakes only, but for the sake of the whole world." (D&C 84:48.) To this the Lord added, "And the whole world lieth in sin, and groaneth under

darkness and under the bondage of sin" (verse 49). Can you see that the Lord is here expressing great hope for a groaning world? He has in mind that we should help.

And how can we help?

WE CAN FIND PEACE IN OUR LIVES AND BRING PEACE TO THE LIVES OF OTHERS AS WE SHARE THE GOSPEL WITH THEM

(19-17) Share the Gospel Without Timidness

"I can think of nobody who has had a fuller life than I have had, and I don't say that boastfully, but gratefully; and I want to say to you that every happiness and every joy that has been worthy of the name has been the result of keeping the commandments of God and observing his advice and counsel. So, as we go forward, each of us, each having an influence with our

neighbors and our friends, let us not be too timid. We do not need to annoy people, but let us make them feel and understand that we are interested, not in making them members of the Church for membership, but in bringing them into the Church that they may enjoy the same blessings that we enjoy." (George Albert Smith in *CR*, Apr. 1948, p. 162.)

How timid was President George Albert Smith? The answer is obvious, but the mixture of boldness with graciousness is best understood from an incident from President Smith's life:

" 'Surely,' as one minister said to me in England many years ago, 'we don't desire you to come over here to preach; we have all the churches that we can fill.' And he said, 'We have all the preachers that we can afford

President George Albert Smith at his Church office desk

President Smith and his counselors, J. Reuben Clark, Jr., and David O. McKay

to pay. Why do you come over here?'

"And my answer to him was, 'My brother, we are over here without financial remuneration to share the gospel of Jesus Christ with the wonderful people who dwell in this part of the world.'

"He asked, 'Why don't you go to the heathens like we do?' And I answered, 'We do.' He asked, 'Where do you go?' And I said, 'We have come right here.'

"He looked somewhat annoyed, and I said to him, 'Now don't be disturbed, my brother. That isn't intended as an offense at all. There are no finer people in the world than you have here, but what is a heathen anyhow?'

"With some hesitation he answered, 'Well, a heathen is a man who doesn't believe in the God of Abraham, Isaac, and Jacob, and Jesus Christ.'

"I said, 'Do you have any people like that here in Great Britain?'

"He dropped his head and said, 'Yes, I am sorry to say we have.'

"Then I said, 'Surely you are not going to complain about us if we come over here to help you convert them. You haven't been able to do it, and that is why we are here. We want them all to understand the gospel of Jesus Christ.' " (George Albert Smith, in *CR*, Oct. 1948, p. 5.)

PRESIDENT SMITH PROPHESIED OF THE MARVELOUS SUCCESS WHICH WOULD COME TO THE WORLDWIDE MISSIONARY WORK OF THE CHURCH

(19-18) We Will Go to Every Part of the World

"We must preach the gospel to the South American countries which we have scarcely touched. We must preach the gospel to every African section that we haven't been in yet. We must preach the gospel to Asia. And I might go on and say in all parts of the world where we have not yet been

permitted to go. I look upon Russia as one of the most fruitful fields for the teaching of the gospel of Jesus Christ. And if I am not mistaken, it will not be long before the people who are there will desire to know something about this work which has reformed the lives of so many people." (George Albert Smith in *CR*, Oct. 1945, p. 119.)

(19-19) The Gospel Will Be Taught in Every Place Through Improved Technology

"Short-wave broadcasting will continue to improve, and it will not be long until, from this pulpit and other places that will be provided, the servants of the Lord will be able to deliver messages to isolated groups who are so far away they cannot be reached. In that way and other ways, the gospel of Jesus Christ our Lord, the only power of God unto salvation in preparation for the celestial kingdom, will be heard in all parts of the world, and many of you who are here will live to see that day." (George Albert Smith in *CR*, Oct. 1946, p. 6.)

(19-20) Millions Will Accept the Truth

"I have traveled in many lands and climes, and wherever I have gone I have found good people, sons and daughters of the living God who are waiting for the gospel of Jesus Christ, and there are thousands, hundreds of thousands, millions of them, who would be accepting the truth if they only knew what we know." (George Albert Smith in *CR*, Oct. 1945, p. 120.)

President Smith loved all men. His love was not in the same category with the feelings of most. He possessed charity, the pure love of Christ. Out of this power in his life he pled with individuals and with mankind generally to turn aside from the unhappy future for which they were headed. The work to which he gave himself unselfishly is still largely incomplete. It is ours to carry on. And we shall need the same feelings for God and man stirring within us as stirred within him, if we expect to do it well.

In the Doctrine and Covenants we are assured, just as President Smith said, that there are many not accepting the gospel only because they "know not where to find it." (D&C 123:12.) In light of the concern and warnings we have studied in this chapter, is it not worth your effort to help these "many" of our Father's children? The Prophet Joseph called it "an imperative duty that we owe to all the rising generation." (D&C 123:11.) In this duty of finding and blessing those who would embrace the gospel, President Smith used his whole life, spent his entire energy, sacrificed whatever and whenever necessary. As he departed this sphere of action, he left for us the eloquent sermon of his own life which commands us to go and do likewise.

UNIT TEN
DAVID O. McKAY
Ninth President of the Church

OVERVIEW

When David Oman McKay was born on September 8, 1873, Brigham Young was the President of the Church. Thus began the mortal career of one who would preside among the Saints.

The McKay (or MacKay) clan developed in the northern highlands of Scotland. There was a royalty of character too in this lineage, for grandparents and parents demonstrated in their early conversion an unswerving loyalty to the gospel. Planted in such rich soil, young David grew strong and straight. He learned the virtue of hard work from his farmer father. Faith in the gospel was ingrained in his heart by the precepts, example, and endurance he saw all around him.

A patriarchal blessing to the thirteen-year-old son of Bishop McKay spoke prophecy: "The eye of the Lord is upon thee . . . thou shalt see much of the world . . . sit in council . . . and preside among the people."[1]

The children were urged to better themselves through education. David took advantage of these hard-won opportunities. When he was twenty-one he entered the University of Utah. Here he debated, played the piano in a musical group, participated on the football team, and began to court a certain Miss Emma Ray Riggs. He graduated as president and valedictorian of his class and was accepted as a faculty member at the Weber State Academy. The call of the Lord to serve as a missionary came at an inconvenient time, but at age twenty-four David O. McKay left all that was so dear to him, including a faculty position offer, and went to his native Scotland. His natural leadership was recognized, and he was called to serve as a district president. A member of his mission presidency prophesied that if he remained faithful he would sit in the leading councils of the Church.[2]

On returning home he took up his duties as a member of the faculty of the

Weber State Academy. On January 2, 1901, he was married to his beloved Emma Ray in the Salt Lake Temple, and a union that was to be an example to the entire Church for sixty-nine years commenced. Seven children were to come to this family.

While Elder McKay was serving in the superintendency of the Weber Stake Sunday School, President Joseph F. Smith told Elder McKay that the Lord wanted him to serve in the apostleship. He was then thirty-two years old. His ministry in the Quorum was to stretch over more than half a century. Immediately his talents as an educator were called upon. He served as counselor in the general Church Sunday School and became Church Commissioner of Education in 1919. To him, teaching was the highest of the professions.

In 1908 and again in 1911 this young apostle was appointed by President Joseph F. Smith to serve on an early correlation committee. In 1916 David O. McKay suffered a severe automobile accident; his face was so badly lacerated that many felt he would be disfigured for life. Heber J. Grant blessed him that he would be completely healed, and he was.

In 1918 his first book, *Ancient Apostles*, was published. Then in 1920, along with Hugh J. Cannon, he left on an unprecedented world tour. He was blessed by his fellow apostles to be "a missionary to travel around the world."[3] He visited the Orient and with apostolic authority dedicated China for the preaching of the gospel. While in the Pacific Islands, Tahitian Saints were able to understand his words in their own language. He was forewarned of fatal danger in Hawaii; and while in the ancient Holy Land of Israel, he prophesied that although the land would run red with blood, the Jews would yet be gathered. This tour gave a world vision to the young apostle, and the universality of the gospel message became even more apparent.

Elder McKay became President McKay in 1934 when his long service in the First Presidency commenced, acting as second counselor to both President Heber J. Grant and President George Albert Smith. He took part in the development of the Church welfare program.

President McKay was sustained as the ninth President of the Church in 1951. Almost immediately the new prophet set out on his world mission. He eventually traveled over a million miles, ranging the earth like a modern Paul. He prophesied of the Saints gathering to stakes in their native lands. He foresaw temples dotting the world.[4] Missionary work was accelerated as every member was encouraged to be a missionary. Literally thousands of chapels were built as his ministry stretched over more and more years and conversions continued; it came to be that the majority of Church members had known no other prophet than David O. McKay. But it was spiritual growth that was most important to the Lord's mouthpiece. He spoke of developing the divine nature. He championed the family and the home and forever riveted upon the minds of the Saints, "No other success in life can compensate for failure in the home."[5] He proclaimed that next to life itself was the priceless boon of free agency and that the Constitution of the United States must be defended.

As David O. McKay traveled over the world his influence was felt in other places besides in the immediate Church. He looked like a prophet to many. A Secretary of State called him the best goodwill ambassador the United States had. Monarchs honored him. Presidents called upon him. Nations gave him their highest awards.

In later years, though somewhat restricted physically through failing health, David O. McKay grew spiritually. He often spoke of zest for life. When he died on January 8, 1970, President Joseph Fielding Smith said that he had become perfect in his life.[6]

CHAPTER 20

ARISE AND SHINE FORTH THAT THY LIGHT MAY BE A STANDARD FOR THE NATIONS

INTRODUCTION

President McKay's mortal life was long—it stretched from the time when the railroad first came to Utah, ending the era of covered wagons, to the landing of the first man on the moon. Here was a man who was to witness the kaleidoscope of history as it sped through the latter days of the second millennium since the coming of the Savior. But David O. McKay was destined not merely to witness these significant times, but to place his unique stamp upon them, to significantly influence them. He was soon brought to the fore in the growing kingdom of God, a kingdom which was destined to fill the earth and be a light to all the world. Before his ministry of over sixty-three years was to end, he would travel over a million miles as an ambassador of Christ. He would preside among the people and would do much to continue the expansion of the boundaries of the Church beyond the western United States to the four corners of the earth. By the time he died, over half of the members of the Church would know no other prophet; stakes would be organized on far-flung continents; temples would begin to dot the earth; and many of the great of the world would know the name of David O. McKay, President of the Mormon Church. But more significant than mere outward signs of progress, this prophet of God was led by revelation to further consolidate and correlate the essence of priesthood power in the Church. A consolidation and strengthening that would lead

the kingdom to move toward that ideal which its Head had given in the beginning was "the coming forth of my church out of the wilderness—clear as the moon, and fair as the sun, and terrible as an army with banners." (D&C 5:14.)

THE CHERISHED EXPERIENCES OF A GROWING PROPHET

(20-1) In Making a Prophet, God Does Not Unmake a Man

The leadership the Lord provided to aid his Church when the time was more fully come for it to begin to "arise and shine forth" was not developed in a vacuum. David O. McKay was born with the qualities that would stand him in good stead when called upon to preside. The cherished experiences of his life would put finishing touches on a preparation that reached back into the eternities.

"The President is blessed with pre-vision. Many a morning he has told me that certain incidents would happen during the day and invariably the impression would become a reality. This pre-vision

has been a helpful guide to him through life." (Emma Ray Riggs McKay, cited in Llewelyn R. McKay, *Home Memories of President David O. McKay,* p. 270.)

(20-2) David O. McKay's Home Life Aided His Development

A grateful prophet paid homage to his parents:

"And it is just as easy for me to realize that one may so live that he may receive impressions and direct messages through the Holy Ghost. The veil is thin between those who hold the Priesthood and those on the other side of the veil. That testimony began, I repeat, in the home in my youth because of the example of a father who honored the Priesthood—and his wife, who sustained him and lived it in the home." (David O. McKay in *CR,* Oct. 1960, pp. 85-86.)

(20-3) A Growing Boy Exercised His Leadership Abilities at an Early Age

Llewelyn R. McKay has written this concerning his father:

"When father was eight years of age, his father received a call to go on a mission. To accept such a call for two or three years away from home was no easy decision to make. Another baby was on its way, and plans had been made to enlarge the house and furnishings. The responsibilities of running the farm were too great to be left to his wife, so when David showed the letter calling him to a mission, he said: 'Of course it is impossible for me to go.' Jennette read the letter, looked at her husband, and said decisively: 'Of course you must accept; you need not worry about me. David O. and I will manage

things nicely!' " (*Home Memories*, pp. 5-6.)

(20-4) David O. McKay Learned Early in Life the Realities of Heavenly Communication to Man

One night while still a young child, David O. McKay became terrified. A thunderstorm was raging; and though he wanted to pray for courage, he was too frightened.

"But I did finally bring myself to get out of bed and kneel and pray to God to protect Mother and the family. And a voice, speaking as clearly to me as mine is to you, said, 'Don't be afraid; nothing will hurt you.' Where it came from, what it was, I am not saying. You may judge. To me it was a direct answer.

"I say it has been easy for me to understand and believe the reality of the visions of the Prophet Joseph. It was easy for me in youth to accept his vision, the appearance of God the Father and his Son, Jesus Christ, to the boy praying. I thought of nothing else. Of course that is real. It was easy for me to believe that Moroni came to him there in the room. Heavenly Beings were real from my babyhood on, and as years came those impressions strengthened by reason and strengthened by the inspiration of God directly to my soul." (David O. McKay, *Gospel Ideals*, pp. 524-25.)

(20-5) A Successful Mission Was an Evidence of Inward Greatness

As a struggling young missionary in Scotland, Elder McKay learned to "act well his part" and thus came to leadership. A counselor in his mission presidency was led to prophesy:

"Let me say to you, Brother David, Satan has desired you that he may sift you as wheat, but God is mindful of you, and if you will keep

In college he played football, piano for a dance band, and was elected president of his senior class

the faith, you will yet sit in the leading councils of the Church." (Cited in Jeanette McKay Morrell, *Highlights in the Life of David O. McKay*, pp. 37-38.)

(20-6) David O. McKay Was Able to Accept an Apostolic Call When He Was Thirty-two Years of Age

After returning from his mission, Elder McKay married his beloved Emma Ray and pursued his career as an educator. He was serving in the Weber Stake Sunday School superintendency when President Joseph F. Smith declared that the Lord wanted him to be a member of the Quorum of the Twelve. In his first address as an apostle he spoke of principles that had brought him personal joy and, though he did not say as much directly, had helped shape his life in preparation for such a calling.

"The man who knows what his duty is and fails to perform it, is not true to himself; he is not true to his

brethren; he is not living in the light which God and conscience provides. That is where we stand, and it comes right home to you; it means me. When my conscience tells me that it is right to go along in a specified line, I am not true to myself if I do not follow that. Oh! I know we are swayed by our weaknesses, and by influences from without; but it is our duty to walk in the straight and narrow path in the performance of every duty. And mark this: Every time we have opportunity and fail to live up to that truth which is within us, every time we fail to express a good thought, every time we fail to perform a good act, we weaken ourselves, and make it more difficult to express that thought or perform that act in the future. Every time we perform a good act, every time we express a noble feeling we make it the more easy to perform that act or express that feeling another time." (*CR*, Oct. 1906, p. 113.)

In the history of this earth only a few have stood at the head of God's people; of the billions through history only a few have been called a prophet.

[Read Numbers 11:29.]

What opportunity is open for all of God's children? If you act well your part, will any blessing be withheld? Can you learn lessons from the life of David O. McKay that will aid you? Can we not all find reason to be excited with the great gift of life?

"To all who believe in a living, personal God and His divine Truth, life can be delightful and beautiful.

"As a matter of fact, it's glorious just to be alive. Joy, even ecstasy, can be experienced in the consciousness of existence. There is supreme satisfaction in sensing one's individual entity and in realizing that that entity is part of God's great creative plan. There are none so poor, none so rich, sick or maimed who may

not be conscious of this relationship." (David O. McKay in *CR*, Apr. 1940, p. 115.)

How does this promise of joy relate to Alma 41:10?

THE EXPANDING INFLUENCE OF AN APOSTLE OF GOD

(20-7) Elder McKay Was Exposed to Priesthood Correlation Very Early

The basic correlation of the kingdom of God, under priesthood power, has always been a first principle with the prophets of God. In 1908 Elder McKay was called by President Joseph F. Smith to serve on a correlation committee. That early experience stayed as an important part of his thinking. Elder Harold B. Lee testified:

"This is a move, which, as I say, has lain close to President McKay's mind and now as the President of the Church he is instructing us to move forward, that we consolidate to make more efficient, and more effective the work of the priesthood, the auxiliaries, and the other units in order that we may conserve our time, our energy, and our efforts toward the prime purpose for which the Church itself has been organized." (*CR*, Oct. 1961, p. 81.)

(20-8) David O. McKay's World Tour of 1920-21 Extended His Vision

"From that day in December 1920, when Presidents Heber J. Grant, Anthon H. Lund, and Charles W. Penrose, and several of the Apostles laid their hands upon President McKay's head and blessed him and set him apart as 'a missionary to travel around the world' and promised him that he should be 'warned of dangers seen and unseen, and be given wisdom and inspiration from God to avoid all the snares and the pitfalls that may be laid for his feet'; that he

David O. McKay and his bride, Emma Ray Riggs

should also 'go forth in peace, in pleasure and happiness and to return in safety to his loved ones and to the body of the Church,' he has experienced the protecting care of our Heavenly Father in all his global ministry." (Cited in David O. McKay, *Cherished Experiences*, p. 37.)

David O. McKay was to testify thus of this world tour and others:

"I have an entirely different viewpoint of these countries now. . . . I realize the responsibility of this Church to proclaim the gospel is world-wide. . . .

"God bless the Church. It is world-wide. Its influence should be felt by all nations. May his spirit influence men everywhere. . . . " (McKay, *Gospel Ideals*, pp. 583-84.)

(20-9) Elder McKay Saw That Missionary Work by All Members Was the Key to the Worldwide Expansion of the Church

"And so with you I say, 'We are not ashamed of the gospel of Christ.' I am looking upon a segment of the Church of Christ who share the responsibility of preaching this gospel to all the world, for we are part of a world-wide organization. This gospel is not confined to Utah, nor Idaho, nor Wyoming, nor California, nor the United States, nor just to Europe, but it is the power of God to salvation to all who believe, and you and I must share part of the responsibility of declaring it to all the world." (David O. McKay, *Stepping Stones to an Abundant Life*, pp. 120-21.)

(20-10) As Chairman of the Utah Centennial Commission in 1947, President McKay Encouraged the Saints to Be Pioneers to a Modern World

It was appropriate that David O. McKay play a leading part in

David O. McKay as a missionary in Scotland

honoring the pioneers of the past; his life itself stretched back to Utah's beginnings. But he was a forward-looking modern prophet when he declared:

"But the best way to honor the pioneers is to emulate and make practical in our lives the ideals and virtues that strengthened and animated their lives. These eternal ideals and principles which they fostered and upheld, even under the most adverse conditions, are as applicable today as they were when emphasized by the pioneer leaders." (David O. McKay in *CR*, Apr. 1947, p. 118.)

David O. McKay often spoke of every person's being a "living light fountain" to all those around them. You have witnessed in these few readings how the light of this one man began early to illuminate those around him. But the Savior encouraged all to "let their light so shine" (Matthew 5:16), and each in his own sphere can bear the light of Christ. Do you let your light shine?

"Every man and every person who lives in this world wields an influence, whether for good or for evil. It is not what he says

alone, it is not alone what he does. It is what he is. Every man, every person radiates what he or she is. Every person is a recipient of radiation. The Savior was conscious of that. Whenever he came into the presence of an individual, he sensed that radiation—whether it was the woman of Samaria with her past life; whether it was the woman who was to be stoned or the men who were to stone her; whether it was the statesman, Nicodemus, or one of the lepers. He was conscious of the radiation from the individual. And to a degree so are you, and so am I. It is what we are and what we radiate that affects the people around us." (David O. McKay in *CR*, Apr. 1963, p. 129.)

As we have studied the lives of each of the presidents, you have found qualities of character in each worthy of emulation. Over and over people spoke of the special feeling that radiated from President McKay. Here was a man who could speak of the effect of people on others.

Obviously, one does not will himself into radiating goodness. One does not say, "Well, I'll just radiate a feeling of light today." We radiate what is on the inside. As you continue your study of President McKay, notice those things which made him what he was. Emulate his life and his commitment, and soon people will also note the spirit you radiate.

AS THE PRESIDING PROPHET, DAVID O. McKAY CONSOLIDATED AND STRENGTHENED THE LORD'S CHURCH

(20-11) The Faith of a New President of the Church

"It is just one week ago today that the realization came to me that this responsibility of leadership would probably fall upon my shoulders. . . .

"When that reality came, as I tell you, I was deeply moved. And I am today, and pray that I may, even though inadequately, be able to tell you how weighty this responsibility seems.

"The Lord has said that the three presiding high priests chosen by the body, appointed and ordained to this office of presidency, are to be 'upheld by the confidence, faith, and prayer of the Church.' No one can preside over this Church without first being in tune with the head of the Church, our Lord and Savior, Jesus Christ. He is our head. This is his Church. Without his divine guidance and constant inspiration, we cannot succeed. With his guidance, with his inspiration, we cannot fail." (David O. McKay in *CR*, Apr. 1951, p. 157.)

(20-12) President McKay Saw Two Great Missions for the Church

"The mission of The Church of Jesus Christ of Latter-day Saints may be considered in two great aspects: (1) the proclamation to the world of the restoration of the gospel of Jesus Christ—the declaration to all mankind that God the Father and his Son Jesus Christ appeared in this dispensation to the Prophet Joseph Smith; (2) the other great purpose of the Church is to translate truth into a better social order or, in other words, to make our religion effective in the individual lives of men and in improving social conditions." (David O. McKay, *Man May Know for Himself*, p. 162.)

(20-13) President McKay Advanced Priesthood Correlation–An Essential Step Forward

As has already been noted, priesthood correlation was near to President McKay's heart from the beginning of his ministry. During his administration as presiding prophet this program was to make significant advances. President Joseph Fielding Smith has written this:

"During the early 1960s a broad program of Church correlation began under President McKay's

He traveled the world over, visiting the Saints

direction to help bearers of the priesthood better fulfill their obligations and responsibilities. Four operating committees were formed to include programs of home teaching, missionary, genealogical, and welfare work. Worthy leaders of the priesthood were called to fill positions on these important general committees and to assist in preparing materials and outlines for leaders in the stakes and wards. Under the priesthood correlation program, quorums and groups were given specific leadership responsibilities. High priests were assigned genealogical work; seventies the missionary program; elders the welfare work; and all quorums the home teaching program. The former ward teaching program was greatly expanded into the new home teaching program, and those assigned as home teachers were given greater responsibilities as spiritual advisers to a group of families.

"An organized program of family home evenings was also introduced as part of the correlation program. A special manual of family lessons was published for every family in the Church, and outlines were offered on how to conduct successful family home evening instruction. Course offerings in all of the auxiliary organizations were correlated so that a unified program of gospel learning is followed in all teaching organizations of the Church.

"The work of priesthood correlation and the new emphasis on family home evenings and home teaching brought a great surge of spiritual growth into the Church and marked a significant era in the Church in strengthening the homes and helping fathers and mothers take their rightful places

An excellent horseman; President McKay loved his Huntsville home

as spiritual leaders of their children." (*Essentials in Church History*, p. 543.)

(20-14) The Grand Purpose of Correlation Programs and All Programs of the Church

President McKay testified thus to the assembled priesthood of the Church:

"As I listened to the very able presentation of the scholarly plan to correlate the studies of the priesthood and auxiliaries of the entire Church, I thought what is the end purpose of all this? I visualized the fact that 30,000 or 40,000 men and boys in priesthood assemblies this night constitute an organization in the world with one great purpose in mind, and that is to fulfill or respond to the call that Jesus gave Nicodemus: ' . . . Except a man be born again, he cannot see the kingdom of God.' And Nicodemus wondered, he could not comprehend it. And Jesus answered, ' . . . Except a man be born of water and of the Spirit, he cannot enter into the kingdom of God.' (John 3:3, 5.)

"In that first sentence, 'Except a man be born again, he cannot see the kingdom of God,' we have the answer to the end and purpose of this great plan. . . . " (*CR*, Oct. 1961, p. 89.)

(20-15) The Church Was Strengthened from Within

The ministry of President McKay was extremely lengthy and only a few important matters will be treated there, but such a retrenchment had been accomplished and such a consolidation effected that President Hugh B. Brown was able to testify as follows:

"I want to say to you, brethren, that in the midst of all the troubles, the uncertainties, the tumult and chaos through which the world is passing, almost unnoticed by the majority of the people of the world, there has been set up a kingdom, a kingdom over which God the Father presides, and Jesus the Christ is the King. That kingdom is rolling forward, as I say, partly unnoticed, but it is rolling forward with a power and a force that will

stop the enemy in its tracks while some of you live." (*CR*, Oct. 1967, pp. 115-16.)

LIKE OTHER PROPHETS BEFORE HIM, PRESIDENT McKAY EMPHASIZED THE CENTRAL ROLE OF THE FAMILY AND THE HOME

(20-16) President McKay's Own Life Was an Example of the Importance of Home and Family

President McKay spoke with authority on marriage and the family and the high role of women. His own marriage, in its mortal phase, stretched over sixty-nine years and became a legend in the Church. Hearts were thrilled when Robert R. McKay testified thus of his father's prophetic call:

"As my father, he has my love and devotion, and I echo the thoughts of my brothers and sisters. As the President of the Church, and as a prophet of our Heavenly Father, he has my obedience as a member of the priesthood, and my sustaining vote.

"I can say this, and act as a personal witness, because in all of my years of close association in the home, on the farm, in business, in the Church, there has never been shown to me one action nor one word, even while training a self-willed horse, which would throw any doubt in my mind that he should be and finally did become the representative and prophet of our Heavenly Father. I leave you that personal witness. . . . " (*CR*, Apr. 1967, p. 84.)

(20-17) President McKay Also Taught the Saints by Precept That the Home Is Central to the Gospel

"One of our most precious possessions is our families. The domestic relations precede, and, in our present existence, are worth more than all other social ties. They give the first throb to the heart and unseal the deep fountains of its love. Home is the chief school of human virtues. Its responsibilities, joys, sorrows, smiles, tears, hopes, and solicitudes form the chief interests of human life. . . .

"When one puts business or pleasure above his home, he that moment starts on the downgrade to soul-weakness. When the club becomes more attractive to any man than his home, it is time for him to confess in bitter shame that he has failed to measure up to the supreme opportunity of his life and flunked in the final test of true manhood. No other success can compensate for failure in the home. The poorest shack in which love prevails over a united family is of greater value to God and future humanity than any other riches. In such a home God can work miracles and will work miracles.

"Pure hearts in a pure home are always in whispering distance of heaven.

"In the light of scripture, ancient and modern we are justified in concluding that Christ's ideal pertaining to marriage is the unbroken home. . . . " (David O. McKay in *CR*, Apr. 1964, p. 5.)

DAVID O. McKAY HELPED TO RAISE THE GOSPEL STANDARD TO ALL THE NATIONS

(20-18) The Doctrine of Gathering During President McKay's Administration

"We are still appealing to people to leave Babylon which signifies spiritual darkness. We are still gathering children of light. We are still gathering scattered Israel. But we are no longer urging emigration to America. On the contrary, we are telling the Saints exactly what the Lord expects of them, namely to build stakes of Zion and to extend the boundaries of his kingdom. In the second period of church history the main work in this respect must be done in the missions. Here great growth must be achieved in order that stakes and wards

President McKay with Cecil B. DeMille and Charlton Heston (Moses)

can be established so that the church organization can be extended over the whole earth. The task of our members lies therefore in the missions in order that we may here prepare for the coming of our Lord. The Book of Mormon tells us that at the second coming of the Lord that believers will be found everywhere on the earth. Although small in number, the Church of the Lamb is spread over the whole earth and it is fortified with righteousness and the power of God. (1 Nephi 14:12-14)" (Der Stern, Nov. 1958, p. 343; translated by Ernest Eberhard, Jr. Italics added. See also Seminary and Institute of Religion booklet Presidents of the Church, p. 104.)

(20-19) A Vision of Temples in Foreign Lands

More temples were built during President McKay's administration than during any previous administration. The number is perhaps not as significant as the location. Temples began to be built throughout the world.

President David O. McKay was a great teacher

Llewelyn R. McKay, the eldest son of President McKay, recorded the following incident which occurred when his father was mission president in Europe in the 1920s:

" . . . father had the vision of a temple being erected for the European members of the Church. I recall asking him if missionaries should persist in encouraging members to leave their homes and move to Zion. 'No,' he answered, 'it is important that the branches be built up, and members should remain and work toward that end. Someday we shall have temples built for them which will be accessible to all, so that the desired temple work can be done without uprooting families from their homelands.' " (Home Memories, p. 33.)

(20-20) David O. McKay Proclaimed the Gospel in Such a Way That the World Could Understand It

There is cause to believe that President McKay communicated

not only to the Church but to much of the world. He was formally educated and had a love for the great authors and writers of the English language. He would teach gospel principles as he quoted Shakespeare or Carlisle or his beloved Robert Burns. His talent as a teacher became evident. Note the following clear articulation of the basic foundation of Mormonism:

"One outstandingly distinguishing feature of this Church is divine authority by direct revelation. The appearing of the Father and the Son to Joseph Smith is the foundation of this Church. Therein lies the secret of its strength and vitality. This is true, and I bear witness to it. That one revelation answers all the queries of science regarding God and his divine personality. Don't you see what that means? What God is, is answered. His relation to his children is clear. His interest in humanity through authority delegated to man is apparent. The future of the work is assured. These and other glorious truths are clarified by that glorious first vision." (McKay, Gospel Ideals, p. 85.)

Near the end of World War II President McKay made this poignant and universal plea:

"I feel that we can join with the poet in saying:

'O Christ, who died to give men life,
Bring that victorious hour,
When man shall use for peace, not strife,
His valor, skill, and power.'

"God grant that the nations of the earth will soon open their eyes, and behold the light of the world and thereby accept in this day the things which belong unto their peace. . . . " ("Will Nations Avert a World War III?", Improvement Era, Nov. 1944, p. 708.)

(20-21) The World Is Confronted with Christ

The central message of all the prophets of all the ages to all the world is that Jesus is the Christ. It was so with David O. McKay.

"A few years ago an incident happened in Edinburgh in the winter of 1909, when no less a personage than the prime minister of Great Britain delivered a lecture. . . .

"The gentleman presented in an interesting manner the fundamental ties that unite the different nations of the world—common knowledge, common commercial interests, the intercourse of diplomatic relationship, and the bonds of human friendship.

"The audience greeted his masterful address with a great outburst of applause. As the presiding officer arose, and was about to express his appreciation, and that of the audience, a Japanese student who was doing graduate work at the University, stood up and leaning over the balcony, said, 'But Mr. Balfour, what about Jesus Christ?'

" . . . The leading statesman of the greatest Christian empire in the world had been dealing with the different ties that are to unite mankind, and had omitted the one fundamental and essential bond. . . .

"Without Jesus of Nazareth, the Crucified Christ, the Risen Lord, the world cannot survive." (McKay, *Stepping Stones*, pp. 158-59, 162.)

(20-22) A Prophet Respected Around the World

David O. McKay looked like a prophet even to those who were not Latter-day Saints. He was well known as the "Mormon Prophet"

President and Sister McKay: an LDS ideal

and even figured among the top five church leaders listed in Dr. George Gallup's opinion poll in 1968. (See Smith, *Essentials in Church History* [1969 ed.], p. 556.) Whether attending a reception hosted by Queen Elizabeth of England or mingling with so-called commoners, President McKay stood out physically and spiritually.

"I remember being in New York when President McKay returned from Europe. Arrangements had been made for pictures to be taken, but the regular photographer was unable to go, so in desperation the United Press picked their crime photographer—a man accustomed to the toughest type of work in New York. He went to the airport, stayed there two hours, and returned later from [the] dark room with a tremendous sheaf of pictures. He was supposed to take only two. His boss immediately chided him, 'What in the world are you wasting time and all those photographic supplies for?'

"The photographer replied very curtly, saying he would gladly pay for the extra materials, and they could even dock him for the extra time he took. It was obvious that he was very touchy about it. Several hours later the vice-president called him to his office, wanting to learn what happened. The crime

photographer said, 'When I was a little boy, my mother used to read to me out of the Old Testament, and all my life I have wondered what a prophet of God must really look like. Well, today I found one.' "—*Arch L. Madsen, president of Bonneville International Corporation* (Cited in "Memories of a Prophet," *Improvement Era*, Feb. 1970, p. 72.)

On President McKay's seventy-eighth birthday, his first as president of the Church, his former colleagues of the Council of the Twelve with whom he had served for forty-five years, expressed their best wishes:

"Throughout your eventful life you have been an inspiration to young and old in the Church. Your humble yet brilliant career in the Lord's work has been a literal fulfillment of the Savior's injunction in the Sermon on the Mount which guided a poet to say:

" 'Hold thy lighted lamp on high,
Be a star in someone's sky.' "

(Cited in McKay, *Home Memories*, p. 251.)

Little wonder that he could speak of radiating light to others and challenge us to do the same.

CHAPTER 21

THAT YE MIGHT BE PARTAKERS OF THE DIVINE NATURE

INTRODUCTION

In chapter 20 you read a statement by David O. McKay in which he said that the one great purpose for the Church was to fulfill the challenge given by the Master to Nicodemus that every man should be born again. (See reading 20-14.) What does it mean to be born again? And why would it be so vastly important in the growth and development of the Church?

By revelation the church is called The Church of Jesus Christ of Latter-day Saints. (See D&C 115:4.) The word *saint* comes from the Latin word *sanctus* from which we get such words as *sanctify* and *sanctification*. In other words, in the fullest sense a saint is one who has been sanctified. Our spiritual goal in this life is to become one of the latter-day "sanctified ones."

It is no small matter to profess sainthood, but this is the goal of those who claim membership in The Church of Jesus Christ of Latter-day Saints. The ancient apostle Paul spoke truly when he said we are "*called* to be saints." (Romans 1:7. Italics added.) President McKay knew that only as members of the Church became saints in the fullest sense would the ultimate aim of the gospel be achieved. Zion could never be established on any other foundation, for sanctification means to be cleansed or purified, and Zion is the pure in heart. (See D&C 97:21.) Many accounts of the administration of this prophet of God herald the physical growth of the Church. As impressive as all this is, President McKay knew that growth of the kingdom was simply a means to

an important end, namely, sanctification and the perfection of the individual. When first sustained as presiding prophet, he spoke of his primary goal. It remains an ideal for all to strive toward, the real ideal of Zion.

"I pledge to you that I shall do my best so to live as to merit the companionship of the Holy Spirit, and pray here in your presence that my counselors and I may indeed be 'partakers of the divine spirit.' " (David O. McKay in *CR*, Apr. 1951, p. 157.)

BY BEING AN EXAMPLE OF ONE WHO PARTOOK OF THE DIVINE NATURE, DAVID O. McKAY WAS AN INSPIRATIONAL INFLUENCE IN THE LIVES OF THE SAINTS

(21-1) The Struggle to Rise

It was not in one single bound that David O. McKay arose to spiritual heights. He too struggled against opposition and endured it. He grappled with a temper that needed taming and overcame it. He strove for a testimony and achieved it. There can be no doubt that Satan desired him as he desires to have all men. (See reading 20-5 in this manual.) David O. McKay was successful in the struggle:

" . . . an upright character is the result only of continued effort and right thinking, the effect of long-cherished associations with Godlike thoughts. He approaches nearest the Christ spirit who makes God the center of his thoughts; and he who can say in his heart, 'Not my will, but thine be done,' approaches most nearly the Christ ideal." (David O. McKay in *CR*, Oct. 1953, p. 10.)

(21-2) What Makes a Man Great?

In Elder McKay's first published book is found the following:

"No man has come to true greatness who has not felt in some degree that his life belongs to his race, and that what God gives him He gives him for mankind.

"If any man seek for greatness, let him forget greatness and ask for truth, and he will find both.

"Nothing can make a man truly great but being truly good, and partaking of God's holiness." (*Ancient Apostles*, p. 3.)

A theme of President McKay's was that "character is greater than intellect" (*Gospel Ideals*, p. 443), and that "to be trusted is a greater compliment than to be loved" (*Treasures of Life*, p. 379). Why is this the case? There is much said in these times about "charismatic" leaders. Can any leader be truly great or even charismatic without integrity of character? (Look up the meaning of the word *charisma* in an unabridged dictionary.) President McKay achieved spiritual power in his life; this is evident. Of an ancient prophet of Israel it is written,

"And Samuel grew, and the Lord was with him, and did let none of his words fall to the ground.

"And all Israel from Dan even to Beersheba knew that Samuel was established to be a prophet of the Lord." (1 Samuel 3:19, 20.)

David O. McKay grew in the ways of the Lord, partook of the divine nature, and became established as a prophet in modern Israel. Here was a man who heard the voice of inspiration. "I heard a voice that I had prayed for as a youth. . . . I heard the voice and got in touch with the Spirit as never before." (David O. McKay, *Cherished Experiences* [1976 ed.], p. 127.)

He received the gift of tongues.

"One of the most important events on my world tour of the missions of the Church was the gift of interpretation of the English tongue to the Saints of New Zealand, at a session of their conference, held on the 23rd day of April, 1921, at Puke Tapu Branch, Waikato District, Huntly, New Zealand.

"The service was held in a large tent, beneath the shade of which hundreds of earnest men and women gathered in anxious anticipation of seeing and hearing an Apostle of the Church, the first one to visit that land.

"When I looked over that vast assemblage and contemplated the great expectations that filled the hearts of all who had met together, I realized how inadequately I might satisfy the ardent desires of their souls, and I yearned, most earnestly, for the gift of tongues that I might be able to speak to them in their native language.

"Until that moment I had not given much serious thought to the gift of tongues, but on that occasion, I wished with all my heart, that I might be worthy of that divine power.

"In other missions I had spoken through an interpreter but, able as all interpreters are, I nevertheless felt hampered, in fact, somewhat inhibited, in presenting my message.

"Now, I faced an audience that had assembled with unusual expectations, and I then realized, as never before, the great responsibility of my office. From the depth of my soul, I prayed for divine assistance.

"When I arose to give my address, I said to Brother Stuart Meha, our interpreter, that I would speak without his translating, sentence by sentence, what I said, and then to the audience I continued:

" 'I wish, oh, how I wish I had the power to speak to you in your own tongue, that I might tell you what is in my heart; but since I have not the gift, I pray, and I ask you to pray, that you might have the spirit of interpretation, of discernment, that you may understand at least the spirit while I am speaking, and then you will get the words and the thought when Brother Meha interprets.'

"My sermon lasted forty minutes, and I have never addressed a more attentive, a more respectful audience. My listeners were in perfect rapport—this I knew when I saw tears in their eyes. Some of them at least, perhaps most of them, who did not understand English, had the gift of interpretation." (McKay, *Cherished Experiences,* pp. 73-74.)

He saw visions.

"The plans for the new temple [Swiss Temple] were ready by the time the site was purchased. President McKay discussed the architecture with Edward O. Anderson, a Church architect, after he had evidently seen the building in a vision. After their initial visit about the design of the temple, President McKay's description was so vivid that the architect was able to draw it as the President had seen it. However, in the process of developing the drawings, some changes crept in. Upon seeing the drawings, President McKay said, 'Brother Anderson, that is not the temple that you and I saw together.' The drawings were changed and the president's original concept of the basic design was carried out. . . . " (*1977 Church Almanac,* p. 245.)

He healed the sick.

" . . . as President McKay held her [Nina Penrod's] right hand with his left hand, he shook hands with many others with his right hand. Sister Penrod said it was very humbling in the extreme to her, yet she felt elated because something wonderful had happened to her, for her arthritis pains were all gone." (McKay, *Cherished Experiences,* p. 157.)

He opened the eyes of the blind.

"If I [Melvin T. Mickelson] were to labor in the service of our Master all the days of my life, I could only repay in part the blessings he has so freely given to me, by the faith and humility of our great leader, President David O. McKay. He, through

the power of the priesthood, made it possible for me to enjoy the blessing of sight." (McKay, *Cherished Experiences*, p. 161.)

He exercised the gift of discernment. Elder Robert L. Simpson tells of his first introduction to President McKay. This introduction took place at the dedication of the New Zealand Temple.

" 'The President extended his firm right hand, and placing his left hand on my shoulder, looked into my eyes and, more than that, into every fiber of my being. After a few seconds, he gave my hand a friendly pump, my shoulder a squeeze, and said, "Brother Simpson, I am pleased to *know* you." Not "I am pleased to *meet* you," but "pleased to *know* you." During the ensuing days and weeks, the memory of this introduction kept recurring. Approximately three months later, while sitting in my office in Los Angeles, my telephone rang and the voice on the other end of the line said, "This is David O. McKay speaking." He said that based on our interview, he had felt impressed to issue a call to return with my family to New Zealand to preside over the people I loved so much.' " ("Memories of a Prophet," *Improvement Era*, Feb. 1970, p. 72.)

The power of God was with him. On one occasion in the South Pacific as he was taking leave of a group of Saints, a remarkable thing happened.

"There the now silent and expectant groups were standing disconsolate as Israel of old bereft of their Moses; he dismounted in the trail and raising aloft his hands as a

David O. McKay as a young Apostle

patriarch of the past, he pronounced a remarkable and soul-stirring benediction, all clear and now partly fulfilled.

"It is the testimony of some who cast their eyes upward momentarily as inspired words flowed in great power from Elder McKay's lips that a halo of brightness rested upon him like a shaft of white light, and certain it is that the borderland of heaven and earth rested in close proximity to the spot where was given this wonderful manifestation and blessing. Each listener's soul throbbed with the conviction of the truth." (McKay, *Cherished Experiences*, pp. 66-67.)

Jesus promised that signs would follow those that believed. (See Mark 16:17.) Would you like to have that kind of spiritual power in your life? How do you suppose David O. McKay won that for himself? Read D&C 63:7-12 for an important key to having these signs of which Jesus spoke. In the following sections of this chapter, David O. McKay can teach you the key to joy and spiritual power, for it is the key he himself used.

President McKay and his counselors Henry D. Moyle and Hugh B. Brown

DAVID O. McKAY TAUGHT THE SAINTS THE MEANING OF TRUE SPIRITUALITY AND LED THEM TO PARAKE OF THE DIVINE NATURE

(21-3) Life's Chief Aim

"Man's chief concern in life should not be the acquiring of gold, or of fame, or of material possessions. It should not be development of physical powers, nor of intellectual strength, but his aim, the highest in life, should be the development of a Christ-like character. . . .

"The true purpose in life is perfection of humanity through individual effort, under the guidance of God's inspiration. Real life is reponse to the best about us." (David O. McKay, cited in Jeanette McKay Morrell, *Highlights in the Life of President David O. McKay,* p. 240.)

(21-4) The Rock upon Which the Church Is Built

"When knowledge acquired by natural effort receives the confirmation of heaven and becomes the possession of

thousands or millions of persons united in a Church with Christ as the Head, the gates of hell cannot prevail against either the individual or the collective body. A consciousness of oneness with God and Truth is the Rock upon which Christ's Church is and ever will be founded. It is revelation through which each 'stone' in the structure is made 'a partaker of the divine nature.' " (David O. McKay, *True to the Faith,* p. 50.)

(21-5) The So-Called "Little Things" Make the Difference

"The spiritual road has Christ as its goal. The individual lives for something higher than self. He hears the Savior's voice saying: 'I am the way, the truth, and the life.' Following that voice he soon learns that there is no one great thing which he can do to attain happiness or eternal life. He learns that 'life is made up not of great sacrifices or duties, but of little things in which smiles and kindness and small obligations given habitually are what win and preserve the heart and secure comfort.' " (*Relief Society Magazine,* June 1941, p. 366.)

(21-6) What Spirituality Is, and Ways to Achieve It

"Spirituality is the highest acquisition of the soul, 'the divine in man—the supreme crowning gift that makes him king of all created things.' It is the consciousness of victory over self, and of communion with the Infinite. To acquire more and more power, to feel one's faculties unfolding, and one's soul in harmony with God and with the Infinite—that is spirituality. It is that alone which really gives one the best in life.

"Spirituality is best manifested in doing, not in dreaming. 'Rapturous day dreams, flights of heavenly fancy, longings to see the invisible, are not so impressive as the plain doing of duty.'

"Every noble impulse, every unselfish expression of love, every brave suffering for the right; every surrender of self to something higher than self; every loyalty to an ideal; every unselfish devotion to principle; every helpfulness to humanity; every act of self-control; every fine courage of the soul, undefeated by pretense or policy; every being, doing, and living of good for the very good's sake—that is spiritual.

"This feeling about a higher life is universal. The search for, and development of, spiritual peace and freedom concerns everyone.

"You lose the soul unless you develop spirituality within. I would advocate these steps in the development of spirituality:

"1. It is man's duty to become master of nature—not its slave. Self-control, and control of environment, are important.

"2. Spirituality and the abundant life are dependent upon acknowledgement of Deity, and upon honor for the Godhead.

"3. There must be the consciousness that God has delegated to man the authority to act in God's name.

"4. There must be a realization that God is the Father of all men, and that He values each soul.

"5. Life is a mission, and it is the duty of every man to make the world better for his having been in it." (McKay, *True to the Faith,* pp. 244-45.)

How do you feel about spirituality in your life? Now that you may have a better comprehension of how to more fully "put on the divine nature," how will it affect you? It was the testimony of President McKay, as it has been of all the prophets, that as a child of God the power is in you to rise to the heights of godliness. But it is *you* who must act, using your agency wisely, choosing to leave spiritual Babylon and become a Zion person. (Read D&C 58:26-30.)

"God gave to man part of his divinity. He gave man the power of choice, and no other creature in the world has it. So he placed upon the individual the obligation of conducting himself

as an eternal being. You cannot think of any greater gift that could come to a man or woman than the freedom of choice. You alone are responsible, and by wielding and exercising that freedom of choice, you grow in character, you grow in intelligence, you approach divinity, and eventually you may achieve that high exaltation. That is a great obligation. Very few people appreciate it. The roads are clearly marked—one offering animal existence, the other life abundant. Yet, God's greatest creation—*man*—often is content to grovel on the animal plane." (David O. McKay in *CR,* Oct. 1969, pp. 6-7.)

DAVID O. McKAY KNEW THAT A SANCTIFIED CHURCH WOULD BRING ABOUT ZION

(21-7) Preparing the People for the Millennial Reign

Thirty-one years before the birth of David O. McKay (1842), Joseph Smith wrote the following to a certain newspaper editor, identifying two great missions of the Church.

"This messenger [Moroni] proclaimed himself to be an angel of God, sent to bring the joyful tidings that . . . the preparatory work for the second coming of the Messiah was speedily to commence; that the time was at hand for the Gospel in all its fullness to be preached in power, unto all nations that a people might be prepared for the Millennial reign." (Joseph Smith, *HC,* 4:536-37.)

Like those who preceded him, President McKay furthered both of these missions. More than ever before, the gospel was preached to the nations, and many were

prepared for the Millennium by putting on the divine nature.

(21-8) Cornerstones of Zion

"The Zion we build will pattern after the ideals of its inhabitants. To change men and the world we must change their thinking, for the thing which a man really believes is the thing which he has really thought; that which he actually thinks is the thing which he lives. Men do not go beyond their ideals; they often fall short of them, but they never go beyond them. . . .

" . . . the Lord designates Zion as ' . . . the pure in heart . . . ' (D. & C. 97:21); and only when we are such, and only when we have such shall Zion ' . . . flourish, and the glory of the Lord shall be upon her.' (Ibid., 64:41.)

"The foundation of Zion then will be laid in the hearts of men; broad acres, mines, forests, factories, beautiful buildings, modern conveniences, will be but means and accessories to the building of the human soul and the securing of happiness.

"Let us then as we draw our plans for Zion today choose what we may call the 'four cornerstones of Zion's inhabitants.'

"*First:* A firm belief and acceptance of the truth that this universe is governed by intelligence and wisdom, and, as Plato said, ' . . . is not left to the guidance of an irrational and random chance.'

"The *second* cornerstone is that the ultimate purpose in God's great plan is the perfecting of the individual.

It is his desire that men and women become like himself.

"The *third* cornerstone is a realization that the first and most essential thing in man's progress is freedom—*free agency.* Man can choose the highest good, or choose the lowest good and fall short of what he was intended to be.

"The *fourth* cornerstone is a sense of responsibility toward other individuals and the social group." (McKay, *Gospel Ideals,* p. 335.)

(21-9) The Celestial Transformation of Society

"Force and compulsion will never establish the ideal society. This can come only by a transformation within the individual soul—A life redeemed from sin and brought in harmony with the divine will. Instead of selfishness, men must be willing to dedicate their ability, their possessions, their lives if necessary, their fortunes, and their sacred honor for the alleviation of the ills of mankind. Hate must be supplanted by sympathy and forbearance. Peace and true prosperity can come only by conforming our lives to the law of Love, the law of the principles of the Gospel of Jesus Christ." (David O. McKay, cited in Morrell, *Highlights,* p. 241.)

Many in the Church have sung the hymn "Shall the Youth of Zion Falter?" They will not! Zion will see fulfillment as the great crescendo of this last dispensation. The great hope of all the prophets of all the ages will be fulfilled. Will you be there? Is your hope one with the prophets?

"If the question were asked this morning, 'In what respect . . . has the Church made the most commendable progress?' I would not answer: *'In financial matters.'* . . .

"I would not say: *'In the increase of the number of new houses of worship.'* . . .

" . . . I would not answer: *'In the increased membership.'* . . .

"I would not answer that the most commendable progress has been *in better understanding among the leaders of municipalities, newspaper editors, and well-informed people generally regarding the purposes,* organization, and contributions of the Church toward peace and the ultimate destiny of the world.

"I would answer that *the most encouraging progress of the Church . . . is seen in the increased number of young people participating in Church activity.* . . .

"Heaven guide you, our Youth, wherever you are. As long as you will keep yourselves pure and spotless and prayerfully and earnestly keep close to your Father in heaven, his Spirit will guide you, magnify you in your youth, and make you a power on the earth for good. Your Father in heaven is ever ready to give you help in time of need and give you comfort and strength if you will approach him in purity, simplicity, and faith. . . .

"I repeat, God bless you, our Youth, that you may send out your thoughts in prayer and faith and receive the assurance that you are anchored to the Infinite, in God our Father and his Holy Son, the Redeemer of the world, I pray. . . . " (David O. McKay in *CR,* Apr. 1961, pp. 5, 8.)

DAVID O. McKAY WAS PERFECTED DURING HIS LIFE

(21-10) Holy Men upon the Earth

Two common extremes are expressed concerning the prophets of God. One is that they are not subject to the frailties of the flesh and walk unflawed through life. The other is that they are merely men. The truth is that they are

President McKay loved children and they loved him

mortal men, subject to human frailty, but, nonetheless, holy men endowed with the power of God; they are the Lord's anointed.

"One young man accosted me by saying, 'Well, Brother McKay, you're just a man after all, aren't you?'

" 'Why, I hope so,' I replied. 'What did you think I am?'

" 'Well, you know, we think of the old Apostles as being different.' "

(David O. McKay, cited in Llewelyn R. McKay, *Home Memories of President David O. McKay,* p. 82.)

(21-11) The Testimony of a Prophet About a Prophet

At the funeral of President McKay, Joseph Fielding Smith extolled his prophet-leader.

"I honor and revere the name and the memory of President David O. McKay.

"For 60 years I sat by his side in the presiding councils of the Church. I came to know him intimately and well, and I loved him as a man and honored him as a prophet.

"He was a true servant of the Lord—one who walked uprightly before his Maker; one who loved his fellowmen; one who enjoyed life and rejoiced in the privilege of service that was his; one who served with an eye single to the glory of God.

"He exemplified perfectly the Old Testament standard: ' . . . what doth the Lord require of thee, but to do justly, and to love mercy, and to walk humbly with thy God?' (Mic. 6:8.)

"As stated editorially in the *Deseret News:* 'If ever a man of modern history left his world better for having lived in it, that man was David Oman McKay.

" 'Wherever he passed, men lifted their heads with more hope and courage. Wherever his voice was heard, there followed greater kindness among men, greater tolerance, greater love. Wherever his influence was felt, man and God became closer in purpose and in action.'

"President McKay was called to the holy apostleship in April 1906 by my father, President Joseph F. Smith, who acted under the inspiration of the Spirit, and he became one of the greatest and most inspired leaders of this dispensation. . . .

"In all his travels President McKay was a perfect gentleman—always kind and considerate, more interested in my comfort than in his own.

"I shall miss him greatly. It does not seem possible that he has left us. But we know he has gone to a joyous reunion with his father and mother and that he is now taking up his labors in the paradise of God as he begins to associate anew with his good friends who preceded him into the realms ahead, with Stephen L Richards and J. Reuben Clark, with George Albert Smith and Heber J. Grant, with Henry D. Moyle and Joseph F. Smith, and a host of others.

"To my mind two statements made by the prophet Lehi exemplify the life of President McKay. He was like a great river, 'continually

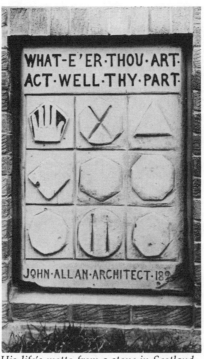

His life's motto from a stone in Scotland

running into the fountain of all righteousness,' and he was like a mighty valley, 'firm and steadfast, and immovable in keeping the commandments of the Lord!' (1 Ne. 2:9-10.)

"I thank God for the life and ministry of this great man. He was a soul set apart, a great spirit who came here to preside in Israel. He did his work well and has returned clean and perfected to the realms of light and joyous reunion. If ever there was a man to whom these words of scriptural benediction might well be said, it was President McKay:

" 'Come, ye blessed of my Father, inherit the kingdom prepared for you from the foundation of the world' (Matt. 25:34), for ye did all things well that were entrusted unto thy care.

"I pray that the peace of heaven may rest with Sister McKay and their family and that the spirit of emulation may abound in the

hearts of all of us for that mighty prophet whose memory is hallowed to us this day." ("One Who Loved His Fellowmen," *Improvement Era*, Feb. 1970, pp. 87-88.)

(21-12) President McKay Purified the Common Clay and More Fully Partook of the Divine Nature

He lifted up his
Common clay,
Purified it,
Made it fit,
Put eternal impress
On it.

With loving care
Prepared it
To be
Exalted.

He taught the
Simple virtues:
Home–a shrine,
Parenthood–a privilege,
Motherhood–divine,
Purity–Godlike.

(S. Dilworth Young, "Thoughts on President David O. McKay, *Improvement Era*, Feb. 1970, p. 77.)

As you have studied the life and teachings of a great prophet of God, you have seen how he has furthered the cause of Zion. It could be truthfully said that David O. McKay was a visionary man. He had a vision of Zion. How is your vision? Are you yourself moving toward Zion? Have you been born again unto the Lord? In reading 21-12 President Smith declared, "I pray that . . . the spirit of emulation may abound in the hearts of all of us for that mighty prophet. . . . " What does this quote mean to you?

While on his world tour in 1920, David O. McKay had a marvelous dream which sets for us the challenge spoken of several times in this unit. He said,

"I then fell asleep, and beheld in vision something infinitely sublime. In the distance I beheld

a beautiful white city. Though far away, yet I seemed to realize that trees with luscious fruit, shrubbery with gorgeously-tinted leaves, and flowers in perfect bloom abounded everywhere. The clear sky above seemed to reflect these beautiful shades of color. I then saw a great concourse of people approaching the city. Each one wore a white flowing robe, and a white headdress. Instantly my attention seemed centered upon their Leader, and though I could see only the profile of his features and his body, I recognized him at once as my Savior! The tint and radiance of his countenance were glorious to behold! There was a peace about him which seemed sublime—it was divine!

"The city, I understood, was his. It was the City Eternal; and the people following him were to abide there in peace and eternal happiness.

"But who were they?

"As if the Savior read my thoughts, he answered by pointing to a semicircle that then appeared above them, and on which were written in gold the words:

President McKay and his wife, Emma Ray

" 'These Are They Who Have Overcome The World—Who Have Truly Been Born Again!'

"When I awoke, it was breaking day. . . . " (McKay, *Cherished Experiences*, p. 102.)

UNIT ELEVEN
JOSEPH FIELDING SMITH

Tenth President of the Church

OVERVIEW

Not unlike Hannah, mother of the Old Testament prophet Samuel, Julina Lambson Smith had greatly desired a son. Having given birth to three lovely daughters, she longed and prayed for a son. She promised the Lord that if he would so bless her she would vow to do all possible to see that the boy was reared to God's service and also that this son would become a credit to the Lord and to his father, Joseph F. Smith.

The Lord blessed the Smith home with a boy who was to be honored with the name of his father, a name that had been reserved for the firstborn son of Julina. And, like Samuel of old, young Joseph took his mother's agreement with the Lord seriously.

In his youth Joseph Fielding drank of the bitter cup of persecution as the infamous federal marshalls came to polygamous homes in Utah, searching for his father and other Church leaders. He recalled that they prowled around their home interrogating and terrorizing the women and children, blighting their lives and precipitating a dark cloud of unhappiness and fear. In such gloomy circumstances, his father was forced into exile almost continuously between Joseph Fielding's eighth and fifteenth years. Thus, when people would express the thought that President Joseph Fielding Smith had a favored youth and consequently he ought to be a great man, he was constrained to admit that they did not understand all the circumstances. His father was a busy man, away from home during most of the formative years of Joseph Fielding's youth because of difficulties with the government of the United States.

Through the first of these lonely, trying years was born an understanding and a courage in young Joseph Fielding that made him one of the latter-day Church's most able defenders. Tried,

tested, and found true and faithful seems to be typical of the life of this great servant of the living God. Three times he married (Louie Emily Shurtliff, Ethel Georgina Reynolds, and Jessie Ella Evans), and three times he experienced the sorrow of losing an eternal companion. Once he also made the supreme sacrifice of his son (Lewis Warren Smith) in the defense of his country.

Sensitive and understanding, he despised misery and suffering everywhere and did all in his power to alleviate it by clothing the naked, feeding the hungry, and visiting those in need. A pillar of strength and encouragement to his family and the Church, he was loved universally. Little children adored him and thought it not strange to be found in the arms of this prophet, for he suffered the little ones to come. Years later they came by the hundreds to honor him and pay their last respects at his death. He had been tempered in the fires of life and had become as tough as rawhide. When he was eighty-nine years of age he slipped on the steps of his apartment and sustained a multiple fracture of his leg. But he was due at a meeting in the temple, so he gritted his teeth and limped the block and a half to the temple, sat through the meeting, and then limped home. Only then would he submit to the medical treatment which others insisted that he have. He later admitted that the meeting had been a little long, and with tongue in cheek he confessed that most meetings are.

Spanning the years since Brigham Young, Joseph Fielding was age twenty-seven when the Wright brothers made their maiden voyage at Kitty Hawk. He viewed the invention of the airplane as fulfillment of prophecy. He loved to fly and thrived on the excitement of supersonic speed. But in a practical sense, his life was a model of simplicity. His interest was in

service and not in money or popularity. He thought little of giving money to those in need but was visibly embarrassed when receiving public recognition. He chose to live in a simple apartment rather than in luxurious surroundings. He preferred walking to riding, and his wife driving their compact car to the chauffeured luxury limousine that was offered him.

An apostle at age thirty-three, he was sustained as president of the Church at age ninety-three. None have been called as the Lord's anointed at a later age or have been better prepared than was Joseph Fielding Smith. In his veins coursed the blood of prophets. In his heart burned the fires of unselfish service to his family and fellowmen. His reminder was that the latter-day prophets are prophets to the entire world, that the world must repent, and that the gospel must be taken to all the world before the coming of the Lord.

Weighty was his message. Constant was his counsel. Unwavering was his faith. Even as many saw his firmness, many others knew his tenderness and love. He could be found with equal comfort hitching a horse to a buggy or studying the Book of Mormon, playing baseball or defending his father from the barbs of evil editors, engaging in a contest of handball with his sons or editing B. H. Robert's *Comprehensive History of the Church,* flying in a supersonic jet fighter or taking a child in his loving arms, patiently tending an ailing child through the night or explaining the mind and will of the Lord on any doctrinal issue.

Other great spirits have walked the earth, but none have stood more firm or have been more faithful than Joseph Fielding Smith—student, author, friend, father, husband, defender, loving counselor, historian, missionary, sportsman, optimist, genealogist, and a foreordained prophet of God.

CHAPTER 22

PROCLAIMING THE DOCTRINES OF THE GOSPEL

INTRODUCTION

The day was July 19, 1876. It was 89 degrees in the shade—if one could find any—and the dusty Salt Lake City streets served as an effective reminder that America, now a century old, was still a frontier. Ulysses S. Grant was in the White House. George Armstrong Custer had met his destiny at the Little Big Horn three weeks before. In just five days ten thousand Saints would meet in the new Tabernacle to commemorate the twenty-ninth anniversary of the arrival of the pioneers in the Valley. They would hear prophetic counsel from their beloved Brother Brigham.

It was the starting of a new life for the Saints—a good start—and the birth of a new son for Elder Joseph F. Smith, a member of the Council of the Twelve. July 19, 1876, found the Smith home on North Temple in a state of anxious anticipation. Julina Lambson Smith was to deliver her firstborn son, who would receive his father's name, his father's voice, and, to an amazing degree, his father's heritage as a missionary, a historian, an apostle, a scriptorian, a counselor in the First Presidency, and eventually, as the presiding prophet.

Joseph Fielding would consider his name sacred, a name which his father proudly bore, as did also his granduncle and great-grandfather (who had been identified by name by none other than Joseph who was sold into Egypt). Oh, how he would honor this name. Never would he allow the use of its abbreviation, Joe.

Who would have guessed that this shy, studious farm boy would be found in his eightieth year streaking across the sky at the controls of a United States Air Force jet? But this was an unusual boy! This was a boy who thought it his duty to walk through life with his hand in the hand of the Lord. Indeed, his sole desire (to learn the will of the Lord in order that he could live it) moved him to read the Book of Mormon twice by the time he was ten years old. When the ball team missed him, they could generally find him in the hayloft reading that book. He read and memorized the *Children's Catechism* (an early Church publication which explained the doctrines of the gospel) and Primary books. Natural and spontaneous, his appetite for learning properly whetted throughout his life, he would become one of the greatest gospel scholars that the Church has known.

"From my earliest recollection, from the time I first could read, I have received more pleasure and greater satisfaction out of the study of the scriptures, and reading of the Lord Jesus Christ, and of the Prophet Joseph Smith, and the work that has been accomplished for the salvation of men, than from

anything else in all the world." (Joseph Fielding Smith in *CR*, Apr. 1930, p. 91.)

Though the world may view a boy as a bundle of energy to be dealt with, a problem to solve, a perpetual dirty face, or a fun-loving child to enjoy, the Lord knows the boy and his destiny, for he is His son. Such was Joseph Fielding Smith as he moved toward his great destiny.

AS A SENSITIVE, TENDERHEARTED BOY, JOSEPH FIELDING SMITH WORKED HARD, OFTEN STOOD ALONE, AND ASSISTED AS A FAMILY PROVIDER

(22-1) Joseph Fielding Worked While Others Rested

Inspired by a disciplined father, Joseph Fielding was, from childhood, an early riser, a practice that lasted throughout his entire life and was his formula for getting things done. Even at the age of ninety-five "he was still his own best sermon on nonretirement. I remember early one winter morning driving to Salt Lake City long before daylight. As I turned a corner near Temple Square, the headlight of my car brought into view an elderly man out walking in the cold, snowy air. It was Joseph Fielding. He was up every morning well before 6 o'clock, and put in a heavy day's work. It was a lifelong habit, and one that he also instilled in his children. 'People die in bed,' he cautioned them. 'And so does ambition.'

" 'Somehow it seemed immoral to lie in bed after 6,' recalls a son. 'Of course, I only tried it once. Father saw to that.' " (Joseph Fielding

241

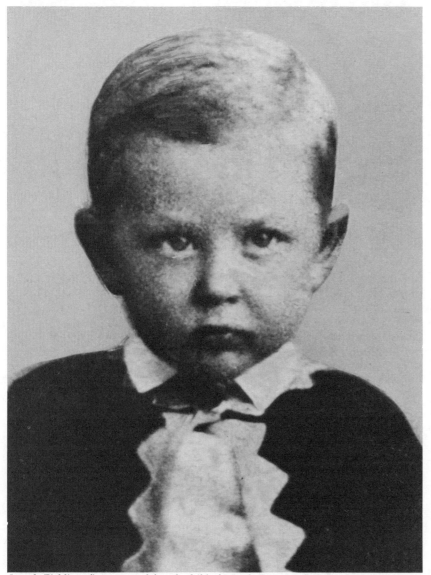

Joseph Fielding–first son and fourth child of Joseph F. and Julina Lambson Smith Smith, Jr., and John J Stewart, The Life of Joseph Fielding Smith, p. 3.)

(22-2) He Was a Master at Capturing Moments That Others Wasted

"Even in advanced age Joseph Fielding Smith was one of the hardest working men I knew. 'How do you manage to get so much done?' I once asked him. 'It's in the bag,' he said. 'In the bag?' I asked. He pointed to a lunch sack. 'I'm a brown bagger.' For years he carried a sack lunch to his office, so he could keep working through the noon hour. 'That gives me an extra 300 hours per year.' " (Smith and Stewart, *Life of Joseph Fielding Smith*, pp. 3-4.)

Suppose you had a job in 1894. The work is hard. The pay is modest. The muscles of an eighteen-year-old get sore and weary. Remember that work in early Utah required walking to and from the job as well as doing your home chores. As you walk slowly home, following a long and difficult day, would you feel like reading and studying the scriptures? Would you be pleasant upon your arrival home, looking for ways to make your younger brothers and sisters happy?

(22-3) Joseph Fielding Was an Industrious, Hard Worker and Generous with His Earnings

"It was a late summer evening in Salt Lake City, in the year of 1894. Joseph Fielding Smith, 18 years of age, had just completed another day of heavy work as a cash boy in the wholesale grocery department in the basement of the Zion's Cooperative Mercantile Institution, at Main and South Temple Streets. He flexed his shoulders, took a deep breath, tried to stand up straight. It was not easy. The hours were long, the work was exhausting, and the pay was pitifully meager. 'I worked like a work horse all day long and was tired out when night came, carrying sacks of flour and sacks of sugar and hams and bacons on my back. I weighed 150 pounds, but I thought nothing of picking up a 200-pound sack and putting it on my shoulders. I was a very foolish fellow, because ever since that time my shoulders have been just a little out of kilter. The right one got a little more "treatment" than the left.'

"But jobs were not easy to find and his family needed all the financial support it could get, from him and his brothers old enough to work. So Joseph felt fortunate to have this job despite the strenuous working conditions and low pay. The daily physical workout might even be good for him in the long run, if it did not kill him first.

"And now, as was his habit, he

stopped by the candy counter and bought a sack of hardtack to take home to Mama and to his younger brothers and sisters. He found pleasure in seeing the little ones' joy at this frequent treat.'' (Smith and Stewart, *Life of Joseph Fielding Smith*, pp. 65-66.)

(22-4) The Moving Drive in His Youth Was to Learn and Accomplish What the Lord Wanted Him to Do

''As Joseph rounded the corner on North Temple Street and headed west down along City Creek, he delighted in the sound of the water rippling along over the rocks. He also noted there was a touch of fall in the air now as dusk settled in on the valley. He would have to remember and wear his jacket to work in the morning. Walking along he pulled from his shirt pocket a small copy of the New Testament that he carried with him constantly, reading it during his noon break and while going to and from work, and in fact whenever he had opportunity. He opened it to his marker in the Book of Acts, Chapter 3, and read a few verses, but the light had grown dim, for the days were getting shorter, a thing he disliked, and it was a strain on his eyes to read, especially while walking. So he put the book back in his pocket. His eyes were not too strong anyway, and it would not do to unnecessarily strain them. There was a lot of reading to get done in the days and years ahead. Instead of reading the rest of the way home he would mentally run through some scriptures that he was trying to commit to memory. Matthew, Chapter 11, 'Come unto me, all ye that labour and are heavy laden, and I will give you rest. Take my yoke upon you, and learn of me; for I am meek and lowly in heart; and ye shall find rest unto your souls. For my yoke is easy, and my

burden light. . . . ' '' (Smith and Stewart, *Life of Joseph Fielding Smith*, p. 67.)

(22-5) He Knew the Fright of Having a Brush with Death

It becomes immediately evident to the viewer that the lives of the Lord's anointed are preserved for their chosen destiny.

''Many of Joseph's youthful hours were spent herding cows near the Jordan River and laboring with his brothers on the family farm in Taylorsville. On one occasion when he and his younger brother, George, were loading hay onto a wagon to take it from the field to the barn, Joseph had a close brush with death. They had stopped on a road by the canal to stack some bales and give the team a drink. Because they had a skittish horse, Joseph told George to stand by the head of the team and hold their bridles until he could climb up and take the reins. Instead, George went back and started up the binding rope. As he did so, the horses started with a sudden jerk and Joseph fell down between the horses on the doubletree.

''The thought, 'Well, here's my finish!' flashed through his mind. But something turned the horses and they ran into the canal, while Joseph was thrown clear of their hoofs and the wheels of the wagon. When he got up, he gave George an honest appraisal of his feelings and then hurried home—shaken, but grateful to be in one piece. His father came out to meet him and wanted to know what difficulty he had encountered, having received a strong impression that his son was in some kind of danger.'' (Joseph F. McConkie, *True and Faithful*, p. 18.)

(22-6) By the Age of Ten, He Was Assisting His Mother in Her Professional Duties

''When his mother returned from the Hawaiian Islands, Joseph was ten years old, and it was at that tender age that he began assisting her in her professional duties as a licensed midwife or obstetrician. Joseph's job was that of stable boy and buggy driver. At all hours of the day or night, when the call came for his mother's services, Joseph was to hitch up the faithful mare 'Old Meg' to the buggy and drive his mother to the home of the confinement case. Here he might wait while she delivered the baby, or, if his mother thought the wait would be too long, she would send him home with instructions on when to return for her. . . .

'' 'Sometimes I nearly froze to death. I marveled that so many babies were born in the middle of the night, especially on cold winter nights. I fervently wished that mothers might time things a little better.' '' (Smith and Stewart, *Life of Joseph Fielding Smith*, pp. 52-53.)

(22-7) The Touch of the Spirit and the Thirst for the Things of the Lord Occurred Very Early in the Life of Joseph Fielding Smith

'' 'I was born with a testimony of the gospel. . . . I do not remember a time when I did not have full confidence in the mission of the Prophet Joseph Smith and in the teachings and guidance of my parents.' This statement is endorsed in a blessing given to him in 1913 by Patriarch Joseph D. Smith.'' (Smith and Stewart, *Life of Joseph Fielding Smith*, p. 56.)

''I remember that one thing I did from the time I learned to read and write was to study the gospel. I read and committed to memory the children's catechism and primary books on the gospel. Later I read the history of the Church as recorded in the *Millennial Star*. I also read the Bible, the Book of Mormon, the Pearl of Great Price,

and the Doctrine and Covenants, and other literature which fell into my hands. . . . I learned at a very early day that God lives; he gave me a testimony when I was a child, and I have tried to be obedient always, with some measure of success." (Cited in McConkie, *True and Faithful,* p. 69.)

"By nature, Joseph was more quiet and studious than his brothers. It was his habit to hurry with his chores so that he could go to his father's library and study." (McConkie, *True and Faithful,* p. 18.)

From the vantage point of hindsight, one quickly comes to the realization that Joseph Fielding Smith entered this life with the shadow of former greatness guiding him to the lofty summits of mortal experience. Indeed, he was blessed of the Lord from his early childhood. He responded to the promptings of the Spirit throughout his life. And his service was accepted of the Lord, for throughout his faithful mortal probation, there issued an inspiration that lifted and edified the Saints for nearly a century. As you study and consider the sections to follow, try to discover what it is that comprises the building of a man like Joseph Fielding Smith.

A NATURAL BORN OPTIMIST, JOSEPH FIELDING LOOKED ON THE POSITIVE SIDE OF LIFE AND WAS QUICK TO SEE THE HUMOR OF AN EVERYDAY EXPERIENCE

(22-8) Joseph Fielding Smith Enjoyed Wholesome Humor

The members of the Church everywhere were well acquainted with this respected theologian, and they welcomed his clear, unmistakable commentary on the scriptures. But there was almost

Joseph Fielding Smith as a missionary, age 23

universal ignorance of his remarkable humorous nature. His innate humor was unaffected and inoffensive. It sprang naturally from real life experiences. Once, for example, after his father had given him a mare named Junie, Joseph Fielding said:

"Junie was one of the most intelligent animals I ever saw. She seemed almost human in her ability. I could not keep her locked in the barn because she would continually undo the strap on the door of her stall. I used to put the strap connected to the half-door of

the stall over the top of the post, but she would simply lift it off with her nose and teeth. Then she would go out in the yard.

"There was a water tap in the yard used for filling the water trough for our animals. Junie would turn this on with her teeth and then leave the water running. My father would get after me because I couldn't keep that horse in the barn. She never ran away; she just turned on the water and then walked around the yard or over the lawn or through the garden. In the middle of the night, I would hear the water running and then I would have to get up and shut it off and lock Junie up again.

"My father suggested that the horse seemed smarter than I was. One day he decided that he would lock her in so that she could not get out. He took the strap that usually looped over the top of the post and buckled it around the post and under a crossbar, and then he said, 'Young lady, let's see you get out of there now!' My father and I left the barn and started to walk back to the house; and before we reached it, Junie was at our side, somewhat to my delight. I could not refrain from suggesting to Father that I was not the only one whose head compared unfavorably with the mare's."
(Cited in Smith and Stewart, *Life of Joseph Fielding Smith*, pp. 53-54.)

(22-9) His New Bride, Jessie Evans, Added a New Dimension of Joy to His Life

Twice before, Joseph Fielding had enjoyed a loving relationship with an eternal companion. Twice before the fragile thread of mortality had broken, temporarily, that eternal union. In the year 1941, at the age of sixty-five, he entered into a third eternal relationship, this time with Jessie Evans.

"When the Tabernacle Choir scheduled a tour to California in

1941, with Richard L. Evans as commentator, Joseph Fielding composed a hilarious letter to Evans charging him with the care and protection of Jessie on the trip: 'You are hereby authorized, appointed, chosen, designated, named, commanded, assigned, ordained and otherwise notified, informed, advised and instructed, *two* wit: . . . ' the letter began, and several paragraphs of nonsense later, 'To see that the said Mrs. Jessie Evans Smith, is permitted to travel in safety, comfort, ease, without molestation and that she is to be returned again to her happy home and loving husband and family in the beautiful and peaceful State of Utah and to her anxious and numerous kindred. . . . '

"Richard L. replied in part, 'Your masterful document of August 15 has cost me a good deal of brow-wrinkling and excruciating concentration. I think without question it will go down in history with the Bill of Rights and the Magna Charta. The remarkable thing about it is, as my legal staff and I have studied it over, that it conveys to me no privileges that I did not already feel free to take and imposes on me no responsibilities that it was not already my pleasure and intention to assume. However, it is a good idea, as many men can testify, to have the consent of a husband before traveling two thousand miles with his wife. . . . ' " (Smith and Stewart, *Life of Joseph Fielding Smith*, pp. 260-61.)

(22-10) Jessie Helped Lighten the Load of This Great Leader and Added Much to His Zest for Living

"Both Joseph Fielding and Jessie enjoyed a colorful cast iron plaque that hung on the kitchen wall of their apartment, stating, 'Opinions expressed by the husband in this household are not necessarily those of the management.' One

time when she was assisting him in his office, when his secretary was on vacation, he tapped her on the shoulder as she sat at the typewriter, and said, 'Remember, Mama dear, *over here you are not* the Speaker of the House!' " (Smith and Stewart, *Life of Joseph Fielding Smith*, p. 261.)

(22-11) Advancing Years Brought Concern to His Family As They Saw No Slackening in the Pace of Their Beloved Brother and Father

"One day a sister of his called on him at the office and scolded him for not taking a nap after lunch. She cited by name half a dozen of his associates who had long done so. 'Yes,' he replied, 'and where are they today? All dead!' " (Smith and Stewart, *Life of Joseph Fielding Smith*, p. 4.)

(22-12) President and Sister Smith Enjoyed Teasing One Another

"There was a direct line of sight between their apartment and his office in the church headquarters building, half a block away. One day as he sat at his desk he received a phone call from Jessie. 'Joseph,' she demanded, 'who is that woman in your office?' 'There is no woman in my office, 'he protested. 'Oh, yes, there is!' she insisted. 'I have my spy glasses focused on you and I know she's there!' President Smith glanced around his office. Near one wall on a pedestal sits a bust of his great-grandmother, Lucy Mack Smith, mother of the Prophet Joseph Smith. 'Jessie, I must confess,' he said. 'You've caught me cold!' He afterward delighted in telling of his guardian angel with binoculars keeping a close watch over him." (Smith and Steward, *Life of Joseph Fielding Smith*, p. 13.)

PHYSICAL ACTION PROVIDED A HEALTHY RELEASE FOR THE ENERGETIC JOSEPH FIELDING SMITH

(22-13) Joseph Fielding Was Interested in Physical Sports and Was Actively Involved in Them Past His Sixty-Fifth Year

"Baseball was Joseph's chief sport as a youngster. He was a member of the Latter-day Saint Sixteenth Ward in the Salt Lake Stake. There was a school in each ward, and each school had a baseball team. 'Our chief "enemies" were the boys of the Fifteenth Ward, which adjoined the Sixteenth Ward, to which I belonged,' he recalls. One of these 'enemies' in the Fifteenth Ward was George Q. Morris, who later became a fellow member of the Council of Twelve. They also competed with a Catholic school.

"Joseph occasionally went fishing, but cared not at all for hunting, perhaps because his father had persuaded him that it was morally wrong to kill for pleasure. One day, however, some of his brothers and friends coaxed him into going rabbit hunting. Reluctantly he shot a rabbit, heard it cry out like a baby, as wounded rabbits often will, was sick at heart, dropped his gun and has never used one since. Like his father, he taught that it is wrong to kill for pleasure." (Smith and Stewart, *Life of Joseph Fielding Smith*, p. 54.)

(22-14) He Gave an Ex-Governor a Lesson in Handball

Herbert B. Maw, an ex-governor of Utah and twenty years younger than Joseph Fielding, shared this interesting insight about a handball game with Elder Smith.

"I thought I would just take it easy on the old gentleman and not beat him too far. Imagine my chagrin when he gave me the trouncing of my life! I thought that I was a good handball player, but I was no competition for him at all." (Cited in Smith and Stewart, *Life of Joseph Fielding Smith*, p. 15.)

Although he was an excellent swimmer, good at tennis and basketball, and enjoyed watching his sons play football, his favorite sport was handball. His son Reynolds added his witness to that of Mr. Maw. He and his brother Lewis played handball against their father, who held one hand behind his back while he "trounced" both of them.

(22-15) One of His Great Enjoyments and Relaxations Was to Fly

Upon his request to see President Smith, a visitor was surprised when the secretary directed him to look at a jet fighter streaking across the sky.

"Oh yes, that's him all right. He's very fond of flying. Says it relaxes him. A friend in the National Guard calls him up and says, 'How about a relaxing?' and up they go. Once they get in the air he often takes over the controls. Flew down to Grand Canyon and back last week, 400 miles an hour!" (Cited in Smith and Stewart, *Life of Joseph Fielding Smith*, p. 2.)

JOSEPH F. SMITH WAS EVER THE TEACHER, CONFIDANT, AND IDEAL OF JOSEPH FIELDING SMITH

Imagine being blessed with a father that you adore. Can you feel the kindly, safe direction from the patriarch of your home, taking you unerringly along the pathway of life? Can you appreciate what an impact it is to be loved, tutored, counseled, and inspired by a prophet-father? Do you understand that this relationship meant more to Joseph Fielding than the wealth of the world?

(22-16) Excellence Was Expected by the Father and Developed by the Son

Letters received by Joseph Fielding from his father reveal even the little qualities President Joseph F. Smith taught his faithful and obedient son. On February 2, 1900, Joseph F. wrote:

"The best school I ever attended is the school of experience. There are some things that seem difficult for me to learn. One thing is English orthography and I see you are a little like me in that regard. Now if I tell you a few words you nearly always spell wrong, the presumption is you will be more careful to spell them right in the future." (Leonard J. Arrington, "Joseph Fielding Smith: The Training of a Prophet" [found in the Church Historical Library], p. 7.)

He then listed such examples as *untill* for *until*; proscribe for *prescribe*; greece for *grease*; shure for *sure*; shugar for *sugar*; and so on. On March 8, 1900 his father advised:

"I scarcely need say to you to make short earnest prayers, short and sincere sermons, and write short letters, concise and to the point, and as often as you can. The difficulty with most people is they are too profuse, both in speaking and writing. We need concentration of mind and thought, and to boil things down. I am pleased to note the improvement you are making." (Arrington, "Joseph Fielding Smith: The Training of a Prophet," p. 7.)

Some advice in a letter dated February 20, 1901, contains some good advice for all of us:

"Always take time to eat your meals and post your journal. I have had experience in these matters. A diary is almost worthless unless written daily. We cannot journalize correctly from memory. Keep your diary up." (Arrington, "Joseph

Joseph Fielding defended his father, President Joseph F. Smith

Fielding Smith: The Training of a Prophet," p. 8.)

(22-17) Joseph Fielding Learned That He Could Ask and Receive

"Joseph F. Smith was a master teacher who spent many hours responding to the questions of his son and seeing that he was properly founded in principles of truth. 'Among my fondest memories,' Joseph Fielding was later to say, 'are the hours I have spent by his side discussing principles of the gospel and receiving instruction as only he could give it. In this way, the foundation for my own knowledge was laid in truth so that I, too, can say I know that my Redeemer lives, and that Joseph Smith is, was, and always will be, a prophet of the living God.'

"And what more fitting place to raise a prophet than the home of a prophet? His mother, Julina Lambson Smith, had been raised in the home of George A. Smith, a cousin and close associate of the Prophet Joseph Smith."
(McConkie, *True and Faithful*, p. 12.)

(22-18) Two Men's Effect upon the Church

Because of his love for his father, Joseph Fielding frequently would quote from him with the same stature and firmness. Joseph Fielding was to extend the voice of his father through long years to come.

"This was the child destined to follow most closely in the footsteps of his father—missionary, historian, apostle, scriptorian, theologian, counselor in the First Presidency, and finally Prophet of the Lord. The voice of the father was to become the voice of the son; jointly, their years in the apostleship would span in an unbroken chain more than a hundred years." (McConkie, *True and Faithful*, pp. 9, 11.)

A loving heart reached out to his father and determined to protect him and ease his burden.

"Until the time of his father's death, Joseph Fielding did all in his power to lighten the heavy load of the Presidency for his father. As an example, to assist in handling the mounting correspondence of the Church, in the evenings after he had completed his own daily work he served without pay as a secretary to his father."
(McConkie, *True and Faithful*, p. 28.)

CAREFULLY SELECTING HIS WEAPON, JOSEPH FIELDING SMITH PICKED UP HIS POWERFUL PEN IN DEFENSE OF FATHER AND CHURCH

Thoughtfully read and consider Alma 31:5. How can it possibly be true that the use of God's word is more powerful, more far-reaching, than the use of military weapons? You will be interested in the answer to this question found through the experience of Joseph Fielding Smith.

(22-19) A Returned Missionary Takes Up the Challenge

At the same time David O. McKay was sustained as a new member of the Council of the Twelve, Joseph Fielding Smith was sustained as assistant Church historian. In this capacity he assisted Anthon H. Lund, Church Historian, in the various activities of that office. One of his jobs was to compile data to be used in defense of Reed Smoot, a Utah Senator and apostle whose right to a Senate seat was being challenged in Washington, D.C.

When Apostle Smoot was exonerated, his defeated opponent became extremely bitter; and through a local newspaper he vented his wrath in the form of

verbal abuses and slander which he heaped upon the Church and in particular upon Joseph F. Smith. So well did young Joseph Fielding present the truth, that the issues were virtually never to be in serious contention again.

"In 1905 Joseph Fielding Smith responded with an open letter to a newspaper report of an interview with R. C. Evans, a member of the first presidency of the Reorganized Church. Both articles were published in the *Toronto Daily Star*. This resulted in a public exchange of letters and a response in the *Saints Herald*. In this debate Joseph Fielding Smith ably defended the Church with sound argument and superior scholarship. Because of the many requests for them, both Mr. Evans' letters and Elder Smith's responses were published in the pamphlet *Blood Atonement and the Origin of Plural Marriage*.

"During the summer of 1906 and 1907, a number of ministers were engaged in missionary work in Salt Lake City and Ogden. These missionaries were extremely vindictive in their references to Brigham Young and subsequent Church leaders. As a result of this agitation, the young people of the Ogden area appealed to their stake presidency, asking that someone make a reply to the assaults. In response to this request, the presidency of Weber Stake invited Joseph Fielding to speak in defense of the faith in the Ogden Tabernacle. The invitation was accepted, and two discourses were delivered on the topic of succession of authority, the first on the tenth of March and the second on the twenty-eighth of April in 1907. These remarks were published in the *Deseret News*; then, due to the many requests made for them, they were published in the booklet form under the title *Origin of the Reorganized Church and the Question*

of Succession." (Booklet, *Presidents of the Church*, p. 112.)

Consider the task of writing a book—the time, the research, the compilation, the careful evaluation, and the problem of pleasing the publishers. While many Church scholars are responsible for only a book or two, President Smith's published works number twenty-five. Not that he aspired to be an author, but he desired to see that the truth was not misunderstood nor cheapened and that noble leaders were not maligned.

Note the interesting evaluation given by his son-in-law, Bruce R. McConkie. Elder McConkie edited a three-volume work of President Smith's entitled *Doctrines of Salvation*, and said this of him:

"Joseph Fielding Smith is the leading gospel scholar and the greatest doctrinal teacher of this generation. Few men in this dispensation have approached him in gospel knowledge or surpassed him in spiritual insight. His is the faith and the knowledge of his father, President Joseph F. Smith, and his grandfather, the Patriarch Hyrum Smith." (Joseph Fielding Smith, *Doctrines of Salvation*, l:v.)

BECAUSE OF HIS STERN REBUKE OF SIN AND SLOTH, MANY ASSUMED THAT THIS GREAT PROPHET WAS HARSH AND WITHOUT FEELING

(22-20) For Many, Joseph Fielding Smith Was an Unknown Man

"In 1970, upon the death of President David O. McKay, Joseph Fielding Smith became tenth president of the Church. At 93, an age when most men have put behind them all earthly cares, he was burdened with the greatest responsibility of his life. For nearly two decades President McKay had been prophet, warming a whole generation with his open, humane, loving inspiration. President Smith by contrast was thought by some to be stern and austere; one writer characterized him as a 'great discomforter,' a man who brought 'a kind of divinely appointed discomfort, a rather unwelcome stirring to righteousness.' " (Preston Nibley, *The Presidents of the Church*, pp. 421-22.)

Sometimes the man seen by the public and the man seen by his family and friends have little similarity to each other. The mission or charge given Joseph Fielding Smith at his ordination to the apostleship may have been a heavy task, but it was one that was taken seriously by this dedicated servant of the Lord.

"Ordained to the special calling of preaching repentance to the people, he accepted the responsibility and remained true to this commission all the days of his life. Because of his uncompromising defense of the Lord's laws and principles, he was considered by many to be austere. President Smith never compromised with sin, but was quick to forgive and extend a hand of fellowship to a repentant sinner. In truth, no man had greater concern and love for each church member." (Smith and Stewart, *Life of Joseph Fielding Smith*, p. vi.)

(22-21) The Man As Known by His Family

The public may be deceived, acquaintances may not recognize the truth, but the inner nature of a man is rarely hidden from his family. Ethel G. Reynolds, whom he married in 1908 and who was the mother of their nine children, described her husband as follows:

"You ask me to tell you of the man I know. . . . I have often thought when he is gone people will say, 'He is a very good man, sincere, orthodox, etc.' They will speak of him as the public knows him. But the man they have in mind is very different from the man I know. The man I know is a kind, loving husband and father whose greatest ambition in life is to make his family happy, entirely forgetful of self in his efforts to do this. He is the man that lulls to sleep the fretful child, who tells bedtime stories to the little ones, who is never too tired or too busy to sit up late at night or to get up early in the morning to help the older children solve perplexing school problems. When illness comes, the man I know watches tenderly over the afflicted one and waits upon him. It is his hands that bind up the wounds, his arms that give courage to the sufferer, his voice that remonstrates with them gently when they err, until it becomes their happiness to do the thing that will make him happy.

"The man I know is most gentle, and if he feels that he has been unjust to anyone the distance is never too far for him to go and, with loving words or kind deeds, erase the hurt. He welcomes gladly the young people to his home and is never happier than when discussing with them topics of the day—sports or whatever interests them most. He enjoys a good story and is quick to see the humor of a situation, to laugh and to be laughed at, always willing to join in any wholesome activity.

"The man I know is unselfish, uncomplaining, considerate, thoughtful, sympathetic, doing everything within his power to make life a supreme joy for his loved ones. That is the man I know." (Cited in Smith and

Stewart, *Life of Joseph Fielding Smith*, pp. 247-48.)

THE MIGHTY FUTURE OF JOSEPH FIELDING SMITH WAS FORESHADOWED AND FOREKNOWN

(22-22) When the Lord Wills, His Prophets Speak

"For an hour or more the Church Presidency and Council of Twelve Apostles, meeting in the Salt Lake Temple in April, 1910, had discussed various men as possibilities to fill the vacancy in the council occasioned by the death of President John R. Winder on March 27, and the subsequent advancement of Apostle John Henry Smith to the Presidency. But to every name suggested there was some exception taken. It seemed impossible to reach any unanimity of feeling in the matter. Finally President Joseph F. Smith retired to a room by himself and knelt in prayer for guidance. When he returned he somewhat hesitantly asked the 13 other brethren whether they would be willing to consider his son Joseph Fielding Smith Jr. for the position. He was reluctant to suggest it, he said, because his son Hyrum was already a member of the council and his son David was a counselor in the Presiding Bishopric. Church members, he feared, would be disgruntled to have another of his sons appointed as a general authority. Nevertheless he felt inspired to offer Joseph's name for their consideration. The other men seemed immediately receptive to the suggestion and sustained President Smith in it." (Smith and Steward, *Life of Joseph Fielding Smith*, p. 174.)

(22-23) Though He Little Realized It, Others Knew That Joseph Fielding Smith Was to Be Chosen of God As an Apostle

" 'At the close of the afternoon session of conference and the adjournment for six months, I received the following note from Sister Susa Young Gates, who has always been a true friend to me and for years has hoped and prayed for me that I might some day be an apostle. "My Beloved Joseph F. Jr. Let me ease the fulness of my joy by telling how grateful I am to God for this beautiful thing. Don't you see now that God is pleased with your earnest, modest labors—and most especially has He not thus indicated His own approval of the grand cause which you have so eloquently espoused? I have felt this coming for some time. I am so happy. Your Aunt Susa." '

"From Apostle-Senator Reed

Joseph Fielding Smith as a young Apostle

Smoot in Washington, D.C. came the telegram, 'God bless you in your apostleship. Be true and loyal to your leader.' And Joseph notes, 'This I shall try always to do. I have also received a number of letters, telegrams, etc., from friends who rejoice at my great blessing, which feeling I believe to be quite universal although there are those who are not pleased. Elder Ben E. Rich, President of the Eastern States Mission [he had earlier been president of the Southern States Mission] who has always been a friend to me, and one year ago predicted that I should be called to this great responsibility, was one of the first to give me the hand of fellowship and his blessing, faith and constant prayers. May the Lord bless him.'' (Cited in Smith and Stewart, *Life of Joseph Fielding Smith*, pp. 178-79.)

The impressive truth is that God whispers his secrets to some so that when his servants are called there may be witnesses. Have you ever had deep impressions pertaining to a prospective bishop or stake president? How does it feel when his name is presented for your sustaining vote? Notice that even though others knew of the divine calling that was to come to Joseph

Fielding Smith, his modesty precluded his accepting that alternative.

''President Francis M. Lyman instructed me in the duties of my calling and told me that I had been called by revelation from the Lord. He said he had watched me for a number of years and while on the trip to Vermont [at the time of the dedication of the Joseph Smith Memorial Monument in December, 1905], both going and coming and while there, he had watched me and felt at that time in his heart that I should some day be an apostle, which prediction has been made by several others, all of which predictions I received lightly and without thought of their fulfillment.'' (Cited in Smith and Stewart, *Life of Joseph Fielding Smith*, p. 179.)

(22-24) The Lord Revealed to Joseph Fielding Smith and to Others That His Will–Not Man's–Had Been Done
'' . . . in a second patriarchal blessing, this one from Patriarch Joseph D. Smith at Scipio, Millard County, Joseph Fielding was told, ' . . . you were called and ordained before you came in the flesh, as an apostle of the Lord Jesus Christ to

represent his work in the earth.' '' (Smith and Stewart, *Life of Joseph Fielding Smith*, p. 181.)

To that same fact, another prophet of God so testified:

''Heber J. Grant, who by then was president of the Church and who was present in the council meeting in the temple the day Joseph was chosen in 1910, assured a group of the correctness of the decision: It was at a Smith family reunion. President Grant pointed to Joseph Fielding and said, 'That man was called by direct revelation of God. I am a witness to that fact.' '' (Smith and Stewart, *Life of Joseph Fielding Smith*, p. 177.)

A humble giant has walked among us. A dedicated defender of truth has blessed our lives. A man of courage and integrity has withstood the winds of mortal injustices. Every Church member of the present or the future has had, or will have, his life touched by the powerful influence of Joseph Fielding Smith. His doctrinal works stand as an eternal monument to him, to his posterity, and to the Church. Consider this man who loved with complete selflessness. Consider this prophet of the living God.

CHAPTER 23

TAKE HEED
UNTO YOURSELVES

INTRODUCTION

"A small girl wriggled out of the crowd and made her way to the President. Soon she was in his arms for a big hug. Quickly a newspaper photographer snapped a picture, and the little girl disappeared back into the crowd.

"The picture appeared unidentified in the Church News. The picture was soon after identified by the child's grandmother, Mrs. Milo Hobbs of Preston, Idaho, in a letter to President Smith.

"On her birthday, Venus Hobbs of Torrence, California, received a surprise telephone call from President and Sister Smith, who were visiting that week in California. They sang 'Happy Birthday' over the phone to her. Venus was delighted at the song, and her parents were touched with tears to think the President of the church would call.

"The parents explained that Venus had been with two aunts at conference, but had slipped away. They feared that she was lost in the crowd. When she returned they asked, 'How did you get lost?'

" 'I wasn't lost,' she said.

" 'Who found you?' they asked.

" 'I was in the arms of the Prophet,' she replied.'' (*Church News*, 8 July 1972, p. 7.)

Immediately, children everywhere recognized the great warmth and love that emanated from President Joseph Fielding Smith. Openly and honestly they felt free to express their love for him. Everywhere he went he had time for

children. They were found in his arms, enjoying his heartfelt hugs, and basking in the security of his love.

Over two-and-a-half million members of the Church had reverently sustained a prophet, seer, and revelator for the first time in nearly nineteen years. At the age of ninety-three, he was the oldest yet to ascend to the presidency.

Some had supposed that the Lord would choose a younger man. They wondered how he could endure the pressures of administering the affairs of the emerging world Church. However, the vigorous profile of President Smith's administration left no lingering question in the minds of the Saints with respect to that concern.

The campus rioting and youthful demonstrations of the sixties were beginning to moderate, but left in their wake was a searching, dissatisfied people looking for something better. The age of the supersonic and jumbo jet airplanes was a reality. It was fitting that one such as Joseph Fielding Smith was called by the Lord in such a day, for his life spanned the days of pioneer life and of horse and buggy to the days of technological and scientific miracles. Here, indeed, was a man to give vision to the Church

and to a rudderless society. Two "youthful" counselors were invited to match strides with this prophet. Harold B. Lee, age seventy-two, and N. Eldon Tanner, age seventy-three. The movement of the new presidency was felt by the members even before that April conference as they responded to the new demands of a growing world Church.

A few months before his death, President Smith's first counselor spoke of him, "As we, President Tanner and I, have been associated with President Smith the past two years, we have marveled at the clarity of his mind, the health of his body, the fact that he could speak well and walk well without difficulty, when most men his age couldn't have done either. . . .

"That we have witnessed time and again, as we were engaged in discussing very serious matters, decisions that should only be made by the president of the church.

"It was then when we saw the sparkling wisdom come to light as he recounted, undoubtedly beyond his own present understanding, things that he called up from the depths of his soul." (*Church News*, 8 July 1972, p. 4.)

His voice was ever clear. His vision was not dimmed. His path was straight and true. For over sixty years he served as a special witness for the Master. He had been called to cry repentance to this generation (see reading 22-20), and he fulfilled that charge faithfully. The Lord confirmed His

acceptance of his ministry by preserving his life and bringing him to the highest of all earthly callings in the kingdom of God. Let us now examine what this great disciple taught us about preparing ourselves for the great and dreadful day of the Lord.

JOSEPH FIELDING SMITH CLEARLY UNDERSTOOD THAT WE LIVE IN THE DAY OF PREPARATION FOR CHRIST'S COMING, A DAY OF WICKEDNESS AND JUDGMENTS

(23-1) Jesus Comes Tomorrow

"I was asked, not long ago, if I could tell when the Lord would come. I answered, Yes; and I answer, Yes, now. I know when he will come. He will come *tomorrow*. We have his word for it. Let me read it:

" 'Behold, *now it is called today until the coming of the Son of Man,* and verily it is a day of sacrifice, and a day for the tithing of my people; for he that is tithed shall not be burned at his coming.' (Now there is a discourse sufficient on tithing.) 'For *after today cometh the burning*—this is speaking after the manner of the Lord—for verily I say, *tomorrow all the proud and they that do wickedly shall be as stubble;* and I will burn them up, for I am the Lord of Hosts; and I will not spare any that remain in Babylon.' (D&C 64:23-24.)

"So the Lord is coming, I say, *tomorrow*. Then let us be prepared. Elder Orson F. Whitney used to write about the *Saturday Evening of Time.* We are living in the Saturday Evening of Time. This is the 6th day now drawing to its close. When the Lord says it is today until his coming, that, I think, is what he has in mind, for *he shall come in the morning of the Sabbath, or seventh day*

of the earth's temporal existence, to inaugurate the millennial reign and to take his rightful place as King of kings and Lord of lords, to rule and reign upon the earth, as it is his right. (See D&C 77:12.)" (Joseph Fielding Smith, *Doctrines of Salvation*, 3:1.)

(23-2) The Day of the Lord Is Near

"I believe that *the coming of the Son of God is not far away,* how far I do not know, but I do know that it is over 100 years nearer than it was when Elijah the prophet came to the Prophet Joseph Smith and Oliver Cowdery in the Kirtland Temple on the 3rd day of April, 1836. Elijah's words point to the fact that we are that much nearer. And this ancient prophet declared that by the restoration of those keys we should know that *the great and dreadful day of the Lord is near, even at our doors.* [D&C 110:16.]

"The world is rapidly coming to its end, that is, *the end of the days of wickedness.* [Joseph Smith—Matthew 4.] *When it is fully ripe in iniquity the Lord will come* in the clouds of heaven to take vengeance on the ungodly, for his wrath is kindled against them. [2 Thessalonians 1:7-9; D&C 29:17.] Do not think that he delayeth his coming. Many of the signs of his coming have been given, so we may, if we will, know that the day is even now at our doors." (Smith, *Doctrines of Salvation*, 3:2.)

(23-3) There Are Numerous Signs of the Approach of the Second Coming

"Many things have taken place during the past one hundred and thirty-six years to impress faithful members of the Church with the fact that the coming of the Lord is near. The gospel has been restored. The Church has been fully organized. The priesthood has been conferred upon man. The various dispensations from the

beginning have been revealed and their keys and authorities given to the Church. Israel has been and is being gathered to the land of Zion. The Jews are returning to Jerusalem. The gospel is being preached in all the world as a witness to every nation. Temples are being built, and ordinance work for the dead, as well as for the living, is performed in them. The hearts of the children have turned to their fathers, and the children are seeking after their dead. The covenants which the Lord promised to make with Israel in the latter days have been revealed, and thousands of gathered Israel have entered into them. Thus the work of the Lord is advancing, and all these things are signs of the near approach of our Lord." (Joseph Fielding Smith in *CR,* Apr. 1966, pp. 12-13.)

(23-4) The Fig Tree Is in Leaf

" 'Watch therefore: for ye know not what hour your Lord doth come. But know this, that if the goodman of the house had known in what watch the thief would come, he would have watched, and would not have suffered his house to be broken up. Therefore *be ye also ready: for in such an hour as ye think not the Son of man cometh.'* [Matthew 24:42-44.]

"So I say to you, my brethren and sisters, and to all who may hear my voice, we are living in the dispensation of the fulness of times. . . .

"I know that there are many, and even some among the Latter-day Saints, who are saying just as the Lord said they would say, 'The Lord delayeth his coming.' [D&C 45:26; 2 Peter 3:3-14.] One man said: 'It is impossible for Jesus Christ to come inside of three or four hundred years.' But I say unto you, Watch.

"I do not know when he is going to come. No man knows. Even the angels of heaven are in the dark in regard to that great truth. [Matthew 24:36, 37.] But this I know, that *the signs that have been pointed out are here.* The earth is full of calamity, of trouble. The hearts of men are failing them. We see the signs as we see the fig tree putting forth her leaves; and knowing this time is near, it behooves me and it behooves you, and all men upon the face of the earth, to *pay heed to the words of Christ, to his apostles and watch,* for we know not the day nor the hour. But I tell you this, it shall come as a thief in the night, when *many of us will not be ready for it.*" (Smith, *Doctrines of Salvation,* 3:52-53.)

(23-5) The Signs of the Times Show That We Live in a Day of Wickedness and Peril

"*The distress and perplexity, bloodshed and terror, selfish ambition of despotic rulers, such as the world has never before seen, all indicate that the great and dreadful day of the Lord is very near, even at our doors.* We have been warned by the prophets from the beginning of time. They have declared, by revelation from the Lord, that *in this present day, confusion, bloodshed, misery, plague, famine, earthquake, and other calamities, would cover the face of the earth.* The Lord told his disciples of these dreadful scenes and said men's hearts would fail them because of these things coming upon the earth [Luke 21:25, 26]. . . .

"It is very evident from what we see daily in the papers that we are living in perilous times. The present condition of the world should not, however, cause us any great surprise, for we have been amply informed that these days are at hand. Only the unbelieving and rebellious against the teachings of

President Smith enjoyed sports

our Lord and his prophets have failed to comprehend these momentous events." (Smith, *Doctrines of Salvation*, 3:19.)

(23-6) *Christ Will Come in a Day of Great Wickedness*

"*When we become ripe in iniquity, then the Lord will come.* I get annoyed sometimes at some of our elders who when speaking say the Lord will come when we all become righteous enough to receive him. *The Lord is not going to wait for us to get righteous.* When he gets ready to come, he is going to come—*when the cup of iniquity is full*—and if we are not righteous then, it will be just too bad for us, for we will be classed among the ungodly, and we will be as stubble to be swept off the face of the earth, for the Lord says wickedness shall not stand.

"Do not think the Lord delays his coming, for *he will come at the appointed time,* not the time which I have heard some preach when the earth becomes righteous enough to receive him. I have heard some men in positions and places of trust in the Church preach this, men who are supposed to be acquainted with the word of the Lord, but they failed to comprehend the scriptures. *Christ will come in the day of wickedness,* when the earth is ripe in iniquity and prepared for the cleansing, and as the cleanser and purifier he will come, and all the wicked will be as stubble and will be consumed." (Smith, *Doctrines of Salvation*, 3:3.)

L. to R.: President Smith and counselors Harold B. Lee and N. Eldon Tanner

JOSEPH FIELDING SMITH ADDED HIS VOICE TO THOSE OF OTHER PROPHETS IN WARNING THE SAINTS AND THE WORLD OF THE COMING JUDGMENTS

(23-7) We Have Been Warned of the Coming Calamities and Told How to Prepare for Them

"We hear occasionally somebody make the statement that things are as bad as they could be, that they could not be worse. I want to tell you they could be worse, a great deal worse. If I read the signs of the times, *we have not suffered yet as much as we are going to suffer, unless we repent.*

"From this stand men have prophesied in the name of the Lord for many decades. President Brigham Young, President John Taylor, President Wilford Woodruff, and others of our leading brethren and presidents of the Church, have raised the warning voice. They have called attention to these present conditions. The Lord has also prophesied of these things, and they have been mentioned by ancient seers and prophets. We have had ample warning. We have been told of the calamities that are coming. We have been taught how we might avoid them, how we might be protected, if we would only hear the counsels that come to us, heed the testimony of truth. If we fail, we cannot escape. . . .

"Do not think that we have reached a condition where things could not be worse. *Unless there is repentance they will be worse.* And so I cry repentance to this people, to the Latter-day Saints, to the people of this nation, and to the nations of the earth everywhere." (Smith, *Doctrines of Salvation*, 3:31-32.)

(23-8) We Must Raise the Voice of Warning

"There is no peace. Men's hearts are failing them. Greed has the uppermost place in the hearts of men. Evil is made manifest on every side, and people are combining for their own selfish interests. Because of this I was glad to hear the warning voice raised by our beloved President [Heber J. Grant] and by his counselors, yesterday, and by others of the brethren who have spoken; for I think this should be *a time of warning,* not only to the Latter-day Saints, but to all the world. *We owe it to the world to raise a voice of warning, and especially to the members of the Church.*" (Smith, *Doctrines of Salvation*, 3:49.)

(23-9) The World Refuses to Heed the Only Way of Escape from the Judgments

"The Lord intends that men shall be happy; that is his purpose. But men refuse to be happy and make themselves miserable, because they think their ways are better than God's ways, and because of selfishness, greed, and the wickedness that is in their hearts; and that is the trouble with us today. The leaders of our nation are struggling and trying to do something to better conditions. I can tell you in a few words just how it can be done, and *it is not going to be done by legislation—it is not going to be done by pouring money out upon the people.*

"Temporary relief is not going to better the situation, because we will still be struggling and fighting and contending with *crime,* with *disease,* with *plagues,* and with *pestilence,* with the *whirlwinds,* and with the *dust storms,* and with the *earthquakes* and everything else coming upon the face of the earth, according to the predictions of the prophets—all because men will not heed the warning voice.

Joseph Fielding Smith about the time he was called as President

"When we quit loving money and get the love of gold out of our hearts and the greed and selfishness, and learn to love the Lord, our God, with all our hearts, and our neighbor as ourselves, and get on our knees and learn to pray and repent of our sins, we will have prosperity, we will have peace, we will have contentment. *But the people will not repent no matter what warning is made, no matter how much their attention is called to these things; the people will not repent because their hearts are set upon evil, and destruction awaits them.*" (Smith, *Doctrines of Salvation*, 3:35-36.)

(23-10) The Saints Can Escape Only Through Obedience

"Do not think for a moment that the days of trial are over. They are not. *If we keep the commandments of the Lord, we shall prosper, we shall be blessed;* the plagues, the calamities that have been promised will be poured out upon the peoples of the earth, and we shall escape them, yea, they shall pass us by.

"But remember the Lord says if we

fail to keep his word, if we walk in the ways of the world, they will not pass us by, but we shall be visited with floods and with fire, with sword and with plague and destruction. *We may escape these things through faithfulness.*" (Smith, *Doctrines of Salvation*, 3:34.)

As you have read these statements by Joseph Fielding Smith you may have sensed why many viewed him as stern and unbending. But ponder this question: Who loves better, the parent who disciplines his child and insists that he eat his vegetables and other good food or the parent who allows the child to eat whatever he wishes? Who is more concerned for the welfare of a person, he who doles out his financial needs and makes him dependent upon the giver or he who stands firm in saying, "If you refuse to work, I cannot help you"? And which prophet truly emulates the love of God, he who says, "What you do is all right, overcome your fears and guilt, God is a loving Father and won't punish you for your errors" (see 2 Nephi 28:7-9; Helaman 13:25-28), or the one who warns, "Repent or misery and calamity will come upon you"? As you continue, notice how Joseph Fielding Smith is deeply motivated by a love of God and a love of his fellowman.

AS WE STUDY THE LIFE AND TEACHINGS OF JOSEPH FIELDING SMITH, WE FIND THE KEYS TO PEACE IN A WORLD OF TURMOIL

(23-11) Repentance Is the Key to Peace in the Latter Days

"We have the means of escape through obedience to the gospel of Jesus Christ. Will we escape? When I see, even among the Latter-day Saints the violation of the laws of the Lord, I fear and I tremble. I have been crying repentance among the stakes of Zion for 30 years, calling upon the people to turn to the Lord, keep his commandments, observe the Sabbath day, pay their honest tithing, do everything the Lord has commanded them to do, to live by every word that proceedeth forth from the mouth of God.

"By doing this we shall escape the calamities.

"I am going to repeat what I have said before, for which I have been severely criticized from certain quarters, that even in this country we have no grounds by which we may escape, no sure foundation upon which we can stand, and by which we may escape from the calamities and destruction and the plagues and the pestilences, and even the devouring fire by sword and by war, *unless we repent* and we keep the commandments of the Lord, for it is written here in these revelations.

"So I cry repentance to the Latter-day Saints, and I cry repentance to the people of the United States, as well as to the people of all the earth." (Smith, *Doctrines of Salvation*, 3:34-35.)

(23-12) Through Study We Can Know What Is Coming and What to Expect

After referring to the terrible judgments described in Jeremiah 25, Elder Smith made this important point:

"I know these are unpleasant things. It is not a pleasant thing even for me to stand here and tell you that this is written in the Scriptures. If the Lord has a controversy with the nations, He will put them to the sword. Their bodies shall lie unburied like dung upon the earth. That is not nice, is it, but should we not know it? Is it not our duty to read these things and understand them? Don't you think the Lord has given us these things that we might know and we might prepare ourselves through humility, through repentance, through faith, that we might escape from these dreadful conditions that are portrayed by these ancient prophets? That is why I am reading them. I feel just as keenly as you do about the condition, and I pray for it to come to an end, but I want it to come to an end right." (Joseph Fielding Smith, *The Signs of the Times*, pp. 154-55.)

(23-13) President Smith Understood the World's Greatest Need

"To the world I say: These are the last days. They are days of trouble and sorrow and desolation. They are days when Satan dwells in the hearts of ungodly men, when iniquity abounds, and when the signs of the times are being shown forth.

"And there is no cure for the ills of the world except the gospel of the Lord Jesus Christ. Our hope for peace, for temporal and spiritual prosperity, and for an eventual inheritance in the kingdom of God is found only in and through the restored gospel. There is no work that any of us can engage in that is as important as preaching the gospel and building up the Church and kingdom of God on earth.

"And so we invite all our Father's children, everywhere, to believe in Christ, to receive him as he is revealed by living prophets, and to join The Church of Jesus Christ of Latter-day Saints. We call upon the world to repent, to worship that God who made them, and to believe the words of those whom he hath sent in this day to proclaim his gospel." (Joseph Fielding Smith in *CR*, Apr. 1972, p. 13.)

President Smith was simultaneously counselor to President McKay and President of the Council of the Twelve Apostles

(23-14) President Smith Outlined the Need for Various People to Change Their Lives

"To the honest in heart in all nations we say: the Lord loves you. He wants you to receive the full blessings of the gospel. He is now inviting you to believe the Book of Mormon, to accept Joseph Smith as a prophet, and to come into his earthly kingdom and thereby become heirs of eternal life in his heavenly kingdom.

"To those who have received the gospel we say: Keep the commandments. Walk in the light. Endure to the end. Be true to every covenant and obligation, and the Lord will bless you beyond your fondest dreams. As it was said by one of old: 'Let us hear the conclusion of the whole matter: Fear God, and keep his commandments: for this is the whole duty of man.' (Eccles. 12:13.)

"To all the families in Israel we say: The family is the most important organization in time or in eternity. Our purpose in life is to create for ourselves eternal family units. There is nothing that will ever come into your family life that is as important as the sealing blessings of the temple and then keeping the covenants made in connection with this order of celestial marriage.

"To parents in the Church we say: Love each other with all your hearts. Keep the moral law and live the gospel. Bring up your children in light and truth; teach them the saving truths of the gospel; and make your home a heaven on earth, a place where the Spirit of the Lord may dwell and where righteousness may be enthroned in the heart of each member.

"It is the will of the Lord to strengthen and preserve the family unit. We plead with fathers to take their rightful place as the head of the house. We ask mothers to sustain and support their husbands and to be lights to their children.

"President Joseph F. Smith said: 'Motherhood lies at the foundation of happiness in the home, and of prosperity in the nation. God has laid upon men and women very sacred obligations with respect to motherhood, and they are obligations that cannot be disregarded without invoking divine displeasure.' (*Gospel Doctrine* [Deseret Book, 1939], p. 288.) Also, 'To be a successful father or a successful mother is greater than to be a successful general or a successful statesman.' (Ibid., p. 285.)

"To the youth of Zion we say: The Lord bless you and keep you,

which most assuredly will be so as you learn his laws and live in harmony with them. Be true to every trust. Honor thy father and thy mother. Dwell together in love and conformity. Be modest in your dress. Overcome the world, and do not be led astray by the fashions and practices of those whose interests are centered upon the things of this world.

"Marry in the temple, and live joyous and righteous lives. Remember the words of Alma: 'Wickedness never was happiness.' (Al. 41:10.) Remember also that our hope for the future and the destiny of the Church and the cause of righteousness rest in your hands.

"To those who are called to positions of trust and responsibility in the Church we say: Preach the gospel in plainness and simplicity as it is found in the standard works of the Church. Testify of the truth of the work and the doctrines revealed anew in our day.

"Remember the words of the Lord Jesus Christ, who said, 'I am among you as he that serveth' (Luke 22:27), and choose to serve with an eye single to the glory of God. Visit the fatherless and the widows in their affliction, and keep yourself unspotted from the sins of the world." (Joseph Fielding Smith in *CR*, Apr. 1972, pp. 13–14.)

PRESIDENT JOSEPH FIELDING SMITH SET ABOUT TO STRENGTHEN THE KINGDOM IN ITS PREPARATION FOR THE LAST DAYS

August 28, 1971, found President Smith with the Saints in England conducting a general conference of the Church for the first time on foreign soil. Notice how he was keenly aware that this historic event was to be a type of that which was to come.

The excitement of the members of the Church was electric, as they had come from many areas of Europe, most at some degree of sacrifice, to hear from the oracle of God. Can you appreciate what it must have felt like to be able to be in the presence of the Lord's representatives for the first time in your life?

"Tearful eyes watched, and voices were muted as President Joseph Fielding Smith stood at the conclusion of the first All-British General Conference. As he stood, the audience came to their feet. No one moved as the Prophet left the stand. It was as though they did not want to leave the spirit that had prevailed in the meeting. There was a sacred air about King's Hall and as a testimony to the spirit the audience burst into spontaneous singing of 'We Thank Thee O God for a Prophet.' The song ended, but the crowd lingered, hungry for the sweetness of the occasion." (*Church News*, 4 Sept. 1971, p. 3.)

(23-15) "... I Will Establish My Church Among Them" (D&C 10:53.)

It is urgent that the gospel be preached to every nation and that there be congregations of Saints established which will provide the means for all nations to be properly warned before the Lord comes again.

"It is a matter of great satisfaction to me and my brethren, that the Church has now grown to the point that it seems wise and necessary to hold General Conferences in various nations. . . .

"The day is long since past when informed people think of us as a peculiar group in the tops of the Rocky Mountains in America. It is true that the Church headquarters is in Salt Lake City, and that the Lord's house has been erected there to which people have come from many nations to learn the law of the Lord, and to walk in His paths.

"But now we are coming of age as a Church and as a people. We have attained the stature and strength, which is enabling us to fulfill the commission given us by the Lord through the Prophet Joseph Smith, that we should carry the glad tidings of the restoration to every nation and to all people.

"And not only shall we preach the Gospel to every nation before the Second Coming of the Son of Man, but we shall make converts and establish congregations of saints among them. . . .

"And so I say, we are and shall be a world Church. That is our destiny. It is part of the Lord's program. 'The covenant people of the Lord,' are 'scattered upon all the face of the earth,' and it is our commission to go into all nations and gather these elect into the Church, and to bring them to a knowledge of their Redeemer, so they shall be heirs of salvation in His kingdom." (Joseph Fielding Smith, cited in *Church News*, 28 Aug. 1971, pp. 3, 7.)

(23-16) A New Era Is Born

Later, in the same conference, President Joseph Fielding Smith emphasized that things are different today. His vision accurately saw a time when the gospel would be taken to other nations through similar conferences.

"Today, however, we have moved into a new era of Church growth and expansion. We are now taking the gospel to the ends of the earth and are seeking to build up the kingdom in every nation and among every people as rapidly as we have the strength to do so. . . .

"We expect to see this growth continue until the gospel becomes a leavening, sanctifying influence throughout this whole land. The gospel is for all men, and the Church shall be established everywhere, in all nations, even to the ends of the earth, before the second coming of the Son of Man." (*CR*, Manchester England Area Conference, Aug. 1971, p. 176.)

"We now come near to the close of a wonderful and memorable conference of the Church here in the British Isles, and I hope this becomes a pattern for what shall be in other nations and places." (*CR*, Manchester England Area Conference, Aug. 1971, p. 175.)

(23-17) President Smith Took Steps to Strengthen the Home

Nothing sounded deeper in the heart of Joseph Fielding Smith than the importance and sanctity of the home. His messages are replete with his counsel to parents and children. One of the first concerns he dealt with as a newly sustained prophet was to bolster the home by strengthening an already revealed institution—family home evening.

"Greater emphasis than ever before was placed on the family. Monday evenings were reserved Churchwide for family home evenings; all other Church activities were scheduled to leave Monday inviolate for the family." (Booklet, *Presidents of the Church*, p. 117.)

In addition to his announcing the desire of the Lord to hold inviolate Monday evenings as the time to gather families around to teach them the gospel, President Smith lovingly entreated parents to take their task seriously.

"We have great concern for the spiritual and moral welfare of all youth everywhere. Morality, chastity, virtue, freedom from sin—these are and must be basic to our way of life, if we are to realize its full purpose.

"We plead with fathers and mothers to teach personal purity by precept and example and to counsel with their children in all such things.

"We ask parents to set an example of righteousness in their own lives and to gather their children around them and teach them the gospel, in their home evenings and at other times." (*CR*, Apr. 1970, pp. 5-6.)

What manner of man was Joseph Fielding Smith? Thoughtfully consider 3 Nephi 27:27. Some saw in President Smith a stern doctrinarian, an unbending judge of righteousness. However, if it could be said that he was a hard man, it must be admitted that he was hard only on the sin, for he was merciful and kind to the sinner. The place of severity in his nature was that he demanded much of himself. He allowed no flabbiness of character so far as his own person was concerned, for his was a godly desire. Can you measure yourself against his standard?

When a compilation of his sermons was published in book form, it was given the title *Take Heed unto Yourself*. It is an appropriate phrase, for it was characteristic of his life—not only his teachings but his own personal commitment to Christ. His writings still serve as an important standard of gospel information, and his life serves as an inspiration to future generations. Of him, President Harold B. Lee said this:

"Truly the greatest monument to him is the great posterity which he has given to the world. I speak honestly and with much thoughtful appraisal of other families when I say that I believe that the Joseph Fielding Smith family, linked with the Smith generations before, have been one of the greatest, if not the greatest, family that has lived upon the earth. I have no doubt but that now he has been welcomed into the company of those who have preceded him and is now finding the joy that one like he is worthy and entitled to receive.

"His passing to me was as near a translation from life unto death as I think we will see in our lifetime experience. He died as he lived and has demonstrated to all of us how one can be so honored and so privileged when he has lived so close to the Lord as has your noble patriarch and father, Joseph Fielding Smith." (Cited in Joseph Fielding Smith, Jr., and John J Stewart, *The Life of Joseph Fielding Smith*, pp. 383-84.)

Children loved his tender nature

UNIT TWELVE

HAROLD B. LEE

Eleventh President of the Church

OVERVIEW

Newsmen waited anxiously on July 7, 1972, for their first press conference with Harold B. Lee, newly ordained President of The Church of Jesus Christ of Latter-day Saints. To them he said, "The safety of the church lies in the members keeping the commandments. There is nothing more important that I could say. As they keep the commandments, blessings will come."[1]

Clifton, Idaho, was an obscure town in 1900; but many great leaders have come from obscure towns, and this one would be known as the birthplace of the eleventh president of the Church. Farm life is strenuous, and young Harold learned early the virtues of hardship, poverty, and toil. Though his youth went unnoticed by the world, he was not unknown to God. Even when a child, the Spirit whispered to him; he was forewarned of dangers and was given wisdom beyond his years. There were years of preparation, obedience, and service.

At the age of eighteen he was principal of a school, and at age twenty-one he was serving in the Western States Mission. The years rushed along. Following his mission, he married Fern Lucinda Tanner, became the father of two daughters, and accepted an appointment to the Salt Lake City Commission.

Later, depression hit the United States. The year was 1930 and Harold B. Lee was thirty-one. Unemployment rose drastically; credit dried up. More than half the members of the Pioneer Stake, where he lived, were out of work. A short time later Harold B. Lee was called as president of the stake. He worried about the welfare of his members, he wept and prayed, and finally inspiration came. Programs were set up to care for those in need, Christmas help was organized, employment opportunities were found. His experience in caring for the people of this stake was, as the future

would prove, in preparation for things to come. Soon he was called to a wider service in the general Church welfare program. Again, with prayer and persuasion and with the blessings of God and his prophet, the program grew and prospered.

Foreordained to be a mighty leader in the kingdom, Harold B. Lee was called as an apostle of the Lord in 1941 and was ordained to this holy assignment by President Heber J. Grant. He toured missions and military bases throughout the world, delivered radio sermons entitled "Youth and the Church" and labored diligently as an advisor to the Primary and Relief Society organizations. He organized two missions in South America and the first stake in England.

In 1961 a call came from President David O. McKay appointing Elder Lee as chairman of the Church Correlation Committee. Past experience had taught him the challenge of such an assignment. With faith and courage he counseled with chosen leaders, struggled in mighty prayer, and formulated a plan that spoke of renewed effort in welfare, missionary work, genealogy, education, home teaching, and family home evening. The entire strength of the Church was being marshalled to bless and sustain the home. It was within the walls of the homes of the Saints that the most important work of eternity would be done. That conviction found expression in his own home as he led his family in gentleness and in love.

Harold B. Lee was a man without arrogance. His humility was that of which the Master spoke. Meekness denotes teachableness, a willingness to submit to whatever the Lord desires; and submit he did. There were years of personal physical suffering, but he kept serving and working. The death of his beloved wife in 1962 was a severe trial. Though this was a great challenge, there was more to come—the death of his daughter Maurine in 1965. Later Elder Lee was to

say, "Only through heartbreak and a lonely walk through the valley of the shadow of death do we really begin to glimpse the path that Jesus walked."[2] But these were days of preparation for things to come.

He was called to the First Presidency in 1970, and two years later was ordained President of the Church. The Church had felt his influence for over thirty years as an apostle, and now they would feel his firm hand at the reins of leadership. He spoke of the priesthood as the greatest power on earth, of the family as the most important of all our labors, of enemies within the Church, and that the safety of the Saints was in giving strict obedience to God's prophet. He could speak of heaven and hell with great power, yet he could also speak with such simplicity that a group of young children would sit almost motionless for an hour as he spoke to them of sacred truths. He had a Christlike combination of love and firmness. With those found in transgression, he reached out in love to help them along the path of repentance. His concern was for the widow, the handicapped, the unmarried—all this because of love. "Never think of me as the head of this Church," he taught. "Jesus Christ is the head of this Church. I am only a man, his servant."[3] His testimony of Jesus Christ was strong enough for many to depend on. A business leader once said to him, "I believe in the Lord, but I do not have a testimony of the living Lord." President Lee replied, "Then you lean on my testimony while you study and pray until your own is strong enough to stand alone."[4]

Though his administration lasted only eighteen months, his teachings and influence in the leading counsels of the Church had been profound for decades. Some felt that his passing was untimely, but the death of a man of God is never untimely. His successor, President Spencer W. Kimball, said at his funeral, "A giant redwood has fallen and left a great space in the forest."[5]

CHAPTER 24

THE CHURCH HAS NEED OF EVERY MEMBER

The Savior said, "By this shall all men know that ye are my disciples, if ye have love one to another." (John 13:35.) Enter now, for a brief moment, into the life of one whose love reached out to everyone in an effort to bring them closer to the Master.

THE EARLY LIFE OF HAROLD B. LEE WAS ONE OF PREPARATION FOR FULFILLING GOD'S PURPOSES

(24-1) Harold B. Lee Was Chosen Before He Was Born, and Was Sent to "Goodly Parents"

"Twenty-five hundred and seventy-two years ago, give or take a year, a prophet accepted of the Lord began to write his history: 'I, Nephi, having been born of goodly parents. . . . ' And then he went on to say, 'I make a record of my proceedings in my days.' (1 Ne. 1:1.) . . .

"And now, so it is today. Beginning his work as the prophet of the Lord, this modern seer and revelator may thus also begin his history: 'I, Harold Bingham Lee, having been born of goodly parents, begin my work.'

"Prophets are born of goodly parents. Before the earth was formed the heavenly hosts gave shouts of joy, both because they could come to the earth and that their leaders were chosen and recognized. . . .

"Said the Lord: 'Abraham, thou art one of them; thou wast chosen before thou wast born.' (Abr. 3:23.) And the Lord designated the others who have been chosen. I do not presume; rather, I am sure, President Lee, thou wast chosen before thou wast born." (S. Dilworth Young in *CR*, Oct. 1972, p. 161.)

(24-2) The Lord Prepared a Lineage Through Which Harold B. Lee Should Come So He Could Inherit the Qualities of Greatness

"I shall speak about genealogy.

"William Lee came from the old sod in 1745. He must have had an unexplained urge, because he would not know really why he came. He might think it was to better his condition.

"He fought in the American Revolution and was wounded. Many of us have ancestors who are reported to have fought in the Revolution, but few of them were wounded. This man was left for dead in the battle of Guilford County Courthouse in the Carolinas in March 1781. Thanks to good nursing he recovered and, as in all good endings, married his nurse. Four sons came to him, one of whom was Samuel, who was the youngest.

"Samuel's sons, Francis, Alfred, and Eli, and their families joined the Church in 1832. . . . They suffered through all the vicissitudes and the troubles and

INTRODUCTION

The path that President Harold B. Lee walked was narrow—even straight. But there was always room for someone else to walk with him. The elderly, the young, the infirm, and the spiritually needy all found his presence a source of strength and aid. To walk with him was to be touched and changed, comforted and challenged.

> The Prophet at Conference
> By Leah S. Neilson
>
> *He stood,*
> *In the newness of his call*
> *And yet serene.*
> *And spoke to us of God—*
> *His witness brimming to his eyes*
> *(A startling hue but oh, so kind).*
> *And we,*
> *Straining to know him,*
> *Searched his words.*
> *Gratitude—*
> *That is the key!*
> *His being is so filled.*
> *And I,*
> *In humble corner where I serve,*
> *Felt that he appreciated me.*
> (*Ensign*, Feb. 1974, p. 27.)

His sister, Verda Lee Ross, said, "Anyone who came into his home was a prince or a princess. He treated them like royalty. He was a most gracious host. It was difficult ever to see him standing while he was with a group, because he would be kneeling down talking to a child or bent over giving comfort to an elderly person. Everyone meant something to Elder Harold B. Lee. He loved people—all people." (From a personal interview with members of the Lee family, conducted by the College Curriculum staff, 6 July 1978.)

persecutions and mobbings of Jackson County, Far West, and Nauvoo, and finally came west. At Winter Quarters their father joined them. He had not joined the Church until this time but joined shortly afterward. Francis married a young woman by the name of Jane Vail Johnson. I shall speak of her later.

"They all came to Utah and settled in Tooele County. They were just getting settled and making things go when they were called by President Brigham Young to St. George, and they went, like all good Latter-day Saints did in those days. But they had not been in St. George very long when they were called to settle in Meadow Valley. That is a place you folks probably have not heard about. It is now known as Panaca, in what they thought was southwestern Utah, but which actually later came to be Nevada. These people, obeying the call, again without question, were the first family to move to Meadow Valley, and they made a dugout house. Sister Young said that you may not know what a dugout house is. I replied that most of the folks would know: One digs a cubical hole in a hillside and covers it with a roof of wooden poles topped with clay.

"Troubles of the few settlers with the Indians caused the authorities in St. George to give them permission to abandon the project, but Sister Jane Johnson Lee refused to leave. She said she was there to stay, and stay they did. Later two Indians came into her dugout home, and one of them, seeing a rifle in one corner of the room, demanded it. Sister Lee refused to give it to him. He started for the gun, but she struck him so hard with a piece of stove wood, it knocked him down. He staggered to his feet and drew his bow,

aiming the arrow at her. She let him have another piece of wood, which smashed the bow and arrow. Both Indians departed.

"Two sons of this brave couple married sisters. Samuel Marion Lee married Margaret McMurrin, and Francis Lee, Jr., married Mary McMurrin. The McMurrins were converts from Scotland who had crossed the plains with the handcart companies. Brother McMurrin, a cooper, which is a man who makes barrels and bends wood, repaired many a handcart wheel en route, which helped get the carts to the valley but delayed him and his family. They also settled in Tooele. Each of the Lee brothers took his bride to Meadow Valley.

"I speak of Margaret's bravery. Eleven times she placed Her life upon the block And offered it that

Harold at age 5

Children might be born. No sterile chamber Where the doctor waits, The anesthetic cone And nurse in readiness, Could be her lot.

"The cabin walls absorbed The agonizing cries, With Death close by. He did not claim her life. Instead he took each child— Each little one to heaven— All eleven. Then came the twelfth.

"For her the light burned Dim, then flickered low, And out— But she had filled her life, and Given all that she could give. Her mission was performed; A son was born, The only child to live.

"He was named his father's name— Samuel Lee. . . .

"Under his grandmother's care the baby Samuel grew into a stalwart boy, and when sixteen went to Clifton, Idaho, in Cache Valley, where he worked on a farm and there later met Louisa Bingham.

"The Bingham family, stalwart in the faith, were pioneers. They endured the hardships of the plains and the difficulties of conquering the new land. They were among the early settlers of Clifton. . . .

"And so, in good time, and in his turn, there came into the family circle on a windy day in late March 1899 a son. They named him Harold Bingham Lee.

"It is fitting this day that we speak briefly of this heritage. The Lord prepared the lineage through which President Lee came that he might inherit their bravery, their loyalty, their integrity, and their devotion to the truth." (S.

Dilworth Young in *CR*, Oct. 1972, pp. 159-61.)

In times of quiet pondering and inner reflection, have you ever questioned your own worth? Have you wondered what it matters that you have lived? Have you asked what a person—especially one of little fame or importance—could do that would change the world significantly?

The world is very large, the problems very complex, the people very numerous. It is only natural that we should ask ourselves, "Can it really make a difference—outside of my own little circle—whether or not I have lived"?

You have read now of Harold B. Lee's grandmother, Margaret. There are some who might suggest that living out one's life in a dugout in some tiny corner of Nevada is hardly one of the world's more illustrious contributions. And certainly many would have said that her sacrifice was too great. Who but those who have endured similar trials could count the cost in suffering, pain, heartbreak? And then finally, after eleven children had died at birth, she brought forth a twelfth child. Yet search the rolls which list the great heroes and martyrs of the world and you will search in vain for the name Margaret McMurrin Lee. Ask any—even people in the Church—to list the names of those who have significantly added to the course and destiny of the kingdom; rarely, if at all, will the name Margaret McMurrin Lee be mentioned.

But now you answer for her, remembering the twelfth child who would father a prophet and seer. Suppose Margaret McMurrin Lee were to ask you, "Did I really make a difference? Does anyone besides the great and the famous really significantly change history?" How would you answer?

(24-3) His Mother's Decisive Action Saved Him from Two Near-Fatal Accidents

"Harold Bingham Lee was the second of their six children. . . . [His mother] Louisa's patriarchal blessing had mentioned her gift of healing, and her inspiration had preserved Harold's life on several occasions. At age eight, his mother sent him for a can of lye, high on a pantry shelf, to make soap with. He slipped and the can tipped its deadly contents all over him. Immediately Louisa grabbed Harold so he wouldn't run, kicked off the lid of a large vat of pickled beets, and splashed cup after cup of red vinegar juice all over his head and body, neutralizing the lye. What could have been a tragedy was averted because of her inspired action.

"While working in the fields in his teens, Harold gashed an artery on a broken bottle. Louisa stopped the bleeding, but the wound became infected. She took a clean black stocking, burned it to ashes, opened his wound, and rubbed the ashes into it very thoroughly. It healed quickly after this." (Jaynann Morgan Payne, "Louisa Bingham Lee: Sacrifice and Spirit," *Ensign*, Feb. 1974, pp. 82-83.)

(24-4) Louisa Saved Her Son from Pneumonia Through Faith and Inspiration

"Louisa bent over her 17-year-old son once more to feel his feverish head and listen to his tight, labored breathing. It was after midnight, and Harold's pneumonia had not seemed to respond to his mother's famous mustard plasters. Anxiety clutched at her heart and she knew she must do something quickly, or her son would die in a few hours.

"She hurried to the back porch and opened a large sack of onions, filled her apron, and went into the kitchen. After slicing a large panful of onions she dumped them into an empty flour sack and covered her son's chest with that wet, juicy sack. Then she prayed and waited for a miracle.

"By morning his breathing was improved, and he was over the crisis." (Payne, "Louisa Bingham Lee," p. 81.)

(24-5) The Voice of God Warned: "Harold, Don't Go over There"

"As a little boy I had my first intimate touch with divinity. As a young boy I was out on a farm, waiting for my father to finish his day's work, playing about, manufacturing things to while away the time, when I saw over the fence into the neighbor's yard some broken-down buildings with the sheds caving in and with rotting timbers. I imagined as a young boy that that might be a castle that I should explore, so I went over to the fence and started to climb through; then I heard a voice as distinctly as you are hearing mine: 'Harold, don't go over there.' I looked in every direction to see where the speaker was. I wondered if it was my father, but he couldn't see me. There was no one in sight. I realized that someone was warning me of an unseen danger—whether a nest of rattlesnakes, whether the rotting timbers would fall on me and crush me, I don't know. But from that time on, I accepted without question the fact that there were processes not known to man by which we can hear voices from the unseen world, by which we can have brought to us the visions of

eternity.'' (Harold B. Lee, "The Way to Eternal Life," *Ensign*, Nov. 1971, p. 17.)

In 1839 the Prophet Joseph Smith sat cold and hungry in a jail in Liberty, Missouri. His heart sorrowed for the suffering of the Saints. Perhaps the Prophet even wondered if his own life would be spared. To him the Lord gave the following comforting words: "Thy days are known, and thy years shall not be numbered less. . . . " (D&C 122:9.) You have just read of experiences in the life of Harold B. Lee that, except for the hand of God, might have taken his mortal life. Were his days, like the Prophet Joseph's, known to God? Who personally intervened in his life so that his years were not "numbered less"? Why was the Lord's eye constantly watching over young Harold? And what of you? Are your days known to the Lord? And do you suppose that he might have a work for you to do? A work significant enough that angels might watch over you? Read D&C 109:22 before answering these questions.

HAROLD B. LEE WAS REARED IN A HOME WHERE LOVE, WORK, AND FAITH WERE TAUGHT

(24-6) Discipline, Frugality, and Industry Were Learned on the Family Farm

Harold B. Lee was reared amid the challenges of rural living. Farm life is difficult and requires much effort and work. During his youth there were few tractors and little power machinery to cultivate, seed, or harvest crops. Life then was truly earned by the sweat of one's brow. Reared under similar circumstances, many boys are unappreciative of the lessons that can be learned from such

experiences; not so with Harold B. Lee. He gained training and blessings that were to be of great importance to his future callings in the Lord's kingdom.

"I have thought of the discipline of the boy and girl of my youthful days in a rural community. We began to 'do chores' shortly after daybreak so we could 'start' with the day's work by sun-up. When the day's work was finished, we had yet to do our evening 'chores,' usually by aid of a lantern. Despite the fact that there were no wages and hours regulations or child labor laws, we did not seem to be stunted from our exertions. Sleep requirements did not admit of too frequent frivolities. Returns from our labors were small and usually came on a once-a-year basis at harvest time. Homes of that day went throughout the summer with but very little ready money but from our cows we were provided

Harold B. Lee as a missionary

milk, butter and cheese; in our granaries there was usually sufficient wheat to be taken to the mill for flour and cereals. We had our own chickens and garden and fruits in season.'' (Harold B. Lee, *Decisions for Successful Living*, pp. 12-13.)

(24-7) Poverty, Trial, and Financial Depression Were Looked upon as Opportunities to Learn and Grow

"Yes, we would have been on the poverty line in those days [during his youth]. But out of that came training and compensations that never could have come, I think, if we had been living in the lap of luxury. We didn't starve. We had things to eat and mother knew how to make over the clothes for her boys. I never had what they called a 'boughten suit' until I went to high school. But I always thought I was well dressed, and I guess we were. And when there came trials when depressions came and we saw great losses, I wondered sometimes. Here, I filled a mission, I came home and I had to walk to school to get an education, and then go down to the University of Utah to finally be able to get a certification in the State of Utah. Ofttimes I walked because I didn't have the money to ride because I needed the money to buy a book. When the end of the term came to trade in the old books for some new, I knew what it was. But out of it, there has come an understanding.'' (Harold B. Lee, Address at Ricks College, 26 Oct. 1973, p. 7.)

(24-8) Louisa's Care and Concern for the Welfare of Her Son Had a Lasting Impression on Harold B. Lee

"I thank God today for my parentage. My father and mother are listening, either in this great assembly or on the radio. . . . I think perhaps this is my way of

paying tribute to the two family names they gave me at my birth, Bingham and Lee. I trust I shall not disgrace those names. I have been blessed with a spendid father and a grand and lovely mother. . . .

"As just a high school boy I went away on a high school debating team. We won the debate. I came back and called mother on the telephone only to have her say: 'Never mind, Son. I know all about it. I will tell you when you come home at the end of the week.' When I came home she took me aside and said: 'When I knew it was just time for this performance to start I went out among the willows by the creek side, and there, all by myself, I remembered you and prayed God you would not fail.' I have come to know that that kind of love is necessary for every son and daughter who seek to achieve in this world. . . . " (Harold B. Lee in *CR,* Apr. 1941, p.120.)

HAROLD B. LEE PASSED THROUGH EXPERIENCES THAT POLISHED HIS CHARACTER AND BROUGHT HIM CLOSER TO THE LORD AND HIS FELLOWMAN

(24-9) The Trying Days of Poverty Saw Him, as a Stake President, Reach Out in Love and Service to the Needy

President Marion G. Romney spoke at the funeral of President Lee and said this:

"Soon after I met him I learned that he then lived in a modest cottage on Indiana Avenue. It was equipped in part with furniture fashioned by his own hands. The other furnishings were made by his accomplished wife. That humble home was hallowed by the love he bore to his sweetheart and two bright-eyed little girls, Maurine and Helen.

"Our nation was at that time in the

An educator, he was an elementary school principal in Idaho

midst of the great depression of the 1930s. He was the president of Pioneer Stake. Few people in the Church were more severely punished by want and discouragement than were the members of his stake. Although harassed with the problems incident to securing for himself and his loved ones the necessities of life, he grappled mightily with the larger problem of looking after the needs of the total membership of his stake.

"Many there were in that day who, having faltered, turned to state and federal governments for help. Harold B. Lee was not among them. Taking the Lord at his word that man should earn his bread in the sweat of his face and convinced that all things are possible to him that believeth, he struck out boldly with the fearless ingenuity and courage of a Brigham Young to pioneer a way whereby his people could, by their own efforts and the help of their brethren, be supplied the necessities of life.

"Directed by the light of heaven,

through building projects, production projects, and a variety of other rehabilitation activities, he gave a demonstration of love for his fellowmen seldom equalled in any generation.

"Those who were close to him in those dark days know that he wept over the suffering of his people, but more than that, he did something for them.

"With all his heart he loved and served his fellowmen. He loved the poor, for he had been one of them. 'I have loved you,' he said. 'I have come to know you intimately. Your problems, thank the Lord, have been my problems, because I know as you know what it means to walk when you have not the money to ride. I know what it means to go without meals to buy a book to go to the University. I thank God now for those experiences. I have loved you because of your devotion and faith. God bless you that you won't fail.' (General Conference address, April 6, 1941.)" ("In the Shadow of the Almighty," *Ensign,* Feb. 1974, p. 96.)

(24-10) Harold B. Lee Sought Earnestly to Know the Needs and Desires of Those He Was Called to Lead

''The first Christmas after I became stake president, our little girls got some dolls and other nice things on Christmas morning, and they immediately dressed and went over to their little friend's home to show her what Santa Claus had brought them. In a few moments they came back, crying. 'What in the world is the matter?' we asked. 'Donna Mae didn't have any Christmas. Santa Claus didn't come.' And then belatedly we realized that the father had been out of work, and there was no money for Christmas. So we brought the little ones of that family in and divided our Christmas with them, but it was too late. We sat down to Christmas dinner with heavy hearts.

''I resolved then that before another Christmas came, we would be certain that every family in our stake had the same kind of Christmas and the same kind of Christmas dinner that we would have.

''The bishops of our stake, under the direction of the stake presidency, made a survey of the stake membership, and we were startled to discover that 4,800 of our members were either wholly or partially dependent—the heads of families did not have steady employment. There were no government make-work projects in those days. We had only ourselves to whom we could look. We were also told that we couldn't expect much help from the general funds of the Church.

''We knew that we had about one thousand children under ten years of age for whom, without someone to help them, there would be no Christmas, so we started to

prepare. We found a second floor over an old store on Pierpont Street. We gathered toys, some of which were broken, and for a month or two before Christmas parents came to help us. Many arrived early or stayed late to make something special for their own little ones. That was the spirit of Christmas giving—one had only to step inside the door of that workshop to see and feel it. Our goal was to see that none of the children would be without a Christmas. We would see that there was Christmas dinner in all the homes of the 4,800 who, without help, would otherwise not have Christmas dinner.

''At that time I was one of the city commissioners. The night before Christmas Eve, we had had a heavy snowstorm, and I had been out all night with the crews getting the streets cleared, knowing that I would be blamed if any of my men fell down on the job. I had then gone home to change my clothes to go to the office.

''As I started back to town, I saw a little boy on the roadside, hitchhiking. He stood in the biting cold with no coat, no gloves, no overshoes. I stopped and asked where he was going.

'' 'I'm going uptown to a free picture show,' he said.

''I told him I was also going uptown and that he could ride with me.

'' 'Son,' I said, 'are you ready for Christmas?'

'' 'Oh, golly, mister,' he replied, 'we aren't going to have any Christmas at our home. Daddy died three months ago and left Mama and me and a little brother and sister.'

''Three children, all under twelve!

''I turned up the heat in my car and said, 'Now, son, give me your

name and address. Somebody will come to your home—you won't be forgotten. And you have a good time; it's Christmas Eve!'

''That night I asked each bishop to go with his delivery men and see that each family was cared for, and to report back to me. While waiting for the last bishop to report, I suddenly, painfully, remembered something. In my haste to see that all my duties at work and my responsibilities in the Church had been taken care of, I had forgotten the little boy and the promise I had made.

''When the last bishop reported, I asked, 'Bishop, have you enough left to visit one more family?'

'' 'Yes, we have,' he replied.

''I told him the story about the little boy and gave him the address. Later he called to say that that family too had received some well-filled baskets. Christmas Eve was over at last, and I went to bed.

''As I awoke that Christmas morning, I said in my heart, 'God grant that I will never let another year pass but that I, as a leader, will truly know my people. I will know their needs. I will be conscious of those who need my leadership most.' '' (Harold B. Lee, *Ye Are the Light of the World,* pp. 345-47.)

(24-11) Through the Death of Close Loved Ones, He Learned More About the Purposes of Suffering

Prophets of God are not immune to the tests and trials of life. They are prepared in the crucible of adversity and suffering. Harold B. Lee's life received the polishing and refinement that can come only from the touch of the Master's hand. Through it all he gained experiences that were for his good and also for the good of the Lord's kingdom. Death, personal physical suffering, and calls that seemed

Harold B. Lee (back row on the right) was active in athletics

impossible were but a few of the experiences necessary for this man of God. His beloved wife of thirty-nine years, Fern, died in 1962. Elder Lee later married Freda Joan Jensen. Three years later he was to meet with the loss of another loved one, his daughter Maurine. Speaking of the anguish of heart of such experiences he said:

"Many times I personally have

wondered at the Master's cry of anguish in the Garden of Gethsemane. 'And he went a little farther, and fell on his face, and prayed, saying, O my Father, if it be possible, let this cup pass from me: nevertheless not as I will, but as thou wilt.' (Matt. 26:39.)

"As I advance in years, I begin to understand in some small measure how the Master must have felt. In the loneliness of a distant hotel

room 2,500 miles away, you, too, may one day cry out from the depths of your soul as was my experience: 'O dear God, don't let her die! I need her; her family needs her.'

"Neither the Master's prayer nor my prayer was answered. The purpose of that personal suffering may be only explained in what the Lord said through the Apostle Paul:

" 'Though he were a Son, yet learned he obedience by the things which he suffered.' " (*CR*, Oct. 1965, pp. 130-31.)

(24-12) Through Physical Suffering He Tapped the Powers of Heaven

"May I impose upon you for a moment to express appreciation for something that happened to me some time ago, years ago. I was suffering from an ulcer condition that was becoming worse and worse. We had been touring a mission; my wife, Joan, and I were impressed the next morning that we should get home as quickly as possible, although we had planned to stay for some other meetings.

"On the way across the country, we were sitting in the forward section of the airplane. Some of our Church members were in the next section. As we approached a certain point en route, someone laid his hand upon my head. I looked up; I could see no one. That happened again before we arrived home, again with the same experience. Who it was, by what means or what medium, I may never know, except I knew that I was receiving a blessing that I came a few hours later to know I needed most desperately.

"As soon as we arrived home, my wife very anxiously called the doctor. It was now about 11 o'clock at night. He called me to come to the telephone, and he asked me how I was; and I said, 'Well, I am very tired. I think I will be all right.' But shortly thereafter, there came massive hemorrhages which, had they occurred while we were in flight, I wouldn't be here today talking about it.

"I know that there are powers divine that reach out when all other help is not available." (Harold B. Lee in *CR*, Apr. 1973, p. 179.)

(24-13) The Tests and Trials He Overcame Brought a Refinement Necessary for His High and Holy Calling

"It was the day when I was ordained to my present calling [Quorum of the Twelve], where my wife and I were invited to the home of one of the brethren for a social evening with others of the First Presidency and the Council of the Twelve. . . . As a part of the evening's entertainment, if that it could be called, each member of the Presidency and the Twelve were asked to recite their experience in being called into the Council of the Twelve or the Presidency. I was amazed as I sat listening to the brethren, beginning with the President and so on through the Twelve, that each was telling my story. They were telling the experience that I at that moment was going through. . . . Then again I began to realize that all must be tested and tried and that there is a certain refinement that is necessary before one qualifies to the highest station to which the Lord would have him called." (Harold B. Lee, "Joseph Smith: His Mission Divine," *Annual Joseph Smith Memorial Sermons*, vol. 2, p. 131.)

(24-14) A Challenging Assignment Led to a Sure Witness of the Savior

"I shall never forget my feelings of loneliness the Saturday night after I was told by the President of the Church that I was to be sustained the next day as a member of the Quorum of the Twelve apostles. That was a sleepless night; there ran through my mind all the petty things of my life, the nonsense, the foolishness of youth. I could have told you about those against whom I had any grievances and who had any grievance against me. And before I was to be accepted the next day, I knew that I must stand

before the Lord and witness before him that I would love and forgive every soul that walked the earth and in return I would ask him to forgive me that I might be worthy of that position.

"I said, as I suppose all of us would say as we are called to such a position, or any position. 'President Grant, do you feel that I am worthy of this call?' And just as quick as a flash, he said, 'My boy, if I didn't think so, you would never be called to this position.'

"The Lord knew my heart and he knew that I was not perfect and that all of us have things to overcome. He takes us with imperfections and expects us to begin where we are and make our lives conform fully with the principles and doctrines of Jesus Christ.

"The following day I went to the temple where I was ushered into the room where the Council of the Twelve meet with the presidency each week in an upper room of the temple. I thought of all the great men who have occupied those chairs and now here I was, just a young man, 20 years younger than the next youngest of the twelve, I was being asked now to sit in one of those chairs. It was frightening and startling.

"And then one of the radio commitee who had a Sunday night program said, 'Now you know that after having been ordained, you are a special witness to the mission of the Lord Jesus Christ. We want you to give the Easter talk next Sunday night.' That was to bear testimony of the mission of the Lord concerning his resurrection, his life, and ministry, so I went to a room in the Church Office Building where I could be alone, and I read the gospels, particularly those that had to do with the closing days and

weeks and months of the life of Jesus, and as I read this I realized that I was having a new experience.

"It wasn't any longer just a story; it seemed as though I was actually seeing the events about which I was reading, and when I gave my talk and closed with a testimony, I said, 'I am now the least of all my brethren and want to witness to you that I know as I have never known before this call came that Jesus is the Savior of this world. He lives and he died for us.' Why did I know? Because there had come a kind of a witness, that special kind of a witness, that may have been that more sure word of prophecy that one must have if he is to be a special witness." (Harold B. Lee, "Speaking for Himself: President Lee's Stories," *Ensign*, Feb. 1974, p. 18.)

(24-15) Harold B. Lee Proved Himself Before God and Before His People

In his first major address as President of the Church, Harold B. Lee looked back at his life and contemplated experiences he had passed through which had sometimes been difficult to understand.

"The day after this appointment, following the passing of our beloved President Smith, my attention was called to a paragraph from a sermon delivered in 1853 in a general conference by Elder Orson Hyde, then a member of the Twelve. This provoked some soul-searching in me also.

"The subject of his address was 'The Man to Lead God's People,' and I quote briefly from his sermon: ' . . . it is invariably the case,' he said, 'that when an individual is ordained and appointed to lead the people, he has passed through tribulations and trials, and has proven himself before God, and before His people, that he is worthy of the situation which he holds. . . . that when a person has not been tried, that has not proved himself before God, and before His people, and before the councils of the Most High, to be worthy, he is not going to step in and lead the Church and people of God. It has never been so, but from the beginning some one that understands the Spirit and counsel of the Almighty, that knows the Church, and is known of her, is the character that will lead the Church.' (*Journal of Discourses*, vol. 1, p. 123.)

"As I have known of the lives of those who have preceded me, I have been made aware that each seemed to have had his special mission for his day and time.

"Then, with searching introspection, I thought of myself and my experiences of which Orson Hyde's appraisal had made reference. Then I recalled the words of the Prophet Joseph's characterization of himself, which seemed somewhat analogous to myself. He said:

" 'I am like a huge rough stone rolling down from a high mountain; and the only polishing I get is when some corner gets rubbed off by coming in contact with something else, striking with accelerated force against religious bigotry, priestcraft, lawyer-craft, doctor-craft, lying editors, suborned judges and jurors, and the authority of perjured executives, backed by mobs, blasphemers, licentious and corrupt men and women—all hell knocking off a corner here and a corner there. Thus will I become a smooth and polished shaft in the quiver of the Almighty. . . . ' (*Teachings of the Prophet Joseph Smith*, p. 304.)

"These thoughts now running through my mind begin to give greater meaning to some of the experiences in my life, things that have happened which have been difficult for me to understand. At times it seemed as though I too was like a rough stone rolling down from a high mountainside, being buffeted and polished, I suppose, by experiences that I too might overcome and become a polished shaft in the quiver of the Almighty. "Maybe it was necessary that I too must learn obedience by the things that I might have suffered—to give me experiences that were for my good, to see if I could pass some of the various tests of mortality." (*CR*, Oct. 1972, pp. 19-20.)

HAROLD B. LEE KNEW THAT THE KEY TO REACHING ALL PEOPLE WAS A LOVE FOR ALL PEOPLE

(24-16) Participate in the Greatest of the Miracles

"The great call has come now in the sermons of the brethren to aid those who are in need of aid, not just temporal aid, but spiritual aid. The greatest miracles I see today are not necessarily the healing of sick bodies, but the greatest miracles I see are the healing of sick souls, those who are sick in soul and spirit and are downhearted and distraught, on the verge of nervous breakdowns. We are reaching out to all such, because they are precious in the sight of the Lord, and we want no one to feel that they are forgotten." (Harold B. Lee in *CR*, Apr. 1973, p. 178.)

(24-17) The Lord Personally Taught President Lee That He Must Love Everyone

During these years of challenge to the Church—challenges that came from growth and from the adversary—the Lord had been preparing Harold B. Lee for the task of extending the love and concern of the Church to every

Latter-day Saint. He learned this lesson as an apostle and as President of the Church.

"I know there are powers that can draw close to one who fills his heart with . . . love. . . . I came to a night, some years ago, when on my bed, I realized that before I could be worthy of the high place to which I had been called, I must love and forgive every soul that walked the earth, and in that time I came to know and I received a peace and a direction, and a comfort, and an inspiration, that told me things to come and gave me impressions that I knew were from a divine source." (Harold B. Lee in *CR*, Oct. 1946, p. 146.)

(24-18) An Experience at a Temple Dedication Had a Profound Effect on His Life

"As I come to you at the closing moments of this conference, I would like to take you back now to just one incident, and I am sorry that I can tell you only a part of it because of the limitations of some things contained therein.

"It was just before the dedication of the Los Angeles Temple. We were all preparing for that great occasion. It was something new in my life, when along about three or four o'clock in the morning, I enjoyed an experience that I think was not a dream, but it must have been a vision. It seemed that I was witnessing a great spiritual gathering, where men and women were standing up, two or three at a time, and speaking in tongues. The spirit was so unusual. I seemed to have heard the voice of President David O. McKay say, 'If you want to love God, you have to learn to love and serve the people. That is the way you show your love for God.' And there were other things then that I saw and heard." (Harold B. Lee in *CR*, Apr. 1973, p. 180.)

(24-19) Harold B. Lee's Heart and Mind Went Out in Love to Every Latter-day Saint

"Now I want to tell you a little sacred experience I had following the call to be the president of the Church. On the early morning thereafter with my wife I kneeled in humble prayer, and suddenly it seemed as though my mind and heart went out to over three million people in all the world. I seemed to have a love for every one of them no matter where they lived nor what their color was, whether they were rich or poor, whether they were humble or great, or educated or not. Suddenly I felt as though they all belonged to me, as though they were all my own brothers and sisters." (Harold B. Lee in *CR*, *Mexico and Central America Area Conference*, Aug. 1972, p. 151.)

> Carefully consider for a moment what type of a man Elder Harold B. Lee was. Can you feel from reading his words that he did indeed love all mankind? Can you now understand why God could inspire him to ask Latter-day Saints to reach out in an effort to activate and involve every Church member?

HAROLD B. LEE EMPHASIZED THAT THROUGH THE ACTIVATION AND INVOLVEMENT OF EVERY CHURCH MEMBER THE FORCES OF RIGHTEOUSNESS CAN BE MARSHALED FOR THE CONFLICT WITH EVIL

(24-20) The Adversary Has Power over His Dominion

"In the preface to the revelations by which the Lord established his work in this dispensation, the predictions of today's horrors were clearly predicted, and the author of the wickedness in this world was revealed. Note what he said: The time is not yet but soon (now this was 140 years ago) when 'all men shall know that the day speedily cometh; the hour is not yet, but is nigh at hand, when peace shall be taken from the earth, and the devil shall have power over his own dominion.' (D&C 1:35.)

"As I say, that was 140 years ago, in 1831. Does anyone here in the sound of my voice doubt, as the Lord foretold, that peace has been taken from the world, and that the devil has power now over his dominion and is ruling with blood and horror upon this earth?" (Lee, "Eternal Life," p. 12.)

(24-21) The Members of the Church Must Prepare Themselves for the Conflict with Evil

"But now the members of this church throughout the world must brace themselves for the never-ending contest between the forces of righteousness and the forces of evil. . . .

"If we follow the leadership of the priesthood, the Lord will fulfill his promise contained in the preface to his revelations, when Satan would have power over his own dominion. This was his promise: ' . . . the Lord shall have power over his saints, and shall reign in their midst, and shall come down in judgment upon . . . the world.' (D&C 1:36.)

"I earnestly urge all our people to unite under the true banner of the Master, to teach the gospel of Jesus Christ so powerfully that no truly converted person could ever be aligned with these controversial concepts and procedures contrary to the Lord's plan of salvation." (Harold B. Lee in *CR*, Oct. 1972, pp. 63-64.)

(24-22) The Church Needs the Faithful Obedience of Every Member to Meet the Challenges of the Day

" . . . I am convinced that the greatest of all the underlying reasons for the strength of this church is that those who keep the commandments of God are 100 percent behind the leadership of this church. Without that united support it would be readily understood that this church could not go forward to meet the challenges of the day. Our call is for the total membership of the Church to keep the commandments of God, for therein lies the safety of the world." (Harold B. Lee in *CR*, Apr. 1973, p. 10.)

Did that last word surprise you? Had you expected President Lee to say, " . . . therein lies the safety *of the Church*"? But he didn't; he said, "therein lies the safety *of the world*." Earlier we talked of how a mere individual could influence the course of history or significantly alter the way things are by the power of his own life. The grandmother of Harold B. Lee influenced history in a quiet way, in a quiet place called Meadow Valley. And what of Harold B. Lee himself? Of course, in the revealing light of history, his name looms large among the many who have been the great builders of the kingdom. But what of those earlier days, the days of his youth in the sleepy little town of Clifton, Idaho? Do you suppose that some of his neighbors and friends might have smiled had you suggested that young Harold's name would someday join the list that included such names as Abraham, Moses, Alma, Nephi, Joseph, and Brigham?

Wouldn't it thrill you to have your grandchildren or your great-grandchildren say of you, "He helped save the world."

Elder Lee in a moment of relaxation

Perhaps you will never be brought to those points of fame and greatness where your name becomes a household word. Perhaps you will never sit in the councils of the General Authorities. Your contribution may be like that of Margaret McMurrin Lee, a contribution of quiet sacrifice and devotion in some little-known place. But what President Lee has just told you is that your sacrifice, your obedience, does matter—not just to the Church and kingdom, but indeed to the very world.

CHAPTER 25
A DEFENSE AND A REFUGE

INTRODUCTION

The Parable of the Village

For long years a village situated high in the mountains had lain isolated and secure. Wars, plagues, and disasters had ravaged the valleys below again and again, with little effect on the villagers. But now a runner had come. "The enemy is coming!" he cried breathlessly. "He destroys all in his path."

An urgent meeting was called, and the village council met to determine how best to defend themselves.

"We must leave our homes and flee even higher!"

"We must scatter and hide until the enemy is gone!" shouted another.

"We are insignificant," responded a third. "Surely the enemy will pass us by."

"We could send a representative," said yet another, "and sue for peace. Even the payment of tribute would be better than death."

One of the wisest of the council raised his hands for silence. When he spoke, he spoke softly and with soberness. "We must this day act with wisdom and courage, for our very existence depends on our decisions here. The enemy is numerous; if we scatter, we shall be hunted and killed like frightened rabbits. The enemy is well supplied; we cannot flee fast enough to outrun his swiftness. To sue for peace is the course of a fool; for the enemy destroys old and young alike with no mercy. And though we are a small and unimportant village, we sit astride the path to future conquests. He cannot pass us by."

"Then let us attack him while still in the foothills," cried one of the bravest of the young men. Again the

wise one shook his head. "Our beloved mountains are our greatest defense; to pit our few against his hordes on lower ground would be futile."

"Then what?" cried the villagers. "What are we to do to save ourselves?"

The village council was now in an uproar at the words of the wise one. "You tell us only what we cannot do," they shouted at him. "Tell us what we can do!"

"What can we do?" he echoed. "We can—nay we must make our stand here at the village. Here it is that we must defeat the enemy."

"But how?" cried the one who wished to sue for peace. "We are so few and the enemy is mighty. He shall roll over us like a flood. We shall be annihilated."

"It is true we are few and that the enemy is mighty. But he is not invincible. The mountains themselves are a great weapon in our land, and while the enemy fights only for gain, we fight for all that is most precious to us. If we unite ourselves we can defeat him and save our homes. But we must fight together; we must fight as one man. Therefore, send word now to every villager. Call on every home and every scattered farm to come. Send runners to the other mountain villages and have them join with us; for if we fall, their destruction will follow. Let every man stand at the

battle line. Let each woman help with food and medical supplies. Even the children can contribute to the victory. We need every hand, every heart. Only in this way can victory be ours."

It was July 1972. Wars, plagues, and disasters threatened people throughout the world. Proposals for peace and relief were numerous. But during these trying times another voice was raised in solemn testimony. Unlike the leader in the parable above, this man was a prophet of God and his name was Harold B. Lee. He too was concerned about war and death. But the war and death he spoke of was spiritual. For years he had raised his voice as an apostle of the Lord and had declared that the only safety for Latter-day Saints in this war for the souls of men was to unite together in a program of defense.

"Almost imperceptibly we see the hand of the Lord moving to do things, and this I construe to be a consolidation of the forces of the Lord under the direction of the prophet, just as in an army, in order to meet a superior force of the enemy in numbers, the forces of our opposition to the forces of evil must be consolidated in order to give them the most effective possible defense.

"We are in a program of defense. The Church of Jesus Christ was set upon this earth in this day '. . . for a defense, and for a refuge from the storm, and from wrath when it should be poured out without mixture upon the whole earth.' (D&C 115:6.)" (CR, Oct. 1961, p. 81.)

Four years later he quoted a prophecy of President Heber C. Kimball's as being applicable to our day:

"President Heber C. Kimball, shortly after the Saints had arrived here in the mountains—and some, I suppose, were somewhat gloating over the fact that they had triumphed for a temporary period over their enemies—had this to say: '. . . we think we are secure here in the chambers of the everlasting hills, where we can close those few doors of the canyons against mobs and persecutors, the wicked and the vile, who have always beset us with violence and robbery, but I want to say to you, my brethren, the time is coming when we will be mixed up in these now peaceful valleys to that extent that it will be difficult to tell the face of a Saint from the face of an enemy to the people of God. Then, brethren, look out for the great sieve, for there will be a great sifting time, and many will fall; for I say unto you there is a *test*, a TEST, a TEST coming, and who will be able to stand? . . .

" 'Let me say to you, that many of you will see the time when you will have all the trouble, trial and persecution that you can stand, and plenty of opportunities to show that you are true to God and his work. This Church has before it many close places through which it will have to pass before the work of God is crowned with victory. To meet the difficulties that are coming, it will be necessary for you to have a knowledge of the truth of this work for yourselves. The difficulties will be of such a character that the man or woman who does not possess this personal knowledge or

witness will fall. If you have not, got the testimony, live right and call upon the Lord and cease not till you obtain it. If you do not you will not stand.

" 'Remember these sayings, for many of you will live to see them fulfilled. The time will come when no man nor woman will be able to endure on borrowed light. Each will have to be guided by the light within himself. If you do not have it, how can you stand?' (*Life of Heber C. Kimball*, pp. 446, 449-450.)" (Harold B. Lee in *CR*, Oct. 1965, p. 128.)

Then, as President of the Church, he gave the following admonition:

"The greatest challenge we have today is to teach the members of this church to keep the commandments of God. Never before has there been such a challenge to the doctrine of righteousness and purity and chastity. The moral standards are being eroded by powers of evil. There is nothing more important for us to do than to teach as powerfully, led by the Spirit of the Lord, as we can in order to persuade our people in the world to live close [to] the Lord in this hour of great temptation." (Cited in *Church News*, 15 July 1972, p. 4.)

In some ways, talk of such conflict is troubling, for you must live through these times. Fathers, mothers, husbands, wives, children—these are most precious to us, and these relationships have great eternal significance. Therefore they become strategic objectives in Satan's war against good. How can one defeat Satan? How can we protect and preserve our families from the forces of evil?

THE LORD CALLS PROPHETS AND SEERS TO GUIDE US IN THE CONFLICT WITH EVIL; HAROLD B. LEE WAS ONE OF THOSE SO CALLED BY THE LORD

(25-1) The Value of Seers

In an interesting discussion between two Book of Mormon personalities, a *seer* is defined as "a revelator and a prophet," and one who "can know of things which are past, and also of things which are to come, and by them shall all things be revealed, or, rather, shall secret things be made manifest, and hidden things shall come to light, and things which are not known shall be made known by them, and also things shall be made known by them which otherwise could not be known.

"Thus God has provided a means that man, through faith, might work mighty miracles; therefore he becometh a great benefit to his fellow beings." (Mosiah 8:16-18.)

Surely in the conflict with evil, seers are needed who can reveal the mind and will of God so that the Saints, through faith, may prepare and become spiritually strong to resist evil. Harold B. Lee was one whose whole life seemed to be an effort to help the people become strong enough to stand against the tides of wickedness. Of him, it was said:

"President Harold B. Lee is a pillar of truth and righteousness, a true seer who has great spiritual strength and insight and wisdom, and whose knowledge and understanding of the Church and its needs is not surpassed by any man." (Joseph Fielding Smith in *CR*, Apr. 1970, p. 114.)

Earlier, Elder Marion G. Romney had said of him:

"Such is Harold B. Lee, who now stands, not at the end of his career

but on its threshold. He knows his course, is recognized for what he is, and is on his way. Behind him is a record of high attainment. Before him, 'hills peep o'er hills, and Alps on Alps arise.' Sustained by the conviction that he lives in the shadow of the Almighty, he will not falter. The future must reckon with Harold B. Lee." (Marion G. Romney, "Harold B. Lee—Apostle of the Lord," *Improvement Era*, July 1953, p. 524.)

Elder Romney's statement was made in 1953. Many of you who are reading this manual were still dwelling in the premortal spheres when Elder Romney made that prophetic statement. You are part of that "future" which must reckon with Harold B. Lee. While it is true that he has died, thus passing the mantle on to others, his teachings can bless you and strengthen you in the challenge that face you. Through his seership he saw conditions that would threaten your spiritual existence and eternal destiny. And through his prophetic office he told you of ways to combat those forces successfully.

HAROLD B. LEE SAW THAT THE ADVERSARY WAS SEEKING TO DESTROY THE FAMILY UNIT

(25-2) The Destructive Influences of the World Are Threatening the Family

"These are challenging times. Around the world there are influences which would strike at the home, at the sacred relationships of husband and wife, of parents and their children. The same destructive influences face our unmarried adult members of the Church.

"How fortunate we are in the midst of all this to have the teachings of our Lord and Savior, Jesus Christ, the head of the Church. His words, and those of his prophets, are ours to help us strengthen our homes and bring more peace and happiness into them.

"There is no other people on the face of the earth, whom I know anything about, who have the lofty concepts of marriage and the sacredness of the home as do the Latter-day Saints. In a revelation given in our day the Lord said: 'Marriage is ordained of God unto man. Wherefore, it is lawful that he should have one wife, and they twain shall be one flesh, and all this that the earth might answer the end of its creation.' (D&C 49:15, 16.)

"There are, however, unmistakable evidences that the same dangers that are abroad in the world are now among us and are seeking to destroy this God-given institution, the home." (Harold B. Lee, *Strengthening the Home* [pamphlet], pp. 1-2.)

(25-3) The Home Is the Key to Peace and the Conquest of Evil

"In the midst of the early persecutions of this church, the Saints sought earnestly from the Lord as to how they were to meet the threats of their enemies.

"The answer came: 'Therefore, renounce war and proclaim peace, and seek diligently to turn the hearts of the children to their fathers, and the hearts of the fathers, to the children.' (D&C 98:16.)

"And then came this significant promise:

" 'And again I say unto you, if ye

President Lee and his wife Freda Joan Lee

observe to do whatsoever I command you, I, the Lord, will turn away all wrath and indignation from you, and the gates of hell shall not prevail against you.' (D&C 98:22.) . . .

"In plain language, then, the Saints were told that to avoid war with their enemies they must renounce war and proclaim peace and to see that this was to begin within the home where fathers and children would be at peace with each other.

"The Lord gave a further promise, saying that when and if all wrath and indignation would be conquered within themselves, the evils of Satan's powers could not successfully assail them.

"He didn't leave us with any question as to the prime place in his church and in the world where this preparation and the battle against evil—unless curbed in the beginning—would break out into armed conflict.

"After giving his law to parents to teach and train their children to walk uprightly before the Lord, he indicated his displeasure relative to those among us who, in his language, 'are idlers . . . and [our] children are also growing up in wickedness; they also seek not earnestly the riches of eternity, but their eyes are full of greediness.' (D&C 68:31.)

"If these words are clearly understood, we have been told where the roots of all evil are to be found." (Harold B. Lee in *CR*, Oct. 1972, pp. 60-61.)

It was Henry David Thoreau who said, "There are a thousand hacking at the branches of evil to one who is striking at the roots." (Walden I.) The world tries to put down evil through various programs of welfare assistance, antipoverty plans, prison reforms, legislative programs, and so forth. The intentions are good and the efforts prodigious, but the results are often disappointing. With their gift of seership, the prophets have seen beyond the symptoms of evil. As you have just read, President Lee pinpointed the home as the prime place to prepare people to overcome evil. To put it into military terms, the home is the most critically strategic point in the battle against Satan. Is it any wonder, then, that the archenemy of righteousness has launched such a determined and widespread attack against the home? President Lee had the vision sufficient to see the roots of righteous living and the threat to those roots in our day. With such a gift we would also expect that we could look to him to discover how to most effectively combat the forces seeking to destroy our homes.

THE CHURCH IS TO ASSIST THE HOME IN ITS DIVINE GOAL OF PERFECTING FAMILY MEMBERS

(25-4) *The Objective of the Church Is to Help the Saints Meet the Problems of the Day*

"There is one grand objective in all this great Church organization that now numbers more than three million persons. That objective is to provide for and to promote the spiritual, temporal and social salvation or welfare of every one who has membership in one of these priesthood or auxiliary groups, and if each such group is moved by the power and righteousness of the principles inherent therein, 'they will have all the power necessary to meet every problem in this modern and changing world.' (Brigham Young.)" (Harold B. Lee, *Decisions for Successful Living*, p. 211.)

(25-5) *Application of the Lord's Plan Will Save Our Families*

" . . . the members of the Church have been given the family home evening plan for family instruction and involvement. Linked with that, he has given us the plan of temporal salvation in the churchwide welfare program, where everyone is to give in labor, money, or service to the full extent of his ability and then receive from out of the bounties, of which each one who needs has been a producer, and then without embarrassment or reticence, he receives according to his need.

"Beyond this the Lord has directed the establishment of children and youth activities and of instruction to mothers and fathers in the auxiliaries and priesthood quorum organizations of the Church, where every means is provided to give to all, as an outside observer said, speaking of the youth activities provided by the Church, 'the opportunity to participate in so many good things that they have little or no time for the evil activities.'

"Any thinking person can see that if these fundamentals of sound social principles are not employed in every community to deal with crime, unemployment, and juvenile delinquency, then the seeds of unrest and bitterness would lead to the ultimate, of which the Lord warned. When these principles of right living and the application of his doctrines of salvation are not heeded, then we must expect that the power of evil will lead to conflict in the family, in the nation, and throughout the world." (Harold B. Lee in *CR*, Oct. 1972, p. 62.)

(25-6) The Sanctity of Our Homes Can Be Protected If We Will Heed the Counsel of the Prophet of God

"Some months ago, millions of watchers and listeners over the world waited breathlessly and anxiously the precarious flight of Apollo 13. The whole world, it seemed, prayed for one significant result: the safe return to earth of three brave men.

"When one of them with restrained anxiety announced the startling information, 'We have had an explosion!' the mission control in Houston immediately mobilized all the technically trained scientists who had, over the years, planned every conceivable detail pertaining to that flight.

"The safety of those three now depended on two vital qualifications: on the reliability of the skills and the knowledge of those technicians in the mission control center at Houston, and upon the implicit obedience of the men in the Aquarius to every instruction from the technicians, who, because of their understanding of the problems of the astronauts, were better qualified to find the essential solutions. The decisions of the technicians had to be perfect or the Aquarius could have missed the earth by thousands of miles.

"This dramatic event is somewhat analogous to these troublous times in which we live. The headlines in the public press only this week made another startling announcement by a presidential commission to the President of the United States. 'U.S. Society Is in Peril.' Many are frightened when they see and hear of unbelievable happenings the world over—political intrigues, wars and contention everywhere, frustrations of parents, endeavoring to cope with social

problems that threaten to break down the sanctity of the home, the frustrations of children and youth as they face challenges to their faith and their morals.

"Only if *you* are willing to listen and obey, as did the astronauts on the Aquarius, can you and all your households be guided to ultimate safety and security in the Lord's own way." (Harold B. Lee in *CR*, Oct. 1970, p. 113.)

Bill and Marsha were two months away from being married in the temple. The anticipation of their own home and family was glorious. But this night their dreams and hopes were being challenged. Bill's roommate, John, questioned the possible success of their marriage. "Children, schooling, finances—how do you know your marriage will survive these problems?" he asked.

Bill and Marsha had already thought that question through. Bill replied, "In the last conference, President Harold B. Lee said that those who follow the counsel of the living prophets will be sustained and guided by the Lord during times of trial and challenge in marriage. We want to establish our home on the counsel of God's prophet."

John didn't think that Bill's answer was sufficient. "I know how strongly you feel about your Church," he said, "but what you have just stated is so idealistic. You've got to be practical. Your prophets give some good sermons on religion, but they don't know that much about marriage in real life and about realistic family problems."

Marsha spoke up. "Bill and I just read the counsel that President Lee gave to a newly married

couple. He told them to end every day with family prayer. By this he meant that the couple was to talk over any difficulties or misunderstandings that had happened during the day. If there were problems, they were to ask each other for forgiveness and then kneel in prayer together and petition the Lord for his blessings. (See *CR, Mexico Area Conference*, Aug. 1972, pp. 121-22.) We feel such counsel is very practical and would go a long way toward creating a happy marriage. There are numerous other examples, too."

John just shook his head. "Well, it seems pretty naive to me. After all, I've tried marriage twice, and it just doesn't work!"

For a long moment Bill looked at his friend. Then very gently he said, "Maybe what you needed was some inspired counsel to build upon."

HAROLD B. LEE SUSTAINED GOD'S PROPHETS AND UNDER THEIR DIRECTION RECEIVED REVELATION AIMED AT PREPARING THE SAINTS FOR TEMPORAL SALVATION

(25-7) He Was Called by the First Presidency to Further Develop Principles That Would Direct the Temporal Salvation of the Saints

The early 1930s were characterized by phrases such as "soup kitchens" and "bread lines." The depression had hit, and 25 percent of the normal labor force of the United States were unemployed. Other countries were in as bad or even worse condition. Church members were not exempt from the effects of this period, for many had grave financial problems. The Pioneer Stake of Salt Lake City, for example, had over 50 percent of its male population unemployed. But

the Lord had been inspiring his prophets to prepare the Church for such times of difficulty, and the president of that very stake, Harold B. Lee, was called to assume an important responsibility in such preparations.

"For the last five glorious, strenuous years, I have labored, under a call from the First Presidency, with a group of men in the development of and the unfolding of what we have called the Church Welfare Plan. . . . It was on April 20th, 1935, when I was called to the office of the First Presidency. That was a year before official announcement of the Welfare Plan was made in this Tabernacle. There, after an entire half day session, at which President Grant and President McKay were present, President Clark then being in the East—they had some communications with him, so that all members of the Presidency were in agreement—I was astounded to learn that for years there had been before them, as a result of their thinking and planning and as the result of the inspiration of Almighty God, the genius of the very plan that is being carried out and was in waiting and in preparation for a time when in their judgment the faith of the Latter-day Saints was such that they were willing to follow the counsel of the men who lead and preside in this Church.

"My humble place in this program at that time was described. I left there about noon-time. . . . I drove with my car up to the head of City Creek Canyon. I got out, after I had driven as far as I could, and I walked up through the trees. I sought my Heavenly Father. As I sat down to pore over this matter, wondering about an organization to be perfected to carry on this work, I received a testimony, on that beautiful spring afternoon, that God had already revealed the greatest organization that ever could be given to mankind [the priesthood], and that all that was needed now was that that organization be set to work, and the temporal welfare of the Latter-day Saints would be safeguarded." (Harold B. Lee in *CR*, Apr. 1941, pp. 120-21.)

(25-8) As He Faithfully Labored Under the Direction of the First Presidency, He Received a Witness That the Welfare Program Was of Great Significance

" . . . I had driven . . . across the mountains to Richfield, for an early morning meeting. At that time

President Harold Bingham Lee

there was an upturn in business, so much so that some were questioning the wisdom of this kind of activity, and why hadn't the Church done it before now? There came to me, in that early morning hour a distinct impression that was as real as though someone had spoken audibly, and this was the impression that came, and has stayed with me through these years: There is no individual in the Church that knows the real purpose for which the program then launched had been intended, but hardly before the Church has made sufficient preparation, that reason will be made manifest, and when it comes it will challenge every resource of the Church to meet it. I trembled at the feeling that came over me. Since that day that feeling has driven me on, night and day, hardly resting, knowing that this is God's will, this is His plan. The only thing necessary today is that the Latter-day Saints everywhere recognize these men, who sit here on the stand, as the fountainheads of truth, through whom God will reveal His will, that His Saints might be preserved through an evil day." (Harold B. Lee in *CR*, Apr. 1941, p. 121.)

One need not read very far into the scriptures to realize that the last days will be days of great calamity and frightening judgments. Nor does one need to read many newspapers or listen to many news broadcasts to realize that calamities and judgments are part of our daily life. We are thus not only threatened by spiritual forces that seek to destroy us, but many of the Saints will have to face temporal threats to life and property and to the survival of their families. Earthquakes, floods, fires, riots, storms—all can bring temporal disaster. But again the prophets and seers

have told you how to prepare for such eventualities. And as you have just seen, Harold B. Lee played a major role in propounding these principles and revelations.

Today most members are familiar with such terms as "welfare plan," "Bishop's storehouse," "year's supply," and so on. Yet many still postpone their obedience to the counsel of the prophets. Elder

Lee said that when he felt how important the welfare program would be in the future, the feeling of urgency had driven him on day and night, hardly allowing him to rest. What changes would there be in the temporal preparation of the Church if every member felt that same driving urgency? What changes would occur in *your* life? Have you followed the counsel of the Brethren concerning temporal preparation?

He was conscious of the world role of the Church

THE PRINCIPLES OF PRIESTHOOD CORRELATION WERE GIVEN BY REVELATION TO HELP THE SAINTS MEET THE CHALLENGES OF THE LAST DAYS

(25-9) Harold B. Lee Played a Significant Role in Developing the Principles of Priesthood Correlation

In 1960, under the leadership of President David O. McKay, the First Presidency sent the following letter to the General Priesthood Committee, which was under the direction of Elder Lee:

"We of the First Presidency have over the years felt the need of a correlation between and among the courses of study put out by the General Priesthood Committee and by the responsible heads of other Committees of the General Authorities for the instruction of the Priesthood of the Church. . . .

"We think that the contemplated study by the Committee now set up should have the foregoing matters in mind. We feel assured that if the whole Church curricula were viewed from the vantage point of what we might term the total purpose of each and all of these organizations, it would bring about such a collation and limitation of subjects and subject matters elaborated in the various Auxiliary courses as would tend to the building of efficiency in the Auxiliaries themselves in the matter of carrying out the purposes lying behind their creation and function.

We would therefore commend to you Brethren of the General Priesthood Committee the beginning of an exhaustive, prayerful study and consideration of this entire subject, with the cooperative assistance of the Auxiliaries themselves so that the

Church might reap the maximum harvest from the devotion of the faith, intelligence, skill, and knowledge of our various Auxiliary Organizations and Priesthood Committees. . . .

"Faithfully your brethren,
David O. McKay
J. Reuben Clark, Jr.
Henry D. Moyle
The First Presidency"

(*CR,* Oct. 1967, pp. 98-99.)

As you read this directive you might well have seen the problem as one of a technical nature, related only to unifying the curriculum efforts of various organizations of the Church. But Elder Lee and others who worked with him took seriously the First Presidency's commendation of "an exhaustive, prayerful study and consideration of this entire subject." In doing so, they found that they were magnified in their stewardships, as they received pertinent revelation for the Saints.

"President McKay sometime ago in talking to the Presidency and the twelve, urged us to give time for more meditation so that we could tune in with spiritual forces that we had a right to and should expect to direct us in our work. He said, 'The best time for me is early in the morning when my mind and body are rested. But when the inspiration comes, and it can come just as clearly as though you were taking down a telephone and dialing in for information; when the Lord tells you what to do, you have to have the courage to do what he instructs you.'

"It is that, President McKay, which has been one of the most humbling experiences of this last year. Under your assignment, I

bear humble witness to the Church I have sought that with all the faith I could muster, I have importuned the Lord. Sometimes the startling nature of my assignment has required courage almost beyond my strength. I come to you tonight subdued in spirit, I come to you with a sincere witness that the Lord is revealing and working through channels that he has appointed. Don't you ever let anybody tell you, the membership of the Church, that the Lord is not today revealing and directing and developing plans which are needed to concentrate the entire forces of this Church to meet the challenge of the insidious forces at work to thwart and to tear down and to undermine the church and kingdom of God." (Harold B. Lee in *CR,* Oct. 1962, pp. 82-83.)

These revealed principles were later known as the principles of priesthood correlation. As these principles were gradually unfolded before the Church, and particularly to the priesthood leaders, it became evident that this was not just an administrative program to facilitate improved communication and a more effective curriculum; it was the design of the Lord to establish a program of defense against some of the insidious designs of the adversary that were intended to thwart and break down the family and the kingdom of God.

Now consider for a moment what could happen in our world if Latter-day Saints would heed the counsel of their prophet leader and sustain these principles of temporal and spiritual salvation.

(25-10) The Lord Revealed Principles That Would Concentrate the Entire Forces of the Church and Bring About Marvelous Developments

"I bear you my solemn witness that I know that God is directing this work today and revealing his mind and will. The light is shining through, and if we can get the priesthood now to come alive and to put into full gear the full strength of the priesthood, we shall see some of the most wonderful developments and some of the greatest things happen to the forces which the Lord can set in motion that we have ever known in this dispensation." (Harold B. Lee in *CR*, Oct. 1962, p. 83.)

(25-11) Elder Lee Indicated Four Important Factors of Priesthood Correlation

"First, we must see that the whole effort of correlation is to strengthen the home and to give aid to the home in its problems, giving it special aid and succor as needed.

"Second, the strength of the priesthood must be fully employed within the total responsibility of priesthood quorums as clearly set forth in the revelations.

"Third, we must survey the purposes lying behind the creation and purpose of each auxiliary organization.

"And fourth, the prime and ultimate objective of all that is done is the building up of a knowledge of the gospel, a power to promulgate the same, a promotion of the faith, growth, and stronger testimony of the principles of the gospel among the members of the Church."
(Harold B. Lee in *CR*, Oct. 1964, pp. 80-81.)

(25-12) Priesthood Correlation Provides the Scaffolding to Support the Home

"Again and again has been repeated the statement that the home is the basis of a righteous life. With new and badly needed emphasis on the 'how,' we must not lose sight of the 'why' we are so engaged. The priesthood programs operate in support of the home; the auxiliary programs render valuable assistance. Wise regional leadership can help us to do our share in attaining God's overarching purpose, 'to bring to pass the immortality and eternal life of man.' (Moses 1:39.) Both the revelations of God and the learning of men tell us how crucial the home is in shaping the individual's total life experience. You must have been impressed that running through all that has been said in this conference has been the urgency of impressing the importance of better teaching and greater parental responsibility in the home. Much of what we do organizationally, then, is scaffolding, as we seek to build the individual, and we must not mistake the scaffolding for the soul." (Harold B. Lee in *CR*, Oct. 1967, p. 107.)

(25-13) Families Are Urged to Hold a Weekly Home Evening

"Greater emphasis on the teaching of the children in the home by the parents was brought forth in what we call the family home evening program. This was not new. Fifty years ago it was given emphasis; and as we went back into history, we found that in the last epistle written to the Church by President Brigham Young and his counselors, it was urged that parents bring their children together and teach them the gospel in the home frequently. So family home evening has been urged ever since the Church was established in this dispensation." (Harold B. Lee in *CR*, Oct. 1967, p. 101.)

(25-14) The Priesthood Quorums Were to Assist the Home Through Home Teaching

"The first step that was made was to place the priesthood in the place where the Lord had placed it: to watch over the Church.

"In the Doctrine and Covenants, Section 20, the Lord said:

" 'The teacher's duty is to watch over the church always, and be with and strengthen them;

" 'And see that there is no iniquity in the church, neither hardness with each other, neither lying, backbiting, nor evil speaking;

" 'And see that the church meet together often, and also see that all the members do their duty.' (D&C 20:53-55.)

"This, you will note by careful reading of this great revelation in its entirety, was to apply to the whole priesthood of the Church.

"The name of home teaching was given to this movement, to distinguish it from ward teaching. . . .

"Home teaching, in essence, means that we consider separately each individual member of the family who constitutes the entire home personnel. Home teaching, as distinguished from ward teaching, is to help the parents with home problems in their efforts to teach their families the fundamentals of parental responsibility, as contrasted with merely bringing a message, a gospel message, to the entire family. Quorum leaders were given the responsibility of selecting, training, and supervising quorum members in visiting with and teaching assigned families of their own quorum members." (Harold B. Lee in *CR*, Oct. 1967, p. 100.)

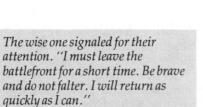

The battle for the village raged on into the late afternoon. Time and again the enemy had hurled their finest troops against the ragged line of villagers. Time and again that line had rallied and had pushed the enemy back. Now, in a brief respite, the villagers looked below as the enemy regrouped, massing forces for what would be their greatest thrust yet. A deep sense of foreboding fell on the villagers. Could they hold the line? There had been many casualties.

The wise one signaled for their attention. "I must leave the battlefront for a short time. Be brave and do not falter. I will return as quickly as I can."

Dismay was clearly evident on the faces of the weary men. "Leave us? But we are facing our most critical test! How can you leave us now?"

The old man nodded slowly. "Yes, I know what is coming. It is the time of greatest crisis. I must go and bring help. We have called for all to

join us, but too often we have called in vain. Too many have ignored the threat of destruction. Some have said the enemy would not come. Others have tarried to secure their farms and homes from harm. Still others have fled to the heights, with fear as their companion." He shook his head sadly. "And some have even deserted to the enemy. Soon the great attack will come. I must go to those who are not here and call them to the line. Every hand strengthens our cause. Every soul adds to the

The Lee family (1941), L. to R.: Sister Fern Lucinda Lee, daughters Helen and Maurine, Elder Lee

assurance of victory. I will send them to you as swiftly as I can."

On December 26, 1973, Elder Harold B. Lee passed from this life into the next. But his mission was accomplished.

"He is like a man assigned to prepare transportation for a difficult journey into unknown lands. In order to insure a safe journey he takes the car completely to pieces, checks every part, puts in stronger gears, changes some of the connections to insure that the power is available in times of difficulty. The car is finally put together. He does the timing and the tuning and supervises the painting. He gets in and test drives it once or twice. Finally he gets out, polishes the last flecks of dust off the radiator cap, brushes off his hands, and contemplates the journey ahead. Then comes the signal, your work is completed. The journey will be safer because of your effort. Your work is over.

"Ours goes on." (Lavine Fielding, "The Long Odyssey," *Ensign,* Feb. 1974, p. 10.)

The Lord promised that "the day cometh that they who will not hear the voice of the Lord, neither the voice of his servants, neither give heed to the words of the prophets and apostles, *shall be cut off* from among the people." (D&C 1:14. Italics added.) In this chapter you have read the counsel of a prophet and seer. Are you heeding the counsel he has given to you? Have you caught the vision of the central value of the home, and are you making conscious and sincere effort to strengthen your own home (even if you have not as yet married and established that home)? Do you see home teaching as an awkward, inconvenient assignment, or do you really consider separately each individual member of the family and help the parents with home problems? Are collecting a year's supply of food and performing other tasks of temporal preparation realities in your life or just something you've got to do "sometime"?

Ammon told King Limhi that a seer would manifest secret things and bring to light hidden things so that men could act in faith and work mighty miracles. (See Mosiah 8:16-18.) But of what value to you is a seer if his counsel is ignored? Consider the words of President Lee himself:

"Now the only safety we have as members of this church is to do exactly what the Lord said to the Church in that day when the Church was organized. We must learn to give heed to the words and commandments that the Lord shall give through his prophet, 'as he receiveth them, walking in all holiness before me; . . . as if from mine own mouth, in all patience and faith.' (D&C 21:4-5.) There will be some things that take patience and faith. You may not like what comes from the authority of the Church. It may contradict your political views. It may contradict your social views. It may interfere with some of your social life. But if you listen to these things, as if from the mouth of the Lord himself, with patience and faith, the promise is that 'the gates of hell shall not prevail against you; yea, and the Lord God will disperse the powers of darkness from before you, and cause the heavens to shake for your good, and his name's glory.' (D&C 21:6.)" (Harold B. Lee in *CR,* Oct. 1970, p. 152.)

UNIT THIRTEEN

SPENCER W. KIMBALL

Twelfth President of the Church

OVERVIEW

Spencer Woolley Kimball was born March 28, 1895, in Salt Lake City. The next January, Utah was granted statehood. The Manifesto was five years old, the economy was going into an upswing, and the Saints were entering an era of relative calm.

But the calm was deceptive, like the eye of a hurricane. Many political, social, and scientific developments that were in their infancy were destined to unleash a revolutionary storm on the world. Not all the effects of a hurricane are harmful, nor have all the social and scientific changes of the last eighty years been harmful. But the pollutions they brought were destined to challenge Spencer W. Kimball when he became the twelfth president of the Church.

There were prophetic moments and intimations, but a casual observer could have described his childhood and early manhood as quite ordinary. There were cows to milk, gardens to weed, and buildings to paint.

Though the childhood was not unusual, the boy himself was not ordinary. He was one who demanded much of himself. In school, church, and at play, his was an excellent and usually the best performance. He abstained totally from whatever would pollute the body. He was president of his deacons quorum and continued in leadership, filling each position with steadfastness and devotion.

Exactly one year after his release from a mission to Missouri, at the age of twenty-three, he was named stake clerk of the St. Joseph Stake in Safford, Arizona. Six years later he was sustained as a counselor in the presidency of that stake, a position he filled for ten years. Later the stake was divided, and he was named president of the new stake. Five and a half years later, after over a quarter of a century in stake leadership, he was called to fill

the sacred office of the apostleship—a special witness of the Savior and minister of the affairs of the general Church. Thirty years in this calling brought him to the office of prophet, seer, and revelator, on December 30, 1973.

Spencer W. Kimball also spent twenty-five successful years in banking, insurance, and real estate. He helped organize the Gila Broadcasting Company and the Gila Valley Irrigation Company and served in important leadership assignments in these ventures. He was a district governor of Rotary International, president of the Safford Rotary Club, a member of the Gila Junior College Board of Trustees, a member of the Arizona Teachers Retirement Board, Vice-President of the Roosevelt Council of Boy Scouts, chairman of the USO, chairman of the United War Fund campaign in Graham County, and master of ceremonies at endless Church and civil functions. As a pianist, he often accompanied the singing. As a singer he was in constant demand. For many years he was a member of a popular quartet called the Conquistadores.

The Lord allowed a great deal of pain and sorrow to temper and mold this chosen man. He was nearly drowned at age ten, lost his beloved mother at age eleven, hovered near death from typhoid at age thirteen, and lost his father at age twenty-nine. Five years after his call to the Council of the Twelve, he suffered a serious heart ailment which forced him into months of inactivity. Here was a physical dynamo, a star athlete, a most active person, threatened with death or cessation of nearly all activity. In the high mountains of Arizona he recuperated among his Indian friends.

But that was not the end of suffering. Some years later he was afflicted with cancer in his throat. The doctors said he would lose his voice, the very focal point of his life and service as an

apostle. With a special blessing from Harold B. Lee, Elder Kimball submitted to surgery. Part of a vocal cord was saved. Then followed months of physical pain and mental anguish as he struggled for restored health and a new voice. When he was ready to try to speak again, he went home to the valley of his youth. There he told about having fallen among "cutthroats" in the east. With this priceless bit of humor, he said good-bye to the past and a new voice began to be heard—no singing, but a beloved, familiar voice with a gravity of sound to match the gravity of his message.

The frailties of the flesh threatened again to stop him short of the calling for which he was being prepared. His heart condition resurfaced and required open-heart surgery to save him. Again President Lee pronounced blessings: life for the patient and divine guidance for the surgeon. Both blessings were fulfilled. A speedy recovery occurred; a prophet was saved. Only two years later he became president of the Lord's church, demonstrating remarkably vigorous health.

Here was a man with a faith like that of David, who could see no reason to run from Goliath, because the Lord was with him. Here was a man of intensive preparation, an individual who, at nine years of age, had systematically memorized scriptures and hymns and had read the Bible from cover to cover when age fourteen. Yet here was a man who felt so inadequate when called to the Council of the Twelve that for eighty-two days—from the time he was notified until the time he was sustained—mornings found him still on his knees after night-long pleadings for mercy, grace, forgiveness, and strength.

Such is Spencer W. Kimball, who has called upon every member to repent—NOW! and to convert the world—NOW!

CHAPTER 26

WHY CALL YE ME, LORD LORD AND DO NOT THE THINGS WHICH I SAY?

INTRODUCTION

A sleepy country town—that would be the way a reporter might describe Thatcher, Arizona. But there never has been anything sleepy about the bright-eyed three-year-old who moved there with his family in May of 1898. True, he might fall asleep at the supper table or wherever else his usually active body came to rest; but his sights were always raised high and his stride always stretched out.

The streets of Thatcher are paved now, but they are still shaded by pecan trees that have grown old with the prophet. Their leafy boughs reach farther now to shade the weary traveler, who can pick up their abundant harvest from the Bermuda grass and eat to his heart's content, because the nuts are not all gathered.

This valley and its citizens claim Spencer W. Kimball as their own, and he reciprocates. Much of him is in the valley and much of the valley is in him. Part of it is in the barren and forbidding desert that broods on the outskirts of the ribbon of green that hard-won water and rigorous toil have wrested away from that desert. But more of it is in the people. Without them the rest would be meaningless. In fact, civilization could not have come to this valley without such people. They were Mormon pioneers—the usual kind, the kind that settled hundreds of places like this valley.

You too have a heritage, or you can acquire one. Will you honor it as nobly as President Kimball has honored his? True, we cannot discount his

foreordination and that he was a "noble and great one." (See Abraham 3:22.) But you also qualified in the premortal world to be offered an opportunity for exaltation (and there is no greater opportunity) if you will accept the challenge of mortality as President Kimball has. President Kimball's life is an ideal prototype.

PRESIDENT KIMBALL DEMANDS OF OTHERS NO MORE THAN WHAT HE HAS ALWAYS BEEN WILLING TO GIVE HIMSELF

(26-1) President Kimball Has Called for Noble Choices and Courageous Endeavor

"I remind you young men that regardless of your present age, you are building your life; it will be cheap and shoddy or it will be valuable and beautiful; it will be full of constructive activities or it can be destructive; it can be full of joy and happiness, or it can be full of misery. It all depends upon you

and your attitudes, for your altitude, or the height you climb, is dependent upon your attitude or your response to situations. . . .

"Remember that those who climb to high places did not always have it easy." (Spencer W. Kimball in *CR*, Oct. 1974, pp. 112-13.)

(26-2) "Are We Prepared to Lengthen Our Stride? To Enlarge Our Vision?"

"My brethren, I wonder if we are doing all we can. . . . Are we prepared to lengthen our stride? To enlarge our vision?

"Remember, our ally is our God. He is our commander. He made the plans. He gave the commandment. Remember what we have quoted thousands of times as told by Nephi:

" 'And it came to pass that I, Nephi, said unto my father: I will go and do the things which the Lord hath commanded, for I know that the Lord giveth no commandments unto the children of men, save he shall prepare a way for them that they may accomplish the thing which he commandeth them.' (1 Ne. 3:7.)" (Spencer W. Kimball, "When the World Will Be Converted," *Ensign*, Oct. 1974, p. 5.)

On the desk of President Kimball sits a plaque on which are inscribed two words: "DO IT!" You have just read President Kimball's challenge to you and to all the Church. As you now begin to study this man of prodigious energy and drive and the events and forces that shaped him, ponder this. Again and again, after being called to the presidency, President Kimball quoted Luke 6:46,

which comprises the title of this chapter. Why could he comfortably use that scripture as a theme? Paul wrote to the Romans, "Thou therefore which teachest another, teachest thou not thyself? thou that preachest a man should not steal, dost thou steal?" (Romans 2:21.)

Notice what President Kimball preaches and teaches: Lengthen your stride. Enlarge your vision. Face adversity and make it work for you. Do it! Why claim to be disciples of Christ when you don't act accordingly.

As you study this man, search for those things which give him the right to teach in such a manner.

(26-3) There Was a Lot to "Live Up To" in the Heritage of President Kimball

"Who is Spencer Woolley Kimball? For a true appraisal, we must go back to his antecedents. He was born in Salt Lake City on March 28, 1895, the son of Andrew Kimball and Olive Woolley. Like Nephi of old, he may thank the Lord that he came of goodly parentage. His two grandfathers were outstanding colonizers and peers among men. Heber C. Kimball was an apostle of the Lord, friend and disciple of the Prophet Joseph, counselor to President Young, and missionary extraordinary for his church; Edwin D. Woolley was a colorful Salt Lake leader, business manager for President Young, and a great bishop of the Thirteenth Ward for a period of forty years. His own father, Andrew Kimball, was likewise a most remarkable man. Energetic and zealous always, as an advocate of the restored gospel, he presided over the mission in the Indian Territory for ten years and at intervals returned to Salt Lake to earn a living for his family. For

twenty-six and a half years, from 1898 to the day of his death, he was president of the St. Joseph Stake of Zion, the stake which had been named at the suggestion of President John Taylor in honor of the Prophet Joseph. His ability as a builder and organizer did much toward the development of a great agricultural empire in eastern Arizona, and in the years of his administration the stake developed from a few wards on the Gila River to some seventeen wards and branches of the church, extending from Miami, Arizona, to El Paso, Texas." (Jesse A. Udall, "Spencer W. Kimball, the Apostle from Arizona," *Improvement Era*, Oct. 1943, p. 590.)

(26-4) His Father Had Intimations of Young Spencer's Future Greatness

"Ten-year-old Spencer Woolley Kimball liked to help his father with the chores. Perched on a stool, the lad sang happily as he milked one of the cows. He was completely oblivious at the moment to his father standing in the barn doorway talking to a neighbor who had just delivered a load of pumpkins for the pigs.

" 'That boy, Spencer, is an exceptional boy,' President Kimball was saying. 'He always tries to mind me, whatever I ask him to do. I have dedicated him to be one of the mouthpieces of the Lord—the Lord willing. You will see him some day as a great leader. I have dedicated him to the service of God, and he will become a mighty man in the Church.'

"Even while milking the cows, Spencer was justifying the faith and confidence of his father, for he was vocalizing with a purpose. On a piece of paper lying on the floor by the milk bucket, he had the words of the hymn he was singing. He practiced thus every day so that

he could learn the words of the Church hymns by heart. He often did the same thing with verses of scripture, memorizing them for future use." (*Church News*, 18 Nov. 1961, p. 16.)

(26-5) President Kimball Has Never Been Willing to Indulge Himself in Less than Perfect Performances

"From childhood he has been most conscientious in his work—nothing short of the best was good enough. For years he had a record of perfect attendance at Sunday School and Primary. One Monday he was in the field tramping hay for his older brothers when the meetinghouse bell rang for Primary.

" 'I've got to go to Primary,' he timidly suggested.

" 'You can't go today; we need you,' they said.

" 'Well, Father would let me go, if he were here,' the boy countered.

" 'Father isn't here,' they said, 'and you are not going.'

"The piles of hay came pouring up, literally covering Spencer, but finally he had caught up; sliding noiselessly from the back of the wagon, he was halfway to the meetinghouse before his absence was noticed, and his perfect record remained unbroken. . . .

" . . . Like Daniel, Spencer has never defiled himself. If you were to ask him point-blank if he had always observed the Word of Wisdom, he would modestly tell you that he had never tasted tea, coffee, liquor nor tobacco." (Udall, "Spencer W. Kimball," p. 591.)

(26-6) He Set Hard Goals at an Early Age

"Let me tell you of one of the goals that I made when I was still but a lad. When I heard a Church leader from Salt Lake City tell us at

conference that we should read the scriptures, and I recognized that I had never read the Bible, that very night at the conclusion of that very sermon I walked to my home a block away and climbed up in my little attic room in the top of the house and lighted a little coal-oil lamp that was on the little table, and I read the first chapters of Genesis. A year later I closed the Bible, having read every chapter in that big and glorious book.

"I found that this Bible that I was reading had in it 66 books, and then I was nearly dissuaded when I found that it had in it 1,189 chapters, and then I also found that it had 1,519 pages. It was formidable, but I knew if others did it that I could do it.

"I found that there were certain parts that were hard for a 14-year-old boy to understand. There were some pages that were not especially interesting to me, but when I had read the 66 books and 1,189 chapters and 1,519 pages, I had a glowing satisfaction that I had made a goal and that I had achieved it.

"Now I am not telling you this story to boast; I am merely using this as an example to say that if I could do it by coal-oil light, you can do it by electric light. I have always been glad I read the Bible from cover to cover." (Spencer W. Kimball in *CR*, Apr. 1974, pp. 126-27.)

(26-7) He Was a Scholar and an Athlete

"The young Spencer grew to maturity at Thatcher. Having completed the public schools he entered the Gila Academy, the institution which had been established by the church early in the colonization of the valley. Later, its name was changed to the Gila Junior College. In 1914 he was graduated with highest honors and

Heber C. Kimball is President Kimball's grandfather

as president of his class. In addition to his scholastic achievements he was a star forward on the basketball team, and many a game was won by his accurate goal-throwing from every angle on the floor." (Udall, "Spencer W. Kimball," p. 591.)

(26-8) He Excelled in Athletics As He Did in Most Other Things

"I am on the basketball court. We play in our overalls and shirts with cheap rubber shoes and with basketballs of our own buying. We have beaten Globe High School on our dirt court, and we have defeated Safford and other high schools. Now, tonight, we Academy boys are playing the University of Arizona team.

"It is a great occasion. Many people come tonight who have never been

before. Some of the townsmen say basketball is a girl's game, but nevertheless they come in large numbers tonight. Our court is not quite regulation. We are used to it, our opponents are not. I have special luck with my shots tonight, the ball goes through the hoop again and again, and the game ends with our high school team the victors against the college team. I am the smallest player and the youngest on the team. I have piled up the most points through the efforts of the whole team in protecting me and feeding the ball to me. I am on the shoulders of the big fellows of the Academy. They are parading me around the hall to my consternation and embarrassment." (Spencer W. Kimball, *One Silent Sleepless Night*, p. 57.)

(26-9) President Kimball Selected a Wife with the Same Care That Characterized All His Important Choices

"How much a man's success depends upon his wife! Elder Kimball has been favored with a charming helpmate who has been constant, patient, full of understanding and encouragement. Her training in, and teaching of, home economics has enabled her to feed and clothe her family well, even though the income sometimes was small. Camilla is the daughter of Edward Christian Eyring and Caroline Romney. They had come to Arizona from Mexico in 1912 as a result of the Mexican revolution. It was in 1917 when she was teaching at the Gila Academy at Thatcher that she met Spencer, and it was not many months before their courtship ripened into marriage. It is said that transplanted flowers are usually the fairest and so it was in her case; the blue-eyed, golden-haired girl with the Spanish name, transplanted from

Andrew and Olive Kimball's family–Spencer W. on his mother's knee

Mexico, blossomed into glorious womanhood as an intelligent, well-trained woman, prominent in her own right. Her church activities are many. In a stake capacity she has served in the presidency of the Primary twelve years, in the presidency of the Mutual five years, and for eight years she was literary class leader in the Relief Society. In a ward capacity she served as literary leader of the Relief Society for eighteen years and at intervals has been a teacher in the Sunday School. She has also been active in civic affairs. . . . '' (Udall, ''Spencer W. Kimball,'' p. 591.)

''The family is the center of all that is important to President Kimball. President and Sister Kimball have

four children. They desired to have more, but that frail footpath of life over which spirits must cross into mortality is often beset with obstacles. It is sometimes very difficult and occasionally not possible to invite a spirit to cross it.'' (Boyd K. Packer, ''President Spencer W. Kimball: No Ordinary Man,'' *Ensign*, Mar. 1974, p. 7.)

There is much more to be told about the roots and branches of President Kimball. For instance, there were the many close calls with death—near drowning, accidents, extremely serious illnesses and operations. And there was the day he and his many brothers and sisters were called home to be told by their

bishop that their mother had died in far-away Salt Lake City, where their father had taken her for special care. And you could share the terror and helplessness of a night soon after when his youngest sister died in his brother's arms.

''There we were, eight of my mother's eleven . . . around the chair, frightened, and praying, and weeping. The doctor was miles away. His horse and buggy could not possibly have brought him there soon enough, and what could he do if he arrived?'' (Quoted by Olive Beth Kimball Mack, ''How a Daughter Sees Her Father, the Prophet,'' Address given at Salt

Lake Institute of Religion, 9 Apr. 1976, p. 4.)

You could also share his trip by railroad to Salt Lake City with his father via San Francisco, and all the other sad and joyous recollections of *One Silent Sleepless Night*. These things would have told you about preparation—preparation of a prophet, preparation by a diligent boy and a diligent man, preparation by a kind Heavenly Father who knew what the boy and the man would become.

And you would see a pattern of how you should respond to your experiences and opportunities.

"President Kimball once said, 'What mother, looking down with tenderness upon her chubby infant does not envision her child as the president of the Church or the leader of her nation! As he is nestled in her arms, she sees him a statesman, a leader, a prophet. Some dreams do come true! One mother gives us a Shakespeare, another a Michelangelo, and another an Abraham Lincoln, and still another a Joseph Smith.

" 'When theologians are reeling and stumbling, when lips are pretending and hearts are wandering, and people are "running to and fro, seeking the word of the Lord and cannot find it"—when clouds of error need dissipating and spiritual darkness needs penetrating and heavens need opening, a little infant is born.' (Conference address, April 4, 1960.)

"And so came Spencer Woolley Kimball. The Lord had managed those humble beginnings. He was not just preparing a businessman, nor a civic leader, nor a speaker, nor a poet, nor a musician, nor a

teacher—though he would be all of these. He was preparing a father, a patriarch for his family, an apostle and prophet, and a president for His church." (Packer, "President Spencer W. Kimball," p. 3.)

HIS LIFE WAS A PREPARATION FOR THE PURPOSES OF THE LORD

(26-10) President Kimball Learned to Do Things Correctly and Thoroughly as a Boy

"There is the harness shed. Pa is very meticulous with the harnesses. They must always be hanging up when not on the horses. The collars must be smooth and clean, the bridles fitting just right, the blinds in place. The harness must be washed with Ivory soap frequently and then oiled, and I learn another important lesson: the leather equipment must never be dry and hard and curled.

"There is the buggy shed. The surrey and the one-seated buggy must always be in shelter from storm and sun, and they must be clean. I learn to wash vehicles and grease them. In a little pocket on the right side of the building is the axle-grease can and dauber. I lift one side at a time to the wooden horse, remove the wheel, grease the axle carefully, replace the nut, and screw it on to keep it in place. The wagons must be similarly treated as often as needed. And they must be painted too. I learn while yet a very small boy how to buy and mix paint and apply it to body and wheels and framework. The hairline of trim paint must be applied with precision. The fences must all be whitewashed and the trellis painted green. The house, the big house, needs paint too, and I climb the high ladders and paint the gable ends of the house and the trim. Pa does most of it at first, then

I gradually come into the program until it is my task almost exclusively. And the barn and granary and harness shed—all must be painted at intervals. Even the mangers." (Kimball, *One Silent Sleepless Night*, p. 20.)

(26-11) As a Youth, He Determined That His Spiritual Life Would Not Be Choked Out by the Weeds of Complacency

"When I was a youngster, a stirring challenge came to me that moved me not a little. I cannot remember who issued the challenge nor under what circumstances it came. I remember only that it struck me like a 'bolt out of the blue heavens. The unknown voice postulated:

" 'The "Mormon Church" has stood its ground for the first two generations—but wait till the third and fourth and succeeding generations come along! The first generation fired with a new religion developed a great enthusiasm for it. Surrounded with bitterness, calumny of a hostile world, persecuted "from pillar to post," they were forced to huddle together for survival. There was good reason to expect they would live and die faithful to their espoused cause.

" 'The second generation came along born to enthusiasts, zealots, devotees. They were born to men and women who had developed great faith, were inured to hardships and sacrifices for their faith. They inherited from their parents and soaked up from religious homes the stuff of which the faithful are made. They had full reservoirs of strength and faith upon which to draw.

" 'But wait till the third and fourth generations come along,' said the cynical voice. 'The fire will have gone out—the devotion will have been diluted—the sacrifice will

have been nullified—the world will have hovered over them and surrounded them and eroded them—the faith will have been expended and the religious fervor leaked out.'

"That day I realized that I was a member of the third generation. That day I clenched my growing fists. I gritted my teeth and made a firm commitment to myself that here was one 'third generation' who would not fulfill that dire prediction." (Spencer W. Kimball in *CR*, Oct. 1969, pp. 18-19.)

(26-12) He Has Set the Example of the Necessary Purging Wrestle

"I believe the brethren were very kind to me in announcing my appointment when they did so that I might make the necessary adjustments in my business affairs, but perhaps they were more inspired to give me the time that I needed of a long period of purification, for in those long days and weeks I did a great deal of thinking and praying, and fasting and praying. There were conflicting thoughts that surged through my mind—seeming voices saying: 'You can't do the work. You are not worthy. You have not the ability'—and always finally came the triumphant thought: 'You must do the work assigned—you must make yourself able, worthy and qualified.' And the battle raged on.

"I remember reading that Jacob wrestled all night, 'until the breaking of the day,' for a blessing; and I want to tell you that for eighty-five nights I have gone through that experience, wrestling for a blessing. Eighty-five times, the breaking of the day has found me on my knees praying to the Lord to help me and strengthen me and make me equal to this great responsibility that has come to me." (Spencer W. Kimball in *CR*, Oct. 1943, pp. 15-16.)

(26-13) Communion with God Is Essential in the Task of Enduring to the End

"After his call to the Twelve he suffered a series of heart attacks. The doctors said that he must rest. He wanted to be with his beloved Indians. Brother Golden R. Buchanan took him to the camp of Brother and Sister Polacca, high in the pines of Arizona, and there he stayed during the weeks until his heart mended and his strength returned.

"One morning he was missing from camp. When he did not return for breakfast, Brother Polacca and other Indian friends began to search. They found him several miles from camp, sitting beneath a large pine tree with his Bible open to the last chapter of the Gospel of John. In answer to their worried looks, he said, 'Six years ago today I was called to be an Apostle of the Lord Jesus Christ. And I just wanted to spend the day with Him whose witness I am.' " (Packer, "President Spencer W. Kimball," p. 4.)

(26-14) A Sense of Humor Helps Get Him over the Rough Spots

"There was a long period of recuperation and preparation. The voice was all but gone, but a new one took its place. A quiet, persuasive, mellow voice, an acquired voice, an appealing voice, a voice that is loved by the Latter-day Saints.

"In the intervening time he could work. During interviews he tapped out on the typewriter answers to questions and spent his time at the office.

"Then came the test. Could he speak? Could he preach?

"He went back home for his maiden speech. He went back to *the* valley. Anyone close to him knows it is not *a* valley, it is *the* valley. There, in a conference of the St. Joseph Stake, accompanied by his beloved associate from Arizona, Elder Delbert L. Stapley, he stood at the pulpit.

" 'I have come back here,' he said, 'to be among my own people. In this valley I presided as stake president.' Perhaps he thought that should he fail, here he would be among those who loved him most and would understand.

"There was a great outpouring of love. The tension of this dramatic moment was broken when he continued, 'I must tell you what has happened to me. I went away to the East, and while there I fell among cutthroats. . . .' After that it didn't matter what he said. Elder Kimball was back!" (Packer, "President Spencer W. Kimball," p. 4.)

(26-15) The Adversary Attempted to Hold Him Back, but President Kimball Prevailed

"On two occasions, each time when he was on assignments to stake quarterly conference, and each time not related to problems incident to the conference, there was unleashed against him the very might of the adversary. He endured during those hours, not to be recorded here, something akin to what his grandfather had experienced when, as an Apostle of the Lord, he opened the work in England, something not unlike the Prophet Joseph experienced as he first knelt in the Grove.

"These trials have made him humbly dependent upon the power of the Lord. To pray with Spencer W. Kimball is an experience!" (Packer, "President Spencer W. Kimball," p. 5.)

(26-16) He Has Helped Countless People by Performing "Spiritual Surgery"

"President Kimball himself is an experienced surgeon of sorts. Not a doctor of medicine, but a doctor of spiritual well-being. Many a moral cancer has been excised, many a blemish of character has been removed, many a spiritual illness of one kind or another has been cured through his efforts. Some on the verge of spiritual oblivion have been rescued by him. He has written a book—literally years in preparation—*The Miracle of Forgiveness.* Many have been protected by the counsel he has written. Countless others have been inspired to set their lives in order and have experienced that miracle." (Packer, "President Spencer W. Kimball," p. 5.)

(26-17) He Loves and Serves Wherever He Can, Leaving No Room for Slothfulness or Neglect

" . . . he holds Arizona in a particular kind of affection—an affection that is mutual, as evidenced by an article which appeared in the *Oasis,* a publication of the Safford Rotary Club, in July 1943, when Spencer was leaving Arizona, after four and one half decades, to return to Salt Lake City:

" 'If there's one man that would be missed in any organization, it is Spencer Kimball, and this is more especially true of the Safford Rotary Club than any other. He's been so faithful and so "on the job" all the time, we often accept him as a fixture—like the president's gavel. Ponder the past of the club for a moment. Who'll be ready to play the piano on call? Who'll put on a program on short notice? Who'll direct community singing for our parties, and what good will a party be without Spencer to be master of ceremonies? . . . Regardless of his religion, every member of the club joins in wishing Spencer godspeed and success in his new work.' " (Richard L.

Evans, "Spencer W. Kimball of the Council of the Twelve," *Improvement Era,* Oct. 1954, p. 708.)

As you can see from the above items, President Kimball has paid the price to speak authoritatively about repentance and righteousness. You may not be able to duplicate his achievements in athletics, poetry, schooling, business, and all the rest; but you can do your best. And who knows what sleeping giant you may find within you? Listen to one who

Spencer Woolley Kimball

knows—whose knowledge is borne of a lifelong commitment—as he tells you how to purge your life of sin and also gives you the key to spiritual power.

PRESIDENT KIMBALL HAS CLEARLY DEFINED TRUE REPENTANCE AND HOW ONE OVERCOMES THE EFFECTS OF SIN IN ONE'S LIFE

(26-18) Repentance Is Not Escape from the Realities of Sin

"Sometimes it is easier to define what something is by telling what it is *not.*

"Repentance is *not* repetition of sin. It is *not* laughing at sin. It is *not* justification for sin. Repentance is *not* the hardening of the spiritual arteries. It is *not* the minimizing of the seriousness of the error. Repentance is *not* retirement from activity. It is *not* the closeting of sin to corrode and overburden the sinner." (Spencer W. Kimball, "What Is True Repentance?" *New Era,* May 1974, p. 4.)

(26-19) All the Steps of Repentance Must Be Performed

"True repentance is composed of many elements, each one related to the others.

"President Joseph F. Smith covered the matter well:

" 'True repentance is not only sorrow for sins and humble penitence and contrition before God, but it involves the necessity of turning away from them, a discontinuance of all evil practices and deeds, a thorough reformation of life, a vital change from evil to good, from vice to virtue, from darkness to light. Not only so, but to make restitution so far as is possible for all the wrongs that we have done, to pay our debts and restore to God and man their

rights, that which is due them from us. This is true repentance and the exercise of the will and all the powers of body and mind is demanded to complete this glorious work of repentance.' '' (Kimball, ''What Is True Repentance?'' p. 4.)

(26-20) Repentance Is Universal and Exacting in Its Demands

''True repentance must come to each individual. It cannot be accomplished by proxy. One can neither buy nor borrow nor traffic in it. There is no royal road to repentance: whether he be a president's son or a king's daughter, an emperor's prince or a lowly peasant, he must himself repent and his repentance must be personal and individual and humble.

''Whether he be lean or fat, handsome or ugly, tall or short, intellectual or less trained, he must change his own life in a real and humble repentance.

''There must be a consciousness of guilt. It cannot be brushed aside. It must be acknowledged and not rationalized away. It must be given its full importance. If it is 10,000 talents, it must not be rated at 100 pence; if it is a mile long, it must not be rated a rod or a yard; if it is a ton transgression, it must not be rated a pound.'' (Kimball, ''What Is True Repentance?'' pp. 4-5.)

(26-21) A Realistic Recognition of Guilt Will Bring Great Remorse

''Consciousness of guilt should bring one to his knees in humbleness with 'a broken heart and a contrite spirit' and in 'sack cloth and ashes.'

''There must be a pricking of conscience, perhaps sleepless hours, eyes that are wet, for Alma says:

'' ' . . . none but the truly penitent are saved.' (Al. 42:24.)

''Remorse and deep sorrow then are preliminary to repentance.

''There must not be rationalization to cover and hide. . . .

''This is important: do let yourself be troubled; let the tears flow; let your heart be chastened. Do not endeavor to excuse yourself in the least point because of your sin. Let the justice of God have full sway in your heart so that it will bring you to the dust in humility.

''There should be the element of shame. . . .

''If there is no pain and suffering for the errors, then there can be no repentance.

''The road to forgiveness is through repentance, and the road to repentance is through suffering, and that road must be kept open.

Spencer (standing, right) enjoyed athletics

Otherwise, the transgressions will invade and finally absorb again.'' (Kimball, ''What Is True Repentance?'' p. 5.)

(26-22) A Forgiving Spirit Is Necessary

''True repentance is to forgive all others. One cannot be forgiven so long as he holds grudges against others. He must be 'merciful unto [his] brethren; deal justly, judge righteously, and do good continually. . . . ' (Al. 41:14.)'' (Kimball, ''What Is True Repentance?'' p. 5.)

(26-23) Until the Change Is Permanent, the Soul Is Still in Jeopardy

''There must be an abandonment of the transgression. It must be genuine and consistent and

continuing. The Lord said in 1832: ' . . . go your ways and sin no more; but unto that soul who sinneth shall the former sins return, saith the Lord your God.' (D&C 82:7.)

"And a temporary, momentary change of life is not sufficient." (Kimball, "What Is True Repentance?" p. 5.)

(26-24) Sometimes Confession to and Punishment by the Church Is Necessary

"The true confession is not only a matter of making known certain developments but it is a matter of getting peace, which seemingly can come in no other way.

"Frequently people talk about time: How long before they can be forgiven? How soon may they go to the temple?

"Repentance is timeless. The evidence of repentance is transformation. We certainly must keep our values straight and our evaluations intact.

"Certainly we must realize that penalties for sin are not a sadistic desire on the part of the Lord, and that is why when people get deep in immorality or other comparable sins, there must be action by courts with proper jurisdiction. Many people cannot repent until they have suffered much. They cannot direct their thoughts into new clean channels. They cannot control their acts. They cannot plan their future properly until they have lost values that they did not seem to fully appreciate. Therefore, the Lord has prescribed excommunication, disfellowshipment, or probation, and this is in line with Alma's statement that there could be no repentance without suffering, and many people cannot suffer, having not come to a realization of their sin and a consciousness of their guilt.

"One form of punishment is deprivation, and so if one is not permitted to partake of the sacrament or to use his priesthood or to go to the temple or to preach or pray in any of the meetings, it constitutes a degree of embarrassment and deprivation and punishment. In fact, the principal punishment that the Church can deal is deprivation from privileges." (Kimball, "What Is True Repentance?" p. 7.)

(26-25) A Life of Action and Service Is a Form of Restitution

"True repentance must include restitution. There are sins for which restitution can be made, such as a theft, but then there are other sins that cannot yield to restitution, such as murder or adultery or incest. One of the requisites for repentance is the living of the commandments of the Lord. Perhaps few people realize that as an important element; though one may have abandoned a particular sin and even confessed it to his bishop, yet he is not repentant if he has not developed a life of action and service and righteousness, which the Lord has indicated to be very necessary: ' . . . He that repents and does the commandments of the Lord shall be forgiven.' " (Kimball, "What Is True Repentance?" p. 7.)

> If you have ever raised a garden you probably have noticed that the weeds tend to choke out the vegetables if there isn't much effort put forth to give the vegetables a proper start. But once the vegetables are well established, they tend to choke out the weeds. Our lives are a lot like that; there isn't much room for the sins if the garden of life is filled with those righteous pursuits which are called for in the advancement of the salvation of our families and neighbors.

(26-26) There Is a Relationship Between Obtaining Forgiveness and Bringing the Law of Forgiveness to Others

"In addition, a sound way to neutralize the effects of sin in one's life is to bring the light of the gospel to others who do not now enjoy it. This can mean working with both inactive members of the Church and nonmembers — perhaps more usually the latter. Note how the Lord has related the forgiveness of sins to the bearing of testimony respecting the latter-day work:

" 'For I will forgive you of your sins with this commandment — that you remain steadfast in your minds in solemnity and the spirit of prayer, *in bearing testimony to all the world* of those things which are communicated unto you.' (D&C 84:61. Italics added.) . . .

" 'Brethren, if any of you do err from the truth, and one convert him;

" 'Let him know, that he which converteth the sinner from the error of his way shall save a soul from death, and shall hide a multitude of sins.' (Jas. 5:19-20.)

"Every person who is beginning the long journey of emancipating himself from the thralldom of sin and evil will find comfort in the thought expressed by James. We could expand it somewhat and remind the transgressor that every testimony he bears, every prayer he offers, every sermon he preaches, every scripture he reads, every help he gives to stimulate and raise others — all these strengthen him and raise him to higher levels." (Spencer W. Kimball, *The Miracle of Forgiveness*, pp. 204-5.)

(26-27) Unlike Reformation, Repentance Should Not Be Approached in a Piecemeal Attitude

"In connection with repentance, the scriptures use the phrase, 'with all his heart' (see D&C 42:25). Obviously this rules out any reservations. Repentance must involve an all-out, total surrender to the program of the Lord. That transgressor is not fully repentant who neglects his tithing, misses his meetings, breaks the Sabbath, fails in his family prayers, does not sustain the authorities of the Church, breaks the Word of Wisdom, does not love the Lord nor his fellowmen. A reforming adulterer who drinks or curses is not repentant. The repenting burglar who has sex play is not ready for forgiveness. God cannot forgive unless the transgressor shows a true repentance which spreads to all areas of his life." (Kimball, *Miracle of Forgiveness*, p.203.)

PRESIDENT KIMBALL HAS IDENTIFIED THE SINS THAT THREATEN US THE MOST

All through the ages people in the fallen world have tended to reject the prophets of God and have set up false prophets of their own who would justify them in their sins. The Bible and the Book of Mormon contain histories of this fault even as it occurred in the nations of Israel. You may remember how Jesus upbraided the scribes and the Pharisees for honoring the dead prophets and rejecting the living prophets: " . . . ye build the tombs of the prophets, and garnish [decorate] the sepulchres of the righteous, And say, if we had been in the days of our fathers, we would not have been partakers with them in the blood of the prophets." (Matthew 23:29, 30.) Then he told them their impending murder of him was worse than anything their fathers had done; it would fill up the measure of their fathers. (See Matthew 23:32.)

The martyr Stephen accused the Jews of always rejecting the prophets. He said, "Which of the prophets have not your fathers persecuted? and they have slain them which shewed before of the coming of the Just One; of whom ye have been now the betrayers and murderers." (Acts 7:52.)

Samuel the Lamanite, as he stood on the wall under divine protection and delivered his accusing message to American Israel, included a similar indictment: " . . . if a prophet come among you and declareth unto you the word of the Lord, which testifieth of your sins and iniquities, ye are angry with him, and cast him out and seek all manner of ways to destroy him. . . . " (Helaman 13:26.) Samuel also pointed out how they gladly followed the "prophets" who told them to indulge themselves in their vices and to follow the evils of the world.

Do you know that each prophet is inspired to tell us what we need now—not yesterday or tomorrow, but now? not necessarily what we want, but what we need? How do you react to the messages of President Spencer W. Kimball and the rest of the prophets of our day? The following items represent some of the recurring themes of President Kimball's warning voice.

(26-28) President Kimball Has Warned Us to Love the Eternal Wealth

"I saw him [a man who had sought for worldly wealth] lying in his death among luxurious furnishings in a palatial home. His had been a vast estate. And I folded his arms upon his breast, and drew down the little curtains over his eyes. I spoke at his funeral, and I followed the cortege from the good piece of earth he had claimed to his grave, a tiny, oblong area the length of a tall man, the width of a heavy one.

"Yesterday I saw that same estate, yellow in grain, green in lucerne, white in cotton, seemingly unmindful of him who had claimed it. Oh, puny man, see the busy ant moving the sands of the sea." (Spencer W. Kimball in *CR*, Apr. 1968, p. 74.)

(26-29) He Has Visited the Ruins of Antiquity and Has Called Us to Turn Back from Following Their Occupants to the Same Fate

"Babylon is no more. Why? Because of unrighteousness— because of unrighteousness! We could continue for hours and tell the stories of Jerusalem, with its temple destroyed time after time; of Rome where we spent interesting days in the Coliseum, going through the noted arches, the underground passages, the catacombs, the great mansions, the bathhouses in which the Romans found their fate in debauchery. We could go back to Nineveh and Babylon. We could visit many places where the Jaredites and the Nephites dwelt, and every time, brothers and sisters, you would find that there was one path which lead them to destruction.

"It's the path of yielding to temptation—to desire—to the flesh. And there is only one path that can keep one from that peril and it is the straight and narrow path which few will find, but which leads to God." (Spencer W. Kimball in *Church News*, 28 Feb. 1951, pp. 4-5.)

(26-30) Only Murder and Denial of the Holy Ghost Are Greater Sins than Unchastity

"What is the greatest, the most abominable sin in the world which [comes] in the lives of people generally. It is the sin of adultery. It deprives them of that which is the most dear and precious thing above all things, chastity and virtue.

"I had a young couple come to me some years ago. They wanted to be married in the temple. They had been for six months prior to this time, unchaste—from the day of their engagement, unchaste. And when it was brought to their attention, (you'll hardly believe this) they said, 'Well, that isn't so wrong is it Brother Kimball?' That isn't so very wrong! That isn't so very wrong is it brother Kimball! Is it possible that any Latter-day Saint boy or girl can arrive at marriageable age and not know that this is the most abominable next to shedding of innocent blood, and the denying of the Holy Ghost, which latter few of us can do. How do we keep that way? How do we get that way?" (Kimball in *Church News,* 28 Feb. 1951, p. 5.)

(26-31) The Miracle of Forgiveness Is a Real Possibility

" . . . the Lord has given us a great promise. This is a gospel of repentance. It is the gospel of forgiveness, but forgiveness doesn't come easy. When one has gone down this wide lane to evil he must come back up the lane, climbing—and it's a hard, hard pull. The way of the transgressor is hard. But if one will fast enough, and pray enough, and weep enough and serve enough, he can come back." (Kimball in *Church News,* 28 Feb. 1951, p. 6.)

"No one knows all that Spencer Kimball does for people—not even Camilla, his wife—not even his brethren. No one knows the extent of the personal funds that he takes from his own pocket for the assistance of the needy, especially for his Lamanite brethren. No one knows of all the letters he writes, of all the meetings he holds, or of all the travel he does—driving, preaching, encouraging, counseling—never sparing himself.

"People in trouble flock to him, both the young and the old, with personal problems. He is early and late at the office. His home is a place where visitors from outside the city find hospitality and sustenance.

"He loves people; he loves sociability; he loves to sing, to play the piano; he loves the greatness of the out-of-doors, and the beautiful and finer things. He loves life—and lives it purposefully.

"He is a man of strength and dignity, of personableness and persuasion—and of faith. He believes that the impossible is possible with the help of God. He knows the profound importance of his calling, and devotes himself to it with a kind of dedication that is rare among men.

"And when Spencer Kimball has visited a stake, those who are responsible for its activities know that they have been visited and instructed and interviewed and taught with a thoroughness that they don't soon forget. And yet they also know that there has been in their presence a kindly and understanding man, a friend with a firm hand and a warm heart, with a lovable nature, an unaffected manner, and a kindly relieving humor. And they know that he has been there, not in the spirit of criticism, but in earnest exhortation, because of his love of God and his love of men.

"This is a rare man—Spencer Kimball—as approachable as a child, as wise as a father, as loving as a gentle brother. And he has not shunned any obligation that he was aware of—as a father, friend, and brother; or as a businessman, citizen, and civic servant—or as an Apostle of the Lord Jesus Christ." (Evans, "Spencer W. Kimball," p. 751.)

Now, knowing this man a little better, do you understand why he can challenge us to lengthen our stride, to purify our lives? Here is a man who can stand and, without flinching, quote the Lord's demand: "Why call ye me, Lord, Lord, and do not the things which I say?" (Luke 6:46.)

Spencer W. (L) as a missionary

CHAPTER 27

WHEN THE WORLD WILL BE CONVERTED

INTRODUCTION

Occasionally someone does something that is so timely and significant that it captures the attention and imagination of many. And in so doing he becomes famous or noteworthy and earns a special niche in history. Usually it is the sort of thing that causes people to ask, "Why didn't I think of that?" It seems so obvious and simple—after it has been announced. But only special people have these great insights.

So, Henry Ford put his "flivver" on an assembly line with vast repercussions for an industry and the future of labor. But that was insignificant when compared to the impact President Kimball's call for a renewed effort in missionary work will have on the world and the Church.

There was about a day and a half left in 1973 when Elder Ezra Taft Benson laid his hands on Elder Spencer W. Kimball's head and set him apart as president of the high priesthood of all the Church and gave him the right to exercise all the keys of the kingdom. In the next few months it became apparent that a much bigger spirit had inhabited President Kimball's body than even his many admirers had guessed. Perhaps his attitude about missionary work illustrated his dynamic leadership more than anything else he did. In April of 1974, he issued a charge and challenge to the Regional Representatives which was talked about for months thereafter. In October of 1974, the *Ensign* reprinted this address which was titled,

"When the World Will Be Converted." In this address President Kimball announced to the whole Church his convictions about missionary responsibility. A filmstrip of this address was prepared and presented in all of the stakes. In it President Kimball reiterated his simple and literal acceptance of the Lord's charge, "Go ye therefore, and teach all nations. . . . "(Matthew 28:19.) Since the Lord commanded it, this work must be done—NOW! That is the electrifying thing about President Kimball—most people plan to get on with it by and by; he means to get at it right now!

The reactions to this talk were interesting. They ranged from "I thought we had been doing pretty good," and "Maybe we aren't converting all that we could," to "Why haven't we looked at it this way before?"

To fully appreciate the position President Kimball has taken on missionary work, you would have to be familiar with the story of David and Goliath. To all the rest of Israel, Goliath was

invincible—anyone could see that. But to David, fear of Goliath was an insult to the God of Israel and to all the past prophets and to the faithful who crossed the Red Sea and came into the land that God had led them to. How could Goliath stand against one who came in the name of the Lord? (See 1 Samuel 17.)

This is the faith of President Kimball. It is foolish lack of faith in the God of Israel to approach the conversion of the world with half measures or to stand in fear and awe at the magnitude of the task. We must not content ourselves by gathering a few grains here and there when the Lord wants the whole field harvested. Do you have a similar kind of faith? The prophets have clearly promised that the world—spiritual Babylon—must be pulled down before the millennial era can begin. Without question this will involve great and disastrous judgments. War, anarchy, calamity, famine—all are listed as part of the coming judgments. Which of us, seeing a flood sweeping down on our neighbor's home, would not cry out a warning? How, then, can we not cry warning to those who are threatened with spiritual and temporal destruction?

Israel must be gathered, the Lamanites healed, the kingdom expanded, the world warned. Little wonder that the prophet calls on us to lengthen our stride, to lift our vision. Can you, like David of old, or President Kimball of our own day, see the possible outcome

through the eyes of faith? Ponder this question as you read the challenges given the Saints by Spencer W. Kimball.

THE WORLD IS DESPERATELY ILL

(27-1) The Lingering Malady of the World Can Be Cured Only by a Special Physician

"Our world is sick. Man, created perfect in the image and likeness of God, his Creator, is ill. He has a lingering and worsening malady. The world needs, oh how it needs, a mechanic. Man needs, oh how he needs, a physician.

"Such mechanics and health specialists need more faith and wisdom and love than the wrench and the hammer and the scalpel and the microscope.

"Yes. We frankly admit there are problems in our world. Serious problems, but they can be corrected and solved. There is a cure and it will cure it all." (Spencer W. Kimball, "The Gospel Solves Problems of the World," Address given at the BYU Ten-Stake Fireside, 26 Sept. 1971, pp. 5-6. The full text of this speech is in the appendix of the course manual for Rel. 130, *Sharing the Gospel*.)

(27-2) The World's Malady Centers in Man Himself

"We read in the papers and hear on TV constantly that the world 'is in an awful mess.' Not true! The world is still most beautiful. It is man who is off center. The sun still illumines the day and gives light and life to all things; the moon still brightens the night; oceans still feed the world and provide transportation; rivers still drain the land, and provide irrigation water to nourish crops. Even the ravages of time have not sloughed off the majesty of the mountains. Flowers still bloom and birds still sing, and

children still laugh and play. What is wrong with the world is man-made." (Spencer W. Kimball, *The Miracle of Forgiveness*, p. 300.)

GOD HAS CALLED PRESIDENT KIMBALL TO CONTINUE AND ACCELERATE THE DIVINE CURE

The quote above (item 27-2) was the next to the last paragraph in

Spencer W. Kimball as an Apostle

a chapter of the book cited in which President Kimball had pointed out how Church members create their own problems through bitterness and hate. He concludes the chapter with the following words:

"It can be done. Man can conquer self. Man can overcome. Man can forgive all

who have trespassed against him and go on to receive *peace* in this life and eternal life in the world to come." (Kimball, *Miracle of Forgiveness*, p. 300.)

These words epitomize both President Kimball and the gospel; they carry the message of hope, they tell what can be done. As you continue studying this chapter, note how President Kimball is always the optimist, the forgiver, the positive voice. He speaks harshly against sin—as do all who truly love—but he pleads continually for the sinful person to come to Christ, the divine healer. The gospel is the cure. The Church is the hospital, the convalescent ward, or the rehabilitation center. But it is more than these, because those who are truly and completely well can be found nowhere else.

The next few items are presented to help you obtain or enlarge your view of President Kimball as the one who has given prophetic leadership in administering the gospel care to a sick world.

(27-3) President Kimball Courageously Declares the Superiority of the Restored Gospel

"I was in Lima. A number of men of the press from the big newspapers circled me in the mission home. . . . And when most of them had made their notes and departed seemingly satisfied, one young upstart remained to question me. . . . He disdainfully asked why the 'Mormon' Church had not cured this world of poverty. Then I turned on him and said something like this:

"Sir! What is this you ask? Do you know where poverty is born, where it resides, where it is nourished? I have traveled over

your country considerably from coastline to highest mountain tops. . . . I have seen your mountain folk barely existing on primitive fare in squalid shacks, with limited food, with an absence from luxury. In your big city I see your mansions and palaces, but I also see your numerous homes of pasteboard, and tin cans, and store cartons and the emaciated bodies of your Indians from inland and upland. I have seen your cathedrals with altars of gold and silver and your beggars on the cold floors of such edifices, with their skinny arms extended and their bony hands cupped and raised to those who come to see or to worship. And you ask *me* about poverty. I have been through the Andes Mountains and wept for the Indians who are still persecuted and deprived and burdened and ignored. They are carrying their burdens on their backs, their commodities to market on their backs, their purchases on their backs. And when they come to your cities, I see them snubbed and ignored and unaccepted. . . . For four hundred years, as the Children of Israel were, they have been in veritable slavery. . . .

" . . . Have their morals improved, their superstitions decreased, their culture richened? Have their ideals heightened? Their ambitions stirred? Their production increased? Their faith enlarged? What have you done for them? How much better off are they today, in the Andes, than when you came four centuries ago? . . .

"He gathered up his papers and pencils.

"I deliberated:

"We have Indians, too—Indians who came from a desert hogan from near-starving conditions—and they are now, in one single generation,

well-dressed, well-educated, filling missions, getting degrees and drawing coveted salaries, filling important responsibilities in community and nation." (Kimball, "The Gospel Solves Problems," pp. 7-8.)

(27-4) He Will Not Let Personal Problems Stand in the Way of the Lord's Work

A lesser man would have let his age and many physical problems take their toll, but to President Kimball they were a preparation. Elder Boyd K. Packer described the effect of these trials in the following words:

"In all of this there has been a remarkable patience and absence of complaint. He has kept his discouragement to himself and would not miss an appointment.

"Those closely associated with him have seen that these problems have had some effect on his working habits, best characterized by a quote from one of the Twelve who said, 'Yes, President Kimball isn't himself. He's cut down from 18 to 17½ hours of work each day.' " ("President Spencer W. Kimball: No Ordinary Man," *Ensign*, Mar. 1974, p. 5.)

(27-5) Curing the World Involves Spreading the Gospel and Converting People to Christ

"If there were no converts, the Church would shrivel and die on the vine. But perhaps the greatest reason for missionary work is to give the world its chance to hear and accept the gospel. The scriptures are replete with commands and promises and calls and rewards for teaching the gospel. I use the word *command* deliberately for it seems to be an insistent directive from which we, singly and collectively, cannot escape." (Kimball, "When the World Will Be Converted," p. 4.)

(27-6) We Have an Obligation to Do Missionary Work

"A mission is not only a privilege and opportunity, but a solemn duty and obligation. My son, you are heavily obligated for the numerous blessings you enjoy, none of which you have provided yourself, like brains and faculties, sight, hearing. You are the recipient of accumulated 'blessings of the ages' and more particularly of the century. More than 140 years your people have suffered and sacrificed to bring our culture to its present height. Your faith and knowledge of truth are the result of missionary work of days gone by which you can repay only by giving to others the same opportunities. Hence, it is well for every worthy and prepared young man, as he grows up, to desire mightily to fill a mission." (Spencer W. Kimball, cited in Lowell Durham, Jr., and Melvin Leavitt, "President Kimball," *New Era*, Feb. 1974, p. 6.)

(27-7) The Obligation to Save the World Through Missionary Work Is an Unlimited Obligation

"What is the significance of the phrase 'uttermost part of the earth'? He had already covered the area known to the apostles. Was it the people in Judea? Or those in Samaria? Or the few millions in the Near East? Where were the 'uttermost parts of the earth'? Did he mean the millions in what is now America? Did he include the hundreds of thousands, or even millions, in Greece, Italy, around the Mediterranean, the inhabitants of central Europe? What did he mean? Or did he mean all the living people of all the world and those spirits assigned to this world to come in centuries ahead? Have we underestimated his language or its meaning? How can we be satisfied with 100,000 converts out of nearly four billion people in the world who need the gospel? . . .

"Certainly his sheep were not limited to the thousands about him and with whom he rubbed shoulders each day. A universal family! A universal command!" (Kimball, "When the World Will Be Converted," pp. 4-5.)

(27-8) Meeting This Worldwide Obligation Will Require a Great Effort in the Church

"The immensity of the work before us is emphasized as we consider the population of the world as it approaches the four billion mark.

"I am under no delusion, brethren, to think that this will be an easy matter without strain or that it can be done overnight, but I do have this faith that we can move forward and expand much faster than we now are. . . .

"When we have increased the missionaries from the organized areas of the Church to a number close to their potential, that is, every able and worthy boy in the Church on a mission; when every stake and mission abroad is furnishing enough missionaries for that country; when we have used our qualified men to help the apostles to open these new fields of labor; when we have used the satellite and related discoveries to their greatest potential and all of the media—the papers, magazines, television, radio—all in their greatest power; when we have organized numerous other stakes which will be springboards; when we have recovered from inactivity the numerous young men who are now unordained and unmissioned and unmarried; then, and not until then, shall we approach the insistence of our Lord and Master to go into all the world and preach the gospel to every creature." (Kimball, "When the World Will Be Converted," pp. 13-14.)

(27-9) President Kimball Truly Believes in the Ultimate Victory of the Gospel

"Now, we have the promise from the Lord that the evil one will never be able to frustrate totally the work that He has commanded us to do.

" 'This kingdom will continue to increase and to grow, to spread and to prosper more and more. Every time its enemies undertake to overthrow it, it will become more extensive and powerful; instead of decreasing it will continue to increase; it will spread the more, become more wonderful and conspicuous to the nations, until it fills the whole earth.' (President Brigham Young, April conference, 1852.)" (Cited in Kimball, "When the World Will Be Converted," p. 13.)

PRESIDENT KIMBALL HAS POINTED OUT THE WORLD'S NEED OF THE GOSPEL TO CURE ITS ILLS

(27-10) The Lord Knew Where Our Errors Would Take Us, and He Provided a Way Back

There seems to have come a too general acceptance of sin and error as the acceptable way of life. But all is not lost. The people could still change patterns and revolutionize the ways of the world and if that be too difficult, then as individuals we can transform our own individual lives and develop for our individual selves a saving and exalting program and this quite independent of others.

"Our Lord knew the weaknesses of mankind and where his errors would take him. The Lord has provided a cure for all ills in His Gospel program." (Kimball, "The Gospel Solves Problems," p. 3.)

(27-11) The Gospel Succeeds Where the "Medicine Man" of the World Fails

His interest for the welfare of the Lamanites began early

"When I was a little boy I remember the medicine man coming around periodically in his one-horse buggy. It was a kind of a hack, enclosed, and he sold patent medicines. He generally had special bottles—a dollar a bottle—which would cure all things: constipation, liver disorders, headache, backache, stomach ulcers, appendicitis, ingrown toenails, summer complaints, heart failure, and all the other things.

"As I grew up I came to realize that nothing he had in his supply could cure all things, but as I grew older and wiser, full of faith, and better informed, I came to know that there is a cure-all; and it reaches far beyond the heart and the liver and the stomach, and the lungs." (Kimball, "The Gospel Solves Problems," p. 6.)

(27-12) The World Has Been Using Cures That Won't Work

"Man tries to find the cures. He uses artificial means. He would stop war by sending no men to war. The Gospel would change men's concepts through love of fellowmen. The world would legislate goodness and make men fear to do wrong. The Gospel would cause men to do right because it makes them happy to do right.

"Man would limit the poor by birth control and abortion. The Gospel would limit the poor by better distribution of the wealth of the world which the Lord says is plenty, and that there is 'enough and to spare.' 'Man's ways are not always God's ways.'

"Man would place the immigration doors of Heaven under strict lock and key with mere men to hold the keys. The Gospel would provide for and take care of immigration and make a happy place for every infant immigrant. The world would give to women business careers with what they call freedom. The Gospel makes of them partners with God in creation and in rearing and training the spirits who have a right to earth life. . . .

"The Lord Jesus Christ came not with a sword, or jail keys, or legal powers. He came not with power of arms or ammunition, but with the law of persuasion. While he preached righteousness the world fought and sinned and died in their stench. The Gospel is to *all* but it is also to *each*. The big frustrated, corrupt and dying world can be cured but the only cure for it is applying the Gospel in our lives. Human nature must be changed and controlled." (Kimball, "The Gospel Solves Problems," p. 3.)

In his books and many sermons, President Kimball has pointed out that the gospel is a cure-all, not only in the sense that it provides a rebirth and complete change of life that begins to take away the weaknesses and false concepts of the carnal man, but it also gives specific remedies for specific ills.

What is the cure for war? A commitment to a Christlike life.

What is the cure for venereal disease? The law of chastity: "Thou shalt not commit adultery or anything like unto it."

What is the cure for broken homes and delinquent children? Great, overwhelming, natural love, as exemplified in family home evenings and other Church practices.

What is the cure for divorce? The law of forgiveness added to obedience to the laws of God and involvement in the programs of the Church.

What will solve economic problems? Such things as tithes and offerings, true charity, the welfare program, and provident living (managing money wisely, planting gardens, etc.).

What will save money as it improves health? The Word of Wisdom.

President Kimball has a unique way of pointing out all of these things and many more. Will you seek out his instructions and learn to defend the gospel as he defends it? Will you try to see that there is no other cure for the ills of the world? And if there is no other, and if you are really concerned about your fellow beings, where will you concentrate your time, talents, and means?

PRESIDENT KIMBALL GIVES INSPIRED AND LOVING LEADERSHIP TO THE HEALING OF THE REMNANTS OF JACOB

(27-13) President Kimball Was Born with a Love for the Indians

"I do not know when I began to love the children of Lehi. It may have come to me at birth, because those years preceding and after I was born, were spent by my father on missions among the Indians in Indian territory. He was president of the mission. This love may have come in those first years of my childhood, when my father used to sing the Indian chants to us children and show us souvenirs from and pictures of his Indian friends. . . .

. . . "We have about a half-million children of Lehi in the islands of the sea, and about sixty million of them in North and South America, about a third of them perhaps, being pure-blood Indians, and about two-thirds are mixtures but they have the blood of Jacob in their veins." (Spencer W. Kimball in *CR*, Apr. 1947, pp. 144-45.)

(27-14) His Patriarchal Blessing Foreshadowed His Leadership in Leading the Lamanites to Their Great Destiny

"It may have come from my patriarchal blessing which was given to me by Patriarch Samuel Claridge, when I was nine years of age. One line of the blessing reads:

" 'You will preach the gospel to many people, but more especially to the Lamanites, for the Lord will bless you with the gift of language and power to portray before that people, the gospel in great plainness. You will see them organized and be prepared to stand as the bulwark "round this people." ' " (Spencer W. Kimball in *CR*, Apr. 1947, p. 144.)

(27-15) President Kimball Has Called upon the Saints to Weep and Work for the Indians, Who Need the Gospel Desperately

"Someone said:

" 'If my pen might have the gift of tears I would write a book and call it "The Indian," and I would make the whole world weep.'

"I hope I may help to make the whole world weep for the children of Lehi. Can one refrain from tears as he contemplates the fall of these people who have been brought down from culture and achievement to illiteracy and degradation: from kings and emperors, to slavery and serfdom; from landowners of vast continents, to indigent wards of governments and peons—from sons of God with a knowledge of God, to rude savages, victims of superstition, and from builders of temples to dwellers in dirt hogans. . . .

"How I wish you could go with me through the Indian reservations and particularly Navajo Land and see the poverty, want, and wretchedness, and realize again that these are sons and daughters of God; that their miserable state is the result, not only of their centuries of wars and sins and godlessness, but is also attributable to us, their conquerors, who placed them on reservations with such limited resources and facilities, to starve and die of malnutrition and unsanitary conditions, while we become fat in the prosperity from the assets we took from them. Think of these things, my people, and then weep for the Indian, and with your tears, pray; then work for him. Only through us, the 'nursing fathers and mothers,' may they eventually enjoy a fulfilment of the many promises made to them. Assuming that we do our duty to them, the Indians and other sons of Lehi will yet rise in power and strength. The Lord will remember his covenant to them; his Church will be established among them; the Bible and other scriptures will be made available to them; they will enter into the holy temples for their endowments and do vicarious work; they will come to a knowledge of their fathers and to a perfect knowledge of their Redeemer Jesus Christ; they shall prosper in the land and will, with our help, build up a holy city, even the New Jerusalem, unto their God.

"Only in our doing all in our power to restore these people to their heritage can we even approach a justification for having taken their promised land." (Spencer W. Kimball in *CR*, Apr. 1947, pp. 145, 151-52.)

(27-16) He Can See the Encouraging Signs of Victory and the Promise of the Future

"This is a new day. There is a new groundswell. We now have Lamanite stake presidents, mission presidents, bishops, high councilors, branch presidents, presidents of auxiliary organizations, and even a General Authority of the Lamanites.

"Now we have numerous thousands of Lamanites. They want only opportunity, only the coming out of the dust.

First Presidency: N. Eldon Tanner, Spencer W. Kimball, Marion G. Romney

"Hear the Indian children singing 'I am a child of God,' and Indian boys who are working; an Indian group singing 'I am a Mormon boy. I might be envied by a king, for I am a Mormon boy.'

"The Lamanites have received a promise that 'Jacob shall flourish in the wilderness, and the Lamanites shall blossom as the rose.' (D&C 49:24.) They will be a nation in a day; the chief shall be converted; the Indians will be ready for redemption.

"Jacob is waiting for us to help him start to flourish. No rose ever blossomed until the root was planted. No nation can ever be born in a day, a month, a year, unless we who can will help them to plant the seed.

"Today the Indian who once walked silently with his head down

is now standing alert, with eyes to the light and confidence and dignity as he looks up." (Spencer W. Kimball, Address given at the Regional Representatives Seminar, 1 Apr. 1977, p. 12.)

"Colombia is said to be about the size of Texas, Arizona, and New Mexico combined. Bogota is 8,630 feet above sea level, and the work is going forward with great rapidity. The mission president there brought this to our attention: that when the plains of Bogota are all brought into cultivation, as they are in Texas, Louisiana, Utah, and the other states, that there is enough room there to have a church like we have in all of America.

"Can you envision ahead, when one country, Colombia, has its acres all cultivated, the mountains conquered, and there is a happy, loving people in that great country—and many other countries the same. We have hardly scratched the surface.

"When Brazil, Argentina, Peru, [and] Chile are peopled with Latter-day Saints in the same proportion, can you imagine what that will be like?" (Ibid., p. 4.)

The world will not be converted by the unconverted. It will be done by those who have courage and conviction like that of Alma, the sons of Mosiah, Paul, and Spencer W. Kimball. It will be done by men who fit the following standard described by President Joseph F. Smith, who himself boldly confessed that he was a "Mormon" while looking down a gun barrel and fully expecting to be shot.

"One of the highest qualities of all true leadership is a high standard of courage. When we speak of courage and leadership we are using terms that stand for

the quality of life by which men determine consciously the proper course to pursue and stand with fidelity to their convictions. There has never been a time in the Church when its leaders were not required to be courageous men; not alone courageous in the sense that they were able to meet physical dangers, but also in the sense that they were steadfast and true to a clear and upright conviction.

"Leaders of the Church, then, should be men not easily discouraged, not without hope, and not given to forebodings of all sorts of evils to come. Above all things the leaders of the people should never disseminate a spirit of gloom in the hearts of the people. If men standing in high places sometimes feel the weight and anxiety of momentous times, they should be all the firmer and all the more resolute in those convictions which come from a God-fearing conscience and pure lives. Men in their private lives should feel the necessity of extending encouragement to the people by their own hopeful and cheerful intercourse with them, as they do by their utterances in public places. It is a matter of the greatest importance that the people be educated to appreciate and cultivate the bright side of life rather than to permit its darkness and shadows to hover over them.

"In order to successfully overcome anxieties in reference to questions that require time for their solution, an absolute faith and confidence in God and in the triumph of his work are essential." (*Gospel Doctrine*, p. 155.)

Can you see how the courage of the great missionaries and leaders has been based on their

conviction that God is with us and we will triumph? One person might have his thoughts and expectations focused on the great economic and political calamities that appear certain to come and may govern his life in a pessimistic manner. But another person may go through the same period with courage and optimism and see only the blessings, the escape from disaster, and the great triumphs of the kingdom. And his *optimism and faith* will be vindicated.

How are you going to pass through the next few decades? Will you live with courage or fear? Will you live so that the great Nephite heroes and the presidents of the Church will be happy to meet you when the Lord calls you home? Will you elders accept the challenge of a mission? Will you sisters be sure you do not contribute to any failure of a boyfriend to go? Will you tell him he must go if he is to marry you? Will you help keep him clean and virtuous as President Kimball has so often challenged you?

EVERY MEMBER OF THE CHURCH MUST COURAGEOUSLY HELP ADMINISTER THE CURE TO THE SICK WORLD

(27-17) President Kimball Gives Full Energy to the Missionary Effort

"In 1975 my wife and I were with President and Sister Kimball in Bogota, Colombia. As we were in the airport for his departure, an airlines representative met with us. Upon being introduced to this fine young man, the prophet extended his hand with these words, 'Young man, I hope the next time I shake your hand you're a member of this

Meditating with the scriptures

church.' Without any hesitation, and with his eyes fixed firmly on those of the prophet, the man replied, 'Sir, so do I!' The President turned to the mission president and obtained a commitment from him to teach the man the gospel. Words President Kimball had spoken to missionaries in Bogota had been exemplified in deed: 'Give full energy and thought to the Lord's work—your lives will be rich because of it.' That day I saw how the prophet's full thought was centered on living the spirit of the calling, as well as carrying out the physical duties that are his." (Rex D. Pinegar in *CR*, Oct. 1976, p. 103.)

(27-18) President Kimball Has Called for Better-Prepared Missionaries

"When I ask for more missionaries, I am not asking for more testimony-barren or unworthy missionaries. I am asking that we start earlier and train our missionaries better in every branch and every ward in the world. That is another challenge—that the young people will understand that it is a great privilege to go on a mission and that they must be physically well, mentally well, spiritually well, and that 'the Lord cannot look upon sin with the least degree of allowance.'

"I am asking for missionaries who have been carefully indoctrinated and trained through the family and the organizations of the Church, and who come to the mission with a great desire. I am asking . . . that we train prospective missionaries much better, much earlier, much longer, so that each anticipates his mission with great joy." (Kimball, "When the World Will Be Converted," p. 4.)

(27-19) The Lord Gave Us Our Voices So We Can Raise Them Up Voluntarily in Promulgation of the Gospel

"While in Argentina in 1975 at the area conference, President Kimball spoke to a large gathering of youth. Shortly after he began, he set aside his prepared text and shared a personal experience with them. He asked them, 'Who gave you your voice?' He then told them about his experience with surgery to save his voice. He explained that the Lord had spared his voice. He said it wasn't the same voice he had once had. He couldn't sing as he had previously enjoyed doing, but he did have a voice. He said his voice wasn't a pretty one, but I tell you it was beautiful in what it taught that night. As he spoke the youth

responded even before the translator could interpret his words. He told those present, 'Serving a mission is like paying tithing; you're not compelled—you do it because it's right. We want to go on missions because it's the Lord's way. The Savior didn't say, "*If* it's convenient, go," he said, "*Go* ye into all the world." ' (Mark 16:15.) President Kimball explained that it was the responsibility of young women to help young men remain worthy and to encourage them to go on missions.

"As the President concluded his remarks he asked, 'Didn't the Lord give you your voice so you could teach the gospel?' He then testified that he had come to know that his voice and our voices are for the declaring of the gospel of Jesus Christ and for testifying of the truths revealed to the Prophet Joseph Smith. President Kimball teaches us the correct perspective of life." (Rex D. Pinegar in *CR*, Oct. 1976, p. 103.)

As you conclude this brief portrayal of some of the experiences, attitudes, and teachings of President Spencer W. Kimball, have you examined your own life to see how much more you could do if you were motivated as he has been motivated? What qualities does he possess that account for prodigious production? One beloved neighbor had this to say

when Elder Kimball was called to the Council of the Twelve:

"President Kimball possesses so many qualities which fit him for church leadership that it is difficult to point out particular traits and say therein lies his success. Two of his outstanding characteristics are, first, his love for people, a love which begets love; people warm to his teachings; his dealings instil confidence; the well-to-do farmer or the humble laborer, the housewife or the adolescent boy or girl, all have confidence in his integrity; and second, his relentless attention to the duties of the day. The great English philosopher, Francis Bacon, once said, 'When the soul resolves to perform every duty immediately, it is conscious of the presence of God.' A kindred idea was expressed by the great American statesman, Daniel Webster: 'The greatest thought that ever entered my mind is that of individual responsibility to God.' The new apostle has lived his life in such a manner that it would appear that he is in the presence of God at all times, and that not for one moment of his busy life has he forgotten his responsibility to his Creator." (Jesse A. Udall, "Spencer W. Kimball, the Apostle from Arizona," *Improvement Era*, Oct. 1943, p. 639.)

Would it not be safe to say that the relentless attention to the duties of the day arise out of love? What makes a wife help her husband serve God? What makes a husband labor to support his wife and children? What motivates children to be obedient? Is not charity (the pure love of Christ) all that endures? Is there any measure of charity that does not involve service? Is not faith too measured by service? If so, who can measure Spencer W. Kimball's faith and love? Only by following the example he follows, that of our Savior, will you fully know Spencer W. Kimball.

God's "voice" to the world

UNIT FOURTEEN

ZION SHALL YET ARISE

OVERVIEW

The Lord revealed to Enoch "all things, even unto the end of the world,"[1] and by the Spirit of God Moses beheld every particle of the earth and all the inhabitants of the earth, "numberless as the sand upon the sea shore."[2] The brother of Jared was shown all things, "even unto the ends of the earth."[3] Similar visions were shown to Joseph Smith. By revelation, he saw the powers of darkness and the awful consequences of disobedience. He saw the future and was instructed as to the majesty and glory of events that would transpire in the last days.

Joseph Smith saw the organization and pattern of the Lord's church in heaven. He apparently comprehended in great detail the structure of the Church as it would eventually be developed. But although he seemed to be familiar with the total pattern of Church organization, the revelation and direction to organize the whole structure did not come to him all at once, but, rather, a little at a time, piecemeal. The Lord revealed line upon line. And because of his acquaintance with the divine pattern, Joseph Smith was able to fit and fashion every particle of the revealed organization into the structure of the whole.

But although Joseph Smith was inspired by his views of the eternal glory and size of the Church, and of the way things would ultimately be, it was not his lot to remain on the earth until the Church was completely developed and operating fully as God intended that it eventually must. He spoke of his ministry as being "in these infant days of the Church."[4] He laid the foundation for others to build upon. Sustained by his assurance that the Church would one day stand as a mighty oak, he planted the tiny seed and nourished it awhile, but then left it in the care of his successors.

Brigham Young said: "The kingdom is organized; and, although as yet no bigger than a grain of mustard seed, the little plant is in a flourishing condition, and our prospects brighter than ever."[5] Later in his ministry, President Young

declared: "What may we expect to grow out of this infant kingdom? We may look forward to all that belongs to greatness and goodness, to might and power, to dominion and glory. Then how jealously we ought to guard the rights of this infant power! How zealous and constant we should be in maintaining its interest and supporting its laws and sacred institutions!"[6] In 1900 President Lorenzo Snow described the Church as being "pretty well along to manhood,"[7] and just a few years later President Joseph F. Smith described the growing process of the Church: "We have passed through the stages of infancy and of irresponsible childhood, and are indeed approaching the condition of manhood and womanhood in our experience in the Gospel of Jesus Christ. . . ."[8] When the Church had been restored for 141 years, President Joseph Fielding Smith was inspired to tell the Saints at the British Area General Conference, "Now we are coming of age as a Church and as a people. We have attained the stature and strength that are enabling us to fulfill the commission given us by the Lord through the Prophet Joseph Smith that we should carry the glad tidings of the restoration to every nation and to all people. And not only shall we preach the gospel in every nation before the second coming of the Son of Man, but we shall make converts and establish congregations of Saints among them."[9]

Maturity brings greater capacity to respond to greater responsiblity. The Lord would expect more of his church after it had passed from infancy to manhood. Indeed, as President Spencer W. Kimball has challenged: "I wonder if we are doing all we can. . . . Are we prepared to lengthen our stride? To enlarge our vision? . . . I think we must change our sights and raise our goals."[10]

Joseph Smith, and those holy and noble souls who were associated under his direction, struggled mightily and endured valiantly to establish the infant Church generations ago. Satan raged, opposition mounted, and nations and people consented to the

martyrdom of the Prophet and Patriarch. Those who succeeded Joseph and his associates labored earnestly to plant branches here and there throughout America and Europe, to set them in order and, as the hatred of the world became intense against them, to assist them to gather to the settlements of the Great Basin. Isaiah had foretold: "Come, my people, enter thou into thy chambers, and shut thy doors about thee: hide thyself as it were for a little moment, until the indignation be overpast."[11] The infant Church did hide, and when the indignation was softened a little and the attention of the race of man was drawn to the banks of the Rhine and to war, and to famine and to science and to all the rest, the little kingdom began to sally forth again. Congregations were raised again throughout America and then Europe. South America, Australia, New Zealand, the islands of the sea, and then Asia and Africa and the Middle East—branches were established, and stakes were organized; Saints were gathered into stakes throughout the earth. Peace and a spirit of refuge settled over the homes and cities of this Church throughout the earth. Fathers, mothers, and children were bound together by baptism, priesthood, and faithfulness. "A cloud and smoke by day and the shining of a flaming fire by night" shall rest upon these homes, these holy places of God's people, "for upon all the glory of Zion shall be a defense."[12] To these hosts of men and women in the stakes of Zion throughout the earth, to these thousands and hundreds of thousands, the Lord commands: "Arise and shine forth, that thy light may be a standard for the nations."[13] Now go to, spread the vision of this kingdom into every ready, receiving heart. Join in the labor until "the earth shall be full of the knowledge of the Lord, as the waters cover the sea,"[14] for "the truth of God will go forth boldly, nobly, and independent, till it has penetrated every continent, visited every clime, swept every country, and sounded in every ear, till the purposes of God shall be accomplished, and the Great Jehovah shall say the work is done."[15]

CHAPTER 28
PUT ON THY STRENGTH O ZION

INTRODUCTION

And so you've come to the end of this study of the presidents of the Church. These are the men whom the Lord "inspired to move the cause of Zion in mighty power for good." (D&C 21:7.) Under their inspired direction, we have seen the kingdom grow from a tiny group of Saints in New York state to a worldwide kingdom operating in scores of countries and speaking many languages. The world has raged, defamed, persecuted, and even martyred in an attempt to stop the stone from rolling forth. But still it rolls, swelling with increasing rapidity under the guidance and direction of living prophets, seers, and revelators; and as Daniel foretold, this stone shall become a great mountain and it shall fill the whole earth. (See Daniel 2:35.)

Were it not for our knowledge of these things, it would be an easy thing to grow discouraged and even frightened as we view the growing evil and deterioration around us. Even the scriptures paint a grim picture of what the future holds for a world that has forsaken God. We read of hailstorms destroying the crops of the earth (D&C 29:16), a time when men shall take up the sword against their neighbors (D&C 45:33), of earthquakes, tempests, famine, and pestilence (D&C 43:25), of warfare so vast that the spoils of battle take seven years to burn (Ezekiel 39:9), of death tolls so vast that permanent burial teams are hired to cleanse the land of the bodies (Ezekiel 39:11-16), of the sun being

darkened and the moon turning to blood (D&C 88:87).

Nor does current news ease our concern as we read of wars hot and cold, of assassinations, terrorism, atrocities, organized crime, political repression, and a thousand other bits of gloomy proof that the world is sick. And yet did you sense something as you read and studied the lives of the prophets? Did you find any sense of gloom or despair in these men? Or was it the opposite? Notice the following sampling of what these men have said about the future:

Heber J. Grant

"While the world is in a state of commotion and there is perplexity among the nations, the Latter-day Saints have no fears for the future. The signs of the times indicate the near approach of the coming of the Lord, and the work that we are engaged in is a preparatory one for that great event." (*CR*, Oct. 1930, p. 5.)

John Taylor

"We are, as the French would say, *enrapport*, with God; that is in communication with God. . . . And while nations shall crumble and thrones be cast down, and the God of heaven arise and shake terribly the earth, while the elements melt with fervent heat in fulfillment of ancient as well as modern prophecy; while these things are going on he will whisper, peace to Zion." (*JD*, 21:100.)

Joseph F. Smith

"You do not need to worry in the least, the Lord will take care of you and bless you. He will also take care of His servants, and will bless them and help them to accomplish His purposes; and all the powers of darkness combined in earth and in hell cannot prevent it. They may take men's lives; they may slay and destroy, if they will; but they cannot destroy the purposes of God, nor stop the progress of His work. He has stretched forth His hand to accomplish His purposes, and the arm of flesh cannot stay it. He will cut His work short in righteousness, and will hasten His purposes in His own time. It is only necessary for us to try with our might to keep peace with the onward progress of the work of the Lord, then God will preserve and protect us, and will prepare the way before us, that we shall live and multiply and replenish the earth and always do His will; which may God grant. . . ." (*CR* Oct. 1905, pp. 5-6.)

As you remember, we began our course of study with a brief introduction to the prophets and patriarchs of all ages and how they had hoped for, longed for, and sought for the day when Zion would prevail and cover the earth. This is why you find

no despair in these men, these prophets who moved the cause of Zion forward. Why should we despair when we also foresee and have the commission and power to bring again Zion—a land of peace, a city of refuge, a place of safety for the Saints (D&C 45:66), a time when peace and prosperity shall reign among all the creations of God (Isaiah 65:21-25), a time when the people of the first Zion shall fall on the necks of the people of the last Zion and rejoice together (Moses 7:63), a time when the great and abominable kingdom of Satan shall destroy itself and Satan shall be bound and have power to tempt no man (D&C 88:94, 110; 101:28).

As you finish your study of the men God has called in this last dispensation to bring this great state of existence into being, we would like to lift your sights and help you get a glimpse of what they have seen and what motivated them on to greatness.

THE PROPHETS AS SEERS HAVE SEEN THE GLORY OF ZION AND HAVE LONGED FOR IT

(28-1) The Souls of Ancient Patriarchs and Prophets Were Fired by the Contemplation of the Glory of the Zion to Be Realized in the Last Days

In the introductory unit to this course, there was quoted from the writings of Joseph Smith a statement which bears repeating here.

"The building up of Zion is a cause that has interested the people of God in every age; it is a theme upon which prophets, priests and kings have dwelt with peculiar delight; they have looked forward with joyful anticipation to the day in which we live; and fired with heavenly and joyful anticipations they have sung and written and prophesied of this our day; but they died without the sight; we are the favored people that God has made choice of to bring about the Latter-day glory; it is left for us to see, participate in and help to roll forward the Latter-day glory, 'the dispensation of the fulness of times, when God will gather together all things that are in heaven, and all things that are upon the earth,' 'even in one,' when the Saints of God will be gathered in one from every nation, and kindred, and people, and tongue, when the Jews will be gathered together into one, the wicked will also be gathered together to be destroyed, as spoken of by the prophets; the Spirit of God will also dwell with His people, and be withdrawn from the rest of the nations, and all things whether in heaven or on earth will be in one, even in Christ. The heavenly Priesthood will unite with the earthly, to bring about those great purposes; and whilst we are thus united in one common cause, to roll forth the kingdom of God, the heavenly Priesthood are not idle spectators, the Spirit of God will be showered down from above, and it will dwell in our midst. The blessings of the Most High will rest upon our tabernacles, and our name will be handed down to future ages; our children will rise up and call us blessed; and generations yet unborn will dwell with peculiar delight upon the scenes that we have passed through, the privations that we have endured; the untiring zeal that we have manifested; the all but insurmountable difficulties that we have overcome in laying the foundation of a work that brought about the glory and blessing which they will realize; a work that God and angels have contemplated with delight for generations past; that fired the souls of the ancient patriarchs and prophets; a work that is destined to bring about the destruction of the powers of darkness, the renovation of the earth, the glory of God, and the salvation of the human family." (*Teachings of the Prophet Joseph Smith,* pp. 231-32.)

(28-2) Generations of Rightous Saints Have Looked with Longing for the Blessing of Zion but Could Not Find It Because of Wickedness

"Holy men of old were looking for Zion and hoping for the dawn of the day of that universal brotherhood, but in vain; they found it not; only wickedness and abominations. They looked for liberty, and found oppression; for brotherly love, and found selfishness; for happiness in righteousness, and found misery. The government of heaven was not on Earth, and, consequently, they felt that they were only 'strangers,' and 'pilgrims' on Earth, 'declaring plainly that they seek a country,' (Heb. 11:14)—a land in which the Lord is the Ruler, and in which they would not be 'strangers' or aliens. Abraham was a stranger in Palestine, though the land was his by promise. The saints are strangers in the world, until the reign of their Lord and Redeemer is established, though the promise is that they shall inherit the Earth." (Hyrum M. Smith and Janne M. Sjodahl, *The Doctrine and Covenants Commentary,* p. 255.)

(28-3) Prophets of This Final Dispensation Have Prayed and Wept in Their Great Desire for Zion to Come Forth in Majesty and Glory

Joseph Smith said:

" . . . I feel to cry mightily unto the Lord that all things which have happened may work together for

Israel is being gathered from the world

good; yea, I feel to say, O Lord, let Zion be comforted, let her waste places be built up and established an hundred fold; let Thy Saints come unto Zion out of every nation; let her be exalted to the third heavens, and let Thy judgment be sent forth unto victory; and after this great tribulation, let Thy blessing fall upon Thy people, and let Thy handmaid live till her soul shall be satisfied in beholding the glory of Zion; for notwithstanding her present affliction, she shall yet arise and put on her beautiful garments, and be the joy and glory of the whole earth." (*Teachings,* p. 27.)

Brigham Young stated:

"We pray continually for the redemption of Zion, for the Lord to hasten the time when we can return and establish the centre Stake of Zion, and build up the great temple of the Lord upon which his glory will rest as a cloud by day, and a pillar of fire by night. We pray that we may be sanctified, that we may be made pure in heart; and we pray that the Lord will teach us his will continually, and reveal unto us precisely his mind, so that we may have the mind of Christ, and know precisely what to do." (*JD*, 9:137.)

ZION SHALL ARISE AND PUT ON HER GARMENTS DURING THIS, THE FINAL DISPENSATION

(28-4) The Greatest Object of Each Latter-day Saint Ought to Be the Building Up of Zion

"We ought to have the building up of Zion as our greatest object. When wars come, we shall have to flee to Zion. The cry is to make haste. The last revelation says, Ye shall not have time to have gone over the earth, until these things come. It will come as did the cholera, war, fires, and

earthquakes; one pestilence after another, until the Ancient of Days comes, then judgment will be given to the Saints. . . . The time is soon coming, when no man will have any peace but in Zion and her stakes.

"I saw men hunting the lives of their own sons, and brother murdering brother, women killing their own daughters, and daughters seeking the lives of their mothers. I saw armies arrayed against armies. I saw blood, desolation, fires. The Son of Man has said that the mother shall be against the daughter, and the daughter against the mother. These things are at our doors." (Smith, *Teachings*, pp. 160-61.)

(28-5) If We Do Not Gather the Saints Out of the World, They Will Be in Great Danger

" . . . without Zion, and a place of deliverance, we must fall; because the time is near when the sun will be darkened, and the moon turn to blood, and the stars fall from heaven, and the earth reel to and fro. Then, if this is the case, and if we are not sanctified and gathered to the places God has appointed, with all our former professions and our great love for the Bible, we must fall; we cannot stand; we cannot be saved; for God will gather out his Saints from the Gentiles, and then comes desolation and destruction, and none can escape except the pure in heart who are gathered." (Smith, *Teachings*, p. 71.)

(28-6) The Place Where the Holy City, the Center Place of Zion, Is to Be Built Has Been Designated by Revelation

"I received, by a heavenly vision, a commandment . . . [to] designate the very spot which was to be the central place for the commencement of the gathering together of those who embrace the

fullness of the everlasting Gospel. . . . after viewing the country [around Jackson County, Missouri], seeking diligently at the hand of God, He manifested Himself unto us, and designated, to me and others, the very spot upon which he designed to commence the work of the gathering, and the upbuilding of an 'holy city,' which should be called Zion—Zion, because it is a place of righteousness, and all who build thereon are to worship the true and living God, and all believe in one doctrine, even the doctrine of our Lord and Savior Jesus Christ. 'Thy watchmen shall lift up the voice; with the voice together shall they sing: for they shall see eye to eye when the Lord shall bring again Zion' (Isaiah lii:8)." (Smith, *Teachings*, pp. 79-80.)

(28-7) The City of Zion Will Be an Eternal City Never to Be Destroyed Nor Overcome

"God intends to have a city built up that will never be destroyed nor overcome, but that will exist while eternity shall endure; and he will point out the pattern and show the order of architecture; he will show unto his servants the nature of the streets and the pavement thereof,

the kind of precious stones that shall enter into the buildings, the nature of the rock and precious stones that will adorn the gates and the walls of that city; for the gates will be open continually says the Prophet Isaiah, that men may bring in the force of the Gentiles. . . .

" . . . Suffice it to say that God by revelation will inspire his servants and will dictate to them the order of the buildings of that city—the number and width of the streets, the kind of houses, the character of the Temple that is to be built therein, the kind of rock, timber and the various materials that will have to be brought from a distance to enter into the composition of that beautiful city." (Orson Pratt in *JD*, 15:365.)

(28-8) Those Living in the Holy City and the Stakes of Zion Will Be Sanctified to the Point Where They Can Behold the Lord

" . . . all of them who are pure in heart will behold the face of the Lord and that too before he comes in his glory in the clouds of heaven, for he will suddenly come to his Temple, and he will purify the sons of Moses and of Aaron, until they shall be prepared to offer in that

Temple site at Jackson County, Missouri

Temple an offering that shall be acceptable in the sight of the Lord. In doing this, he will purify not only the minds of the Priesthood in that Temple, but he will purify their bodies until they shall be quickened, renewed and strengthened, and they will be partially changed, not to immortality, but changed in part that they can be filled with the power of God, and they can stand in the presence of Jesus, and behold his face in the midst of that Temple." (Orson Pratt in *JD*, 15:365-66.)

(28-9) The Savior Will Not Come in Glory Until Zion Is Built Up and Prepared to Receive Him

"*Behold the Bridegroom cometh.* GO YE OUT TO MEET HIM! The 'wise virgins' are awaking; their lamps are trimmed; they walk not in the dark, but, with 'a light to their feet and a lamp to their path,' they are hastening to the place appointed; for it is written, 'The Redeemer shall come to Zion.'

"The time is close at hand.
. . . God will cut his work short in righteousness. The day and hour are not revealed; but 'when the Lord hath built up Zion, then will he appear in his glory.' " (Charles W. Penrose, cited in Roy W. Doxey, *Zion in the Last Days*, p. 81.)

Pause now to consider the importance of the following scriptures in connection with what you have read.

First read Moses 7:17-21.

1. Is Zion a place or a condition? (vs. 17, 18)

2. What constitutes Zion? (vs. 18)

3. Ultimately, what does Zion, and only Zion, become? (vs. 21)

4. What is the earth destined to become? (D&C 88:17, 25, 26)

5. What vision of President Kimball's is revealed in his talk "When the World Will Be Converted"? (See *Ensign,* Oct. 1974, pp. 2-14.)

Now turn to Matthew 5:8.

1. Who are the only people that can see God?

2. Then what kind of people must establish Zion?

To verify and expand your last answer, consider D&C 101:17-19.

Now read D&C 97:15-23.

1. Where will the pure in heart see God? (vs. 16)

2. What is Zion? (vs. 21)

For nearly 150 years the prophets have tried to lead the Saints to purity. Do you now understand why? How would you evaluate the Church's progress? Now comes the hard question, How are you doing? Take another moment and consider the implications of D&C 105:9-11, 37 in your life. How are you doing in each of the five areas noted in verses 10 and 39? Consider what the Lord is waiting for. Read verses 31 and

32. Are you willing to be pure, that you might become a member of that great army of peace?

BEFORE THE SECOND COMING OF THE LORD, ZION SHALL HAVE BEEN ESTABLISHED IN MAJESTY, DOMINION, AND POWER

(28-10) Zion Shall Be as a City Set upon a Hill

"This latter-day Zion is to be like a city set upon a high hill, and lighted with the glory of God: she will give light to all the surrounding nations. This will be, not only an intellectual, spiritual light, enlightening the mind, but a light that will be seen with the natural eyes: Hence Isaiah says, that 'the Lord will create upon every dwelling place of Mount Zion, and upon her assemblies, a cloud and smoke by day, and the shining of a flaming fire by night.' (Isaiah iv. 5.) That this literal manifestation of the glory of the Lord in a cloud, and smoke, and fire, is to take place while yet the wicked nations are on the earth, is evident from the following prediction of the same prophet—'Arise, shine; for thy light is come, and the glory of the

The New Jerusalem was seen by prophets of old

Lord is risen upon thee. For, behold, the darkness shall cover the earth, and gross darkness the people: but the Lord shall arise upon thee, and his glory shall be seen upon thee.' (Isaiah lx. 1, 2.) Thus, while darkness covers the earth, and gross darkness the people, the glory of the Lord will be literally seen in the form of a cloud and smoke by day, and a flaming fire by night, not merely upon the temple, but upon all the dwelling places of the city, and upon all her assemblies. . . .

"Such a scene as this the earth has never realized, but it must come to pass before the Savior appears." (Orson Pratt, *A Series of Pamphlets on the Doctrines of the Gospel,* pp. 257-58.)

(28-11) The Fame of Zion Shall Encompass the World and the Light of the Glory Affect the People

" . . . that true light which is of God, will be rendered visible to the eyes of all the inhabitants of that city. And shall I limit it there? No. The light will shine so conspicuously from that city, extending to the very heavens, that it will in reality be like unto a city set upon a hill that cannot be hid, and it will have quite a tendency to strike terror to all the nations of the earth. Will all see it? No, some may be too far off, beyond the ocean, to behold that miraculous light that will shine forth in this city, but I will tell you the effect it will have upon the kings, queens, rulers, congressmen and judges of the earth—they will hear of it by telegraph; the news will be flashed over the civilized nations of the earth, but they will not believe it. They will say, 'Let us cross the ocean, and let us see this thing that is reported to us by telegraph; let us see whether it is so or not.' Well, when they get within a day or two's journey of the city they will be alarmed. Some of these kings and

nobles, when they see the light shining forth like the northern lights in the arctic regions, illuminating the whole face of the heavens—when they see this light shining forth long before they reach the city, fear will take hold of them there, says the Psalmist, in the 48th Psalm, they will become weak, and their knees will smite together like the knees of Belshazzar. They will try to haste away from the glory of God and from the power of God, and to get out of the country as soon as possible. Fear and terror will be upon them. It will have an effect upon many other kings and nobles, more pure in heart, more honest, that are willing to receive the truth; it will have a different effect upon them. . . . " (Orson Pratt in *JD,* 24:29.)

(28-12) The Inhabitants of Zion Shall Excel in Wisdom, Knowledge, the Arts, and Science

"We believe that we shall rear splendid edifices, magnificent temples and beautiful cities that shall become the pride, praise and glory of the whole earth. We believe that this people will excel in literature, in science and the arts and in manufactures. In fact, there will be a concentration of wisdom, not only of the combined wisdom of the world as it now exists, but men will be inspired in regard to all these matters in a manner and to an extent that they have never been before, and we shall have eventually, when the Lord's purposes are carried out, the most magnificent buildings, the most pleasant and beautiful gardens, the richest and most costly clothing, and be the most healthy and the most intellectual people that will reside upon the earth. This is part and parcel of our faith. . . . " (John Taylor in *JD,* 10:147.)

"When Zion is established in her beauty and honour and glory, the

kings and princes of the earth will come, in order that they may get information and teach the same to their people. They will come as they came to learn the wisdom of Solomon." (John Taylor in *JD,* 6:169.)

(28-13) At the Commencement of the Millennium, the Zion of Enoch Will Unite with the Zion Established on the Earth

"You know in the days of Enoch the Lord placed the people upon the high places and mountains, and they flourished, and He blessed them, and called them Zion because there was no poor among them, and the Lord was in their midst.

"Now the Latter Day Zion is to be built up according to the same pattern, so far as circumstances will permit, for we expect that the Zion which was built up by Enoch, that had no poor in it, will come down again at the commencement of the Millennium to meet the Zion here, according to the song in the Book of Covenants, 'The Lord has brought up Zion from beneath, the Lord has brought down Zion from above,' and they shall gaze upon each other's countenances, and see eye to eye. . . .

"Let us prepare ourselves for the coming of Enoch's Zion, that we may have the same order of things among us that they had in the beginning. Then, again, it will be a glorious thing in many other respects." (Orson Pratt in *JD,* 2:103-4.)

ALL THE PROPHETS OF THIS DISPENSATION HAVE GUIDED THE CHURCH FORWARD IN LAYING THE FOUNDATION FOR THE ESTABLISHMENT OF ZION

(28-14) The Prophets Have Guided the Work of Gathering the Honest in Heart Out of Spiritual Babylon

Babylon and Zion are counter cultures. There can be no compromise between the two, for Zion must be holy, pure, unalloyed—it must be all Zion and nothing else. So, too, those who build Zion. They cannot be tainted with Babylon but, rather, must forsake and flee her. And so the cry has gone out, "Prepare ye, prepare ye, O my people; sanctify yourselves; gather ye together. . . .

"Go ye out of Babylon; gather ye out from among the nations. . . .

"Go ye forth unto the land of Zion, that the borders of my people may be enlarged, and that her stakes may be strengthened, and that Zion may go forth unto the regions round about." (D&C 133:4, 7, 9.) The prophets have continually sought to bring the pure, the honest, out of spiritual Babylon, that they might be sanctified and bring forth Zion.

(28-15) The Prophets Will Be Instructed by the Lord as to How and Where the Saints Will Be Gathered to Build Zion

" . . . the Lord has clearly placed the responsibility for directing the work of gathering in the hands of the leaders of the Church, to whom He will reveal His will where and when such gatherings would take place in the future. It would be well, before the frightening events concerning the fulfillment of all God's promises and predications are upon us, that the Saints in every land prepare themselves and look forward to the instruction that shall come to them from the First Presidency of this church as to where they shall be gathered. They should not be disturbed in their feelings until such instruction is given to them as it is revealed by the Lord to the proper authority." (Harold B. Lee, *Ye Are the Light of the World*, p. 167.)

"Unto every nation, and kindred, and tongue, and people"

THE RIGHTEOUS MUST HEED THE PROPHETIC CALL TO FLEE BABYLON AND GATHER TO THE STAKES IN PREPARATION FOR THE ESTABLISHMENT OF ZION

(28-16) The Term "Gathering" Refers Not Only to the Idea of Concentrating but Also of Coordinating

The dictionary lists a variety of meanings for the word *gather*, but generally just two meanings present themselves as probably more relevant than any others in understanding the use of the term as it applies to Zion: (1) "to bring together into a crowd, group, body, or mass, . . . concentrate, collect," and (2) "to summon up, muster together, . . . bring together and coordinate." (*Webster's Third New International Dictionary*, 1969 ed., s.v. "gather.") In summary, the two definitions are to concentrate and to coordinate.

Both of these definitions have been a part of the gathering policy of the Church. During the first few decades after the Restoration, the prophets stressed the need for concentration for the purpose of safety. However, the purpose was

also to coordinate the activities and resources of the Saints so that the work of the Church might advance more rapidly.

In the last few decades the emphasis has been on coordination. The Church is sufficiently strong under today's conditions that a concentration into one geographical location is not demanded at present. But with the rapid expansion of the Church, the idea of coordinating the resources, power, and strength of the Saints has received emphasis so that Zion might come forth in glory.

(28-17) Having Completed the Period of Preparation for Its Worldwide Mission, the Church Is Now Commanded to Build Up the Kingdom in Every Nation

"The Church of Jesus Christ of Latter-day Saints is a world church. The gospel is for all men everywhere. Every soul is precious in the Lord's sight. It is his will that all shall repent and serve him and be saved in his eternal kingdom.

"In the beginning days of this dispensation, of necessity, so that his Saints might be preserved and strengthened, the Lord gathered them to the American continent. The foundations were laid for the future world church.

"In the days of our fathers we were few in number and the Lord gathered us into selected areas to train us for our worldwide mission. That day of preparation is behind us. The command has now been given to go into all the world and build up the kingdom in every nation and among every people.

"In our day we are called to accept the gospel, to join with the Saints, and to remain in the nation of our natural inheritance. In our day we are called to build up the kingdom at the ends of the earth, so that the revelation shall be fulfilled which

says that when the Lord comes he will find 'the church of the Lamb of God . . . upon all the face of the earth.' In that day the number of the Saints will be 'few' as compared to the forces of evil, but they will, nonetheless, be established among all nations, kindreds, tongues, and people. (See 1 Nephi 14:11-12.)

"And you may rest assured that when these Saints are well established, as they will be, in all parts of the earth, they will be organized into stakes of Zion. These stakes will then be the gathering place for the righteous in the various nations." (Bruce R. McConkie in *CR, Stockholm Sweden Area Conference*, Aug. 1974, pp. 90-91.)

(28-18) The Gathering of Israel Consists in Coming to a Knowledge of the Truth and Joining the True Church, yet Remaining in One's Native Land

" 'Now I call your attention to the facts, set forth in these scriptures, that the gathering of Israel consists of joining the true church; of coming to a knowledge of the true God and of his saving truths; and of worshiping him in the congregations of the Saints in all nations and among all peoples. Please note that these revealed words speak of the *folds* of the Lord; of Israel being gathered to the lands of their inheritance; of Israel being *established in all their lands of promise;* and of there being congregations of the covenant people of the Lord in *every nation, speaking every tongue,* and *among every people* when the Lord comes again.'

"Elder McConkie then concluded with this statement, which certainly emphasizes the great need for the teaching and training of local leadership in order to build up the church within their own native countries:

" 'The place of gathering for the

Zion is to be established in every nation

Mexican Saints is in Mexico; the place of gathering for the Guatemalan Saints is in Guatemala; the place of gathering for the Brazilian Saints is in Brazil; and so it goes throughout the length and breadth of the whole earth. Japan is for the Japanese; Korea is for the Koreans; Australia is for the Australians; every nation is the gathering place for its own people.' " (Bruce R. McConkie, cited by Harold B. Lee in *CR*, Apr. 1973, pp. 6-7.)

(28-19) The Church Correlation Program Was Revealed to Facilitate the Gathering of Israel and the Establishment of Zion

"Priesthood correlation is the closest blueprint yet in mortality to the plan presented in the grand council of Heaven before the world was created, and is the most effective utilization thus far of the special keys given to the Prophet Joseph Smith in the Kirtland Temple. . . . *Priesthood correlation is to prepare for the second coming of Jesus Christ.*" (N. Eldon Tanner, remarks at Priesthood Genealogy Committee training session, Dec. 1963.)

GOD HAS FOREORDAINED THE DISPENSATION OF THE FULNESS OF TIMES TO REALIZE THE FULNESS OF THE GLORY OF ZION

(28-20) This Dispensation Shall Not Fail to Bring Forth Zion and Prepare a People for the Return of the Lord

"This is the only dispensation that God has ever established that was foreordained, before the world was made, not to be overcome by wicked men and devils." (Wilford Woodruff in *JD*, 17:245.)

Concerning this Brigham Young has said:

"The powers of earth and hell have striven to destroy this kingdom from the earth. The wicked have succeeded in doing so in former ages; but this kingdom they cannot destroy, because it is the last dispensation—because it is the fulness of times. It is the dispensation of all dispensations, and will excel in magnificence and glory every dispensation that has ever been committed to the children of men upon this earth. The Lord will bring again Zion,

redeem his Israel, plant his standard upon the earth, and establish the laws of his kingdom, and those laws will prevail." (*JD,* 8:36.)

Did the significance of what you just read strike you? This dispensation *will not fail!* Before going on, consider a profound fact revealed to the prophet Nephi. Read 1 Nephi 14:10. According to the revelation, what are the only two options open to a person in mortality? Could Nephi's statement be put another way—that there is either Zion or Babylon and one must choose between them? Which is the proper choice?

The answer may seem obvious, even elementary; but is it? You might liken the modern situation to a game in which two teams are pitted against each other in deadly struggle. Only one of the teams will win; the other will lose. You may choose either team on which to play. If you pick the losing team, you will forfeit eternal life. If you choose the winning team, you will gain eternal life. But the problem is that the members of the losing team do not all wear the same uniform. It appears that there are many teams. Your choice would be simple if they all wore black hats or signs saying "losing team." But they don't. And some uniforms are very appealing. Some of the uniforms even include "white hats" and appear to be like those of the winning team. How are you going to choose the winning team? What part will the prophet play in assisting you in your choice?

You may wish to consider one last point. God has decreed that Zion will triumph. This means that no matter what color the hat

or how nice the uniform, if you choose any team other than Zion you will lose it all in the end. Zion will win with you or without you, but win it will! If you want to be part of the winning team, the readings that follow will tell you what you must do. Consider them carefully.

(28-21) The Latter-day Saints Are the Pioneers Who Must Labor to Prepare the Way for Zion

"We talk and read about Zion, we contemplate upon it, and in our imaginations we reach forth to grasp something that is transcendant [*sic*] in heavenly beauty, excellency and glory. But while contemplating the future greatness of Zion, do we realize that we are the pioneers of that future greatness and glory? Do we realize that if we enjoy a Zion in time or in eternity, we must make it for ourselves? That all who have a Zion in the eternities of the gods organized, framed, consolidated, and perfected it themselves, and consequently are entitled to enjoy it." (Brigham Young in *JD,* 9:282.)

(28-22) Zion Must First Be Built Within the Heart, Then Must Radiate Out to Purify and Prepare the Earth

"Zion is here, it is in my heart—peace dwells with me and good principles will prevail there until all evil is overcome even in all the earth. . . . Now remember this, that we will have Zion when all wickedness is gone. We have got to fight, fight, fight until we gain a victory over ourselves." (Brigham Young, cited in *Journal of Wilford Woodruff,* 20 July 1851. Church Historical Library. Punctuation, capitalization, and spelling standardized.)

"Whenever we are disposed to give ourselves perfectly to

righteousness, to yield all the powers and faculties of the soul (which is the spirit and the body, and it is there where righteousness dwells); when we are swallowed up in the will of Him who has called us; when we enjoy the peace and the smiles of our Father in Heaven, the things of His Spirit, and all the blessings we are capacitated to receive and improve upon, then we are in Zion, *that is Zion.* . . .

" . . . I need not tell these things, but if every heart were set upon doing right, we then should have Zion here. I will give you my reason for thinking so. It is because I have had it with me ever since I was baptized into this kingdom. I have not been without it from that day to this. I have therefore a good reason for the assertion I have made. I live and walk in Zion every day, and so do thousands of others in this Church and kingdom, they carry Zion with them, they have one of their own, and it is increasing, growing, and spreading continually. Suppose it spreads from heart to heart, from neighborhood to neighborhood, from city to city, and from nation to nation, how long would it be before the earth would become revolutionized, and the wheat gathered from among the tares." (Brigham Young in *JD,* 1:3-4.)

(28-23) The Saints Are Responsible for Preparing Not Only Their Hearts, but Also Their Homes and Communities for the Glory of Zion

"When we conclude to make a Zion we will make it, and this work commences in the heart of each person. When the father of a family wishes to make a Zion in his own house, he must take the lead in this good work, which it is impossible for him to do unless he himself possesses the spirit of Zion. Before he can produce the work of sanctification in his family, he must

sanctify himself, and by this means God can help him to sanctify his family.

"There is not one thing wanting in all the works of God's hands to make a Zion upon the earth when the people conclude to make it. We can make a Zion of God on earth at our pleasure, upon the same principle that we can raise a field of wheat, or build and inhabit. There has been no time when the material has not been here from which to produce corn, wheat, etc., and by the judicious management and arrangement of this ever-existing material a Zion of God can always be built on the earth. . . .

"My spiritual enjoyment must be obtained by my own life, but it would add much to the comfort of the community, and to my happiness, as one with them, if every man and woman would live their religion, and enjoy the light and glory of the Gospel for themselves, be passive, humble and faithful; rejoice continually before the Lord, attend to the business they are called to do, and be sure never to do anything wrong.

"All would then be peace, joy, and tranquility, in our streets and in our houses. Litigation would cease, there would be no difficulties before the High Council and Bishop's Courts, and courts, turmoil, and strife would not be known.

"Then we would have Zion, for all would be pure in heart." (Brigham Young, *Discourses of Brigham Young*, pp. 118-19.)

(28-24) Through Constant Striving, the True Latter-day Saints Are Preparing to Establish Zion Even Faster Than Did Those of Enoch's Day

"The very man who walked and talked with and knew the God of

heaven, and knew and understood all about making this earth had associates who were associated with Enoch, and yet twenty-five years of the travel and experience of Enoch with his people had not advanced them so far, in my opinion, as this people have advanced in the same time, taking into account the difference of traditions and other advantages.

"They had not a diversity of languages, but all spoke one language; they were not trained in the various traditions in which we have been, for they received only one from Adam. . . .

"Yet Enoch had to talk with and teach his people during a period of three hundred and sixty years, before he could get them prepared to enter into their rest, and then he obtained power to translate himself and his people, with the region they inhabited, their houses, gardens, fields, cattle, and all their possessions." (Brigham Young in *JD*, 3:320.)

(28-25) The Knowledge That Zion Will Come Forth Should Sustain the Saints During Turbulent Times Such That They Are Not Troubled

"I hope we are all familiar with these words of the Lord and with his predictions concerning other coming events, such as the building of the new Jerusalem and the redemption of the old, the return of Enoch's Zion, and Christ's millennial reign.

"Not only do I hope that we are familiar with these coming events; I hope also that we keep the vision of them continually before our minds. This I do because upon a knowledge of them, and an assurance of their reality and a witness that each of us may have part therein, rests the efficacy of Christ's admonition, 'be not troubled.'

"It has always been faith in a lofty goal and confidence that it may be attained that have held people on the rugged course to high attainment. It was the assurance that they could obtain the land flowing with 'milk and honey' that held Moses to the task of leading Israel through the wilderness. It was faith that they could obtain the 'land choice above all others' (see I Ne. 2:20) that led Lehi and his colony through the desert and across the sea. It was the vision of Zion as it shall yet be that sustained the pioneers as they trudged across the plains. Paul says that even Jesus himself endured the cross 'for the joy that was set before him.' (Heb. 12:2.)" (Marion G. Romney in *CR*, Oct. 1966, p. 52.)

You have now concluded a course of study of the lives of the presidents of the church of Jesus Christ, the lives of the men who have become prophets, seers, and revelators. Before completing your course of study, pause now to review and reflect on the importance of these men. Of course, being humble and modest men, they would prefer that you not hold them in too high esteem. In fact, they would wish to defer all glory and honor to the Lord, as did President Joseph F. Smith when he said, "[The Lord] is at the helm; there is no mortal man at the helm of this work." (*Gospel Doctrine*, p. 136.) And the point they make is a good one. You should rejoice that you belong to the church which is directed and governed by the Savior and Redeemer. Note their counsel to you as you too contemplate the establishment of Zion.

"In relation to events that will yet take place, and the kind of trials, troubles, and sufferings which we shall have to cope with, it is to me a matter of very

little moment; these things are in the hands of God, he dictates the affairs of the human family, and directs and controls our affairs; and the great thing that we, as a people, have to do is to seek after and cleave unto our God, to be in close affinity with him, and to seek for his guidance, and his blessing and Holy Spirit to lead and guide us in the right path. Then it matters not what it is nor who it is that we have to contend with, God will give us strength according to our day." (John Taylor in *JD*, 18:281.)

"Are you prepared for the day of vengeance, to come, when the Lord will consume the wicked by the brightness of his coming? No. Then do not be too anxious for the Lord to hasten his work. Let our anxiety be centered upon this one thing, the sanctification of our own hearts, the purifying of our own affections, the preparing of ourselves for the approach of the events that are hastening upon us. This should be our . . . daily prayer, and not to be in a hurry to see the overthrow of the wicked.
. . . Seek not to hasten it, but be satisfied to let the Lord have his own time and way, and be patient. Seek to have the Spirit of Christ, that we may wait patiently the time of the Lord, and prepare ourselves for the times that are coming. This is our duty." (Brigham Young, in *Deseret News* [Weekly], 1 May 1861; see also Brigham Young, *Discourses of Brigham Young,* p. 117.)

"Now, I have asked myself, this being the time to prepare for the millennial reign, how shall we set about to prepare a people to receive the coming of the Lord? As I have thought seriously about that matter, I have

reached two or three sure conclusions in my own thinking. This preparation demands first that a people, to receive the coming of the Lord, must be taught the personality and the nature of God and his Son, Jesus Christ. . . .

"To my thinking, another requisite of that preparation to receive the Lord at the beginning of his millennial reign demands that the people be taught to accept the divinity of the mission of Jesus as the Savior of the world. . . .

" . . . [There is] still another requirement, as I see it, for a

people to be prepared to receive the Savior's coming. We must be cleansed and purified and sanctified to be made worthy to receive and abide that holy presence. . . .

"And now, finally, there is still one thing more that is necessary, to my thinking, before that preparation is made for the millennial reign. We must accept the divine mission of the Prophet Joseph Smith as the instrumentality through which the restoration of the gospel and the organization of the Church of Jesus Christ was accomplished." (Harold B. Lee in *CR*, Oct. 1956, pp. 61-62.)

He will receive Zion unto himself

APPENDIX A
COME: LET ISRAEL BUILD ZION

Elder Bruce R. McConkie
of the Council of the Twelve

The following sermon was given by Elder McConkie on 27 February 1977 in Lima, Peru. President Spencer W. Kimball was desirous that it be printed for the membership of the Church.

We are in the midst of a period of change and realignment where one of the basic doctrines of the Restoration is concerned.

We were directed in the day of Joseph Smith to do one thing with reference to the gathering of Israel and the building up of Zion. Today we are counseled to turn away from the past and do something entirely different.

It is somewhat with us as it was with the disciples in the meridian of time—Jesus first commanded them to preach the gospel to the lost sheep of the house of Israel only; they were forbidden to take the message of salvation to the gentiles. Then he reversed his direction and commanded them to go into all the world and to preach the gospel to every creature, Jew and gentile alike.

As the New Testament account shows, there was a period of a quarter of a century or so in which the early saints—Peter, Paul, James, the Twelve, and all the leading Brethren included—struggled to envision the new decree, the decree that revealed to them that others besides the chosen people of Israel were entitled to the blessings of the gospel and that the gentiles were equal candidates for salvation with them.

Something akin to this is going on in the Church today. Since the coming of Moses to Joseph Smith and Oliver Cowdery, on the third day of April, 1836, in the Kirtland Temple, since the conferral upon mortal men, by that holy prophet, of the keys of the gathering of Israel and of the leading of the ten tribes from the land of the north, we have been using our talents and means and strength to recover the remnant of that once favored nation.

Some considerable success has attended our labors; we have built the Lord's holy house in the tops of the mountains; and all nations have begun to flow unto it. Swift messengers have gone to nation after nation seeking the lost sheep of Israel and inviting them to come "to the mountain of the Lord, to the house of the God of Jacob," so they might be taught in his ways, and walk in his paths, preparatory to the great day when "out of Zion shall go forth the law, and the word of the Lord from Jerusalem." (Isa. 2:3.) Many of the house of Ephraim have been gathered and in due course those of the other tribes will come to receive their blessings, "and be crowned with glory, even in Zion, by the hands of the servants of the Lord, even the children of Ephraim." (D&C 133:32.)

Now, if those of us who have been gathered again into the sheepfold of Israel are to play the part assigned us in the Lord's eternal drama concerning his people, we must know that some things relative to the gathering of Israel are past, some are present, and yet others are future. We ought not to struggle through a quarter of a century or so trying to determine, as did the New Testament saints in an analogous situation, what part we should play in the building up of Zion.

The gathering of Israel and the establishment of Zion in the latter days is divided into three periods or phases. The first phase is past; we are now living in the second phase; and the third lies ahead. Prophecies speak of them all. If we do not rightly divide the word of God, as Paul's expression is, we will face confusion and uncertainty. If on the other hand we correctly envision our proper role and know what should be done today, we shall then be able to use our time, talents, and means to the best advantage in building up the kingdom and preparing a people for the second coming of the Son of Man.

The three phases of this great latter-day work are as follows:

Phase I—From the First Vision, the setting up of the kingdom on April 6, 1830, and the coming of Moses on April 3, 1836, to the secure establishment of the Church in the United States and Canada, a period of about 125 years.

Phase II—From the creation of stakes of Zion in overseas areas, beginning in the 1950s, to the second coming of the Son of Man, a period of unknown duration.

Phase III—From our Lord's second coming until the kingdom is perfected and the knowledge of God covers the earth as the waters cover the sea, and from then until the end of the Millennium, a period of 1,000 years.

We live in the age of restoration. Peter calls it "the times of restitution," meaning the period or time in the earth's history when that which once was shall be restored in all its original glory and perfection. He says the things to be restored include "all things, which God hath spoken by the mouth of all his holy prophets since the world began." (Acts 3:21.) And there are few things of which Israel's prophets have spoken with more fervor and zeal than the latter-day gathering of the house of Jacob and the part that favored people will play in the building of Zion again on earth.

Many things have already been restored, and many things are yet to be restored. Israel has been gathered in part, but in many respects the greatest part of the gathering of Israel is ahead. The foundations of Zion have been laid, but the promised City of Holiness has yet to be built. We have done some of the things destined to be accomplished in this dispensation; we are now engaged in doing the very things reserved for our time; and there are many things ahead to be done by our children and grandchildren and by all those who shall build on the foundation we are now laying.

In view of these principles, and so that members of the Church who live outside the United States and Canada would know why they are now counseled to remain in their own nations and not gather to an American Zion, I gave the following talk in the Lima Peru Area Conference:

We are grateful beyond any measure of expression for the very excellent work being done in the Church here in South America. We extend our high commendation to the noble men who serve as Regional Representatives of the Twelve, as stake presidents, as bishops, and in other responsible positions in the stakes and wards. We feel that a foundation has been laid for great progress and development. We foresee a day when the Church will be a very substantial influence in all these great nations. It is a matter of great gratification that stakes of Zion have been organized here. We hope to see the stakes increase in number and in effectiveness.

I shall speak of the gathering of Israel and of the building up of Zion in the last days. As we all know, the Lord scattered Israel among all the nations of the earth because they forsook him and broke his commandments. As we also know, he is now gathering in the lost sheep of Israel and laying upon them the obligation to build up his latter-day Zion.

This gathering of Israel and this building of Zion in the last days occurs in stages. The early part of the work, which involved gathering to the United States and building stakes of Zion in North America, has already been accomplished. We are now engaged in gathering Israel within the various nations of the earth and in establishing stakes of Zion at the ends of the earth. This is the work that is now going forward in all of the nations of South America and of which I shall now speak.

By the mouth of an ancient prophet, and from the lips of one who lived 3,000 years ago, the Lord sent a message to us. The holy man of old who spake as he was moved upon by the Holy Ghost said these words: "This shall be written for the generation to come"; it is sent to "the people which shall be created," to a people who "shall praise the Lord." (Ps. 102:18.)

We are that people, a people who once again receive revelation, a people to whom God has given anew the fulness of his everlasting gospel, in consequence of which we praise his holy name forever.

The message which has come to us is that the Lord will "have mercy upon Zion: for the time to favour her, yea, the set time, is come." The message is that "when the Lord shall build up Zion, he shall appear in his glory." (Ps. 102:13, 16.)

Now, if I may be properly guided by the power of the Spirit—a thing which I devoutly desire—I shall speak of the manner in which the Lord will build up Zion, the manner in which the Lord is having mercy upon Zion, and the part we are expected to play in the building of Zion.

As is clear from the inspired account, Zion shall be built up—she shall obtain that perfection and glory which is hers—when the Lord appears in his glory. She shall then become as she once was. This will be during the Millennium when the restoration of all things is completed. Zion shall be perfected after the second coming of Christ.

But in the meantime, and as of now, the Lord has laid upon us the responsibility to lay the foundation for that which is to be. We have been commissioned to prepare a people for the second coming of the Son of Man. We have been called to preach the gospel to every nation and kindred and tongue and people. We have been commanded to lay the foundations of Zion and to get all things ready for the return of Him who shall again crown the Holy City with his presence and glory. Our call to all men everywhere is: "Come to Zion, come to Zion, and within her walls rejoice." (*Hymns*, no. 81.)

Now, what is Zion, and where shall she be established? On what ground shall we build her walls? Where shall we place her gates and strong towers? Who shall dwell within her portals? And what blessings shall rest upon her inhabitants?

Truly the scripture saith, "The Lord loveth the gates of Zion more than all the dwellings of Jacob. Glorious things are spoken of thee, O city of God. . . . And of Zion it shall be said, This and that man was born in her: and the highest himself shall establish her." (Ps. 87:2-3, 5.)

Zion has been established many times among men. From the day of

Adam to the present moment—whenever the Lord has had a people of his own; whenever there have been those who have hearkened to his voice and kept his commandments; whenever his saints have served him with full purpose of heart—there has been Zion.

Our first scriptural account relative to Zion concerns Enoch and his city. That prophet of transcendent faith and power lived while father Adam yet dwelt in mortality. It was a day of wickedness and evil, a day of darkness and rebellion, a day of war and desolation, a day leading up to the cleansing of the earth by water.

Enoch, however, was faithful. He "saw the Lord," and talked with him "face to face" as one man speaks with another. (Moses 7:4.) The Lord sent him to cry repentance to the world, and commissioned him to "baptize in the name of the Father and of the Son, which is full of grace and truth, and of the Holy Ghost, which beareth record of the Father and the Son." (Moses 7:11.) Enoch made converts and assembled a congregation of true believers, all of whom became so faithful that "the Lord came and dwelt with his people, and they dwelt in righteousness," and were blessed from on high. "And the Lord called his people Zion, because they were of one heart and one mind, and dwelt in righteousness; and there was no poor among them." (Moses 7:18.)

Please note: Zion is people, Zion is the saints of God; Zion is those who have been baptized; Zion is those who have received the Holy Ghost; Zion is those who keep the commandments; Zion is the righteous; or in other words, as our revelation recites: "This is Zion—the pure in heart." (D&C 97:21.)

After the Lord called his people Zion, the scripture says that Enoch "built a city that was called the City of Holiness, even ZION"; that Zion "was taken up into heaven" where "God received it up into his own bosom"; and that "from thence went forth the saying, Zion is fled." (Moses 7:19, 21, 69.)

After the Lord's people were translated—for it was people who were caught up into heaven, not brick and mortar and stone, for there are better homes already in heaven than men can build on earth—after these righteous saints went to dwell beyond the veil, others, being converted and desiring righteousness, looked for a city which hath foundation, whose builder and maker is God, and they too "were caught up by the powers of heaven into Zion." (Moses 7:27.)

This same Zion which was taken up into heaven shall return during the Millennium, when the Lord brings again Zion; and its inhabitants shall join with the New Jerusalem which shall then be established. (See Moses 7:62-63.)

That many of these truths about Zion were known and taught in ancient Israel is clear from the many references in Isaiah and the Psalms and elsewhere. Isaiah made particular mention of stakes of Zion which would be established in the day of restoration.

As is well known, ancient Israel was scattered among all the nations of the earth because they forsook the Lord and worshipped false gods. As is also well known, the gathering of Israel consists of receiving the truth, gaining again a true knowledge of the Redeemer, and coming back into the true fold of the Good Shepherd. In the language of the Book of Mormon, it consists of being "restored to the true church and fold of God," and then being "gathered" and

"established" in various "lands of promise." (2 Ne. 9:2.) "When they shall come to the knowledge of their Redeemer, they shall be gathered together again to the lands of their inheritance." (2 Ne. 6:11.)

Two things are accomplished by the gathering of Israel: First, those who have thus chosen Christ as their Shepherd; those who have taken upon themselves his name in the waters of baptism; those who are seeking to enjoy his Spirit here and now and to be inheritors of eternal life hereafter—such people need to be gathered together to strengthen each other and to help one another perfect their lives.

And second, those who are seeking the highest rewards in eternity need to be where they can receive the blessings of the house of the Lord, both for themselves and for their ancestors in Israel who died without a knowledge of the gospel, but who would have received it with all their heart had opportunity afforded.

Manifestly in the early days of this dispensation, this meant gathering to the mountain of the Lord's house in the tops of the mountains of North America. There alone were congregations strong enough for the Saints to strengthen each other. There alone were the temples of the Most High where the fulness of the ordinances of exaltation are performed.

However, in the providences of Him who knoweth all things, in the providences of Him who scattered Israel and who is now gathering that favored people again, the day has now come when the fold of Christ is reaching out to the ends of the earth. We are not established in all nations, but we surely shall be before the second coming of the Son of Man.

As the Book of Mormon says, in the

last days, "the saints of God" shall be found "upon all the face of the earth." Also: "The saints of the church of the Lamb and . . . the covenant people of the Lord"—scattered as they are "upon all the face of the earth"—shall be "armed with righteousness and with the power of God in great glory." (1 Ne. 14:12, 14.)

We are living in a new day. The Church of Jesus Christ of Latter-day Saints is fast becoming a worldwide church. Congregations of Saints are now, or soon will be, strong enough to support and sustain their members no matter where they reside. Temples are being built wherever the need justifies. We can foresee many temples in South America in process of time.

Stakes of Zion are also being organized at the ends of the earth. In this connection, let us ponder these truths: A stake of Zion is a part of Zion. You cannot create a stake of Zion without creating a part of Zion. Zion is the pure in heart; we gain purity of heart by baptism and by obedience. A stake has geographical boundaries. To create a stake is like founding a City of Holiness. Every stake on earth is the gathering place for the lost sheep of Israel who live in its area.

The gathering place for Peruvians is in the stakes of Zion in Peru, or in the places which soon will become stakes. The gathering place for Chileans is in Chile; for Bolivians it is in Bolivia; for Koreans it is in Korea; and so it goes through all the length and breadth of the earth. Scattered Israel in every nation is called to gather to the fold of Christ, to the stakes of Zion, as such are established in their nations.

Isaiah prophesied that the Lord "shall cause them that come of

Jacob to take root; Israel shall blossom and bud, and fill the face of the world with fruit." The Lord's promise is: "Ye shall be gathered one by one, O ye children of Israel." (Isa. 27:6, 12.)

That is to say—Israel shall be gathered one by one, family by family, unto the stakes of Zion established in all parts of the earth so that the whole earth shall be blessed with the fruits of the gospel.

This then is the counsel of the Brethren: Build up Zion, but build it up in the area where God has given you birth and nationality. Build it up where he has given you citizenship, family, and friends. Zion is here in South America and the Saints who comprise this part of Zion are and should be a leavening influence for good in all these nations.

And know this: God will bless that nation which so orders its affairs as to further his work.

His work includes the building up of Zion in the last days. He has commissioned us to do that work for him. The foundations of Zion have already been laid in North America, in South America, in Europe, in Asia, in the South Pacific and in every place where there are stakes of Zion. But Zion is not yet perfected in any of these places. When she is perfected, it will be as it was with Zion of old—the Lord will come and dwell with his people.

Our tenth Article of Faith says, "We believe in the literal gathering of Israel." This gathering occurs when the lost sheep of Israel come into the Church. It occurs when their sins are washed away in the waters of baptism, so that once again they have power to become pure in heart; and Zion is the pure in heart.

Our Article of Faith says that "We believe . . . in the restoration of the Ten Tribes." This is in the future. It will occur when the Lord brings again Zion, according to the promises.

Our Article of Faith says "that Zion (the New Jerusalem) will be built upon this [the American] continent." This also is future and will occur after the Lord's people have gained strength and influence and power in all the nations whither he hath scattered them.

Our Article of Faith says "that Christ will reign personally upon the earth; and, that the earth will be renewed and receive its paradisiacal glory." This also is future, a day which we devoutly desire and seek. (Article of Faith 10.)

Each one of us can build up Zion in our own lives by being pure in heart. And the promise is, "Blessed are the pure in heart: for they shall see God." (Matt. 5:8.) Each one of us can extend the borders of Zion by gathering our friends and neighbors into the fold of Israel.

These things of which we speak are part of a great plan and program of the Lord. He has known the end from the beginning. He has ordained and established the system which is now in operation. He has scattered his chosen people in all the nations of the earth. And now through his goodness and grace in this, our day, by the opening of the heavens, by the ministry of holy angels sent from his presence, by his own voice speaking from heaven, by the pouring out of the Holy Ghost—by all these means—he has once again restored the fulness of his everlasting gospel. He has called us out of darkness into the marvelous light of Christ. He has commanded us to build up Zion anew. He has commanded us to overcome the world. He has commanded us to

330

forsake every evil thing. He has made us his agents and representatives. He has commissioned us to go out and find the lost sheep of Israel. He wants us to invite them to gather with the true Church and with the Saints of God.

This is a work of great magnitude and importance. There is no work like it in all the world. The gospel of the Lord Jesus Christ is the greatest thing in heaven or on earth. We rejoice in the glorious truths of heaven we have received. We praise the Lord for his goodness and grace. And we know within ourselves of the truth and divinity of these things.

By the revelations of the Holy Spirit to my soul, I know this work in which we are engaged is true. I know the Lord's hand is in it. I know that success will attend our labors. The day will come when the knowledge of God covers the earth as the waters cover the sea. We are the most blessed and favored people on earth. God grant us the wisdom, God grant us the fervor and devotion, God grant us the zeal and good sense to go forth on his errand living the gospel ourselves and saving our own souls, and offering these glorious principles of salvation to his other children. This is the Lord's work. It is true, and I so testify in the name of the Lord Jesus Christ. Amen. (*Ensign,* May 1977, pp. 115-18.)

**President Spencer W. Kimball
Welfare session, Saturday, April
1, 1978**

*This is our perspective: "The end result
of our labors . . . is the building of a
Latter-day Zion."*

My dear brothers and sisters, what
a beautiful sight you are! The
radiance of your faces and the
beauties of nature on this Temple
Square make my heart swell with
thanksgiving for the blessings of
the Lord. As we meet together in
conference, I hope the spirit of
gratitude permeates all we do and
say, for truly the Lord delights to
bless those who love and serve
him. (See D&C 76:5.)

With the help of the Lord, I should
like to remind us of several truths
and obligations that should never
be forgotten by us as leaders and as
a people. Following these
reminders, I should like to talk
about the building of Zion through
sacrifice and consecration.

First, may I remind bishops of the
vital need to provide recipients of
welfare assistance with the
opportunity for work or service
that thereby they may maintain
their dignity and independence
and continue to enjoy the Holy
Spirit as they benefit from Church
Welfare Services self-help efforts.
We cannot be too often reminded
that Church welfare assistance is
spiritual at heart and that these
spiritual roots would wither if we
ever permitted anything like the
philosophy of the dole to enter into
our Welfare Services ministrations.
Everyone assisted can do
something. Let us follow the order
of the Church in this regard and
insure that all who receive give of
themselves in return.

May we be on guard against
accepting worldly substitutes for
the plan to care for his poor in this,
the Lord's own way. As we hear
talk of governmental welfare

reforms and its myriads of
problems, let us remember the
covenants we have made to bear
one another's burdens and to
succor each according to his need.
President Romney, our dean of
Welfare Services, gave good
counsel when several years ago he
made this statement:

"In this modern world plagued
with counterfeits for the Lord's
plan, we must not be misled into
supposing that we can discharge
our obligations to the poor and the
needy by shifting the responsibility
to some governmental or other
public agency. Only by voluntarily
giving out of an abundant love for
our neighbors can we develop that
charity characterized by Mormon
as 'the pure love of Christ.' (Moro.
7:47.) This we must develop if we
would obtain eternal life."
(*Conference Report,* Oct. 1972, p.
115.)

No "ism" should confuse our
thinking in these matters. As a
reminder of Church policy
regarding individuals receiving
government or other forms of
charity, may I emphasize the
following declaration of principle:

"The responsibility for each
member's spiritual, social,
emotional, physical, or economic
well-being rests first, upon
himself, second, upon his family,
and third, upon the Church.
Members of the Church are
commanded by the Lord to be
self-reliant and independent to the
extent of their ability. (See D&C
78:13-14.)

"No true Latter-day Saint, while
physically or emotionally able, will
voluntarily shift the burden of his
own or his family's well-being to
someone else. So long as he can,
under the inspiration of the Lord
and with his own labors, he will
work to the extent of his ability to
supply himself and his family with

the spiritual and temporal
necessities of life. (See Gen. 3:19, 1
Tim. 5:8, and Philip. 2:12.)

"As guided by the Spirit of the
Lord and through applying these
principles, each member of the
Church should make his own
decisions as to what assistance he
accepts, be it from governmental or
other sources. In this way,
independence, self-respect,
dignity, and self-reliance will be
fostered, and free agency
maintained." (Statement of the
Presiding Bishopric, as quoted in
Ensign, March 1978, p. 20.)

Underlying this statement is the
recurring theme of self-reliance.
No amount of philosophizing,
excuses, or rationalizing will ever
change the fundamental need for
self-reliance. This is so because:

"All truth is independent in that
sphere in which God has placed
it, . . . as all intelligence also;
otherwise there is no existence."
(D&C 93:30.) The Lord declares
that herein lies "the agency of
man" (see D&C 93:31), and with
this agency comes the
responsibility for self. With this
agency we can rise to glory or fall to
condemnation. May we
individually and collectively be
ever self-reliant. This is our
heritage and our obligation.

The principle of self-reliance
stands behind the Church's
emphasis on personal and family
preparedness. Our progress in
implementing the various facets of
this personal and family
preparedness is impressive, but
there are still far too many families
who have yet to heed the counsel to
live providently. With the arrival of
spring we hope all of you will put in
your gardens and prepare to enjoy
their produce this summer. We
hope you are making this a family
affair, with everyone, even the
little ones, assigned to something.

There is so much to learn and harvest from your garden, far more than just a crop itself. We also hope that you are maintaining your year's supply of food, clothing, and where possible, some fuel and cash savings. Moreover, we hope that you are conscious of proper diet and health habits, that you may be fit physically and able to respond to the many challenges of life. Would you see to it that in your quorum and Relief Society meetings the principles and practices of personal and family preparedness are taught.

We wish to remind all the Saints of the blessings that come from observing the regular fast and contributing as generous a fast offering as we can, and as we are in a position to give. Wherever we can, we should give many times the value of the meals from which we abstained.

This principle of promise, when lived in the spirit thereof, greatly blesses both giver and receiver. Upon practicing the law of the fast, one finds a personal well-spring of power to overcome self-indulgence and selfishness. May I refer you to Bishop Victor L. Brown's masterful talk on this subject given last welfare conference and published in the November 1977 *Ensign*.

Now, brothers and sisters, would you put aside for a moment the pressing demands of this day and this week, and permit me to establish some very important perspectives about welfare services. For many years we have been taught that one important end result of our labors, hopes, and aspirations in this work is the building of a Latter-day Zion, a Zion characterized by love, harmony, and peace—a Zion in which the Lord's children are as one.

The vision of what we are about

and what should come of our labors must be kept uppermost in our minds as we learn and do our duty in the present implementation of welfare service. This applies equally to all Church activities. In the fifty-eighth section of the Doctrine and Covenants the Lord shares with us a glimpse of this Latter-day Zion:

"Ye cannot behold with your natural eyes, for the present time, the design of your God concerning those things which shall come hereafter, and the glory which shall follow after much tribulation.

"For after much tribulation come the blessings. Wherefore the day cometh that ye shall be crowned with much glory; the hour is not yet, but is nigh at hand. . . .

"Behold, verily I say unto you, for this cause I have sent you—that you might be obedient, and that your hearts might be prepared to bear testimony of the things which are to come;

"And also that you might be honored in laying the foundation, and in bearing record of the land upon which the Zion of God shall stand; . . .

"And after that cometh the day of my power; then shall the poor, the lame, and the blind, and the deaf, come in unto the marriage of the Lamb, and partake of the supper of the Lord, prepared for the great day to come.

"Behold, I, the Lord, have spoken it." (D&C 58:3-12.)

This day will come; it is our destiny to help bring it about! Doesn't it motivate you to lengthen your stride and quicken your pace as you do your part in the great sanctifying work of the kingdom? It does me. It causes me to rejoice over the many opportunities for service and sacrifice afforded me

and my family as we seek to do our part in establishing Zion.

In the earliest years of this dispensation the people faltered in attempting to live the full economic plan of Zion, the united order. Because of their transgressions, the Lord chastened them in these words:

"Behold, they have not learned to be obedient to the things which I required at their hands, but are full of all manner of evil, and do not impart of their substance, as becometh saints, to the poor and afflicted among them;

"And are not united according to the union required by the law of the celestial kingdom;

"And Zion cannot be built up unless it is by the principles of the law of the celestial kingdom; otherwise I cannot receive her unto myself." (D&C 105:3-5.)

The Lord further counsels that we must learn obedience and be developed in character before he can redeem Zion. (See D&C 105:9-10.)

A few verses later in this same revelation, the Lord repeats the law of Zion in these words and with this promise:

"And let those commandments which I have given concerning Zion and her law be executed and fulfilled, after her redemption.

"And inasmuch as they follow the counsel which they receive, they shall have power after many days to accomplish all things pertaining to Zion." (D&C 105:34, 37.)

The length of time required "to accomplish all things pertaining to Zion" is strictly up to us and how we live, for creating Zion "commences in the heart of each person." (*Journal of Discourses*, p. 283.) That it would take some time to learn our lessons was seen by the

prophets. In 1863 Brigham Young stated:

"If the people neglect their duty, turn away from the holy commandments which God has given us, seek their own individual wealth, and neglect the interests of the kingdom of God, we may expect to be here quite a time—perhaps a period that will be far longer than we anticipate." (*Journal of Discourses*, 11:102.)

Unfortunately we live in a world that largely rejects the values of Zion. Babylon has not and never will comprehend Zion. The Lord revealed our times to the prophet Mormon, who recorded this statement in a closing chapter of the Book of Mormon:

"Behold, I speak unto you as if ye were present, and yet ye are not. But . . . Jesus Christ hath shown you unto me, and I know your doing.

"For behold, ye do love money, and your substance, and your fine apparel, and the adorning of your churches, more than ye love the poor and the needy, the sick and the afflicted." (Morm. 8:35, 37.)

This state of affairs stands in marked contrast to the Zion the Lord seeks to establish through his covenant people. Zion can be built up only among those who are the pure in heart, not a people torn by covetousness or greed, but a pure and selfless people. Not a people who are pure in appearance, rather a people who are pure in heart. Zion is to be in the world and not of the world, not dulled by a sense of carnal security, nor paralyzed by materialism. No, Zion is not things of the lower, but of the higher order, things that exalt the mind and sanctify the heart.

Zion is "every man seeking the interest of his neighbor, and doing all things with an eye single to the glory of God." (D&C 82:19.) As I

understand these matters, Zion can be established only by those who are pure in heart, and who labor for Zion, for "the laborer in Zion shall labor for Zion; for if they labor for money they shall perish." (2 Ne. 26:31.)

As important as it is to have this vision in mind, defining and describing Zion will not bring it about. That can only be done through consistent and concerted daily effort by every single member of the Church. No matter what the cost in toil or sacrifice, we must "do it." That is one of my favorite phrases: "Do It." May I suggest three fundamental things we must do if we are to "bring again Zion," three things for which we who labor for Zion must commit ourselves.

First, we must eliminate the individual tendency to selfishness that snares the soul, shrinks the heart, and darkens the mind. President Romney recently referred to the tragic cycle of civilization, a cycle propelled by anyone who seeks for power and gain. Was it not this that led Cain to commit the first murder "for the sake of getting gain"? (Moses 5:50.) Is not this the spirit of the anti-Christ in which "every man prospered according to his genius, and . . . every man conquered according to his strength; and whatsoever a man did was no crime"? (Al. 30:17.) Did not Nephi single this out as the spirit which led his generation to destruction:

"Now the cause of this iniquity of the people was this—Satan had great power, unto the stirring up of the people to do all manner of iniquity, and to the puffing them up with pride, tempting them to seek for power, and authority, and riches, and the vain things of the world." (3 Ne. 6:15.)

If we are to avoid their fate, we

must guard against the very things that caused their downfall. The Lord himself declared to our grandparents: "And again, I command thee that thou shalt not covet thine property." (D&C 19:26.)

He further counseled his young church by saying:

"Behold, I, the Lord, am not well pleased with many who are in the church at Kirtland:

"For they do not forsake their sins, and their wicked ways, the pride of their hearts, and their covetousness, and all their detestable things, and observe the words of wisdom and eternal life which I have given unto them." (D&C 98:19-20.) It is incumbent upon us to put away selfishness in our families, our business and professional pursuits, and our Church affairs. I am disturbed when I hear of stakes or wards having difficulty dividing equity in welfare projects or making equitable storehouse commodity production assignments. These things should not be. Let us resolve today to overcome any such tendencies.

Second, we must cooperate completely and work in harmony one with the other. There must be unanimity in our decisions and unity in our actions. After pleading with the Saints to "let every man esteem his brother as himself" (D&C 38:24), the Lord concludes his instructions on cooperation to a conference of the membership in these powerful words:

"Behold, this I have given unto you as a parable, and it is even as I am. I say unto you, be one; and if ye are not one ye are not mine." (D&C 38:27.)

If the Spirit of the Lord is to magnify our labors, then this spirit

of oneness and cooperation must be the prevailing spirit in all that we do. Moreover, when we do so, we are told by the Prophet Joseph Smith that "the greatest temporal and spiritual blessings which always come from faithfulness and concentrated effort, never attended individual exertion or enterprise." (*Teachings of the Prophet Joseph Smith*, p. 183.) There are few activities in the Church that require more cooperation and concerted effort than Welfare Services. Whether it is rallying to find employment for a displaced quorum member, toiling on a production project, serving as a lead worker at a Deseret Industries, or accepting foster children in the home, it is cooperation and mutual concern that determines the overall success of the Storehouse Resource System.

Third, we must lay on the altar and sacrifice whatever is required by the Lord. We begin by offering a "broken heart and a contrite spirit." We follow this by giving our best effort in our assigned fields of labor and callings. We learn our duty and execute it fully. Finally we consecrate our time, talents, and means as called upon by our file leaders and as prompted by the whisperings of the Spirit. In the Church, as in the welfare system also, we can give expression to every ability, every righteous desire, every thoughtful impulse. Whether a volunteer, father, home teacher, bishop, or neighbor, whether a visiting teacher, mother, homemaker, or friend—there is ample opportunity to give our all. And as we give, we find that "sacrifice brings forth the blessings of heaven!" (*Hymns*, no.

147.) And in the end, we learn it was no sacrifice at all.

My brothers and sisters, if we can do this, then we will find ourselves clothed in the mantle of charity "which is the greatest of all, for all things must fail—

"But charity is the pure love of Christ, and it endureth forever; and whoso is found possessed of it at the last day, it shall be well with him." (Moro. 7:46-47.)

Let us unite and pray with all the energy of heart, that we may be sealed by this bond of charity; that we may build up this latter-day Zion, that the kingdom of God may go forth, so that the kingdom of heaven may come. This is my prayer and testimony in the name of Jesus Christ. Amen. (*Ensign*, May 1978, pp. 79-81.)

 # BIBLIOGRAPHY

Anderson, Joseph. *Prophets I Have Known*. Salt Lake City: Deseret Book Co., 1973.

Babbel, Frederick W. *On Wings of Faith*. Salt Lake City: Bookcraft, 1972.

Backman, Milton V., Jr. *Joseph Smith's First Vision*. Salt Lake City: Bookcraft, 1971.

Bennett, Frances Grant. *Glimpses of a Mormon Family*. Salt Lake City: Deseret Book Co., 1968.

Cheesman, Paul R. *The Keystone of Mormonism*. Salt Lake City: Deseret Book Co., 1973.

Clark, James R., comp. *Messages of the First Presidency of The Church of Jesus Christ of Latter-day Saints*. 6 vols. Salt Lake City: Bookcraft, 1965-75.

Conference Report of The Church of Jesus Christ of Latter-day Saints. Cited as *CR*.

Cowan, Richard O., and Andersen, Wilson K. *The Living Church*. Provo, Utah: Brigham Young University Printing Service, 1974.

Cowley, Matthias F. *Wilford Woodruff*. Salt Lake City: Bookcraft, 1964.

Craven, Avery, and Johnson, Walter. *The U.S. Experiment in Democracy*. Chicago: Ginn and Co., 1950.

Doxey, Roy W. *Zion in the Last Days*. 2d ed. Salt Lake City: Bookcraft, 1968.

Gates, Susa Young, and Widtsoe, Leah D. *The Life Story of Brigham Young*. New York: The Macmillan Co., 1930.

Grant, Heber J. *Gospel Standards*. Compiled by G. Homer Durham. Salt Lake City: Deseret Book Co., 1969.

Hinckley, Bryant S. *Heber J. Grant: Highlights in the Life of a Great Leader*. Salt Lake City: Deseret Book Co., 1951.

Hunter, Milton R. *Brigham Young, the Colonizer*. Salt Lake City: Deseret News Press, 1940.

Jenson, Andrew. *Latter-day Saint Biographical Encyclopedia*. 4 vols. Salt Lake City: Andrew Jenson History Co., 1901-36.

Johnson, Benjamin F. *My Life's Review*. Independence, Missouri: Zion's Printing and Publishing Co., 1947.

Journal of Discourses. 26 vols. London: Latter-day Saints' Book Depot, 1855-86. Cited as *JD*.

Kimball, Edward L., and Kimball, Andrew E., Jr. *Spencer W. Kimball*. Salt Lake City: Bookcraft, 1977.

Kimball, Spencer W. *Faith Precedes the Miracle*. Salt Lake City: Deseret Book Co., 1972.

___. *The Miracle of Forgiveness*. Salt Lake City: Bookcraft, 1969.

___. *One Silent Sleepless Night*. Salt Lake City: Bookcraft, 1975.

Lee, Harold B. *Decisions for Successful Living*. Salt Lake City: Deseret Book Co., 1973.

___. *Stand Ye in Holy Places*. Salt Lake City: Deseret Book Co., 1974.

___. *Ye Are the Light of the World*. Salt Lake City: Deseret Book Co., 1974.

Lundwall, N. B., comp. *A Compilation Containing the Lectures on Faith*. Salt Lake City: N. B. Lundwall, n.d.

McConkie, Bruce R. *Doctrinal New Testament Commentary*. 3 vols. Salt Lake City: Bookcraft, 1965-73.

___. *Mormon Doctrine*. 2d ed. Salt Lake City: Bookcraft, 1966.

McConkie, Joseph F. *True and Faithful*. Salt Lake City: Bookcraft, 1971.

McKay, David O. *Ancient Apostles*. Salt Lake City: Deseret Book Co., 1964.

___. *Cherished Experiences*. Compiled by Clare Middlemiss. Salt Lake City: Deseret Book Co., 1955.

___. *Gospel Ideals*. Salt Lake City: Deseret Book Co., 1953.

___. *Man May Know for Himself*. Compiled by Clare Middlemiss. Salt Lake City: Deseret Book Co., 1967.

___. *Stepping Stones to an Abundant Life*. Compiled by Llewelyn R. McKay. Salt Lake City: Deseret Book Co., 1971.

___. *Treasures of Life*. Compiled by Clare Middlemiss. Salt Lake City: Deseret Book Co., 1962.

___. *True to the Faith*. Compiled by Llewelyn R. McKay. Salt Lake City: Bookcraft, 1966.

McKay, Llewelyn R., comp. *Home Memories of President David O. McKay*. Salt Lake City: Deseret Book Co., 1956.

Morgan, Dale L. *The Great Salt Lake*. Albuquerque: University of New Mexico Press, 1947.

Morrell, Jeanette McKay. *Highlights in the Life of President David O. McKay*. Salt Lake City: Deseret Book Co., 1966.

Mouritsen, Dale C. *A Defense and a Refuge*. Provo, Utah: Brigham Young University Publications, 1972.

Nibley, Preston. *Brigham Young, the Man and His Work*. 3d ed. Independence, Missouri: Zion's Printing and Publishing Co., 1944.

___. *Presidents of the Church*. 13th ed. rev. and enl. Salt Lake City: Deseret Book Co., 1974.

Pratt, Orson. *Masterful Discourses and Writings of Orson Pratt.* Compiled by N. B. Lundwall. Salt Lake City: N. B. Lundwall, n.d.

——. *A Series of Pamphlets on the Doctrines of the Gospel.* Chattanooga, Tennessee: Printed for the Southern States Mission, 1899.

Presidents of the Church. Salt Lake City: Department of Seminaries and Institutes of Religion, n.d.

Roberts, B. H. *A Comprehensive History of The Church of Jesus Christ of Latter-day Saints.* 6 vols. Provo, Utah: Brigham Young University Press, 1957.

——. *The Life of John Taylor.* Salt Lake City: Bookcraft, 1963.

Romney, Marion G. *Look to God and Live.* Compiled by George J. Romney. Salt Lake City: Deseret Book Co., 1971.

Romney, Thomas C. *The Life of Lorenzo Snow.* Salt Lake City: Deseret Book Co., 1955.

Smith, Eliza R. Snow. *Biography and Family Record of Lorenzo Snow.* Salt Lake City: Deseret News Co., 1884.

Smith, Hyrum M., and Sjodahl, Janne M. *The Doctrine and Covenants Commentary.* rev. ed. Salt Lake City: Deseret Book Co., 1972.

Smith, Joseph. *History of The Church of Jesus Christ of Latter-day Saints.* Edited by B. H. Roberts. 7 vols. Salt Lake City: The Church of Jesus Christ of Latter-day Saints, 1932-51. Cited as *HC.*

——. *Teachings of the Prophet Joseph Smith.* Compiled by Joseph Fielding Smith. Salt Lake City: Deseret Book Co., 1938.

Smith, Joseph F. *Gospel Doctrine.* Edited by John A. Widtsoe et al. Salt Lake City: Deseret Book Co., 1939.

Smith, Joseph Fielding. *Doctrines of Salvation.* Compiled by Bruce R. McConkie. 3 vols. Salt Lake City: Bookcraft, 1954-56.

——. *Essentials in Church History.* 24th ed. Salt Lake City: Deseret Book Co., 1950.

——. *The Progress of Man.* Salt Lake City: The Genealogical Society of Utah, 1936.

——. *The Restoration of All Things.* Salt Lake City: Deseret Book Co., 1945.

. *The Signs of the Times.* Salt Lake City: Deseret Book Co., 1952.

——. *Take Heed to Yourselves!* 2d ed. Salt Lake City: Deseret Book Co., 1966.

Smith, Joseph Fielding, comp. *Life of Joseph F. Smith.* 2d ed. Salt Lake City: Deseret Book Co., 1938.

Smith, Joseph Fielding, Jr., and Stewart, John J. *The Life of Joseph Fielding Smith.* Salt Lake City: Deseret Book Co., 1972.

Smith, Lucy Mack. *History of Joseph Smith.* Edited by Preston Nibley. Salt Lake City: Bookcraft, 1956.

Speeches of the Year. Provo, Utah: Brigham Young University Press.

Spencer, Clarissa Young, and Harmer, Mabel. *Brigham Young at Home.* Salt Lake City: Deseret Book Co., 1940.

Talmage, James E. *Articles of Faith.* 46th ed. Salt Lake City: The Church of Jesus Christ of Latter-day Saints, 1965.

——. *Jesus the Christ.* 38th ed. Salt Lake City: Deseret Book Co., 1970.

Taylor, John. *The Gospel Kingdom.* Compiled by G. Homer Durham. 4th ed. Salt Lake City: Bookcraft, 1964.

——. *Three Nights' Public Discussion . . .* Liverpool: John Taylor, 1850.

Wait, Mary Van Sickle. *Brigham Young in Cayuga County, 1813-1829.* Ithaca, New York: DeWitt Historical Society of Tompkins County, 1964.

Watson, Elden Jay. *Manuscript History of Brigham Young, 1801-1844.* Salt Lake City: Elden Jay Watson, 1968.

——. *Manuscript History of Brigham Young, 1846-1847.* Salt Lake City: Elden Jay Watson, 1971.

West, Emerson Roy. *Profiles of the Presidents.* Salt Lake City: Deseret Book Co., 1972.

Widtsoe, John A. *Priesthood and Church Government.* rev. ed. Salt Lake City: Deseret Book Co., 1936.

Woodruff, Wilford. *The Discourses of Wilford Woodruff.* Edited by G. Homer Durham. Salt Lake City: Bookcraft, 1946.

Young, Brigham. *Discourses of Brigham Young.* Compiled by John A. Widtsoe. 1966 ed. Salt Lake City: Deseret Book Co., 1954.

 # FOOTNOTES FOR OVERVIEWS

UNIT 1

1. Matthew 23:29-33; Acts 7:51-53; Helaman 13:24-28.

2. Moses 7:63, 64.

3. Moses 6:49-68.

4. Moses 6:17, 41.

5. Moses 7:17.

6. D&C 107:54.

7. Moses 7:69.

8. Genesis 18:19.

9. Hebrews 11:10.

10. Hebrews 11:13.

11. Hebrews 8:11.

12. Joseph Smith, *HC*, 4:540.

13. Habbakuk 2:14.

UNIT 2

1. D&C 128:21.

2. D&C 21:7, 8.

3. Brigham Young, *Discourses of Brigham Young*, comp. John A. Widtsoe, 1966 ed. (Salt Lake City: Deseret Book Co., 1954), p. 467.

4. B. H. Roberts, *A Comprehensive History of The Church of Jesus Christ of Latter-day Saints*, 6 vols. (Provo, Utah: Brigham Young University Press, 1957), 2:286.

5. Smith, *HC*, 6:343.

6. Mosiah 5:13.

7. D&C 6:30.

UNIT 3

None

UNIT 4

None

UNIT 5

1. Heber J. Grant, *Gospel Standards*, comp. G. Homer Durham (Salt Lake City: Deseret Book Co., 1969), p. 20.

2. Wilford Woodruff, *The Discourses of Wilford Woodruff*, ed. G. Homer Durham (Salt Lake City: Bookcraft, 1946), pp. 272-73.

3. Matthias F. Cowley, *Wilford Woodruff* (Salt Lake City: Bookcraft, 1964), pp. 564-65.

4. Preston Nibley, *The Presidents of the Church*, 13th ed. rev. and enl. (Salt Lake City: Deseret Book Co., 1974), p. 101.

5. D&C 118:6.

UNIT 6

1. Cited in LeRoi C. Snow, "Devotion to a Divine Inspiration," *Improvement Era*, June 1919, p. 654.

2. Thomas C. Romney, *The Life of Lorenzo Snow* (Salt Lake City: Deseret Book Co., 1955), p. 135.

3. "Characteristic Sayings of President Lorenzo Snow," *Improvement Era*, June 1919, p. 651.

4. "Characteristic Sayings," p. 651.

UNIT 7

1. Joseph Fielding Smith, comp., *Life of Joseph F. Smith*, 2d ed. (Salt Lake City: Deseret Book Co., 1938), p. 449.

2. Joseph F. Smith, *Gospel Doctrine*, ed. John A. Widtsoe et al. (Salt Lake City: Deseret Book Co., 1939), p. 511.

3. Smith, comp., *Life of Joseph F. Smith*, p. 280.

4. Joseph Fielding Smith, Jr., and John J Stewart, *The Life of Joseph Fielding Smith* (Salt Lake City: Deseret Book Co., 1974), p. 124.

UNIT 8

1. Preston Nibley, *The Presidents of the Church*, 13th ed. rev. and enl. (Salt Lake City: Deseret Book Co., 1974), p. 255.

2. Nibley, *Presidents of the Church*, pp. 227-28.

3. Bryant S. Hinckley, *Heber J. Grant: Highlights in the Life of a Great Leader* (Salt Lake City: Deseret Book Co., 1951), p. 125.)

4. Hinckley, *Life of a Great Leader*, p. 262.

UNIT 9

1. Robert K. McIntosh, "An Analysis of the Doctrinal Teachings of President George Albert Smith" (master's thesis, Brigham Young University, 1975), p. 22.

2. George Albert Smith, *Improvement Era*, May 1950, p. 412.

3. George Albert Smith in *CR*, Apr. 1946, pp. 181-82.

4. Personal interview with Edith Elliott, daughter of President Joseph Fielding Smith, 30 June 1972.

UNIT 10

1. Jeanette McKay Morrell, *Highlights of the Life of President David O. McKay* (Salt Lake City: Deseret Book Co., 1966), p. 26.

2. Morrell, *Highlights*, pp. 37-38.

3. Personal interview with Robert McKay by C. Gary Bennett, August 1977.

4. Llewelyn R. McKay, comp., *Home Memories of President David O. McKay* (Salt Lake City: Deseret Book Co., 1956), p. 33.

5. David O. McKay, "The Words of a Prophet," *Improvement Era*, Feb. 1970, p. 85.

6. Joseph Fielding Smith, "One Who Loved His Fellowmen," *Improvement Era*, Feb. 1970, p. 88.

UNIT 11
None

UNIT 12

1. *Church News*, 15 July 1972, p. 3.

2. Harold B. Lee, "Building Your House of Tomorrow," *Speeches of the Year* (Provo, Utah: Brigham Young University Press, 13 Feb. 1963), p. 11.

3. Cited in Gordon B. Hinckley, "Harold Bingham Lee: Humility, Benevolence, Loyalty," *Ensign*, Feb. 1974, p. 90.

4. Cited in Hinckley, "Harold Bingham Lee," p. 90.

5. Spencer W. Kimball, "A Giant of a Man," *Ensign*, Feb. 1974, p. 86.

UNIT 13

None

UNIT 14

1. Moses 7:67.

2. Moses 1:28.

3. Ether 3:25.

4. Joseph Smith, *HC*, 1:207.

5. Smith, *HC*, 6:354.

6. *JD*, 9:171.

7. *CR*, Apr. 1900, p. 2.

8. *CR*, Apr. 1909, p. 2.

9. *CR*, Manchester England Area Conference, Aug. 1971 p. 5.

10. "When the World Will Be Converted," *Ensign*, Oct. 1974, pp. 5, 14.

11. Isaiah 26:20, 21.

12. 2 Nephi 14:5.

13. D&C 115:5.

14. Isaiah 11:9.

15. Smith, *HC*, 4:540.

AUTHOR INDEX

SMITH, JOSEPH F. (Patriarch)

SMITH, JOSEPH FIELDING (Tenth President of the Church)

YOUNG, BRIGHAM

SUBJECT INDEX

L

example of George Albert Smith's, 19-18
George Albert Smith's teachings, 19-18 to 19-20
hardships for John Taylor, 8-4
in all parts of the world, 19-18
of Joseph F. Smith, 15-5 to 15-7
of Lorenzo Snow, 12-10 to 12-14
of Wilford Woodruff, 11-2
obligation to do, 27-6
priesthood correlation, 20-13
renewed effort called for, Intro. to chap. 27
require great effort, 27-8
responsibility of all members, 20-9
responsibility to all nations, 20-8
Spencer W. Kimball's expanded program of, 27-5 to 27-9
Spencer W. Kimball gives full energy to, 27-17
to go to all people, 27-7
voices are to prieach gospel, 27-19
without purse or scrip, 8-5; 8-8; Overview, Unit 5; 12-11

Missouri, 21-10

Moral Cleanliness, 14-7

Mormon Battalion, 9-2 [Box]

Mormonism Compared to Ancient Christianity, 12-8

Moroni, Intro. to Chap. 4
as Joseph Smith's teacher, 3-10
visit to Joseph Smith, 3-9

Moses, 2-3

Motherhood, 23-14

N

Name, 1914 [Box]

Nauvoo, 6-20

Nauvoo Neighbor, 8-10

O

Obedience
first condition for becoming pure, 1-6
Joseph Smith encouraged in by his father, 3-11
leads to safety and security, 25-6
learned by suffering, 24-15
necessary from every member, 24-22
only path to godhood, 13-8
Saints can escape calamities through, 23-10

Obedience to the Lord, 4-11; 4-12

P

Parable
of Good Samaritan, 18-15 [Box]
of the Village, Intro. to Chap. 25

Parents Entreated to Teach Children, 23-17

Patriarchal Order, 14-9

Patriotism Strained Among Saints, 9-2

Peace
comes only through gospel, 16-18
George Albert Smith's teachings on, 1913 to 19-17
if we know our lives are righteous, 19-14
keys for true, 19-13
Spirit of God necessary for, 19-9
to be taken from the earth, 24-20
United Nations charter as way to, 19-8 [Box]

Pearl of Great Price
contains account of First Vision, 3-5
Vision of the Redemption of the Dead, 15-15

Perfect, Overview, Unit 10

Perfection
mortality is school of, 13-10
our duty to improve each day, 13-14
trials necessary for, Overview, Unit 7

Persecution of Brigham Young, 6-23

Peter, James, and John Restore Melchizedek
Priesthood, 4-7

Pioneers, 20-10

Plural Marriage
debate over doctrine of, 9-7
doctrine brought persecution, 9-11
doctrine established, 8-9
example of Joseph F. Smith's family, 14-10 to 14-15

Poverty, 27-3

Pratt, Parley P.
critical of Joseph Smith, 8-3
preached gospel to John Taylor, 8-2

Prayer
David O. McKay received direct answer, 20-4
end each day with family, 25-6
John Taylor prayed for true gospel, 8-1
Wilford Woodruff received answer to, 10-4

Presidency of Church
second apostolic, 9-8
to be reorganized, 5-14

President of the Church
cannot lead Church astray, 11-10 [Box]

Joseph Fielding Smith oldest man to become,
Overview, Unit 11; Intro. to Chap. 23
presides over the whole Church, Intro. to course
senior apostle becomes, 5-16
special gifts and talents of, 2-18
the Lord's mouthpiece on earth, Intro. to course

President of the Quorum of the Twelve as President of
the Church, 5-12

President of the United States, 8-10

Priest, 10-6

Priesthood
no danger from righteous, 16-20
put into full gear, 25-9

Priesthood Correlation
advanced by David O. McKay, 20-13
David O. McKay on committee in 1908, 20-7
development of, 25-8
four important factors of, 25-10
to support home, 25-11

Prophecy, 3-12

Prophet
as watchman, Intro. to course
can never lead Saints astray, 2-6
David O. McKay recognized as one, 20-22
definition of, Intro. to course
do not worship the, 3-17
Joseph Smith as a, 3-12
may not be permitted to say all he knows, Intro. to
course
no one can take his place, 2-5
role of in last dispensation, Chap. 2
shall be to us "instead of God," 2-3
will guide Saints through frightening events, 2-7

Prophets
all seek to establish Zion, Overview, Unit 1
demonstrate lifelong commitment to Christ, 1-11
desire to build the kingdom of God, 1-11
foreordained in premortal world, 2-17
inspired by promise of Zion, 1-10
rejected because of their weaknesses, 2-2
rejected by people of fallen world, 26-27 [Box]
will tell where and how to build Zion, 28-15
Protection for Those Who Keep the Commandments,
19-15

Q

Queen Contests, 26-31

R

Refinement Comes Through Tests and Trials, 24-13

Reformation, Overview, Unit 1

Renovation of Earth, 2-13

Repent
call upon the world to, 23-13
people will not, 23-9

Repentance, 26-18 to 26-27
as Lord's way to peace, 19-8
blessings dependent on, 19-12
choice between clamity and, 19-7
definition of—not an escape, 26-18
Joseph Fielding Smith had special calling to preach,
22-20
key to peace in latter days, 23-11
must include restitution, 26-25
must spread to all areas of life, 26-27
necessary for peace and happiness, 19-9
necessary to avoid calamities, 23-7
necessary to prevent sorrow, 19-6
only way to avoid calamity, 19-8
remorse and sorrow preliminary to, 26-21
requires forgiveness of others, 26-22
required permanent change, 26-23
sometimes requires confession and punishment,
26-24
steps of, 26-19
universal and exacting, 26-20

Revelation
arguments against new, 8-6
distinguishing feature of Church, 20-20
key to Wilford Woodruff's missionary work, 11-2
Manifesto came through, 11-10
of all things given to Enoch, Moses, brother of
Jared, Joseph Smith, Overview, Unit 14
returns to earth, 3-7
rock upon which Church is built, 11-6; 21-4
to every individual, 11-6
to Joseph Smith as foundation of Church, 16-27
to Wilford Woodruff, 11-1 to 11-6

Reynolds, Ethel G.
describes husband Joseph Fielding Smith, 22-21
wife of Joseph Fielding Smith, Overview, Unit 11

Riggs, Emma Ray
married David O. McKay, 20-6
wife of David O. McKay, Overview, Unit 10

Richards, Willard
counselor to Brigham Young, Intro. to Chap. 7
hid John Taylor's wounded body, Intro. to Chap. 8

Ridicule, 3-7

S

Sacred Grove Purchased, Overview, Unit 9

Sacrifice
    brought blessings, 4-10; 4-11
    Heber J. Grant's willingness to, 16-19
    necessary to produce faith, 12-28 [Box]
    whatever is required by the Lord, 1-11

Safety in Following the Living Prophet, 2-9

Saints
    burdens of, 4-8
    colonize the Rocky Mountain Valleys, 7-8
    colonized 800,000 square miles in ten years, 7-9
    definition of, Intro. to Chap. 21
    establish Mormon colonies in Mexico, 9-12
    establish settlements in Canada, 9-12
    feel spirit of gathering, 8-7
    greater sacrifice required from, 4-9
    many decide not to pay tithing, 12-17
    motivated by concept of Zion, 2-1
    must prepare hearts, homes, and communities for
        Zion, 28-23
    plagues with persecution, 9-12
    preserved from unrighteous oppression, 9-6
    see rewards of the faithful, 13-16

Salem, 1-7

Samuel
    prophet of the Lord, 21-2 [Box]
    rejected by Israelites, 2-10 [Box]

Sanctification
    of human family, 2-13
    of Saints, Intro. to Chap. 21

Satan
    desired to have David O. McKay, 21-1
    sought to destroy Wilford Woodruff, 10-8
    to have power over his dominion, 24-20
    tried to stop work of the Lord, 11-7
    unleashing all forces, Intro. to Chap. 6

Savior, 28-9

Scripture, Intro. to course

Scriptures, 26-6

Sealing Families Together, 11-11

Second Coming of Christ
    days of wickedness precede, 23-5
    in a day of great wickedness, 23-6
    is near, 23-2; 23-4
    is tomorrow, 23-1
    no man knows when, 23-4
    numerous signs of, 23-3
    warning to watch and be ready, 23-4

Seer
    definition of, 25-1
    of what value if counsel ignored, 25-13

Seership, Intro. to course

Selfishness, 17-18

Self-Reliance, 17-20

Sense of Humor
    of Brigham Young, 6-19; 7-15
    of Spencer W. Kimball, 26-14

Service Is the Secret of Success, 16-25

Shurtliff, Louie Emily, Wife of Joseph Fielding Smith,
    Overview, Unit 11

Signs to Follow Those Who Believe, 21-2 [Box]

Smith, George A.
    grandfather of George Albert Smith, 18-1
    in George Albert Smith's dream, 19-14 [Box]

Smith, George Albert
    aided sufferers of World War II, 18-8 [Box]; 18-9
    becomes President of the Church, Intro. to Chap. 18
    birth of, Overview, Unit 9
    concern for Lamanites, 18-11
    concern for those disaffected with Church, 18-12
    demonstrated charity, Intro. to Chap. 19
    examples from his life, Chap. 18
    example of faith, Chap. 19-16 [Box]
    examples of his love, 18-13 to 18-15
    healed of typhoid fever, 19-9 [Box]
    learned from his father, 18-2
    love for human family, Intro. to Chap. 18
    married Lucy Woodruff, Overview, Unit 9
    met Brigham Young, 18-1
    never dishonored name, 19-14 [Box]
    overview of life, Overview, Unit 9
    patriarchal blessing excerpt, Overview, Unit 9
    personal mission as prophet, Intro. to Chap. 18
    prophetic warnings, Chap. 19
    sent Ezra Taft Benson to Europe, 18-10
    special gifts of, 2-18 [Box]
    sustained and upheld Constitution, Overview,
        Unit 9
    teachings on missionary work, 19-18 to 19-20
    teachings on peace, 19-13 to 19-17
    taught and lived love, 18-3 to 18-8
    tributes to, 18-9 [Box]
    writes list of goals in life, 18-2 [Box]

T

Y

Z